Land, Development and Design

Paul Syms

Foreword by Sir Peter Hall

Blackwell
Science

© 2002 by Blackwell Science Ltd,
a Blackwell Publishing Company
Editorial Offices:
Osney Mead, Oxford OX2 0EL, UK
  Tel: +44 (0)1865 206206
Blackwell Science, Inc., 350 Main Street, Malden, MA
02148-5018, USA
  Tel: +1 781 388 8250
Iowa State Press, a Blackwell Publishing Company, 2121
State Avenue, Ames, Iowa 50014-8300, USA
  Tel: +1 515 292 0140
Blackwell Publishing Asia Pty Ltd, 550 Swanston Street,
Carlton South, Melbourne, Victoria 3053, Australia
  Tel: +61 (0)3 9347 0300
Blackwell Wissenschafts Verlag, Kurfürstendamm 57,
10707 Berlin, Germany
  Tel: +49 (0)30 32 79 060

First published 2002 by Blackwell Science Ltd

Library of Congress
Cataloging-in-Publication Data
is available

ISBN 0-632-06484-6

A catalogue record for this title is available from the British
Library

Set in 11/13pt Bembo
by DP Photosetting, Aylesbury, Bucks
Printed and bound in Great Britain by
TJ International, Padstow, Cornwall

For further information on
Blackwell Science, visit our website:
www.blackwell-science.com

Maps reproduced from Ordnance Survey mapping on
behalf of the Controller of Her Majesty's Stationery Office
© Crown Copyright MC 100003836.

Contents

Foreword

by Sir Peter Hall, Director of the Institute of Community Studies

One of the strangest and saddest features about urban development in Britain is that it is traditionally seen by all the actors as some kind of war game, in which private developers fight to make as much money as possible while public planners use every possible means to stop them. This should not be necessary, and in other European countries – such as the Netherlands, widely admired for the quality of much of its development – it does not seem to be the case. Part of the problem, no doubt, lies in the adversarial character that the planning process has acquired, far from the ideas of those who framed the historic 1947 Town and Country Planning Act, but part lies in the nature of professional education. Planners are trained in planning schools, developers in schools of surveying, and very seldom do the two professional streams come together.

There is thus a chicken and egg problem: the two professions are reared on significantly different literatures, so authors write for one market or the other. This is compounded by a basic lack of literature on the development process: there is an extraordinary dearth of books that describe this process as the developer experiences it, either for the budding surveyor-developer or the intending planner.

Paul Syms has written to fill this gap, and is to be congratulated on doing it so thoroughly and so clearly. His book concentrates primarily on brownfield development, because that is where current priorities lie and where some of the greatest complexities arise, but in his carefully chosen case studies he does not ignore greenfield development either. It will immediately and justifiably become a standard text for every student and professional who wants to understand the land development process and its outcomes.

Preface

My objective in writing *Land, Development and Design* was to produce an up to date text for use by both students and practitioners in the surveying and town planning disciplines. I wished to concentrate on the reuse of urban land, in line with the emerging policies relating to increasing densities and greater reliance on public transport – what I have called regeneration of the built environment. However, it would have been wrong to totally ignore greenfield development and many of the issues discussed in the book are equally relevant to greenfield sites. One of the masterplanning case studies in Chapter 14 also deals with a major new greenfield project – Cambourne in Cambridgeshire.

Inevitably, given my interests, part of the book deals with the problems surrounding the redevelopment of land affected by contamination. It is not intended to be a technical treatise on dealing with contamination, rather it is aimed at the developer, surveyor and town planner, all of whom need to know what to look for in technical reports. Nevertheless, I hope that the book will be of interest to engineers, environmental scientists and the regulators in environmental health departments and the Environmental Agencies, providing them with an insight into the development process.

Land, Development and Design is divided into four parts. Part One consists of three chapters, which introduce the development process and describe planning policies as they currently exist in England. The approach to the development process is based on the eleven phases of development, as they relate to the re-use of land, which Peter Knight and I first described in our book *Building Homes on Used Land*[1].

Part Two opens with site assembly and putting together the professional team before moving on to site assessment, risk analysis and the remediation of contaminated land. The feasibility study is discussed in the first chapter of Part Three. Here I have taken a fairly straightforward approach to the subject of

---

[1] Based on research for the Joseph Rowntree Foundation and published by RICS Books.

financial appraisals, similar to that which a property developer might adopt in the early stages of a project. For readers who wish to extend their reading in this area there are a number of good texts on advanced valuations. Planning and environmental regulation, the thorny subject of waste management licensing, development finance and joint ventures, tendering and contracts are also considered in Part Three, which concludes with a look at marketing and selling the development.

Part Four deals with design issues in the first three chapters. I must stress that it is not intended as a handbook for urban designers or architects, as there are plenty of people far more competent than myself to write for these audiences. Instead, I have looked at some aspects that are of interest to me, and I hope to others in the field of development.

The last chapter in Part Four brings the reader up to date with the proposed changes to the town planning regime in the 2001 planning Green Paper and its 'daughter papers'.

When I started to write this book in the early summer of 2001 I was conscious of the fact that a great many changes had taken place during the preceding couple of years in terms of Government policies relating to property development in the urban environment. I was also aware that even more changes, concerning town planning policies and the reuse of urban land, were likely to be proposed over the ensuing months and years. I could have decided to defer writing the book until all the new policy ideas had been either implemented or abandoned but that would have resulted in a delay of several years. Therefore I agreed with Julia Burden, Deputy Publishing Director at Blackwell Publishing, that we would have a 'cut-off' date of the end of December 2001. In the event, writing extended into the first few weeks of January 2002 and I should like to thank Julia and the team at Blackwell for their patience in respect of the constantly changing manuscript of the last few weeks. I am also grateful to the technical reviewers for their helpful comments.

As with my earlier book, *Contaminated Land: the practice and economics of redevelopment*[2], I have included checklists at the end of each chapter. Many people commented to me about the usefulness of these in *Contaminated Land* and I hope that the checklists in this book are equally helpful to the reader.

A great many people have helped in the production of this book and it is not possible to name them all but I should like to mention a few. My good friend Tim Abbott of Abbott and Associates, civil engineering quantity surveyors, wrote Chapter eleven on Tendering and Contracts. I cannot claim any expertise in this subject and I am grateful to Tim for his help. I should also like to thank the team at Taylor Young Urban Design, especially Andy Clarke, for producing the mini masterplan used in Chapters 5 and 8.

---

[2] Blackwell Science, 1997.

Dr Sarah Macnaugton of Bio-wise suggested some of the remediation and treatment case studies in Chapter seven, whilst others were provided by QDS and Knight Environmental. Staff members at N.M. Rothschild & Co, Ansbacher & Co and the Royal Bank of Scotland spent time explaining the approaches adopted by their banks when financing development projects. Gwyn Griffiths of the Welsh Development Agency provided the Port of Barry joint venture case study.

David Gray of the East of England Development Agency and Sue Arnold of Ipswich Borough Council both provided me with information for the Ipswich case study, as too did the Concept Centre team and Terry Farrell & Partners for the Cambourne Study. I am also extremely grateful to the various developers, architects and town planners who assisted me with the other design case studies.

I should like to thank everyone who provided photographs and other illustrations used throughout the book. Their copyright is noted in the Acknowledgements after the references section. Where possible I have tried to provide Internet 'weblinks', so as to enable the reader to follow up topics in more detail. These weblinks are listed at the end of Chapter 2.

I should like to thank my colleagues at Sheffield Hallam University, who made suggestions as to what should be included in the book and allowed me the time to undertake the writing. Finally, I should like to thank my wife and collaborator, Janice, for her perseverance in reading countless drafts and for suggesting a number of the topics covered in the book. Without her help the final outcome would not have been achieved.

Biographical note

Paul Syms is Professor of Urban Land Use in the School of Environment and Development at Sheffield Hallam University. He has extensive practical experience in the field of re-using previously developed land and buildings, having established his own consultancy practice in 1986. He still continues to practise, acting mainly as an expert witness.

Paul originally qualified as a valuer and then went on to research a Masters degree in Economic Geography at the University of Manchester. His doctorate from Sheffield Hallam University was awarded in respect of his research into the development and valuation of contaminated land. His work on urban regeneration has been extensively published in the United Kingdom and overseas. Paul is frequently invited to speak at conferences and seminars on the subject of re-using land.

Part One
Planning and Development

Introduction

This part introduces the reader to the preliminary development stages, and to the planning process. The Government is committed to making radical changes to the planning process, criticised by many developers as a major cause of delays in getting developments under way. The process can indeed be very lengthy, regardless of whether the site in question is a greenfield or a previously used site and can be a very emotive issue.

Chapter 1 describes the development process and introduces eleven phases of development. Each of these phases is then covered more fully elsewhere in the book.

Chapter 2 deals with planning policies and comments in detail on land for housing, having briefly set out the Urban Task Force's recommendations. PPG3 has only been in effect for a relatively short time but the aim of this guidance is to encourage the reuse of previously used land wherever possible.

Chapter 3 considers the inception of the project, commencing with an idea or a piece of land, through the process of market research and initial assessment of the likely rents or prices that might be achieved.

Planning is returned to in the final chapter of the book with a summary of the proposals contained in the December 2001 Planning Green Paper.

Chapter 1
The Development Process

1.1 Introduction

> 'We calculate that, on current policy assumptions, the Government is unlikely to meet its own target that 60% of new dwellings should be built on previously developed land. Achieving this target is fundamental to the health of society. Building more than 40% of new housing on greenfield sites is both unsustainable and unacceptable. It will lead to further erosion of the countryside. It will also increase traffic congestion and air pollution, accelerate the depletion of natural resources, damage biodiversity and increase social deprivation within our towns and cities.'
>
> (Lord Rogers of Riverside, Introduction to *Towards an Urban Renaissance*, Urban Task Force, 1999)

Urban regeneration is not just about renewing and revitalising the built environment in our towns and cities. It must also address issues involving the economic and social well-being of the community and should also take account of cultural backgrounds. Without having regard for economic, social and cultural aspects, property development projects may not meet the needs of the community and may be unsustainable in the long run, notwithstanding any short-term profitability that might be achieved. They may even fail to produce a development profit.

The purpose of this book is to focus upon the property development process. It does this mainly by considering the reuse of previously developed land. The book does not seek to examine in depth economic, social and cultural issues but, where these might have a significant bearing on a property development, they are flagged up for the reader's attention. Checklists are provided at the end of each chapter, highlighting the issues raised and are intended to assist developers, planners, surveyors and others involved in the execution of development projects.

It is often the case that planners see property developers as greedy, money-grabbing individuals without a thought for the wider good. They seek planning permissions which are impossible to deliver and in unrealistic time-scales. On the other hand, developers sometimes regard planners as being obstructive, lacking an understanding of development issues and overly constrained by local plans and Unitary Development Plans (UDPs). In practice, however, they both have important roles to play in the development process.

There may well be faults on both sides but, in many cases, the problem is due to a lack of communication and a failure to see the other person's point of view. This chapter looks at the development process and seeks to identify areas where conflicts may arise. In view of policies that focus development attention on the reuse of previously developed sites, and because development of such sites tends to be more complex than greenfields, the chapter concentrates on the redevelopment process, although most of the points are equally applicable to greenfield development.

A number of authors, including Adams (1994) and Cadman and Topping (1995), have looked at the property development process. Adams approached the subject from the viewpoint of the planner working within and in response to property markets. He also considered development models described by previous authors, such as Barrett *et al.* (1978) and Gore and Nicholson (1985). Cadman and Topping's objective was to describe the development process, enabling the reader to obtain a complete overview. They identified the following main stages:

(1)   Initiation
(2)   Evaluation
(3)   Acquisition
(4)   Design and costing
(5)   Permissions
(6)   Commitment
(7)   Implementation
(8)   Let/manage/dispose

They also emphasised that these stages may not always follow this sequence and often overlap or repeat.

The stages described by Cadman and Topping apply to speculative development situations, where a developer might not seek an occupier until construction is well advanced, or even completed. Where a development is pre-let or pre-sold, the letting, management and disposal stage might come much earlier in the development process, possibly even preceding the initiation stage in situations where a developer receives an enquiry from a prospective occupier and then seeks a site in order to satisfy the demand. It is also more appropriate to greenfield development than to the generally more complex processes associated with the redevelopment of 'brownfield' or 'previously developed' land and buildings.

For successful redevelopment to take place it is usually important for each phase of the process to have been completed, or a definable objective to be achievable, before committing too far to the subsequent phases. However, this should not preclude work on the later phases being undertaken at earlier points in the project; indeed, this is often essential if a successful development is to be created. For example, early discussions with the local planning authority will reduce the risk of the developer finding out after the planning application has been submitted that the proposed development runs contrary to an impending policy change or is affected by some future road improvement. Early discussions with environmental regulators will also enable the developer to ascertain whether or not they have any particular concerns relating to the site or its environs.

The basis adopted in the book for describing the redevelopment process is the 11 phases approach outlined in the book *Building Homes on Used Land* (Syms & Knight, 2000). These are shown in summary in the box below and discussed in more detail in the next section.

Box 1.1   The eleven phases of the redevelopment process

- Phase 1: Project inception
- Phase 2: Site acquisition and site assembly
- Phase 3: Site assessment
- Phase 4: Risk analysis
- Phase 5: Detailed design
- Phase 6: Feasibility study
- Phase 7: Planning and regulatory approvals
- Phase 8: Land and development finance
- Phase 9: Tendering
- Phase 10: Construction
- Phase 11: Sales and marketing

1.2   The phases of redevelopment

The redevelopment process should be seen as consisting of 11 phases, many of which are interdependent upon each other. As the focus is on reusing land, site assessment, including investigation, risk analysis and development funding are identified as additional discrete phases within the development process.

Property developers are in business to make profits. The level of profit should be commensurate with the risks involved and should produce a return for the capital employed. Therefore a development that is pre-let or pre-sold will involve less risk than one which is entirely speculative and the developer may be able to accept a reduced profit. The amount of profit required will depend on each individual project and the developer concerned but 15–20% of the end value of the development may be used as a 'rule of thumb'.

Developments that are partly pre-let or pre-sold (or are grant-aided) may be at the lower end of the profit range whilst speculative projects will be at the higher end. Profits on fully pre-let or pre-sold schemes may be lower than 15%, especially if the developer has been in competition to secure the tenant. Profits on housing developments or commercial developments constructed in several phases may also appear to be lower, when compared against end value, but may in fact be significantly higher if considered in terms of returns on capital employed, which may be 'rolled over' several times during the course of the development.

1.2.1   *Phase 1: Project inception*

This phase includes the initial idea, site identification, preliminary design, tentative demand studies, initial costs and development appraisals, etc. The developer may start off with a specific site or building but equally well may commence with something far less tangible, such as an idea. The developer may have identified a 'gap in the market', possibly from feedback received as a result of other developments, or as the result of a visit to other towns or countries.

Design at this stage may consist of no more than a few simple sketches and the financial costing would be equally basic 'back of an envelope' calculations. The market research may have been simply obtaining the views of local estate agents, possibly people the developer has worked with on other occasions and with whom a relationship of trust has developed.

From these initial concepts a more detailed development idea will emerge, or the developer will decide to abandon the project. In this early phase, members of the development team, architect, engineer, cost consultant and estate agent, may well be working 'at risk', with their future remuneration being based on the expected viability of the project.

If the project is to succeed, the developer must be prepared to act in a flexible manner to achieve the redevelopment of 'previously used' or 'brownfield' land and buildings. This may entail changing the type of scheme to be developed and 'what if' alternatives need to be reflected in the development appraisals. It is possible that sites identified for residential development in local plans or Unitary Development Plans are in fact unsuited to that type of use, due to contamination or other problems in the ground. In such situations it is also important for planners and other regulators to adopt a similarly flexible approach when allocating land uses to previously developed sites, whilst taking care not to adversely compromise planning policies or environmental considerations.

1.2.2 *Site acquisition and site assembly*

This is relatively straightforward if the intention is to acquire a single site that is being actively marketed but it becomes more complex with increasing numbers of ownerships and interests, possibly several of which might exist in the same piece of land, e.g. freehold, long leasehold and occupational lease. The developer will be reluctant to make major financial commitments to site assembly unless there is some degree of certainty in being able to acquire all the ownerships and interests, as well as some certainty in obtaining planning permission. This requires carefully negotiated options and conditional contracts to secure the site or sites.

There are important differences between options and conditional contracts. Under an option the developer secures control over the land for a specified period of time, usually related to the planning process, during which the owner is prevented from selling except to the developer or, at least, from selling it without the developer's consent. A price formula may be included, based on the number of dwellings or the floor area of the commercial development. The developer is normally responsible for obtaining planning permission and for all the costs involved, including any appeals. Having obtained the planning permission the developer can then decide whether or not to proceed with the purchase. This is the major difference between options and conditional contracts; under the latter, once planning permission has been granted for at least the minimum number of residential units or the floor area specified in the contract, the contract goes unconditional and the developer has to complete the purchase within a specified time period. The developer has the possibility of forfeiting the contract deposit but this is likely to be much larger than the fee paid under the option agreement.

One of the main problems attaching to site assembly is that landowners may have completely unrealistic ideas about the value of their land but, equally, they may be trapped by historic valuations and the fact that the land is used as collateral against bank borrowings or other loans. The landowner may thus appear to be intransigent in holding out for the maximum payment. Letters of intent, options and conditional contracts must be carefully worded, clearly identifying who is to do what and who will be responsible for bearing what proportion of the costs. Otherwise the developer may be in an impossible position if it is not possible to obtain the planning permission or development density needed to meet the owner's demands.

1.2.3   *Phase 3: Site assessment*

This is the very important investigation phase, to determine whether or not the site is affected by contamination and, if so, the extent to which it may affect the development. The National House-Building Council (NHBC) now requires its members to undertake geotechnical and geoenvironmental investigations of *all sites* if the builder wishes to have the benefit of the Buildmark warranty. This phase also includes assessment of available service infrastructures. It is important to identify any access or site constraints, including any underground obstructions, which may affect the development.

A properly planned investigation is essential, starting with a study of the historical uses on the site and examination of map records from the earliest development. All site assessments should then be followed by a 'walkover' survey. Only then can an intrusive investigation be designed.

In some cases it will be necessary for intrusive investigations to be undertaken in several stages, developing the site assessment in the light of knowledge obtained from the earlier work. Whilst it may be desirable to obtain a 'fixed price' quotation from the environmental consultant or the site investigation contractor, this may not always be possible, especially if the extent of laboratory testing cannot be determined at the outset. If possible, intending developers should talk to previous owners, employees, tenants and local residents, as they may be able to assist in locating unexpected deposits of waste material.

1.2.4   *Phase 4: Risk analysis*

Where the presence of contamination has been disclosed as a result of the site investigation, it is necessary to determine the extent to which it might affect the development. For this purpose the possibility of any source (or contaminant)–pathway–receptor linkage needs to be considered. This is the analysis and reporting phase that can only follow the site assessment phase. If any contamination has been found the report should include recommendations as to remediation strategy. This work should be undertaken by developing conceptual models of any significant contaminant pathways and identifying the possible receptors, including building site operatives, residents, visitors and workers on commercial developments. All possible linkages should be considered. It may not be necessary to remove all contamination from the site; it may be feasible to break or remove the pathway instead. This option must, however, be considered in the context of how it is likely to be viewed by future purchasers, tenants or investors. The possibility of the site being contaminated in the legal sense, in accordance with Part IIA of the Environmental Protection Act 1990, should be considered (see Chapters 6 and 9).

Remediation strategies should be prepared on the basis of suitability for use and careful consideration should be given to any planning conditions that might be imposed. Quite often developers submit site investigation reports and remediation strategies as part of the planning application. Most planners will need specialist help in dealing with these reports, either from their environmental health colleagues or from outside consultants. Similarly, developers and development surveyors will need to obtain specialist advice.

1.2.5   *Phase 5: Detailed design*

Only when the foregoing phases have been substantially completed can the project move to the detailed design phase. This will involve reworking the original ideas to take account of discovered ground conditions and other possible constraints, such as the inability to acquire, or redevelop, the entire site.

It will be necessary for the project team to examine the layout of the site and be prepared to consider alternative remediation strategies given different layouts or reuse of land. On sites affected by landfill gas, it will be necessary to address the gas protection, venting and monitoring measures at an early stage, as part of the integrated design process. If monitoring is required, then the development will probably be better suited for 'managed' (usually rented) housing or for commercial use. Developers and regulators should agree in advance the duration of any monitoring, or the criteria to be achieved before monitoring is discontinued. Different local authorities may have different ideas in respect of monitoring, often driven by their previous experience.

Community considerations are most important during this phase and it may be appropriate to arrange public exhibitions and meetings to discuss the proposals before they are finalised.

1.2.6   *Phase 6: Feasibility study*

Although the development team should have been taking account of the financial implications of any changes brought about as a result of earlier phases in the development, it is only now that a full and accurate feasibility study can be produced. Having completed the site assessment and having identified all potential pollutant linkages, the revised design should be the subject of a comprehensive review, involving all members of the development team.

It is possible that a considerable period of time, at least several months and possibly more than a year, will have elapsed since the project inception phase and it may be advisable to undertake a new demand study, especially if the nature of the development proposal has undergone any significant changes.

The review will involve a complete reassessment of detailed design and costs, as well as consideration of any competing schemes that may be under construction or in planning stages. Many developers use commercially available computer packages to model the financial implications of changes, whilst others have developed in-house packages or use computer spreadsheets.

1.2.7   Phase 7: Planning and regulatory approvals

Although it is only now that a full planning application can be submitted, developers would be ill-advised to leave it until this point to establish contact with the planning department. There is, however, a degree of wariness, or even mistrust, on the part of many developers. They feel that if they talk to the planning officer at an early phase in the process, their ideas will become public knowledge, as members and other agencies are asked for their views, and that competitive advantage will be lost. As a result developers sometimes leave it until the last moment to submit an application, then they want a decision in six to eight weeks, leading to friction all round. Intending developers also need to be aware of the fact that, when considering the redevelopment of previously developed land, other regulatory approvals may be required (e.g. waste management licences) and these may take even longer than planning permission to obtain.

It should be recognised that applications involving the remediation of soil contamination through the planning process may involve the need to satisfy the council's environmental health department and the Environment Agency as well as the planning officers. This will inevitably take longer than for an application on an uncontaminated site. Ideally therefore, developers should establish contact with the planners during the inception phase but some understanding regarding confidentiality as to the development proposals may be needed.

Close liaison between developers and regulators during the earlier phases should ensure that the necessary information regarding land condition has been collected and can be presented in support of the applications. The ways in which existing planning guidance on contaminated land is applied do vary between authorities but it is important, from the developer's point of view, to ensure that all relevant information is available and is fully understood by the regulators. The need, or otherwise, for waste management or mobile plant licences should be identified as early as possible.

1.2.8   Phase 8: Land and development finance

Relatively few developers fund projects entirely from their own resources and developers who need to raise finance are unlikely to leave it until this stage before considering approaches to banks or other financial institutions. It will be necessary to identify appropriate sources, including possible partners (e.g. sources of grant aid) and to negotiate funding agreements at an earlier stage of the project but only now will they be in a position to conclude the financing arrangement. Larger developers often have a 'rolling facility' and do not have to seek funding for each individual project.

Interest charges on development projects are generally calculated by reference to the London Interbank Offered Rate (LIBOR), the rate banks charge for lending money to each other. Development finance will be charged at a percentage above LIBOR, the actual margin depending upon the financial standing and 'track record' of the developer. This type of financing is referred to as 'debt' and may produce around 70% of the funding for the project. Other types include equity, where the financial institution takes a stake in the project in return for finance; and 'mezzanine', usually at a higher interest rate, used where funding in excess of 70% is needed.

Banks and other financial institutions are probably more prepared to provide development finance for 'previously used' sites than they were a few years ago, but there are still a few exceptions. Financiers will, almost certainly, require full site investigation reports and may insist on appointing their own environmental consultants to comment upon the reports. They may also wish to oversee the remediation works. There may be some reluctance to provide finance for projects that involve innovative, or relatively untried, remediation methodologies. Possible sources of grant aid should be identified and negotiations commenced as soon, as possible after project inception. Remember, even if the land is included at nil cost the project may still not be viable without some public sector support. It may also be necessary to arrange insurance to protect purchasers or investors against any deficiencies in the site remediation, including the possibility that some contaminants may have been overlooked.

1.2.9   Phase 9: Tendering

This includes the selection of suitable contractors and decisions relating to single or multiple contracts (e.g. site remediation, infrastructure, construction). The form of contract, for example whether or not it includes contractor's design, also forms part of this phase. Members of the development team have important roles in the tendering process, and advising on contract documentation etc.

The appointment of contractors with experience of site remediation can be beneficial for redevelopment projects, as they may be able to suggest ways of undertaking the work. The tendering process will inevitably vary, with some developers having established relationships with contractors, leading to a negotiated contract, whilst others will undertake a full competitive tendering process. Either way, the scope of the work should be adequately described in the tender documents.

1.2.10   Phase 10: Construction

This includes: site remediation, monitoring and auditing; site infrastructure, construction, landscaping, etc. In many respects the construction phase may seem straightforward after all the earlier phases. However, the lack of complications during the construction phase may be largely due to the careful planning and organisational work that has preceded it.

The site remediation/preparation works must be properly supervised and, most important where decontamination is involved, must be fully recorded. Ideally this will involve maintaining photographic and written records, including sketches of where contaminants, or other site constraints such as old services or underground obstructions, were located. Developers should be aware that debris from previous uses, including glass, metal and plastics, can be just as harmful to building workers and small children as chemical contaminants and should be removed as part of the remediation contract.

1.2.11   Phase 11: Sales and marketing

It is unlikely that a developer will leave this to the very end of the project but it is only now that a saleable or lettable product has been produced. Ideally the sales and marketing team should have been involved since project inception and they should certainly have had an input into the detailed design phase. Reports from the sales team may also be essential in securing development finance.

This phase should also include communication of information regarding site history, site investigations and remediation works, to purchasers, tenants and investors. Developers will have different ways of dealing with this. Some will be quite open about the site history, including 'before' photographs in the sales office and on brochures, whereas others will only provide information as part of the package sent to purchasers' solicitors. Either way, it is important to be open with information relating to the site and its development, as any attempt at concealment is likely to have an adverse effect once it is discovered. As a general rule openness is probably the best policy, otherwise buyers may feel that the developer is trying to hide something.

1.3   Summary

Redevelopment of 'previously developed' land and buildings is complex, involves risks and some degree of flair. It also means that those involved need to understand each other's objectives and constraints. Good communication is often the key to success.

The second chapter in Part One outlines government policies and legislation having a direct bearing on the development process. Part Two (Chapters 4 to 7) looks specifically at land-related issues, including site assembly, site investigation and risk analysis. Available site remediation and treatment options are also reviewed in this part. Part Three (Chapters 8 to 12) covers the development process from the feasibility study to sales and marketing. Part Four (Chapters 13 to 16) deals with design issues, looking at traditional and innovative layouts, development densities and sustainability. Several case studies, of both greenfield and brownfield developments are described. The book concludes with a chapter setting out the proposed changes to planning policies.

Chapter 2
Planning and Development Policies

2.1 Introduction

'The land use planning system, and the decision makers within it, play a key role in national life. They determine where and in what form development can occur, protect key environmental assets, and establish the location of essential infrastructure.'

(CBI, 2001)

The above quote from the CBI (formerly the Confederation of British Industry) planning brief *Planning for productivity*, emphasises the importance of the planning system in ensuring the availability of land for commercial developments. The brief, which is supported by the British Property Federation (BPF), the House Builders Federation (HBF) and the British Chambers of Commerce (BCC), states that there are around 150 000 planning applications a year for commercial developments in England: 'But for business, the planning system is too slow, involves too many uncertainties and often results in poor decisions.' Highlighting the problems, the brief proposes a ten-point action plan, which is discussed later in this chapter.

The importance of planning is also recognised by Government:

'A key role of the planning system is to enable the provision of homes and buildings, investment and jobs in such a way which is consistent with the principles of sustainable development. It needs to be positive in promoting competitiveness while being protective towards the environment and amenity. The policies which underpin the system, summarised [in Planning Policy Guidance Note 1], seek to balance these aims. It will frequently be the case, in relation to a particular development proposal, that several economic, environmental, social or other factors need to be taken into account. This requires a framework which promotes consistent, predictable and prompt decision making.'

(DTLR, 2001a, paragraph 1)

This chapter was written during what may be regarded as an important period in the development of English town planning policies. The preceding 18 months had seen the publication of an Urban White Paper (DETR, 2000a), new planning policies in relation to housing development (DETR, 2000b) and extensive guidance relating to design and urban capacity. Many of the developments in policy and guidance are referred to in this and succeeding chapters. However, policies and guidance are not static, therefore this chapter can only provide an outline of planning policies and guidance, as they existed in the autumn of 2001. In order to ascertain the latest situation readers are advised to consult the various websites listed in the Weblinks at the end of this chapter.

Opening the debate on the future of planning, Stephen Byers, the Secretary of State for Transport, Local Government and the Regions, described the importance of planning in the following terms:

'Planning is fundamental to the way our cities, towns and villages look, the way they work and the way they interconnect. Getting planning right means that our goals for society are easier to achieve. Good planning can have a huge beneficial effect on the way we live our lives.'

(Byers, 2001)

The British system of town planning is now over 50 years old and, in the view of the Government, is in need of a radical overhaul. The intention of opening a debate was therefore to inform Government thinking, leading to the publication of a Green Paper on planning in the autumn of 2001. This is referred to later in this chapter. First, however, current planning policies are considered.

2.2 Planning Policy Guidance Notes

In England, the Department of the Environment, Transport and the Regions issues various statements relating to planning policy, including Planning Policy Guidance Notes (PPGs) covering many different aspects of development (see Box 2.1). It is not the purpose of this chapter to examine each of these in detail, but some of the more important development aspects are outlined. The actual guidance notes can be downloaded from *www.databases.dtlr.gov.uk* and double-clicking on the title of the appropriate guidance note.

The PPGs play a major part in guiding local planning authorities and intending developers. Whilst all are important in their context, some PPGs are more relevant to the generalities of development than others that are more specialist in their application. Reference is made in this and subsequent chapters to the implications for development arising out of different PPGs.

PPG1 sets out the Government's approach to planning and to sustainable development, seeking to deliver the objective of achieving, now and in the future, economic development to secure higher living standards while protecting and enhancing the environment. The most commonly used definition is 'development that meets the needs of the present without

Box 2.1   Planning Policy Guidance Notes.

- PPG01   General Policy and Principles
- PPG02   Green Belts
- PPG03   Housing
- PPG04   Industrial and Commercial Development and Small Firms
- PPG05   Simplified Planning Zones
- PPG06   Town Centres and Retail Developments
- PPG07   The Countryside: Environmental Quality and Economic and Social Development
- PPG08   Telecommunications
- PPG09   Nature Conservation
- PPG10   Planning and Waste Management
- PPG11   Regional Planning
- PPG12   Development Plans
- PPG13   Transport
- PPG14   Development of Unstable Land
- PPG14A   Annex 1: Landslides and Planning
- PPG15   Planning and the Historic Environment
- PPG16   Archaeology and Planning
- PPG17   Sport and Recreation
- PPG18   Enforcing Planning Control
- PPG19   Outdoor Advertisement Control
- PPG20   Coastal Planning
- PPG21   Tourism
- PPG22   Renewable Energy
- PPG22A   Annexes to PPG22
- PPG23   Planning and Pollution Control
- PPG24   Planning and Noise
- PPG25   Development and Flood Risk

compromising the ability of future generations to meet their own needs' (World Commission on Environment and Development, 1987). It also emphasises the importance of urban regeneration and the reuse of previously developed land as important objectives in supporting more sustainable patterns of development and the Government's commitment to:

- 'concentrating development for uses which generate a large number of trips in places well-served by public transport, especially town centres, rather than in out-of-centre locations; and
- preferring the development of land within urban areas, particularly on previously-developed sites, provided that this creates or maintains a good living environment, before considering the development of greenfield sites.'

(PPG1, 1997, paragraph 7; see DTLR, 2001a)

2.3   Planning policies relating to the development of urban land

The Green Paper *Household Growth: where shall we live?* (DETR, 1996a) addressed the problem of providing development land in order to satisfy the growth in demand for housing, expected as a result of the 1992-based Household Projections. These showed that the number of households in England was expected to grow by 4.4 million (23%) over the 25 years 1991 to 2016, to reach 23.6 million by 2016. The underlying population was expected to increase by 3.6 million over the same period (DETR, 1996a, p. 5).

The reasons given for household growth formation exceeding the increase in population were given as:

- a reduction in marriage rates, only partly offset by cohabitation;
- people marrying at a later age or not marrying at all;
- an increase in divorce and separation;
- single (never-married) mothers;
- young people leaving home at a younger age; and
- people living longer. (See DETR, 1996a, pp. 13–17.)

In numerical terms the greatest increases in household formation were expected to be in London and the South-East, Hampshire, Greater Manchester and West Yorkshire. In some parts of the country, particularly the South-East this would result in considerable pressure being placed on greenfield land for housing development. According to the Green Paper (see DETR, 1996a, p. 18):

- Around 169 000 ha, or 1.3% of England's area, are projected to change from rural uses to urban uses between 1991 and 2016, equal to about 6800 ha per year.
- By 2016 about 11.9% of England's land area is projected to be in urban uses compared with an estimated 10.6% in 1991.
- Between 1991 and 2016, households are projected to increase by 23% but land in urban uses is projected to increase by 12.2%. The difference is explained primarily by the recycling of land in urban uses.

The figure for expected growth in household formation was later revised in a downward direction, to 3.8 million, for the 25-year period 1996–2021 (DETR, 1999). Although a reduction, the revised projection still represented a 19% increase in household formation and, numerically, exceeded the population growth projection for the same period.

The Green Paper considered a number of options for future development, assessing the merits of:

- urban infill;
- urban extensions;
- key village extensions and multiple village extensions;
- new towns and new villages.

It concluded that all of these options would need to be considered as potential elements of a response to the latest household projections. The extent to which they are appropriate, and the degree to which they will be able to make a substantive contribution to the scale of development needed, will vary from area to area (DETR, 1996a, pp. 35–38).

The Green Paper also sought views as to whether or not an 'aspirational target' of 60% of new homes to be built on previously-used land could be achieved 'or whether we could do better' (DETR, 1996a, p. 40), recognising that there existed a wide variation in land reuse, with the average for London being 83%, whilst in the East Midlands it was only 32%.

PPG6: *Town Centres and Retail Development*

Planning Policy Guidance Note 6, *Town Centres and Retail Developments*, places the emphasis on a plan-led approach to promoting development in town centres, both through policies and the identification of locations and sites for development. It stresses the need for a sequential approach to the selection of sites for development, for retail, employment, leisure and other key uses in town centres and support for local centres. Thus, in the absence of a planning brief, when identifying a site for retail development, if a developer is proposing an out-of-centre development the onus will be on the developer to demonstrate that he has thoroughly assessed all potential town centre options (PPG6, DETR, 1996b, paragraph 1.10). This means that where suitable sites, or buildings for conversion, are available in town centres, preference should be given to the redevelopment of these (followed by edge of centre, district and local centres) before out-of-centre locations are considered.

A study by CB Hillier Parker, on behalf of the National Retail Planning Forum, the British Council of Shopping Centres and the DETR, has examined how the sequential test set out in PPG6 is being applied in practice and its effects on retail development (CB Hillier Parker, 2000). The objectives were to establish the availability of evidence on policy and practice before and after introduction of the sequential approach and then to test the quality of that evidence to arrive at conclusions on the effects of the policy measure. The research consisted of the following:

- In-depth interviews with 12 local authorities.
- A detailed review of the documentary evidence they provided.
- In-depth interviews with six retail developers, seven food retailers and six non-food retailers.
- Analysis of the documentation provided by the private sector.
- In-depth analysis of the Inspector's conclusions and decisions taken at nine public inquiries into major retail developments.
- An outline review of a further 20 Planning Inquiry decisions.

From this study the conclusion was reached that local plan policies and decisions for retail development have changed to incorporate the sequential approach. However, further research is needed addressing the definition of edge-of-centre, into the availability of town centre sites, the flexibility of retailers and the capacity of town centre and edge-of-centre locations to accommodate new retail development.

Mixed-use development is promoted by PPG6, retaining key town centre uses and maintaining urban vitality. The vitality and viability of town and district centres depend on:

- retaining and developing a wide range of attractions and amenities;
- creating and maintaining an attractive environment;
- ensuring good accessibility to and within the centre; and
- attracting continuing investment in development or refurbishment of existing buildings. (PPG6, DETR, 1996b, paragraph 2.2.)

In order that these objectives may be achieved, the planning system should provide a positive framework to encourage appropriate investment in town centres, through the development of town centre strategies and development plans and by facilitating site assembly. The Government wishes to attract investment into upgrading existing buildings and high-quality new development, including an increase in housing in town centres. A set of indicators for measuring the vitality and viability of town centres is included in PPG6 and these are reproduced in Box 2.2. They provide baseline and time-series information on the health of the centre, allow comparison between centres and are useful for assessing the likely impact of out-of-centre developments.

PPG13: Transport

PPG13 deals with transport and opens by making the point that our quality of life depends on transport and easy access to jobs, shopping, leisure facilities and services. It goes on to say that we need a safe, efficient and integrated transport system to support a strong and prosperous economy. But the way we travel and the continued growth in road traffic is damaging our towns, harming our countryside and contributing to global warming (PPG13, DETR, 2001 paragraph 1).

The objectives of the guidance are to integrate planning and transport at the national, strategic and local level. In order to deliver the objectives of this guidance, when preparing development plans and considering planning applications, local authorities should:

- actively manage the pattern of urban growth to make the fullest use of public transport, and focus major generators of travel demand in city, town and district centres and near to major public transport interchanges;
- locate day-to-day facilities which need to be near their clients in local centres so that they are accessible by walking and cycling;
- accommodate housing principally within existing urban areas, planning for increased intensity of development for both housing and other uses at locations which are highly accessible by public transport, walking and cycling;
- ensure that development comprising jobs, shopping, leisure and services offers a realistic choice of access by public transport, walking, and cycling, recognising that this may be less achievable in some rural areas;
- in rural areas, locate most development for housing, jobs, shopping, leisure and services in local service centres which are designated in the development plan to act as focal points for housing, transport and other services, and encourage better transport provision in the countryside;

Box 2.2   Measuring the health of town centres.

- **Diversity of uses.** How much space is in use for different functions, such as offices; shopping; other commercial, leisure, cultural and entertainment activities; pubs, cafés and restaurants; hotels; educational uses; housing – and how has that balance been changing?
- **Retailer representation and intentions to change representation**. It may be helpful to look at the existence and changes in representation including street markets, over the past few years, and at the demand from retailers wanting to come into the town, or to change their representation in the town, or to contract or close their representation.
- **Shopping rents**. Pattern of movement in Zone A rents within primary shopping areas (i.e. in retail units the retail value for the first 6 m depth of floorspace from the shop window).
- **Proportion of vacant street-level property**. Vacancies can arise even in the strongest town centres, and this indicator must be used with care. Vacancies in secondary frontages and changes to other uses will also be useful indicators.
- **Commercial yields on non-domestic property (i.e. the capital value in relation to the expected market rental)**. This demonstrates the confidence of investors in the long-term profitability of the centre for retail, office and other commercial developments. This indicator should be used with care.
- **Pedestrian flows**. The numbers and movement of people on the streets, in different parts of the centre at different times of the day and evening, who are available for businesses to attract into shops, restaurants or other facilities.
- **Accessibility**. The ease and convenience of access by a choice of means of travel, including the quality, quantity and type of car parking, the frequency and quality of public transport services, the range of customer origins served and the quality of provision for pedestrians and cyclists.
- **Customer views and behaviour**. Regular surveys of customer views will help authorities in monitoring and evaluating the effectiveness of town centre improvements and in setting further priorities. Interviews in the town centre and at home should be used to establish views of both users and non-users of tile centre. This could establish the degree of linked trips.
- **Perception of safety and occurrence of crime**. This should include views and information on safety and security.
- **Town centre environmental quality**. This should include information on problems (such as air pollution, noise, clutter, litter and graffiti) and positive factors (such as trees, landscaping, open spaces).

Source: PPG6 Town Centres and Retail Developments; DETR, 1996b

- ensure that strategies in the development and local transport plan complement each other and that consideration of development plan allocations and local transport investment and priorities are closely linked;
- use parking policies, alongside other planning and transport measures, to promote sustainable transport choices and reduce reliance on the car for work and other journeys;
- give priority to people over ease of traffic movement and plan to provide more road space to pedestrians, cyclists and public transport in town centres, local neighbourhoods and other areas with a mixture of land uses;
- ensure that the needs of disabled people – as pedestrians, public transport users and motorists – are taken into account in the implementation of planning policies and traffic management schemes, and in the design of individual developments;
- consider how best to reduce crime and the fear of crime, and seek by the design and layout of developments and areas to secure community safety and road safety; and
- protect sites and routes which could be critical in developing infrastructure to widen transport choices for both passenger and freight movements. (PPG13, DETR, 2001, paragraph 6)

The guidance note recommends that local authorities should seek to ensure that strategies in the development plan and the local transport plan are complementary. In doing this, consideration of development plan allocations and local transport priorities and investment should be closely linked. Local authorities should also ensure that their strategies on parking, traffic and demand management are consistent with their overall strategy on planning and transport.

Land uses that are major generators of travel demand in city, town and district centres should be concentrated near to major public transport interchanges. Transport interchanges that are in city, town and district centres should generally be preferred over out-of-centre interchanges, which should not be a focus for land uses which are major generators of travel demand.

Local authorities should actively manage the pattern of urban growth and the location of major travel-generating development in such ways as to make the fullest use of public transport. This may require the phasing of sites being released for development, so as to coordinate growth with public transport improvements and ensure it relates well to the existing pattern of development.

Local authorities should also take into account the potential for changing overall travel patterns, for instance by improving the sustainability of existing developments through a fully coordinated approach of development plan allocations and transport improvements. Day-to-day facilities which need to be near their clients should be located in local and rural service centres, with safe and easy access, particularly by walking and cycling. Such facilities include primary schools, health centres, convenience shops, branch libraries and local offices of the local authority and other local service providers.

Some of the related design issues raised by PPG13 are discussed in Chapter 13.

2.4   The Urban Task Force

On the subject of development densities, the Urban Task Force view was that 'we must change the way in which we respond to the concept of urban density' (Urban Task Force, 1999, p. 59). Standard development densities in England are between 20 and 30 dwellings per hectare, although in some areas such as Bloomsbury and Islington in London densities can rise to as high as 100–200 dwellings per hectare. Contrast this with the most compact and vibrant European city, Barcelona, which has an average density of about 400 dwellings per hectare (Urban Task Force, 1999, p. 59).

The Urban Task Force considered the potential for derelict and vacant land and vacant buildings to be redeveloped or converted for residential use. Defining derelict land as 'damaged' but justifying reclamation, the Task Force estimated that, based on National Land Use Database (NLUD) figures, about 5600 ha in England could be redeveloped for housing which could produce 164 000 new dwellings. Vacant land, i.e. land that is less damaged by previous development activities could, on the same basis, provide about 5300 ha capable of accommodating 150 000 housing units. Vacant residential and commercial buildings could contribute a further 250 000 units (Urban Task Force, 1999, pp. 179–184). All of these figures are based on current development densities of around 28–30 units per hectare (12 units per acre) but, as will be shown in later chapters, significantly higher densities can be achieved. Therefore derelict and vacant land, and vacant buildings, could provide even more dwellings if developed to higher densities.

The Urban Task Force, appointed by Deputy Prime Minister (and the then Secretary of State for the Environment) John Prescott and chaired by Lord Rogers of Riverside, considered the issue of reusing land, together with the question of development densities for urban development. It concluded that the planning system should be the main tool for managing the land supply (Urban Task Force, 1999, p. 212) and that:

- most contaminated land is capable of safe remediation using modern technology at reasonable cost;
- the present barriers to redevelopment are largely to do with perception of risk;

- we have to simplify and consolidate the regulatory systems which seek to protect the environment from the consequences of contamination;
- we should promote greater standardisation in the way we manage the risks involved in redeveloping contaminated sites, and thereby promote a better and consistent understanding of the situation. (Urban Task Force, 1999, p. 237)

Many of the recommendations made by the Urban Task Force have subsequently been put into effect, either by the Government or by other organisations. For example, recommendation 76 urged the piloting of standardised land condition statements, to provide more certainty and consistency in the management and sale of contaminated and previously contaminated land; a consortium of organisations (including the RICS, the ICE, Royal Society of Chemistry and representatives from the banking, insurance and development industries) has since completed work on a standard form of Land Condition Record and an accreditation body has been established, see *www.silc.org.uk*. The Government's full response to the Urban Task Force recommendations is contained in the Urban White Paper *Our Towns and Cities: the future* (DETR, 2000a).

2.5   Land for housing

Four years after the Green Paper, *Household Growth: where shall we live?* (DETR, 1996a) the 60% 'aspirational target' was adopted into policy, as part of a revised Planning Policy Guidance note on Housing (PPG3). This set out the Government's objectives:

'The Government intends that everyone should have the opportunity of a decent home . . . to promote more sustainable patterns of development and make better use of previously-developed land[2.1] the focus for additional housing should be existing towns and cities.'

(DETR, 2000b, p. 5)

[2.1] Previously developed land is that which is or was occupied by a permanent structure (excluding agricultural or forestry buildings), and associated fixed surface infrastructure. The definition covers the curtilage of the development. Previously developed land may occur in both built-up and rural settings. The definition includes defence buildings and land used for mineral extraction and waste disposal where provision for restoration has not been made through development control procedures. (PPG3 – Housing, p. 27). The definition specifically excludes land and buildings used for agriculture or forestry and previously used land where the remains of any structure or activity have blended into the landscape.

The ways in which local authorities should seek to achieve these objectives include:

- Planning to meet the housing requirements of the whole community.
- Ensuring the provision of greater diversity in terms of types and tenure of housing.
- Seeking to create 'mixed' communities.
- Providing sufficient housing land but giving priority to reusing previously developed land.
- Creating more sustainable patterns of development by building in ways which exploit and deliver accessibility to public transport.
- Placing the needs of people before cars and reducing the dependence upon cars.
- Promoting good design in housing to produce high-quality living environments.

2.5.1   Predicting demand

The previous policy of 'predicting' the demand for housing over the lifetime of a Unitary Development Plan (UDP) or Structure Plan, and 'providing' land in order to meet that prediction, is to be replaced by 'plan, monitor and manage'. The intention here is to keep the demand for housing land under regular review, with the level of housing provision and its distribution being based on a clear set of policy objectives, linked to measurable indicators of change. Monitoring would be the basis on which regional planning bodies (RPBs) would formulate and review their housing policies on a not less than five-yearly basis. Regional Planning Guidance (RPG) and development plans should provide clear guidance as to the location of new housing development, including expected areas of major growth. Structure plans and UDPs should identify growth areas and distribution of housing land at a district level. Local Plans and UDPs should identify sites, and buildings suitable for conversion, at a local level sufficient to meet housing requirements after making allowance for 'windfall' sites. These objectives are likely to be reinforced, and to some extent changed, as a result of the Planning Green Paper (see Chapter 16).

So far as the allocation of land for housing development is concerned, the presumption is that previously developed sites (or buildings for reuse or conversion) should be developed before greenfield sites. The guidance note sets a national target for 60% of additional housing to be provided on previously developed land and through the conversion of buildings by the year 2008. In following the principles of the policies, when allocating land for development in local plans and UDPs, local planning authorities should assess the potential and suitability of sites against the following criteria:

- The *availability of previously developed sites* and empty or underused buildings and their suitability for housing use.
- The *location and accessibility* of potential development sites to jobs, shops and services by modes other than the car, and the potential for improving such accessibility.
- The *capacity of existing and potential infrastructure*, including public transport, water and sewerage, other utilities and social infrastructure (such as schools and hospitals) to absorb further development and the cost of adding further infrastructure.
- The *ability to build communities* to support new physical and social infrastructure and to provide demand to sustain appropriate local services and facilities.
- The *physical and environmental constraints on development of land*, including, for example, the level of contamination, stability and flood risk, taking into account that such risk may increase as a result of climate change.

(DETR, 2000b, p. 13)[2.2]

This is known as the 'sequential test' approach to the allocation of land for development and the exception to this principle will be where previously developed sites perform so poorly in relation to these criteria as to preclude their use for housing (within the relevant plan period or phase) before a particular greenfield site.

Windfall sites are those that have not been specifically identified for residential development in the local plan or UDP because they were in some alternative use (e.g. industry, school or hospital) at the time the relevant plan was prepared. Such sites may comprise a significant proportion of the previously developed sites becoming available within a local authority's area. Local authorities should seek to make allowance for different types of windfalls, based on past trends, with no allowance being made for greenfield windfalls. It may also be appropriate for authorities to consider reallocating for housing development land that is currently allocated to other uses, such as employment, where that land cannot realistically be taken up for that use during the plan period.

In order to make the best use of available resources, local authorities should avoid the inefficient use of land. This implies increasing development densities beyond the current average of 25 dwellings per hectare. Local authorities should therefore seek to encourage densities of between 30 and 50 dwellings per hectare, and greater intensity of development at places with good public transport accessibility such as city, town, district and local centres or around

---

[2.2] Emphasis as in the original text.

major transport nodes. Car parking standards at no more than 1.5 off-street spaces per dwelling would be in line with Government policies.

PPG3 recognises that not all development can take place within urban areas but the extent to which development should take place outside existing areas will depend upon the overall need for housing land, the capacity of existing urban areas to accommodate additional housing and the efficiency with which land is developed. Only a limited amount of housing can be expected to be accommodated in expanded villages, for example where it can be demonstrated that additional housing will support local services, such as schools or shops, that would become unviable without some modest growth. Additional housing may also be provided in rural areas to meet specific requirements, such as affordable housing, and to help secure a mixed and balanced community. Rural developments will have to be designed sympathetically and be laid out in keeping with the character of the area.

The provisions for rural development within the guidance note will account for only a very small percentage of the demand for new housing and it is clear that virtually all new developments will be within existing urban areas, competing for land against other uses. In the view of some commentators this 'broad-brush' approach is nonsensical (Straw, 1999) as many towns are physically incapable of accommodating all the Government's sought uses. Straw contends that the historic fabric of many towns would be at risk from major new development and that not all uses are capable of coexisting – exemplified by the rising concerns of inner-city residents over development that generates activity late into the evening.

2.5.2   Suitability for use

A major thrust of Planning Policy Guidance Note 3 is to encourage the reuse of previously used land in preference to developing on greenfield sites. If the guidance is heeded by local planning authorities, developers are likely to encounter pressure to increase development densities, rather than the other way round as has often been the case in the past. In some cases developers may feel that the move towards reducing car-parking provision will have a detrimental impact on the viability of developments. They may also feel that some land is not suitable for residential use, either physically or in terms of perception, because of the nature of contaminants present in the ground or the previous use of the site.

In the UK, Government policy dealing with land contamination is based on the 'suitable for use' approach, which consists of three elements:

(1)   *Ensuring that land is suitable for its current use.* In other words, identifying any land where contamination is causing unacceptable risks to human health

and the environment, assessed on the basis of current use and circumstances of the land, and returning such land to a condition where such risks no longer arise (i.e. 'remediating' the land).

(2) *Ensuring that the land is made suitable for any new use, as planning permission is given for that new use.* In other words, assessing the potential risks from contamination, on the basis of the proposed future use and circumstances, before official permission is given for the development and, where necessary, to avoid unacceptable risks to human health and the environment, remediating the land before the new use commences.

(3) *Limiting requirements for remediation to the work necessary to prevent unacceptable risks to human health or the environment in relation to the current use or future use of the land for which planning permission is being sought.* In other words, recognising that the risks from contaminated land can be satisfactorily addressed only in the context of specific uses of the land (whether current or proposed), and that any attempt to guess what might be needed at some time in the future for other uses is likely to result in premature work (thereby risking distorting social, economic and environmental priorities) or in unnecessary work (thereby wasting resources).

DETR Circular 02/2000, Annex 1, pp. 7–8, (DETR, 2000c)[2.3]

The first of these elements is intended to be addressed by the 'contaminated land legislation' – Part IIA of the Environmental Protection Act 1990 – and the second by the town planning process, including Planning Policy Guidance Notes. The third element is a statement confirming that land should be decontaminated only to the extent that it should not cause harm in its existing or immediately proposed use. In this context it is not intended that the policy should 'second-guess' future development that might occur on the land by insisting on a higher standard of remediation than might otherwise be required.

2.6 Effect of the Government's current planning policies

At the time of writing, October 2001, the policies set out in PPG3 have been in effect for little over one year and it is therefore rather early to determine whether or not they have been fully effective. However, some early inferences can be drawn. Straw's (1999) comments, referred to above, were made in response to the consultative draft of PPG3 and before the new policies came into effect. More recent press comment has attacked PPG3 as a 'Stalinist new regulation' which is smothering new developments in red tape and demands

---

[2.3] Emphasis as in the original text.

for 'mixed communities' and 'sustainable development' (Anon, 2001), resulting in a shortfall of 55 000 new homes completions in the previous year, against an average demand of 200 000.

The National Statistics Bulletin 'Land Use Change in England', published in July 2001, provides an indication of how the policies are working (see Box 2.3 below).

The Council for the Protection of Rural England (CPRE, 2001) has published a report that looks at the first year of policy implementation in respect of PPG3. It is based on a questionnaire survey of local planning authorities (154 responses, 50% response rate) and contains the following key findings:

Box 2.3   Key points from Land Use Change Bulletin No. 16 (provisional estimates for 2000, Office for National Statistics, 2001).

Changes to residential use
- In 2000, 57% of all new dwellings were provided on previously developed land and through conversions, and 47% of land changing to residential use was previously developed. Both trends have remained stable over the last few years.

Density of dwellings built
- In 2000, dwellings were built at an average density of 28 dwellings per hectare on previously developed land, and 22 dwellings per hectare on land not previously developed. This is similar to the average over the period since 1989, when the dwellings data were first collected.
- Over the same period, nearly half of all new dwellings were built at densities of less than 30 dwellings per hectare; these dwellings were built on three-quarters of all land used for housing.

Changes within green belts and flood risk areas
- Each year between 1995 and 1998, 2–3% of all new dwellings and 5–6% of all land changing to residential use was within green belts, which cover 13% of England. Half of the green belt land changing to residential use was previously in urban use.
- Each year since 1995, about 11% of all new dwellings and 9% of all land changing to residential use was within flood risk areas.

Changes to urban and rural uses
- Changes to rural uses are recorded more slowly so a complete picture is available only up to 1996. In the four years up to 1996, an average of about 38 000 ha (0.29% of the area of England) per year changed use. Of these, 15% were changes from rural to urban use.

News release 25 July 2001, DTLR, website, *www.dtlr.gov.uk*

(1)   Government Ministers have signalled their clear intent to see PPG3 delivered on the ground in speech after speech and backed this up with a new Greenfield Direction (DETR Circular 08/00 (see DETR, 2000c)) to inform them of all major greenfield proposals.

(2)   Half of local authorities have not undertaken an urban capacity study (see DETR, 2000d) and barely one quarter have reviewed density or design policies, parking standards or employment land allocations.

(3)   There is enough rural land earmarked by the planning system to accommodate the demands of the top 80 housebuilders for six years without using a single urban site. Almost no action is being taken to withdraw existing greenfield sites from the system and nobody knows where they are.

(4)   The Government is setting adequate regional targets to meet its national target of 60% of housing on previously developed land but actual performance has been stuck at 57% since 1995.

(5)   Regional plans are still being based on projections of household demand despite the Government's desire to kill off predict-and-provide planning. Local authorities and Inspectors seek clearer guidance on the new plan, monitor and manage approach.

(6)   The Government has not intervened on more than 60% of all major greenfield housing developments since 7 March 2000, thereby allowing the development of over 15 000 houses on 671 ha of rural land. Decisions on a further 4750 homes on 233 ha are outstanding (report date March 2001).

(7)   Local authority councillors are poorly informed about PPG3 and only one in seven has been offered training in its implications.

(8)   Local councils continue to give planning consent for low-density greenfield housing development where brownfield alternatives exist and planning Inspectors are not ensuring the consistent implementation of the new guidance.

(9)   Government Regional Offices have contributed fully to reviews of Regional Planning Guidance on the implications of PPG3 but are inconsistent and unreliable in policing its implementation on the ground.

(10)   Local councils are proving reluctant to review local plans to take on board the new guidance despite the strongest encouragement for them to do so.

(PRE, 2001)

2.7   The CBI ten-point action plan

Taking the right decision at the right time is a key factor in business success but, according to the CBI, the planning system has not kept pace with economic change. Clearly businesses will be disappointed when planning permission is refused (about one in ten applications) but criticisms are not driven solely by 'sour grapes', rather the principal concern is with the way in which the decision is made. The CBI sees three distinct, yet interrelated ways in which the planning system is failing its users:

(1)   It is too slow, too often, on decisions that matter.
(2)   The process involves too many uncertainties.
(3)   There is too much scope for poor decisions.

(CBI, 2001)

Viewed from the perspective of the local planning authority, prospective developers often leave it too late to discuss their proposals, or do not even seek to enter into any discussions prior to submitting a planning application and then expect a decision within six to eight weeks (see Syms, 2001). Developers are also seen as being prone to submitting unrealistic applications that do not accord with UDPs and Structure Plans.

Therefore, in trying to address the problems inherent in the planning system, the ten areas for action and the principal changes proposed by the CBI are as follows.

(1)   *Making local plans more relevant to business*
    (a)   Impose a deadline for completion of plans, enforceable by strict penalties.
    (b)   Plans to be shorter, more strategic and more flexible in nature
    (c)   Increase economic input in plans to reflect Regional Economic Strategy priorities.
    (d)   Keep plans up to date through regular reviews.
    (e)   Ensure consistency with other policies such as transport.

(2)   *Ensuring regional and national economic priorities are implemented effectively at the local level*
    (a)   Local plans should incorporate development sites regarded as priorities by the RDAs.
    (b)   RDAs should actively develop the economic case for priority developments.
    (c)   RDAs should be statutory consultants on local plans and strategic developments.
    (d)   Economic input needed in respect of individual planning applications.
    (e)   Review the regional planning process to determine the role it could play in planning for major projects.

(3)   *Promoting more informed political participation in the planning process*
   (a)   Greater delegation of decisions from members to officers; committees should concentrate on larger or controversial projects
   (b)   Base delegation decisions on majority decisions of the planning committee, rather than total unanimity.
   (c)   Ensure that planning officers' advice is given due consideration by committee.
   (d)   Better dissemination of what is in the local plans and where development opportunities exist.
   (e)   Economic development officers should be given a greater input in the planning process.
   (f)   Training on business needs and planning regulations should be mandatory for councillors sitting on planning committees.

(4)   Reducing the decision-making load on the system
   (a)   Widen rules on 'permitted development' and 'deemed consent'.
   (b)   Review the Use Classes Order to take account of modern practices and requirements.
   (c)   Adopt a more flexible approach for some types of developments, (e.g. within the designated boundaries of business parks).
   (d)   Adopt more effective and more widespread use of Simplified Planning Zones.

(5)   *Making planning obligations more transparent and fair*
   (a)   Clearer national guidelines needed, requiring local authorities to be more explicit about their aims.
   (b)   Greater consistency needed between local authorities in the way they negotiate planning obligations, share and encourage good practice.

(6)   *Introducing procedural deadlines and more effective performance standards*
   (a)   Measure and set separate targets for decisions in respect of household and commercial planning applications.
   (b)   Place more emphasis on targets measuring the quality of the decision.
   (c)   Best Value framework indicators should set more demanding targets for minimising the number of applications lost on appeal.
   (d)   Establish rigorous time limits for the key parts of the planning process.

(7)   *Enhancing local authorities' capabilities and resources*
   (a)   Encourage innovative ideas to overcome shortfalls in the numbers and quality of planning officers.

    (b)   Reduce the use of 'area teams', giving flexibility to assign officers with the right skills to deal with commercial applications, regardless of location.

    (c)   Bring in specialists or consultants where necessary to advise on major applications.

    (d)   Outsource some work during busy periods, rather than downgrade the level of service.

(8)   *Providing better incentives and penalties to improve performance*

    (a)   Reward success for significant progress in meeting targets for processing commercial applications.

    (b)   Incentivise local authorities to ensure that local plans are in place and are regularly reviewed.

    (c)   Where planning decisions, made against officers' advice, are overturned on appeal, local authorities to pay compensation for the cost of the delay.

(9)   *Making the planning system easier for businesses to use*

    (a)   Simplify the process to ensure that a suitably skilled planning officer leads an application the right way through the process.

    (b)   Adopt new methods, such as an internet 'planning portal', so that applicants can track the progress of their application.

    (c)   Offer pre-submission discussions to applicants, with clear guidance to businesses.

    (d)   Encourage businesses to provide sufficient information early on in an application, without the need to repeat to other statutory bodies.

    (e)   Use a 'decision in principle' mechanism so that finance can be secured and get a project under way.

(10)   *Improving local authorities' and statutory bodies' understanding of business needs*

    (a)   Promote use of the best practice Planning Users' Concordat.

    (b)   Enable, through education, training and industrial secondments, a better understanding of business, on the part of planning officers and committee members, including the economics and finance of developments.

Overall, the CBI Planning for Productivity paper received very positive responses. Some of these were from unexpected sources as, for example, the CBI thought that local authority representatives might have been put out by criticisms of the inefficient ways in which local authority planning departments operated, but a number of planning staff wrote in support of the paper. Not surprisingly these comments were particularly in support of what the CBI had said about lack of resources.

Business organisations including the British Property Federation, The British Chamber of Commerce and the House Builders Federation, expressed support for the paper and went as far as endorsing it, with their respective logos displayed on the back of the paper. Support was also received from the RICS, RIBA and the Environmental Services Association.

The Royal Town Planning Institute (RTPI) also supported most of what was in the CBI paper, but did not agree with all of the recommendations, as shown by this extract from *Planning* magazine:

> 'RTPI public affairs director David Rose said that much of the CBI's demands are sensible. "They are not saying that planners have to work harder"; he added, "They recognise that authorities need more staff and resources." But Rose criticised the CBI's suggestion that authorities should be penalised for failing to get up-to-date plans in place.'
>
> (Rose, 2001).

The CBI was pleased with the immediate response from Government and two days after the launch of the CBI paper, Stephen Byers gave a speech on the Government's plans to reform the planning system.

> 'Local planning departments have over half a million direct customers a year applying for planning permissions. But the performance of individual authorities is highly variable. It simply cannot be right for similar planning applications to take days to decide in one authority and weeks in another. Nor can it be right for time-critical business decisions to be given the same priority as an application for a garage extension.
>
> Business tells me that what they need most of the planning system is speed, certainty, transparency and quality of decisions. None of these requirements seem remotely unreasonable. They are what we all want of planning. And they are no more than we would expect of any other public service.'
>
> (Byers, 2001)

The good response to the CBI paper was probably due to two reasons:

(1)   It was well-timed and caught the wave of discontent about the planning system at the right time.
(2)   The CBI consulted a large number of organisations when preparing the paper and did not limit itself to views from businesses.

The issues relating to the need to update the planning system are discussed further in Chapter 16.

2.8   Summary

This chapter provides a brief overview of the planning policies that are currently shaping development in the UK and especially in England. It cannot hope to have covered all of the issues that are likely to impact upon development proposals. Developers and their development teams need to be aware of planning policies and indeed some of the philosophy underlying the policies, as ignorance is unlikely to result in a good development.

As mentioned in the introduction, planning policies are in a state of change and intending developers need to ensure that they are consulting the latest versions of guidance notes and other documents. Many complaints have been expressed about the development plan system – UDPs, Structure Plans and local plans – often regarding the time involved in bringing these from inception to adoption. Developers often regard them as being out of date before they even come into force and this can lead to conflict, resulting in planning refusals and appeals.

Many argue that there is not enough brown land to satisfy demand, that many of our old industrial sites have already been reclaimed, that the cost of reclamation is too high or that sites are in the wrong places (Rogers & Power, 2000, p. 157). While there may be some truth in these arguments, it does not mean that opportunities to redevelop previously developed land should be ignored or rejected.

In some parts of the country there is certainly not enough brown land to satisfy demands for residential and commercial developments, so greenfield land has to be used. But the same principles of increasing development densities should also apply to such land, albeit not to the same high densities as may be appropriate in inner urban areas – perhaps moving to densities of 40–50 housing units per hectare (16–20 units per acre) on greenfield land would be a start. So far as existing brown land is concerned, it is almost inevitable that developers will tackle the easiest sites first, leaving harder sites until later; indeed Government policies and grant aid have tended to encourage this to happen. Reclamation costs will be higher for the most severely damaged land, although the development of new techniques may bring down the costs and Government policies may encourage landowners to take a proactive approach towards preparing land for redevelopment.

2.9   Checklist

- Does the proposed development make the best use of the site?
- Does it comply with the development plan for the area?
- Does it accord with planning policies?

- Does it favour the use of brownfield land in inner urban areas, before fringe of settlement or greenfield development?
- Town centre sites are likely to be given planning preference to out–of–town locations; how will this affect the proposed development?
- Transport issues must be considered when preparing development plans.
- Windfall sites may need to be allowed a change of use to ensure their redevelopment.

Throughout this chapter, reference has been made to relevant Internet websites. The Internet provides an invaluable source of information for students and practitioners involved with planning and development. Web addresses are sometimes prone to change but the following table lists the weblinks referred to, in this and succeeding chapters, all of which were correct at the end of 2001.

Planning and Development Weblinks.

Name	Web address
ArcExplorer	www.gis.com/software/free
Associated British Ports (ABP)	www.abports.co.uk
Association of Geo-technical and Geo-Environmental Specialists (AGS)	www.ags.org.uk
Bio-wise	www.dti.gov.uk/biowise
British Market Research Association (BMRA)	www.bmra.org.uk
Bruntwood Estates	www.bruntwood.co.uk
Bryant Homes	www.bryant.co.uk
Business Geographics	www.geoweb.co.uk
Cambourne Concept Centre	www.cambourne-uk.com
Central Office of Information	www.coi.gov.uk
Certa (Insurance)	www.certa.com
Charles Close Society for the Study of Ordnance Survey Maps	www.charlesclosesociety.org.uk
Circle Systems (computer software)	www.circsys.com
Civic Trust	www.civictrust.org.uk
Customs and Excise (VAT and Landfill Tax)	www.hmce.gov.uk
Department for the Environment, Food and Rural Affairs (DEFRA)	www.defra.gov.uk
Department for Transport, Local Government and the Regions (DTLR)	www.dtlr.gov.uk
DTLR databases	www.databases.dtlr.gov.uk
East of England Development Agency (EEDA)	www.eeda.org.uk

Contd

Planning and Development Weblinks *Continued*

Name	Web address
EG Property Link	www.propertylink.co.uk
Environmental Regulations (England and Wales)	www.netregs.environment-agency.gov.uk
ESRI, California	www.esri.com
Estates Gazette interactive	www.egi.co.uk
George Wimpey plc	www.wimpey.co.uk
Health and Safety Executive	www.hse.gov.uk
HM Treasury	www.hm-treasury.gov.uk
HM Treasury – Finance Bill 2001 – Tax relief for contaminated land remediation	www.hm-treasury.gov.uk/financebill/2001
Insignia Richard Ellis	www.richardellis.co.uk
Joseph Rowntree Foundation	www.jrf.org.uk
King Sturge & Co	www.kingsturge.co.uk
Lambert Smith Hampton	www.lsh.co.uk
Landmark Information Group	www.landmarkinfo.co.uk
Landmark Information Group – Promap	www.landmarkinfo.co.uk/promap
Law Society	www.lawsociety.org.uk
Market Research UK Ltd	www.mrscotland.co.uk
National Housing Federation	www.housing.org.uk
National Land Use Database (NLUD)	www.nlud.org.uk
Nicholas Grimshaw & Partners	www.ngrimshaw.co.uk
Office of National Statistics (ONS)	www.statistics.gov.uk
ONS Neighbourhood Statistics	www.statistics.gov.uk/neighbourhood
Planning Policy Guidance Notes (PPGs)	www.planning.gov.uk
Royal Institute of British Architects (RIBA)	www.riba.org.uk
Royal Institution of Chartered Surveyors (RICS)	www.rics.org
Royal Town Planning Institute (RTPI)	www.rtpi.org.uk
Secured by Design	www.securedbydesign.com
Sheffield One (urban regeneration company)	www.sheffield1.com
Specialists in Land Contamination (SiLC)	www.silc.org.uk
Terry Farrell & Partners	www.terryfarrell.com
The new Bull Ring, Birmingham	www.thenewbullring.co.uk
United States Environmental Protection Agency (USEPA)	www.epa.gov
Urban Splash	www.urbansplash.co.uk

Chapter 3
Project Inception

3.1 Introduction

A new property development may come about in many different ways. Larger developers have teams of land buyers seeking sites that meet their requirements and such developers will routinely be offered sites by landowners or their agents. Some, such as major housebuilders, work on a regional basis and the land buyers will be seeking sites that meet their company's specific requirements to meet specific market profiles and to accommodate standard ranges of houses.

Residential and commercial developers will seek to maintain a land bank, so as to ensure that the essential raw material of land is sufficient to maintain the company's expected rate of production. That rate of production will also fluctuate according to the state of the market, increasing to meet strong demand and reducing in times of falling demand. Responses to market fluctuations will inevitably suffer from time lags.

Increasing production in order to meet strengthening demand will generally be more difficult than reducing production. The ability to increase demand will be determined by factors such as planning permission on land held in land banks and the availability of suitable labour and materials. Slowing down production on the other hand will depend largely on the developer's contractual position with contractors undertaking the construction work.

Financing arrangements also have a bearing on the ability to increase or decrease the rate of development. Proposals to significantly increase the rate of production may be regarded by the developer's financial backers as over-extending the company's resources and management capabilities, and so the banks or other funding institutions may seek to control the rate of expansion by controlling the money supply. In a market downturn the developer may have already acquired the site and be making interest payments, or accumulating even more debt in the form of 'rolled up' interest. The developer then has to decide whether or not to increase the debt, and associated risk, by proceeding to build out the development, or wait until there are signs of an upturn in the market. This type of decision calls for very careful judgement on the part of the developer: build too early and the development will remain unsold or unlet; build too late and the development will miss the upturn in the market. The decision-making processes involved are discussed more fully in Chapter 8.

3.2   Land for development

The extent to which developers are prepared to make significant financial commitments to land acquisition will depend on a number of factors including planning permission, the availability of off-site infrastructure and the state of the market. For example, if the land already has planning permission with frontage to a main road in which all services are available and the market is strong, developers will compete with each other to secure the site. If, however, the land is simply allocated for development at some future date, lacks a viable road access and services, and the market is weak, developers are less likely to commit funds to outright purchase.

It also follows that land acquired with planning permission and infrastructure in a competitive situation will be more costly than the alternative site where development may be several years away. Therefore developers will seek to secure land well in advance of requirements, obtain planning permission themselves, or seek to improve existing permissions, and ensure that they are not competing with other developers for the right to develop that land.

Land banks can therefore be divided into two categories: current, usually land with planning permission and ready for immediate or short-term development; and strategic, where planning permission does not exist, major infrastructure works may be required and development may be many years into the future. Table 3.1 gives an indication of the current and strategic land banks of ten major housebuilders.

In assembling their strategic land banks developers will wish to minimise their financial commitments and are therefore less likely to commit to outright purchase. Instead they prefer to leave the owner in occupation of the land, or in receipt of the agricultural rents, and enter into an option agreement or conditional contract, making only a downpayment that would be very small in relation to the full development value of the site. Options and conditional contracts are discussed more fully later in this chapter.

By no means all land acquired by developers is obtained through the efforts of teams of land buyers seeking to secure land identified for future development in UDPs and local plans. Smaller developers may not even employ dedicated land buyers, with the site identification and acquisition being the responsibility

Table 3.1 Housing completions and land banks of ten major housebuilders.

Company	Completed homes in latest report	Change from previous report ±%	Current land bank: plots	Strategic land bank: plots or acres as shown	Years supply based on latest figures	Comments
Barratt	9 980*	+7	33 000 (a net increase of 1600 in six months)	—	3.3 years	6590 plots acquired in the half year to Dec. 2000
Bellway	4 538*	+3	16 500 (an increase of 1000 in six months)	—	3.64 years	—
Countryside	743	−19.58	4 100	16 900	28.26	Completions include 102 joint ventures. Average cost per serviced plot £52k, (approx. 20% of selling prices) up from £45k
Crest Nicholson	1 731	−28.53	7 280	12 562	11.46	Land bank increased from 11 680 previous year
Alfred McAlpine	4 072	—	8 344 (up from 7 587)	6 598 under option	3.67	Includes partnership housing of 986 units
Persimmon	13 000–14 000 (restructuring at time of report)	—	10 888	In excess of 20 000	3.77	Average cost of current land bank £23 181 per plot
Redrow	3 338	+7	13 500	27 000	12.13	6000 plots in strategic land bank allocated in local plans

Contd

Table 3.1 Continued.

Westbury	4 355	+1.68	12 700	11 500	5.56	Average cost of current land bank £27 350 per plot
Wimpey/McLean	10 823	−6.75	33 450 plots	10 700 acres (4 348 ha)	3.09 (current only)	Strategic land bank increased by 550 acres (223 ha) since previous year
David Wilson	3 604	−0.5	13 500	—	3.75	—
Totals	43 184	—	153 262	94 560 plots plus 10 700 acres (4348 ha) 190 000 plots	3.55 years current plus in excess of 4.4 years strategic	—

Notes: 1. The information contained in the table is based on the latest published accounts of the companies concerned. The most recent information is March 2001 and the oldest is December 1998.

2. Some of the developers quote production figures as 'sales' and some as 'completions'. It is not always clear whether the latter means physical completion or sales. For the purpose of this table they have been treated as the same.

3. Ten developers are detailed, all quoted on the Stock Exchange; they include the largest developers but are not necessarily the 'top ten' in terms of numbers of units produced.

4. Most of the information obtained was based on annual figure but some completions were taken from half-yearly figures. These have been used to extrapolate annual figures and are marked with an asterisk (*).

of a small team of development executives, who will then work up the feasibility of the project and may even remain involved with it right through to completion. For these smaller developers, and for at least part of the development programme of larger developers, 'windfall' sites will play an important part. These are sites that were not envisaged as being available for redevelopment at the time the UDP or local plan was prepared. They may have been in use for many different purposes, such as manufacturing plants, retail units or schools, and their closure, or relocation, was not contemplated at the time the relevant plan was prepared. These previously developed or brownfield sites can be expected to play an increasing part in property development activities in the UK.

Another source of development land may be available to developers who are also property investors. When leases come to an end the developer/investor is faced with three choices: to re-let the building as it is; to refurbish or modernise the building before re-letting; or to redevelop the site. Thus it will be necessary for the developer/investor to decide on the most appropriate course of action, given the state of the market and the relative costs involved.

3.3   Assessing the market potential

The same larger developers that employ teams of land buyers are also likely to have in-house capabilities in respect of market research and analysis. The research techniques employed may be quite sophisticated, with demographic studies being used to forecast trends in family formation, births, employment and age of the community. These will be used to determine the type of product that will be required, whether it be housing for new families, singles or retirees, or to meet employment needs in the form of speculative offices or industrial units.

The smaller developer is less likely to have the services of an in-house market research team and will either have to appoint a specialist research organisation, or rely on his or her own experience plus the advice of other professional advisers, such as local estate agents. Many developers possess almost a 'sixth sense' for knowing what will work in their marketplace. They have either produced a well-tried and highly respected product, or they have the knack of being able to identify a niche in the market. One of the most disastrous things a developer can do, however, is to assume that just because a type of development has worked before, it will work again, even in a similar or nearby location.

For example, the fact that a speculative 5000 square metre industrial building let to a 'household name' before construction was completed does not mean that the development of a similar building half-a-mile down the road will be equally successful. The first building might simply have been developed at a time when a local company was seeking to relocate, or when the tenant had a need for a building to satisfy a particular need, such as a new contract. It may have soaked up all of the latent demand in the area, with there being no underlying demand for industrial buildings. The intending developer therefore needs to analyse the historical take-up of buildings with particular care.

3.3.1 *Market research*

At its simplest, market research may consist of nothing more than the property developer looking at what is currently on the market, what has sold or let well over the last 12 months and what new developments are proposed. Questions might be asked of local and national estate agents as to how they view the prospects for a particular type of development product. This might be backed up by some economic and demographic information about the area but little more in terms of identifying potential demand. Taken altogether this limited research might give some indication as to how the project might be received in the marketplace but it will be fairly unstructured.

All too often this is how developers undertook market research in the past but this is changing. Banks and other financial institutions will require market research that is more robust and, ideally, research that includes a degree of testing amongst the target market. This research might be either quantitative or qualitative. It can also be strategic or site specific.

Regardless of the type of research undertaken, the researcher and the project team need to understand what is required from the research and, in order to reach an informed position, they all need to recognise the limitations of the research. The example in Box 3.1 shows what can happen if the perception of some members of a project team differs from that of the other members.

In the example in Box 3.1 the project had started with an idea for a building to fit a specific site; this had then evolved through trying to fit an operating concept into a specific location. The concept itself was from the USA and was untried, at least at the scale envisaged, in the UK. It might have worked but, due at least in part to the differences in perception, it was not tested.

Quantitative research might include face-to-face interviews, in the street or some specific location, such as a shopping centre. The sampling frame can be pre-defined, in terms of size, age and gender, and the results might provide an indication as to the demand for a particular type of housing development. Telephone interviews, enquiring about expansion/contraction and possible relocation decisions might assist in assessing demand for a commercial or industrial development, although firms are often wary about responding to this type of questioning. This type of survey work can be designed to be very

Box 3.1   Research for a new development concept.

Some years ago the author was instructed to undertake background research for a major urban renewal project. The proposal was to develop an international trade mart and the architect had designed a dramatic new building modelled on a mart in Los Angeles. As a concept, the idea was new to the UK and the background research involved examining a number of different trade mart operations in the USA and elsewhere, across a range of manufactured goods, including furniture, clothing and electronics. The research undertaken was both qualitative and quantitative, including interviews and financial information relating to existing trade marts. As well as examining the economic operations of trade marts, the visual appearance was considered to be very important and a photographic presentation accompanied the final report.

When the research report was presented, one of the directors of the development consortium asked 'Where are all the people?'. He had been thinking that the development would be something like a retail shopping centre, whereas in fact the trade mart concept comprised a large number of small wholesale showrooms under one roof, some of which looked like shops but others presented an appearance closer to offices, whilst the number of buyers visiting the mart would be a tiny percentage of the number of visitors needed to produce a successful retail centre.

Clearly the misconception had also existed in the minds of other directors of the development consortium as, a few weeks later, the project was abandoned.

specific in terms of location of the firms questioned. Self-completion questionnaires circulated by inclusion in magazines, at conferences or via other media such as email, provide other quantitative data, although there may be some difficulty in assessing the total population size to which the responses relate.

Qualitative market research includes group discussions and focus groups, individual interviews and business-to-business surveys. These are more likely to provide an indication of the general state of the market but nevertheless may assist in finalising the design of the product or the mix of units, e.g. the number of two-bedroom as opposed to one-bedroom apartments, or office suites of less or more than 100 square metres in floor area.

Background information to support the market research can be obtained from Government publications such as Economic Indicators and Populations Estimates from National Statistics, *www.statistics.gov.uk*. Of particular benefit might be the new Neighbourhood Statistics service from National Statistics, providing information at district and ward-based levels, *www.statistics.gov.uk/ neighbourhood*. Press releases from the Central Office of Information (COI), can provide further useful background, see *www.coi.gov.uk*.

For residential developments it might be appropriate to probe people's intentions to move house within the next 12 months, and the type of accommodation they might require. This can be achieved by including specially tailored questions in omnibus surveys, such as the monthly ones carried out in Scotland by Market Research UK Ltd, see *www.mrscotland.co.uk/omnibus.html*. Surveys of this type provide fairly coarse background information, on a national or regional basis, as to market trends, which can then be refined by telephone surveys targeted by post code sector.

Regardless of how it is undertaken, the objectives of market research should be to identify and quantify the potential market for the proposed product and to gain an understanding of how it might be received. This will enable the development team to adjust the product to suit the market. For example, the research and historical figures might show an annual demand for offices in the general location of the development of around 5000 square metres per annum, rising by about 5% per annum. Given that assessment it would probably be totally inappropriate to develop 15 000 square metres in a single building, unless the research has also identified a possible relocation target, in which case pre-letting might be more appropriate than a speculative development.

Appointing the right market research organisation is important. The British Market Research Association has over 200 members and claims to account for around 80% of the UK market research industry, see *www.bmra.org.uk*. Throughout the whole of the market research process it should be borne in mind that even the smallest development will probably take a minimum of one year from the date of the research until the first accommodation is available; this time lag needs to be taken into account. The objective therefore will be one of endeavouring to predict what the market will be like when the first phase of the development is ready for sale or lease. The market researcher and the developer will also have to take account of the cyclical nature of property markets, with peaks and troughs of demand.

When the proposed development involves the reuse of previously developed land, developers, as short-term risk-takers, occupy a pivotal position in terms of stimulating initial confidence in the property market and in creating opportunities for longer-term investors within urban regeneration areas. Unfortunately these investment opportunities often do not materialise, as relevant market data concerning returns are invariably inadequate (Adair *et al.*, 1998, p. 46). This is because the main investment market for real estate, and for which data is available, is focused on 'prime property' – that is, buildings let to quality tenants in sought-after locations. In contrast, many urban regeneration projects, by their very nature, are likely to be in what are perceived to be secondary locations and may attract tenants of lower standing.

3.3.2   *Geographical information systems (GIS)*

> 'GIS is a technology that presents and processes information in a spatial context, defined by the coordinates of location on the globe. GIS is both an analytical and communications tool, which allows people to understand and see relationships that would otherwise be difficult to grasp. With GIS, users can consider more information and see more complex relationships. GIS can display a prodigious quantity of information on the scale, concentration, frequency and relationships between, and the attributes of, people, organi-zations, political jurisdictions, and communities. The relationships between the factors studied may be either expressly acknowledged or constructed purely for analytical purposes. GIS is integral to internet applications, many real estate processes and a myriad of processes that extend beyond real estate.'
>
> (Roulac, 1998, p. 1)

Geographical information systems are computer systems that are used for capturing, storing, checking, integrating, manipulating, analysing and dis-playing data relative to the Earth's surface. Several different software packages are available including, MapInfo from Business Geographics, *www.geoweb.co.uk*, and ArcView from Californian company ESRI, *www.esri.com*. ESRI also supply free downloadable software, ArcExplorer, which performs some basic GIS functions enabling users to use their own data or to browse over the Web, *www.gis.com/software/free_software.html*. Ordnance Survey maps are available in electronic format from PRODAT, a Landmark Information Group company, *www.landmarkinfo.co.uk/promap*.

GIS systems operate in a series of map layers linked to databases; one map layer may show the topography of the ground, which can then be overlaid with other layers showing the road network, land uses, ownerships, town planning data, floodplains, etc. They typically include points, lines and polygons (closed lines representing areas on the map). For each of these map features there is also an entry in an accompanying database, and each entry can have multiple characteristics or attributes. For convenience, the database can be thought of as a spreadsheet, with the map features as spreadsheet rows and the feature attributes as spreadsheet columns (Landis, 1998, p. 6).

For most GIS users, probably the most important GIS capability is pre-sentation mapping, showing geographic features on a map and assigning data values or ranges to those features. GIS enables the user to zoom into or out of different levels of detail and to produce hard copy, paper, maps at different scales and definition. Another important use for GIS is through the use of maps as organising tools for large databases, such as the National Land Use Database (NLUD) in England, *www.nlud.org.uk*, developed as a partnership between DETR, Ordnance Survey, the local government Improvement and Development Agency and English Partnerships. In this use, mapping becomes a tool for users to query tabular databases, reorganise data into different spatial units, keep records of spatial data and compare information across different features or databases (Landis, 1998, p. 8). NLUD can be accessed to obtain the location of brownfield sites. As well as showing the location of sites on a map, the database gives details of previous land use and planning status.

For the intending property developer GIS can be used for a number of purposes, including:

- to determine how location affects property values;
- to list and display properties currently on the market;
- to record and present data relating to historic transactions;
- to display changes in growth patterns in towns and cities;
- to record and display town planning data;
- to show the location of local services, such as shopping centres and libraries in relation to the proposed development; and
- to show the location of existing or proposed competing developments.

3.3.3   Market analysis

The extent to which a developer will undertake comprehensive market research at the project inception stage will vary for many different reasons. A developer working in a well-defined local market, say producing mid price range houses in a single town or city, may need to undertake very little research and will probably be able to base the site acquisition decision on the company's own performance figures. In contrast, a developer from outside the area, wishing to break into what might be a lucrative market potential, would be well-advised to undertake extensive market research and to apply a great deal of care in analysing the results.

Regardless of whether the developer is familiar with the local market or not, the following ten factors are fundamentals that any intending developer would be well-advised to take into account:

(1) *Population change* – consider whether the population in the town or city and the wider region or subregion is increasing or decreasing; a reducing population is likely to be accompanied by a declining market.

(2) *Economic change* – consider whether the comparative wealth of the town

or city might be increasing or decreasing relative to the region or sub-region; and on a national basis, an improving economy may bring demands for enhanced specifications in developments.

(3)   *Employment change* – determine if any major employers in the area have recently signalled an intention to expand or decrease their activities; closures or downsizing are likely to result in a downturn in demand.

(4)   *Employer vulnerability* – consider whether the area is dependent on a single employer or industry and the extent to which local employment might be affected by national or international events.

(5)   *Market prices* – review changes in rents and prices for industrial, office, retail and residential properties and determine whether these are keeping pace with, exceeding or falling behind inflation; changes in one sector may have a lagged impact on other sectors.

(6)   *Investment yields* – changes in the returns that investors require from different forms of property investment, and how they compare with other forms of investment, will provide an indication of how they view the market in the area, although probably only on a regional or sub-regional basis.

(7)   *Infrastructure changes* – works such as new motorway connections and airport expansions are likely to have a positive impact, whilst abandonment of a proposed bypass may have a negative effect.

(8)   *Land availability* – a plentiful supply of land, allocated in the UDP or local plan, for the use proposed by the developer, with no real competition probably indicates a weak market.

(9)   *Existing planning permissions* – evidence of unimplemented planning permissions for similar uses is also evidence of weakness in the market.

(10)   *Specification comparison* – consider how the specification of competing developments compares with the proposed project; assess whether innovative ideas have succeeded or failed.

These ten factors apply to all forms of development, regardless of whether the developer is planning a residential scheme, a new business park or a retail centre. Intending developers need to recognise the potential impact that changes in one sector may have on other sectors and be conscious of differences within sectors; for example, a weak demand for industrial buildings may be somewhat concealed by a strong demand for warehouse premises in good motorway locations, both within the same general sector.

Depending on the type of development, it will be necessary to take account of other factors in the market analysis. The location, and quality, of schools will be important factors in analysing the potential success of a residential development aimed at young families, whereas proximity to doctors and pharmacists may be more important in a sheltered housing scheme for the elderly.

Shopping and leisure facilities will be important factors to consider in commercial projects. The lack of such facilities is an often-voiced complaint heard from employees working in out-of-centre business parks. Whilst the lack of such facilities may be of little concern to the decision-makers, who may be quite happy to consume a lunchtime sandwich at their desks, it may represent a serious problem for other members of staff, especially those with young families who have limited time in which to shop or exercise. Lack of such facilities may also result in recruitment problems for tenants and have an eventual impact on demand or rents.

Transport and accessibility are both factors that will need to be considered in the market analysis, with differing impacts according to the type of development proposed. As discussed in Chapter 2, these are major planning policy issues and it is likely that increasing pressures to reduce private car usage will be brought to bear. Developers will therefore need to consider the extent to which national and local policies or pressures might affect the development by the time it is completed. For example, the introduction of bus lanes might result in increased congestion in the remaining road space available to cars, until the drivers feel defeated, leave the car at home and resort to public transport. This situation, and the possible introduction of charges for taking private vehicles into city centres, might have serious detrimental impacts on the viability of a development that places heavy reliance on the car.

Mixed-use schemes have often been resisted by developers, on the principle that they are difficult to fund. However, planning policies are strongly in favour of such projects and they are becoming more acceptable to funding institutions. As part of the market analysis, intending developers need to have regard for the scale and massing of their development, as well as the use or mix of uses, in relation to proposed projects on adjoining sites. Potential purchasers of sub-urban-scale two-storey houses are unlikely to respond with enthusiasm if a five-storey office building constructed close to their boundary overshadows them.

3.4 Forecasting rents and prices

Property markets are cyclical – they rise, peak then enter a downward slope before reaching a low point and starting to rise again. It is often said that property development market research is only undertaken when the market is on the downward part of the cycle and, to some extent at least, this is understandable. If the market is on the upturn, especially in very buoyant conditions, the market research may be out of date even before it has been fully collated and analysed. The developer may therefore feel justified in saying that the research is meaningless, as he can achieve almost any price or rent he likes to name. In a falling market on the other hand, the developer may be faced with either having to discontinue operations for a time or producing a product that is better or more desirable than those offered by competitors – thus market research is more likely to be taken into account.

It is not always possible to identify rising and falling markets in such clear-cut terms, especially if the rises and falls are not steep, or if the market is close to a peak or a trough. Well-designed market research should be able to assist the developer in assessing the state of the market for the proposed product and whether or not it is possible to forecast any potential for growth in rents or prices over the development period.

The Data Analysis tools in Microsoft Excel can be used to analyse data on historical transactions and trend lines extended to predict future performance for rents and prices, but such projections should be used with caution. Transaction data need to be researched and processed with great care, so as to ensure the closest possible conformity in terms of property size, location and specification. Rents and prices may require dissection, stripping out rent-free periods, fitting-out allowances, developer financing and other concessions, in order to arrive at true comparison figures. Where possible, comparisons should be made with other classes of property, as a market turndown in one class of property may lag a year or more behind other classes.

3.5   Summary

Developers might complain about the problems of site assembly but, according to the *Daily Telegraph*'s City Comment, they are shedding crocodile tears. Because planning permission is so hard to win, big housebuilders have specialist departments to accumulate land with planning permission and, as demonstrated earlier in this chapter, the resultant land banks can represent several years' supply of that most important raw material – *land*. Land banks are well-named – for a housebuilder, they are better than money, and many make more profit from the rising profit on plots than building on them (Collins, 2002).

Market research is important in order to estimate the likely demand for the development, especially as it is likely to be many months or even years before the buildings are ready for occupation. During the course of the project it may be necessary to revise the scheme in order to cater for changes in demand – flexibility is the keyword.

All developers are in the business of taking risks, although some are more risk-averse than others, but risk-taking does not mean they should be fool-hardy. There can be no substitute for good market research and careful analysis of the data produced by that research. Nevertheless, developers, planners, bankers and everyone involved in the development process have to recognise that research and analysis cannot guarantee success – if they could then there would be little justification for development profit.

Property market research is made much easier through use of the internet to obtain background research and statistical information from government and other sources. The larger firms of commercial and residential estate agents have their own research departments and some allow free access to research reports via their websites. These can provide background or market-specific information. GIS can assist in the analysis of data and in the way it is presented to bankers, planning authorities and potential customers.

Spreadsheets and computer packages can assist the analysis of market research data but the intending developer should not rely solely on computerised projections. Experience and judgement, as well as an understanding of wider economic and social factors, can be just as important in assessing the viability of a new development.

3.6   Checklist

- Commission a land-use study of the area.
- Analyse historical take-up in the market.
- Undertake robust market analysis.
- Be cautious of any projections as to rents, yields or prices.
- Make full use of technology such as GIS and the internet when putting together development proposals.

Part Two
Land

Introduction

This part considers the 'land' aspects of development. Land is the essential raw material of any property development project and its acquisition, investigation and preparation can be fraught with many difficulties. Even land that previously has not been developed can present the intending developer with insurmountable problems. Recognising the difficulties that may arise in respect of ground conditions, the National House-Building Council requires its members to undertake site investigations on both brownfield and greenfield sites if they wish to benefit from the Buildmark Warranty.

Chapter 4 describes the process of finding the site and acquiring it for development. Land assembly problems and purchase agreements are considered. The roles of the key members of the development team are described and an indication is given as to their likely fees.

Chapter 5 deals with site assessment and investigation, not so much from the perspective of how to carry it out but rather from the position of the intending developer or the planning officer confronted with technical reports. It describes the essential elements that should be contained in such reports and refers to current guidance and good practice.

Chapter 6 examines 'risk' in the context of the development project, dealing not only with normal commercial risks but also those associated with land contamination. The 'contaminated land legislation', Part IIA of the Environmental Protection Act 1990, and its implications for developers are outlined.

Chapter 7 looks at the remediation options that may be available to the developer. As a general rule, developers need to deal with contamination as quickly as possible but excavating the contaminated soil and removing it to landfill may not be the only option. It may be feasible to leave the contamination on site and modify the development so as to ensure that it is securely contained.

Chapter 4
Site Assembly and the Professional Team

4.1 Introduction

The development project may commence with no more than a concept, an original thought on the part of the developer, or something that he or she has seen work elsewhere. At this stage the developer might not have a particular site in mind or even a specific location. He or she simply may have a general idea as to the part of the town or city in which the scheme should be located, for example 'within walking distance of the town centre' or 'close to the river'.

Land is the essential raw material of all property development projects and few developers will rely solely on acquiring land that is offered on the open market by estate agents or advertised in the press. Site finding and land assembly requires a proactive approach and is often very complex. This chapter looks at some of the problems involved and suggests ways in which they may be resolved.

In order to assess the development of a particular site, or to determine the viability of a particular concept, the developer will need to engage the services of a multi-disciplinary professional team. It will often be necessary for at least some of the team members to be involved during the early project inception and site assembly stages. The roles of team members are considered in this chapter.

4.2 Finding and acquiring the site

Finding a suitable site may be relatively straightforward, assuming that there is a ready supply of development land on the market. An ample supply may, however, indicate weak demand or, alternatively, few of the available sites may be suitable for the proposed development and there may be stiff competition from other developers. So the developer may have to resort to finding sites that are not on the open market and possibly assembling the site from several different parcels of land, potentially with a number of different interests in each parcel.

The developer may commission a land-use study of the area, aimed at identifying how the land is being used at present, as well as any areas of vacant or underutilised land and buildings. The study should also identify any potential 'bad neighbour' uses in the area that might have an adverse effect on the project. The study should include an examination of current, but unimplemented, planning consents in the area and all outstanding proposals. Instead of commissioning a third party to undertake the study, the developer might use its own internal resources, with members of staff driving, or walking, round the area in order to find a suitable site. Well-established developers, with a track record for a particular type of development, or in a locality, will also be offered land direct by landowners, or via their agents.

Having found a suitable site the developer must then decide how to approach the owner. If the property is publicly available for sale, with a board fixed to the building, or a particular agent is known to act for the company that owns the property, then the way forward is quite clear. If, however, no agent is involved the developer (or his agent) will need to make an approach to the owner. In either case the developer will need to decide whether to make a direct approach or to use an agent who will be under instructions to keep the developer's identity confidential during the early stages of the negotiations.

The need for confidentiality will vary according to the nature of the development proposed and the number of parcels or interests to be acquired. Consideration will have to be given to the possible need to relocate existing occupiers, owners or tenants, as well as the costs or compensation that might be involved. It is not unusual, in a redevelopment situation, to find that negotiations will involve a freeholder, one or more long leaseholders (with interests from 99 to 999 years) and numerous occupational tenants or licensees. Multiply this across several parcels, or buildings, making up the development site and the opportunities for one or more people to oppose the development are myriad.

There is also the possibility that it may not be possible to identify the owner of the reversionary freehold interest, or indeed one or more of the intermediate long leaseholders. The developer will then have to decide how best to resolve the problem. If, for example, the freeholder cannot be found but the owner of a 999-year lease from the 1850s is prepared to sell, then it may be appropriate to consider creating a new 750-year lease in order to be able to sell the development to an investor. Care needs to be taken when creating such subsidiary interests that the original lease does not contain covenants requiring the freeholder's consent for the creation of subsidiary interests or redevelopment of the property. If it does, then the developer will have to apply to the Lands Tribunal for removal of the restrictive covenants and it may also be appropriate to take out insurance against the eventuality of the freeholder reappearing.

4.3   Land values and owner aspirations

In a 1993 study of grant regimes aimed at stimulating redevelopment in inner cities, the consultants, Price Waterhouse, observed that existing land values are also perceived to be a significant constraint to inner city development and regeneration (Price Waterhouse, 1993, p. 16). Eight years later land value and the aspirations of site owners were seen as the third most important factor in the redevelopment of brownfield land (Syms, 2001, p. 49), after project viability and advice on remediation methods. There was also strong support for easier land assembly procedures and the use of compulsory purchase powers.

A somewhat different picture was presented by Adams *et al.* (1999) who, in a study of development in four cities (Aberdeen, Dundee, Nottingham and Stoke-on-Trent), found that 53% of landowners had either encouraged or significantly encouraged redevelopment, and only 17% had discouraged redevelopment (Adams *et al.*, 1999, pp. 7–9). Whilst, at first sight, this might appear to be a very different situation, the researchers found that most of the owners considered to have significantly encouraged redevelopment also took a proactive role in seeking redevelopment, through actions such as site assembly and seeking planning permission. Those considered to have encouraged redevelopment intended either to complete necessary actions themselves at a later date or to pass the task over to others (Adams *et al.*, 1999, p. 9). Taking actions to assemble sites, say through landowners working together, and obtaining planning permission will normally have the effect of adding value to the land and thereby enable the seller to justify a higher expectation when selling to a developer.

A notable aspect affecting the willingness of landowners to sell previously developed land to developers for redevelopment, is the possibility that they would have to accept a price that is below the most recent valuation of the property. Land and buildings used for manufacturing purposes are subject to periodic valuations, either by directors or in-house valuers, or by independent chartered surveyors. As part of the production assets of the business they may have a substantial value, even after allowing for annual depreciation but, if the manufacturing operations come to an end, that value may be difficult to realise. There may be no demand from other manufacturing concerns and the buildings may not be suitable for conversion to other uses. The only option may be to demolish and redevelop.

Demolition can be very expensive, even if value is obtainable from salvage materials such as stone, slate and steel. Present-day health and safety laws mean that demolition contractors have to take greater steps to protect their employees and the public than they might have done, say, a decade or more ago, requiring expenditure on scaffolding and site fencing that might not have been incurred previously. Dealing with underground obstructions, such as foundations and large machinery bases, and with contamination will add to the cost. The landowner and the developer both need to be wary of the demolition contractor who offers to demolish the buildings down to ground level for a very attractive price, removes everything of any salvage value and leaves the biggest headaches unseen under the ground. Electricity, gas, water, telephone and drainage infrastructures may all have been adequate for the premises while in manufacturing use but may be woefully inadequate for any new development.

The costs involved in overcoming all of these problems and preparing the site for redevelopment will have to be borne as part of the development project. The developer almost certainly will not be prepared to accept a reduced profit out of the scheme and may even require an enhanced profit as a contingency against any unforeseen difficulties. As demonstrated in Chapter 8, all of these costs in site preparation will be deducted from the price the developer is able to pay for the site. Therefore instead of receiving a sum at least equivalent to the value of the premises in their previous use, or even a handsome uplift for development potential, the landowner may be disappointed to receive a substantially reduced offer.

In situations such as this, the landowner may be well-advised to commission his own site investigation and to obtain tenders for demolition and site preparation. It may even be advantageous for the landowner to fully prepare and service the site, with the help of a suitably qualified development team, and only then sell on to a developer. An alternative may be for the developer to enter into an 'open book' arrangement with the landowner, whereby all the development costs are freely disclosed, and to agree that a percentage of the profit above a predetermined level is payable to the landowner – known as an overage agreement.

4.3.1   *Tax relief for reclaiming contaminated land*

The introduction in the March 2001 Budget of tax relief at the rate of 150% in respect of expenditure on the remediation of contaminated land – Section 70 and Schedules 22 and 23 of the Finance Act 2001, *www.legislation.hmso.gov.uk/ acts/acts2001/10009* – should have the effect of encouraging landowners to voluntarily remediate land and return it to beneficial use. Only expenditure on land that is wholly or partly in a contaminated state can qualify for tax relief and that expenditure has to be in respect of relevant land remediation undertaken directly by the company or on its behalf. Expenditure on employee costs, directly in respect of the remediation, on materials and on subcontracted remediation can be included. The expenditure can only be included if it would not have been incurred had the land not been in a contaminated state.

For the purpose of obtaining tax relief:

> 'land is in a contaminated state if, and only if, it is in such a condition, by reason of substances in, on or under the land, that–
> a) harm is being caused or there is a possibility of harm being caused; or
> b) pollution of controlled waters is being, or is likely to be caused.'
>
> (HM Treasury, 2001, Schedule 22, 3(1))

It should be noted that this definition differs from the one contained in Part IIA of the Environmental Protection Act 1990 (see Chapter 6), in that the harm, or likelihood of harm, does not have to be 'significant'. Therefore it would appear only necessary to demonstrate that a possible pollutant linkage exists, with an attendant possibility for harm (however slight) or pollution, in order to qualify for tax relief.

4.3.2   Use of compulsory powers

When the owners of interests in the land cannot be found, or are unwilling to agree to sell, the local authority may be prepared to use its powers of compulsory purchase to assist in site assembly. These powers are contained in section 226(1)(a) of the Town and Country Planning Act 1990, which enables local authorities, subject to the approval of the Secretary of State, to acquire land in their area which 'is suitable for and is required in order to secure the carrying out of development, redevelopment or improvement'. The process of compulsory purchase is lengthy and costly, therefore the willingness of local authorities to use their powers may depend on the importance with which they view the proposed development.

In considering the limitations of the existing system of compulsory purchase, City University Business School, in research commissioned by the DETR, identified a number of difficulties:

- *Lengthy time-scales* – with the Compulsory Purchase Order (CPO) process taking an average of three years and longer for larger schemes.
- *User dissatisfaction with the CPO process and outcome* – the process seems to promote a confrontational stance.
- *Problems with dispute resolution procedures* – a more accessible forum and one which provides 'binding mediation' was suggested.

- *Blighting effect of CPOs that are not implemented* – the process may result in land values falling and the proposed development becoming no longer viable.
- *Conflict-ridden nature of the CPO process* – no incentive to cooperate and some owners taking a 'belligerent attitude' in order to delay the process.
- *Resistance of a very high proportion of local authorities* to the use of CPO powers – a lack of political will, related to factors such as a lack of capital receipts, spending power and time constraints.

A Government-appointed Compulsory Purchase Advisory Group subsequently examined the problems surrounding the existing process and made a number of recommendations (Raggett, 1999). Yates (2001) has reviewed those recommendations and conducted a survey of local authorities, Regional Development Agencies and private sector developers. She concluded that the main disincentives to using compulsory purchase in complex urban regeneration schemes were the time involved in the CPO process, the lack of spending power/funding, lack of private sector commitment, and the unrealistic aspirations of owners. These same factors were also the main obstacles and reasons for failing to deliver regeneration schemes.

Following discussions with the DETR and the Lord Chancellor's Department, the Law Commission has undertaken a preliminary study and has published a scoping paper in which it states:

'There is general agreement that current law and practices are cumbersome and convoluted. The long lead-time not only generates uncertainty and financial loss for the current landowners but it also makes the procedure unattractive to potential investors as a means of assembling land for major infrastructure or regeneration schemes.'

(Law Commission, 2001)

It is clear therefore that, where the proposed development site is made up of many parcels and multiple interests, site assembly can be a lengthy process. The last thing the developer wants is to reach agreement with the one remaining owner, or holder of an interest, only to find that the first person to have agreed is no longer in favour of the project and is no longer prepared to sell. This calls for carefully drafted agreements to safeguard the developer's position. The problems associated with site assembly and the process of compulsory purchase have been considered as part of the Planning Green Paper (see Chapter 16).

4.4   Agreements for the purchase of development sites

In assembling sites or building up their 'land bank' developers will wish to spend as little money as possible and will only expect to pay out full development value for land that is ready for immediate development. For land that is likely to be developed in the medium to longer term, say three to ten years, they will generally endeavour to secure control of the land for the lowest sum possible. They will therefore need to enter into some form of agreement with the landowner(s). The forms of agreement are probably as diverse as there are developers for sites but they fall into three broad categories:

(1)   options
(2)   conditional contracts
(3)   rights of 'first refusal'.

A further alternative considered in this section is the possibility of 'land pooling', whereby the landowners unite together in the common objective of securing the redevelopment of their land.

4.4.1   *Options*

Appendix 1 contains an example option agreement, with explanatory notes giving more detail about specific clauses or sub-clauses. Options of this type are generally used where land does not have planning permission and is outside the existing development envelope. Similar types of agreement may also be used in situations where land is zoned for development but cannot be developed immediately for some reason or other, for example the lack of physical infrastructure such as roads or services. They are less likely to be used in situations where land already has planning permission, unless the developer wishes to try to obtain a new or revised consent that produces a higher value, for example a higher density development or a more upmarket type of scheme.

Because the development, and thus the opportunity to achieve a profit, may be several years away the developer will wish to keep the option fee to a minimum. The fee may bear no relationship to the value of the land itself. In the case of the example agreement the £25 000 fee was approximately 50% of the present value of the site as grazing land and 0.5% of the potential development value of £5 000 000 but it was not arrived at by any reference to these figures. The developer will also usually expect to pay the landowner's surveyor and legal fees in connection with the option agreement.

Options provide the developer with freedom of choice; for example, a developer may fulfil all its obligations under the agreement, incurring considerable cost, and still decide not to take up the option. This rarely happens but could occur in situations where the market in a certain area has gone into what is perceived as 'terminal decline' from which it is unlikely to recover within a realistic time-scale, or where the agreement has been so badly drafted as to commit the developer to paying a figure that is wildly in excess of current market value.

4.4.2   *Conditional contracts*

These are more likely to be used in situations where the land already has planning permission, or is zoned for development that can commence within the fairly near future, say within two years. Conditional contracts are binding contracts for sale that become unconditional when a certain specified event, or the last of a series of events, takes place. The events might include the grant of planning permission for a specified number of dwellings, the approval of a remediation strategy for a brownfield site, the completion of a section 106 agreement requiring no more than 20% of the site to be developed for social housing, or the completion of a new infrastructure provision (e.g. a road, a light rapid transit stop or a new bus service).

Conditional contracts will almost certainly specify a price to be paid for the land, or a very precise formula for calculating the price. Such a formula is likely to comprise a base figure for the site, assuming a specified number of dwellings, plus an 'overage' figure for an increase in permitted floor area, each additional unit given planning permission, or an additional payment for every 1% reduction in the social housing provision specified in the section 106 agreement. Without a clearly defined mechanism for determining the price, a conditional contract would be fraught with problems and may be unenforceable.

This contrasts with option agreements where a price is less likely to be stated, although a formula may be included. In its original form the example agreement in Appendix 1 contained a complex clause for determining the price, based mainly around the treatment of land within the development (or on other land) allocated for social housing provision. The use of a reference to the RICS Appraisal and Valuation Manual obviates the need for such a clause because the Independent Expert will have to take into account all factors relating to the market and the planning permission.

4.4.3   *Rights of 'first refusal'*

Probably far less frequently used than options or conditional contracts, rights of first refusal or pre-emption may be regarded as a last resort by a developer who cannot persuade a landowner to enter into a more binding arrangement. As with an option, a right of first refusal can be registered as a charge against the land. Under such agreements the landowner has to offer the developer the opportunity to purchase the land, either at a specified price or, more likely, by reference to a formula or 'open market value' as in the option. Such agreements do not prevent the landowner from offering the land for sale in the open market but the developer party to the agreement would, normally, have to be given the opportunity to match the best offer received from a third party.

Unlike options where only the developer can withdraw from the agreement if all conditions relating to obtaining planning permission have been complied with, the right of first refusal agreement leaves the landowner in control of the situation. Under such agreements, if the landowner simply fails to take any action to market the land the agreement cannot be implemented, even though the developer may have expended a considerable sum in obtaining planning permission. Such agreements are unlikely to be used in situations where planning permission already exists, unless the developer wishes to seek a 'higher value' consent. They are highly speculative from the developer's perspective and this type of agreement, especially if poorly drafted, may be worthless.

A variation on the right of first refusal may be in conjunction with an option and could be appropriate in situations where the landowner does not wish to sell at the present time but may wish to do so at some foreseeable date in the future. For example, the owner of a manufacturing business may wish to retire in five years' time, at which point he intends to sell the business and realise maximum development potential out of the site by seeing it redeveloped for housing. He may therefore enter into a right of first refusal for a specified period of five years, during which time the developer will seek planning permission, and grant an option exercisable in the fifth year only, with completion to coincide with sale of the business. The developer has the security of knowing that the site will become available on a certain date but that if, for any reason, the owner wishes to sell at an earlier date then the site has to be offered to him first.

4.5   Land pooling

The idea of landowners pooling their resources in order to assemble a developable site is not new. If all parties to a pooling arrangement can expect to receive a tangible benefit from the arrangement, such as a more regular plot shape or an increase in value, then in theory pooling should work to everyone's advantage and be freer from problems than other forms of site assembly. In practice, however, this may not always be the case as some landowners may be unwilling to enter into a pooling arrangement or have an unrealistic idea of the value of their land.

Research carried out under the auspices of the Urban Villages Forum and led by Dr Nathaniel Lichfield, Professor Emeritus at the University of London and a partner in Dalia and Nathaniel Lichfield, Chartered Town Planners, has considered how land pooling may be encouraged in order to persuade owners to participate in joint action. In a paper based on the research, Connellan (2001) identifies three ways in which land is currently assembled for major development, redevelopment and rehabilitation projects, being a process of establishing a new ownership through the acquisition of property interests or control over all the relevant constituent parts of a development site:

(1) *Direct compulsion* – the use of compulsory purchase powers or the threatened use of such powers in order to reach an agreement.
(2) *Indirect compulsion* – action through the planning system, using development control to encourage owners of fragmented sites to assemble their land (DETR, 1999b, PPG6, paragraphs 1.6 and 1.13).
(3) *The voluntary approach* – whilst recognising that 'the free market in land operates reasonably efficiently for small sites held by one or two owners' the author argues that 'voluntary land assembly is a viable option only in certain circumstances ... but it can be fundamentally flawed, in circumstances where a "hold out owner" can prevent unified control over the relevant site being created' (Connellan, 2001, p. 3).

The researchers considered forms of land pooling used in other countries and, in addition to purely voluntary arrangements, identified three categories:

(1) Public authority inspired, controlled and compulsorily effected (German model).
(2) Voluntary but having recourse to an authorised framework (French model).
(3) Authorised framework designed on majority rules (overriding dissenters and enforcing participation) and instigated by a nucleus of owners (Japanese model).

They concluded that the French and Japanese models were of particular interest because they combine and integrate voluntary and compulsory elements. Although different they tend to operate on the basis of:

• readily available knowledge and advice on the land pooling process (the framework of such process having been established by Government authorisation);
• a scheme acceptable to the planning/local authority;
• the scheme must be viable (in terms of market economics or with the aid of subsidy);

- the scheme is backed by required majority of owners (usually a two-thirds majority by land value and area) with any dissenting minority disempowered;
- sufficient incentives by way of expectations of profits (or reallocation of acceptable plots) with safeguards on risk-avoidance and ultimate tax benefits;
- requirements of public authorities for extractions of any land – planning gain, impact fees and the like – are not so demanding as to damage the required incentives to owners and to any development organisation;
- early and active participation of a development organisation, which will underwrite the risk and organise an economic, efficient and effective development process;
- acceptable (and rapid) process for determining compensation (i.e. share apportionment, plot reallocation, or buying-out dissenters) within minimum scope for disputes; and
- the recommended scheme must be sufficiently all-embracing and flexible to cope with all the various facets which political decisions entail.

(Connellan, 2001, p. 7)

The evidence compiled by the research team suggested that assisted land pooling of the type described above could be effective in encouraging development, redevelopment and rehabilitation in accordance with planning hopes and expectations. To be successful, land pooling needs to be achieved through a suitable vehicle and an authorised framework whereby the owners are persuaded to participate in joint action. It is suggested that consideration should be given to key issues, including:

- the *carrot* is the expectation of favourable terms (compensation, profits, relocation, tax benefits, etc.) and the *stick* is the prospect of being left behind in the most likely event of the scheme going forward;
- the accepted principle is that if a required majority is in favour of the plan which is acceptable to the planning authority, the residual minority cannot abort the scheme;
- any dissenters are dealt with on an equitable basis (i.e. no less favourably than on compulsory acquisition terms);
- a policy of risk-avoidance to the owners (on any composite redevelopment scheme) is pursued by involving a development organisation early in the process as an active *participant and an acceptor of risk* – which will obviously entail a measure of profit-sharing with that organisation.

(Connellan, 2001, p. 8)

Thus the outcome of a land pooling scheme should be to provide each landowner with either a more developable piece of land, which may be either larger or smaller than the original holding, an enhancement in the value of the land and/or a share in the profit achieved by the development.

4.6   Legal advice

Regardless of the number of interests to be acquired and the nature of the proposed development, the intending developer will need to obtain legal advice in order to ensure that the appropriate legal agreements are entered into. Larger developers have their own in-house legal teams, or firms of solicitors with whom they have a close working relationship; other developers will need to appoint someone appropriate to the task in hand. This may be a firm, or individual, specialising in development projects. In an interview survey, reported in Syms (2001, p. 42), one of the solicitors interviewed stated that he did nothing else other than act for developers acquiring development sites, usually brownfields, leaving his partners and other members of staff to undertake the other property work. His reason for this was that he enjoyed the complexities involved.

When the proposed development site is one that has been previously developed, and especially where the possibility of contamination exists, developers need to obtain the best legal advice they can. Keeping (2001) considered the problems that beset the purchasers of potentially contaminated land, as they and their advisers grapple with the implications of a constantly shifting regulatory framework. Over the course of the ten years from 1991 (when the Environmental Protection Act 1990 came into force) to 2001 a state of uncertainty has existed, first over the nature of contaminated land legislation and second, over the degree of rigour with which it will be implemented by the regulatory authorities.

Keeping considered the liabilities of those who acquire contaminated land, whether knowingly or unknowingly, and the advice they receive from their legal advisers. He undertook a survey of the conveyancing practitioners in 231 legal firms, of differing sizes, located in London and the provinces. In his survey he enquired as to the extent and nature of environmental enquiries which solicitors were currently including in their preliminary enquiries (Keeping, 2001, p. 255). He found that the extent and nature of such enquiries varied dramatically between organisations, scc Table 4.1.

Some of the findings from his study were as follows:

- It appeared to be more efficient to use a number of specific 'core' enquiries which are made for every transaction, rather than to rely on a standard list of preliminary enquiries
- A minority of solicitors tended to be 'overzealous' when narrowing their selection of enquiries.

Table 4.1 Indication of the range of preliminary enquiries made by conveyancer relating to contaminated land. (Keeping, 2001)

Type of firm	Larger London (n=51)	Mid-sized London (n=40)	Larger provincial (n=113)	Smaller provincial (n=27)	Percentage of all firms making each enquiry (n=231)
Land-use details					
Previous uses/activities	28	26	96	16	72
Uses/activities on adjacent sites	21	17	74	2	49
Reclaimed/filled site?	19	24	80	5	53
Which processes (and are they prescribed)?	37	26	50	9	53
Water abstraction?	17	7	21	1	20
Waste/effluent disposal on site	42	29	111	20	87
Site storage					
Active/disused tanks	35	23	79	17	59
Toxic/hazardous waste	42	23	83	3	65
Prescribed and/or hazardous substances	33	16	82	1	57
Environmental audits					
Site audits/studies/sampling	37	34	106	20	85
Aware of actual/potential leaching or migration	19	6	42	2	30
Details of remediation undertaken on site	22	2	64	2	39
Confirmations					
Polluting matter entering water source	21	22	64	11	51
Licences and consents					
Details of relevant licences/consents	31	22	92	19	72
Confirmation of compliance	40	23	82	9	67
Environmental insurance	11	6	51	6	32
Complaints					
Complaints received	27	15	70	4	50
Actions/claims					
Due to pollution	29	26	104	19	77
Proceedings for statutory nuisance	39	21	84	18	70
Civil proceedings due to state of land	23	14	60	7	45
Have NRA/EA carried out or are they likely to carry out work?	20	7	45	7	34

- A very small number (3%), all provincial firms, did not make any environmental enquiries.
- Some 72% of conveyancing practices sought information on past land uses.
- Only 59% made enquiries as to the existence of storage or waste disposal tanks on the site, although 85% did enquire about environmental audits.

- A total of 71% requested details relating to licences and consents under environmental legislation.

Developers rely heavily on the advice and services of legal advisers during the process of acquiring freehold, leasehold and other interests in land for development. Keeping concluded that many conveyancers, while meeting the reasonable minimum that the Law Society might expect the reasonable and competent practitioner to achieve, are not acting much in excess of this, if at all. A significant proportion of firms are failing to raise even the most obvious and pertinent enquiries, such as details about a site's previous uses (Keeping, 2001, p. 261).

Since Keeping undertook his research the Law Society has published a 'warning card' to all solicitors, in which a warning is given that solicitors should be aware of the requirements of Part IIA of the Environmental Protection Act 1990 (see Chapter 6), although they cannot provide clients with conclusive answers. In the view of the Law Society, the warning card conforms to best practice and solicitors must exercise their professional judgement to determine the applicability of the advice to each matter in which they are involved and, where necessary, they should suggest that the client obtains specialist advice. Legal agreements relating to the sale and transfer of land affected by the presence of contaminants will need careful drafting, particularly where they deal with the transfer of liabilities (see Chapter 6).

4.7   The professional team and fees

The very first concept drawings and cost estimates prepared during the inception phase will probably be sketches and calculations prepared by the developer – 'back-of-the-envelope' – but very soon it will be necessary to appoint a professional team to work up the ideas and assess their viability. At this early stage the fee arrangements between the developer and the specialist consultants may be very loose, especially if they have worked together on previous projects, and the consultants may even be prepared to undertake the work 'at risk' without any fee payments, in the expectation of fees if the project goes ahead. Before long, however, it will be necessary for the developer to enter into formal agreements with the consultants; these should clearly state the roles and responsibilities of the consultants concerned, the basis of their fees and the stages at which they will be paid, e.g. finalisation of concept design, planning approval, start on site.

The nature of the professional team employed on a property development project and the individual roles of the consultants will vary according to the size and nature of the project. The basis of fees payable to the consultants will also vary according to the nature of the work and the basis of procurement used in respect of the construction contract. The key members and their roles in a brownfield redevelopment project might be as described in the following subsections.

4.7.1   Architect

Responsible for designing the general layout of the development and the buildings, the architect is a key member of the professional team and usually one of the first members to become involved in the project inception phase. The architect may also be responsible for supervision of the work on site and historically was seen as the overall project manager for the development.

The Royal Institute of British Architects (RIBA) publishes recommended fee structures for architects and payment schedules according to different stages of the work. Generally fees for redevelopment projects are likely to be around 4–5% of the value of the construction contract but it may be possible to negotiate lower percentages, especially where there is a long-standing relationship between developer and architect. For housing schemes, involving large numbers of houses constructed to relatively few designs, say 100 plus houses and not more than six standard designs, the fee arrangement may be a fixed sum for the estate layout and for each house design, with the developer being responsible for on-site supervision. Additional fees may be payable to the architect in respect of detailed drawings and revisions to the designs. If the project involves the refurbishment and conversion of existing buildings, especially those subject to listing, then the architect's fees might increase significantly, say to 6–8% of the contract value or even higher if particularly complex restoration work is involved.

Ideally, the architect who undertakes the initial design work should see the project through to completion but this may not always be the best course of action. For example, an architect may be very good at producing the concept drawings used for the initial project appraisal and even working the scheme up to the submission of the planning application, but may be less able to deliver the detailed design in a form that will ensure commercial viability. This can lead to friction between the developer and the architect. There may be a contractually binding situation or the developer may feel morally bound to keep the architect employed on the project. Either way can lead to poor design as compromises are reached, and the financial failure of the project.

A more appropriate solution may be to terminate the agreement, with the architect being paid for work completed to date, and to appoint a new architect for the detailed design work, even if this means a revision of the planning permission. Difficult situations of this nature are less likely to arise where the developer and architect have worked together on previous projects. They may be more likely to occur when the architect has been appointed as the result of a design competition; the winner may have considerable flair and ability in winning the competition but be less able to deliver the finished product.

4.7.2   *Consulting engineer*

A civil or structural engineer will be responsible for designing the foundations of the new buildings and ensuring their stability. The engineer might also be responsible for designing the steel or concrete frames for the buildings but quite often this responsibility is passed to the specialist contractor who will construct the frame. The role of the consulting engineer might also include detailed design of the road layout and services but for larger or more complex schemes specialist highways engineers and services engineers will be employed for these tasks. The highways engineer's role would include traffic flow counts and negotiating road junctions and car parking requirements with the highways and planning authorities. The services engineer will be involved in agreeing infrastructure supply and requirement capacities with the utility providers and these, in turn, might insist on doing some of the design work themselves.

Where existing buildings are concerned the structural engineer will have to undertake a detailed survey of the structure and, where major alterations are proposed, may have to design a completely new internal frame to fit within the existing walls. This may also involve underpinning the existing foundations or constructing new foundations for the internal structures.

As with the architect, the consulting engineer's fees will vary according to the nature of the work involved but are likely to be between 1.5% and 2.5% of the contract value. Fees for specialists such as the highways and services engineers will be in addition. These may be calculated on daily rates according to the seniority of the staff involved, quoted as a lump sum or, occasionally, as a percentage of the specific work involved rather than the full project cost.

In addition, the consulting engineer will normally be responsible for employing specialist site investigation contractors to drill boreholes and undertake laboratory tests to ascertain the bearing capacity of the ground. With previously developed sites, especially those involving contamination, this responsibility may be shared with the environmental consultant (see section 4.7.6 and Chapters 5 and 6).

4.7.3   *Landscape architect*

For some projects landscaping design may be included in the architect's brief but for larger and more complex projects the employment of a suitably qualified landscape architect is likely to be essential. Planning permission for the project may include a condition requiring the submission and approval of a landscaping scheme before the development commences and, in some cases, it may even be necessary to undertake some landscaping, such as earth mounding or perimeter planting, before construction commences.

The role of the landscape architect is not simply about deciding where to plant some trees and the species to use. It includes not only soft landscaping, such as planting, but also hard surfaces in the form of paving, street furniture, sculpture and other works of art that might be included in the development. The landscape architect may also be required, possibly in consultation with an arboriculturist, to advise on the retention, removal or pruning of existing trees on the development site.

The fees payable to the landscape architect will depend largely upon the nature of the work involved.

4.7.4   *Quantity surveyor*

Responsibility for cost estimates, cash flows and ensuring that the development is constructed in accordance with the budget is that of the quantity surveyor, who should also be able to advise the developer on the appropriate form of contract for procuring the construction work (see Chapter 11). The quantity surveyor's role has changed significantly over recent years, with many members of this profession preferring to call themselves 'construction cost consultants'. There is less reliance on voluminous Bills of Quantities and more on Performance Specifications. As with the architect, the quantity surveyor's involvement should commence early in the inception phase, so as to have an input in developing the design of the project in a cost-effective manner. This might simply involve giving advice as to the likely cost per square metre for buildings of the type proposed, up to preparing elemental cost plans for the development.

Fees payable to the quantity surveyor will depend on the nature of the service required – in some instances quantity surveyors become virtual or actual project managers – and the scale and nature of the development. They will also vary according to the type of contract entered into with the main contractor, for example whether or not it includes contractor's design. In general though, the quantity surveyor's fees are likely to be between 1.5% and 2% of the value of the construction contract, excluding any project management role.

4.7.5   *Project manager*

Not all development projects will have a dedicated project manager; in less complex projects this role may be taken by one of the other members of the professional team, and in many cases the project may be managed directly by a member of the developer's own staff. Developers are more likely to employ full-time project managers on larger projects and these may be provided by specialist project management firms. The project manager may be responsible for recommending and negotiating the appointments of the other members of the professional team.

The project manager's fees will depend on when he or she is appointed; for example, the project manager might not be appointed until the detailed design has been finalised but in other cases might be involved from the inception stage. Based on a percentage of the development cost, the fee for project management might be between 1.5% and 4% depending upon the precise role and the complexity of the project. It might also be based on a weekly or monthly rate for the duration of the project, plus a performance bonus.

4.7.6   *Environmental consultant*

Any development project involving the reuse of previously developed land requires the involvement of an environmental consultant, or at least a consulting engineer or a laboratory with environmental capabilities. The role of the environmental consultant will include designing the geo-environmental site investigation, supervising the works, liaising with the laboratory in respect of the analysis of soil and water samples and interpreting the results of the investigation. The environmental consultant may also be called upon to make recommendations in respect of any site remediation or treatment that may be required and for major developments to prepare an Environmental Impact Assessment in respect of both the site preparation works and the development itself as part of the planning process. The environmental consultant should be retained to produce a monitoring report and/or a post–completion audit of any remediation works undertaken on the site.

Fees payable to the environmental consultant will usually be a lump sum for the consultant's report, plus additional sums for borehole contractor, hire of excavator sampling and laboratory analyses. Total costs will vary significantly according to the previous uses that have existed on the site and the extent of any contamination. However, as a part of the overall development cost the environmental work is fairly insignificant, possibly 0.5 to 1%, but done properly it can be the most important factor in the success of the project (see Chapter 5).

4.7.7   *Estate agent*

All too often developers overlook the input that can be provided by the person who will be responsible for selling or letting the product that will be produced by the project. The agent can provide an invaluable insight into the nature of the accommodation that is likely to be required by the market when it becomes available in say 18 months or two years' time. Developers frequently instruct agents who have introduced them to the site and, whilst they may have an obligation (contractual or moral) to appoint them to handle the sales and letting, they do need to consider whether the introducing agent is the best firm to achieve the required results. It may well be that another agent may have better knowledge of the local market, or of the proposed product, in which case consideration should be given to a joint agency instruction.

Traditionally, the estate agent has relied on performance-related fees for his or her remuneration. Typically these have been 1.5–2.5% of the sales figure (or a fixed sum per unit for new housing), and 10% of the first full year's rental for industrial or commercial properties (15% for joint agency), plus advertising, site boards, brochures, promotion and other marketing costs. Nowadays this is changing; if the agent is involved from the project inception phase a consultancy fee (say 0.5% of the estimated value of the project, or a fixed sum) may be payable for marketing and product advice, possibly with a reduced fee becoming due on the sale or letting.

4.7.8 Other players

In addition to the foregoing key players, property development projects are likely to involve the members of other professions. A *solicitor* will be needed to handle the site acquisition and future sales, or to prepare a standard draft lease for industrial or commercial properties. A *town planning consultant* will be required for complex or contentious projects, and for redevelopment schemes, especially those in historic cities, the services of an *archaeologist* may be required. Specialist *market research* and *economics* consultancies may be required to advise on long-term projects, including those that involve a mix of uses.

4.7.9 Total fees

The total fees payable to the key members of the professional team, excluding specialist consultants, are likely to be around 8% for the most straightforward types of development, rising to 18% or higher for complex projects, including the renovation and conversion of listed buildings. A study by BCIS found that the average fees paid to consultants on construction projects amount to 9.2% of the construction cost (BCIS, 2001). This finding was based on a sample of over 1500 projects completed between 1998 and 2000. The most frequent fee per project was 10% of the final account.

4.8   Summary

A development project may start off with an idea or concept evolved by the developer, or it may start with a parcel of land and the question 'What can we do with this?'. Regardless of how the development originates, the project inception and site assembly phases need careful handling if the developer is to be assured of success.

The developer may be in the process of accumulating a land bank, either for development immediately or to ensure an adequate supply of land for the future. Major housebuilders tend to hold or control sufficient land to meet their requirements for several years ahead.

Site assembly can be a complex and lengthy process, requiring clearly worded agreements so as to ensure that all necessary interests in the land can be acquired. Having the right professional team is of the utmost importance and trying to save on fees might be counterproductive and detrimental to the success of the development.

Having the right development team is essential to the success of the project. Fees are an unavoidable part of the project expenditure and developers should not skimp on these; value for money should however be expected. It can sometimes be advantageous to employ a team that has worked together before but the developer and/or project manager needs to be alert for any complacency that might creep in. With the different disciplines involved in carrying out a property development project there is the potential for professional disputes and disagreements to arise. These need to be tackled as early as possible; otherwise they are likely to have a damaging effect on the project. It is important that all team members try to understand the roles and responsibilities of the other professions that make up the team.

4.9   Checklist

- Be conscious of the constraints or pressures that might influence the price a landowner is seeking.
- If appropriate, consider some form of overage or profit share.
- Be aware of the different types of agreement that can be used; more than one type of agreement might be necessary to assemble a single site.
- Ensure that appropriate legal advice is obtained.
- Assemble a professional team at an early stage.

Chapter 5
Site Assessment

5.1 Introduction

It is essential that any investigation of a previously developed site commence with an historical study of the previous uses of the site. Industrial activities on land in major industrial towns and cities in the UK may extend back over 200 years or even longer. During that time many activities could have taken place that might have a material effect on the development potential of the land.

The historical study provides the framework against which the detailed geotechnical and geo-environmental investigations may be designed and evaluated. It will enable the site investigator to design the investigation so as to target more accurately possible constraints affecting the development potential of the site. These constraints might include underground machinery bases and redundant services. Site access, which was suitable for the previous use on the site, may not be acceptable for the proposed use and will thus present another constraint. The historical study should also enable the reader of the site investigation report to determine whether likely areas of contamination have been investigated and this chapter focuses primarily on the contamination aspects.

Any intending developer, or planning officer, should be extremely wary of a site investigation report that does not contain an historical study and, unless satisfied by further enquiries, probably would be well-advised to reject the report.

The process of carrying out a comprehensive environmental investigation on a contaminated site has been described by Syms (1997, Chapter 4), and there is also a wealth of guidance in this area. Rather than describing the process, therefore, the purpose of this chapter is to illustrate what the non-specialist reader should be looking for in a site investigation report. Where appropriate, reference is made to relevant guidance but it is not the intention of this chapter to teach the reader how to undertake investigations. Previously developed sites

75

can present many complex problems in terms of site investigation and it is important that the client, whether developer or landowner, and the investigator both have a clear understanding as to what is required from the investigation. Getting it right at this stage may be essential to the viability of the project.

5.2   The historical study

This involves a study of historical maps and other records, so as to determine how the site has developed over the years and to ascertain whether or not any geographical features have changed and why this might have occurred. Several phases of building construction might have occurred during 200 years of industrial history, and features such as lakes, ponds and watercourses might have disappeared. Site levels might have undergone significant change, possibly as the result of the on-site disposal of waste materials, or through the import of wastes from nearby industries so as to fill hollows or reduce gradients. Storage tanks may be shown on one map but have disappeared by the date of the next map, or underground tanks might have replaced them.

Careful examination of map features and an understanding of the abbreviations that describe them are essential to learning about the previous uses of the land. In the 1882 map extract in Figure 5.1 is a circular feature described as *S.H.*, which the site investigator initially identified as a 'shaft'. Given the part of the country in which the site was located, with a long history of mining, this was not an unreasonable assumption and the feature could well have been a ventilation shaft from a mine. However, the roughly kidney-shaped feature to the east was something of a puzzle. On checking with Ordnance Survey, it was found that *S.H.* was in fact a summer house, not a shaft, and the adjoining feature was probably an ornamental lake. This was later confirmed by the intrusive investigation and the 'lake' probably started out as a clay pit, of which there were many in the area.

The historical maps may also provide a positive indication of previous uses, with descriptions such as 'foundry', 'locomotive works' or 'tannery' but they might simply say 'works' or 'depot' with no further indication of the activities that took place on or around the premises being investigated. A much more laborious and painstaking investigation may now be required, involving a visit to the local library. Trade directories, listing the occupiers of properties and their trades street by street, property by property, can be invaluable sources of information. Figure 5.2, shows an example page from one such directory.

It is important that the historical study considers not only the proposed development site itself but also current and historical uses in the surrounding area. An area of one kilometre around the site under investigation is often

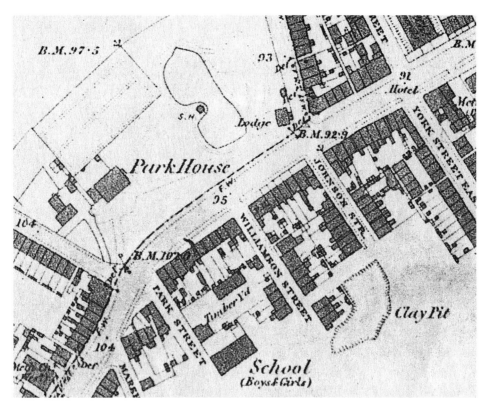

Figure 5.1 1882 map.

suggested as an appropriate radius for the study but in some cases it may be necessary to look even further afield for potential sources of contamination.

Industrial wastes, such as ashes and slags from furnaces, were often used to make up levels on neighbouring land or as hardcore under buildings. Ash may also be found under sports fields where it was used to form a drainage layer. These ashes and slags are frequently contaminated with elevated concentrations of heavy metals, such as arsenic, lead and copper. Other wastes that may be deposited in the area surrounding the now defunct industries might include spent oxide from coal gasification plants, tannery waste containing animal fats and elevated concentrations of chromium and residues from glassworks and dyeworks.

Investigators also need to consider other ways in which contaminants may have travelled to sites some distance away. For example, the prevailing wind in the UK is from the south-west and airborne contamination may have been carried from factory chimneys to result in particulate deposits contaminating land lying several miles to the north-east. This may especially be the case with

ST. HELENS,

SUTTON, PEASLEY CROSS, ECCLESTON, PARR, WINDLE, RAINFORD, HAYDOCK, CRANK, AND NEIGHBOURHOODS.

ST. HELENS is a municipal borough, market town, and chapelry, situated at the junction of, and comprising part of, the four townships of WINDLE, SUTTON, PARR, and ECCLESTON; 201¼ miles N.W. from London, 31¾ S. from Lancaster, 30¾ S.W. from Preston, 21 W. by S. from Manchester, 9 S.W. from Wigan, 12 E. by N. from Liverpool, 10½ W. from Warrington, 88¾ N.N.W. from Birmingham, and 120¾ S. by E. from Carlisle. This town, originally a village of little note, has risen into importance from the manufacture of crown, plate, flint, and bottle glass, it being the principal seat of this trade in the United Kingdom. The Union Plate Glass Company, the London and Manchester Plate Glass Company, the British Plate Glass Company, and the St. Helens Crown, Sheet, and Plate Glass Company are extensive concerns, covering a large area of ground and employing a great number of hands. The plates of glass cast here are of great dimensions, and the glass is as brilliant and perfect in every respect as the French or Venetian plates. Copper smelting is also carried on here extensively, and there are also several very extensive manufacturing chemists' and alkali works. The earthenware, terra-cotta, and sewage pipe manufactories of Messrs. Doulton & Co. Mr. David Horn, and others are extensive. Watch movements of great excellence are made here, and there are iron and brass foundries, breweries, and a ropery. A handsome and commodious new Town Hall, with municipal and police offices, has lately been erected at a cost of about £50,000. Two newspapers published here are largely circulated in the district. The cheapness and abundance of coal, the proximity of Liverpool, with the facility afforded by railway for the conveyance of coal, manufactures, and merchandise have greatly contributed to the prosperity of the establishments in St. Helens and its vicinage. The town is lighted with gas and supplied with water, but not so abundantly as desired. St. Helens is now a municipal borough, a charter of incorporation having been granted on the 30th January, 1868. The district incorporated includes the whole of the townships of Sutton and Parr, and extends so far into Windle as to include Cowley Hill and the part known as the "City," and in Eccleston so as to include the rapidly improving district known as St. Ann's. The total area of the new borough comprises 6,558 acres—viz. Windle, 690 acres; Eccleston, 510 acres; Sutton, 3,725 acres; Parr, 1,633 acres; and contained within its boundary in 1878 55,000 inhabitants. At the courts leet and baron held in November for Windle by Lord Robert Gerard, lord of that manor, peace officers are appointed for the district; and a county court is held every alternate Tuesday for the recovery of debts. The churches under the Establishment are—St. Mary's, Church street; St. Thomas's, Peter street; and Holy Trinity, Parr Mount. The Baptists, Independents, Presbyterians, Methodists, the Society of Friends, Christian Brethren, and Roman Catholics have their respective chapels. Sunday schools are established in connection with all the places of worship, and there are National and infants' schools, and others for the children of Roman Catholics (who are a numerous body); and also richly endowed day schools in connection with the Independents, conducted on the British principle. The market is held on Saturday, and the fairs on the first Tuesday after Easter week, and the Saturday following September 11.

RAINFORD is a township in the parish of Prescot, West Derby hundred, about five miles N.W. from St. Helens and seven S.E. from Ormskirk, with two railway stations adjoining. The church is a plain square building. The living, a perpetual curacy, is in the gift of the vicar of Prescot. There is also a chapel for Independents. In the township are an endowed school for boys, a National school for girls, and one connected with the Independents. There are several collieries in the township. Acreage, 5,893; population in 1871, 3,336.

PARR is a township in the parish of Prescot, about one and a half miles from St. Helens. The church of St. Peter, which was destroyed by fire, is re-built on another site, and is a very handsome stone structure. The living is a perpetual curacy. In connection with the church there is a National school. There is also one for Roman Catholics. Several collieries, large alkali works, and copper works are in the township. Acreage, 1,601; population in 1871, 9,281.

SUTTON is a township in the parish of Prescot, extending to within a mile eastward of that town, and forming part of St. Helens. In this township is the County Asylum, and there are copper smelting works, manufactories of crown and flint glass, earthenware and fire clay goods, and iron and brass foundries. Acreage, 3,616; population in 1871, 10,905.

ECCLESTON township is situated like Sutton, being bounded by Prescot and St. Helens, and contains some excellent stone quarries, coal mines, and earthenware manufactories; also a flint and crown glass manufactory. Acreage, 3,387; population in 1871, 13,832.

WINDLE is a township, part of which is comprised in St. Helens. Near to old Windleshaw Abbey is the cemetery. There are collieries, large chemical works, &c, in the township. Acreage, 2,907; population in 1871, 15,016.

POST OFFICE, MARKET STREET,

NATHANIEL TATE GREY, Post Master.

ARRIVALS.

From London (night mail) and all parts at seven morning.
From London, Midland and Southern Counties, Liverpool, Manchester, Warrington, Preston, Wigan, and Southport at half-past one afternoon.
From Liverpool, Manchester, Cheshire, Lancashire, Yorkshire, day mail from Ireland, at half-past five afternoon.

DESPATCHES.

To Liverpool at five minutes past nine morning.
To Manchester, Derby, Nottingham, Leicester, and all parts of Lancashire and Yorkshire at ten morning.
To North-West of England (north of Preston) and Scotland at eleven morning.
To London, Warrington, Midland, and Southern Counties at fifteen past eleven morning.
To Liverpool and Southport at twenty minutes past two afternoon.
To Liverpool at a quarter-past five evening.
To Corwen, Llangollen, Ruabon, and Wrexham at twenty minutes past seven evening.
To London and all parts at thirty minutes past nine evening.

Money Order and Telegraph Office and Savings Bank.

Post Office, CRANK, John Middlehurst, *Post Master.*—Letters arrive (from St. Helens) at eight morning, and are despatche thereto at seven evening.

Money Order and Telegraph Office and Savings Bank.

Post Office, HAYDOCK, John Richardson, *Post Master.*—Letters from all parts arrive (from St. Helens), at eight morning and are despatched thereto at six evening.

Money Order and Telegraph Office and Savings Bank.

Post Office, PEASLEY CROSS, James Sheffield, *Post Master.*—Letters arrive (from St. Helens) at half-past ten morning, and are despatched at seven evening.

Money Order Office and Savings Bank.

Post Office, RAINFORD, Jane Middlehurst, *Post Mistress.*—Letters from all parts arrive (from St. Helens) at half-past eight morning, and are despatched thereto at ten minutes past six evening.

Money Order Office and Savings Bank.

Post Office, SUTTON OAK, Frank Briggs, *Post Master.*—Letters from all parts arrive (from St. Helens) at seven morning and half-past six evening, and are despatched thereto at half-past ten morning and half-past six evening.

Money Order Office and Savings Bank.

Post Office, Marshalls Cross, SUTTON, James Dixon, *Post Master.*—Letters arrive (from St. Helens) at a quarter-past eight morning, and are despatched thereto at five minutes past six evening.

Letters for THATTO HEATH and ECCLESTON should be addressed "*via* PRESCOT."

NOBILITY, GENTRY AND CLERGY.

Abbott Miss Kate, 23 Boundary rd
Allen Miss Ann, 26 Bickerstaffe st
Allen Mr. John Fenwick, Peasley vale, Sutton
Ansdell Mr. John, Cowley House
Ansdell Mr. Thomas F. Cowley hill
Arratt Mr. Alexander, Sunny side, Cowley hill
Baxter Mr. Henry, Rainhill
Belsher Mr. Robert, Windle st. Cowley hill
Bernard Mr. John, Denton's green
Binney Mr. Hudson A. Sutton
Biram Mr. Benjamin, Peasley House
Bishop Mr. Charles Joseph, Cowley hill
Bishop Mrs. Ellen, Hill side, Cowley hill
Bishop Mr. Samuel, Cowley hill
Bishop Mr. Samuel Richardson, Cowley hill
Blinkhorn Mr. John W. Park House, St. Ann's
Blinkhorn Mr. Wm. Sutton grange, Sutton
Booth Mr. John, Eccleston
Bramwell Mr. Edward, Cowley hill
Brewis Mr. Thomas, Cowley hill
Briscoe Walter, Esq. Sherdley Hall, Sutton
Campbell Mr. Henry, St. Ann's
Carr Rev. Edward G. Denton's green
Carroll Rev. Anthony, St. Ann's Monastery, Sutton
Cook Mr. Johnson, Cowley mount
Cook Mr. Joseph (mayor), Cowley mount
Cook Mr. Robert, St. Ann's
Cook Miss Sarah, 104 Cropper's hill
Cook Mr. Thomas, jun. Cowley hill
Cook Mr. Thomas, Cowley hill
Cook Mr. William, West View ter. North rd
Cotton Mr. John, Cowley hill
Crockett Rev. Robert P. Eccleston

780 1 n

Figure 5.2 Example page from an 1870s trade directory.

coal-burning industries that used coal with high sulphur content, producing elevated sulphate concentrations in affected soils.

All of these and other aspects need to be taken into account when undertaking the historical study. The Contaminated Land Report (CLR No. 3) *Documentary Research on Industrial Sites*, prepared for the Department of the Environment, provides guidance on the identification of the past uses of a site from maps and other sources (RPS Consultants, 1994). An invaluable history of map-making in Britain, the scales used and a guide to the symbols and abbreviations on historical maps is *Ordnance Survey Maps: a concise guide for historians* (Oliver, 1993), *www.charlesclosesociety.org.uk*. Also of interest is *Ordnance Survey Maps: a descriptive manual*, by J.B. Harley (1975); this is out of print but copies may be obtainable from second-hand booksellers.

5.2.1 A practical example

Figures 5.3(a)–(f) show the changes that took place in an area of St Helens over the period 1849–1992.

In 1992 a potential development site at the centre of the map extract (Figure 5.3(f)) was almost devoid of buildings. The site has an area of 6.312 ha and is bounded to the north by a dismantled railway. The eastern boundary is formed by the disused St Helens Canal (a lock is shown just to the north of the site), the southern boundary by Standish Street and the western boundary by an existing railway line.

To the north of the site is a depot, precise use unknown, which has a tank on the site adjacent to the railway. Further north is another section of disused canal and beyond that a series of earthworks are shown. North-east of the site are two further depots, a warehouse and a works; the precise use of these properties cannot be determined from the map. A gas works is shown to the east, on the opposite side of the canal, and railway land extends southwards from the site. Residential streets, a park, bowling greens, playground and recreation ground are located to the west, beyond the railway lines. A corporation yard, glass works, works and reservoir are situated to the north-west. All of these uses are within 500 m of the property under investigation and if the map analysis were extended to 1000 m radius, various other depots, warehouses, works and tanks would be recorded.

It is clear from the analysis of the 1992 map that many different uses existed in this area and that it is not possible to accurately identify these from map analysis alone. Figure 5.3(a) takes the investigation back to the earliest available map (1849) showing development in the vicinity of the site.

The first point to note from the 1849 map is that a substantial part of the site itself is occupied by the Pocket Nook Union Plate Glass Works and that the site

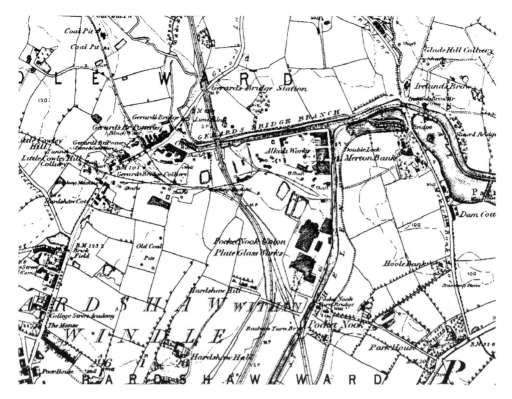

Figure 5.3 Maps of St Helens showing the changes between the dates: (a) 1849.

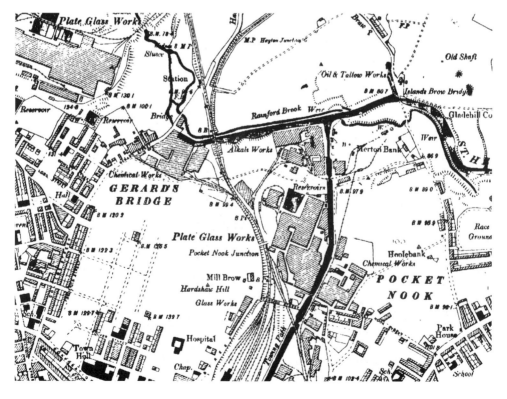

Figure 5.3 (b) 1894.

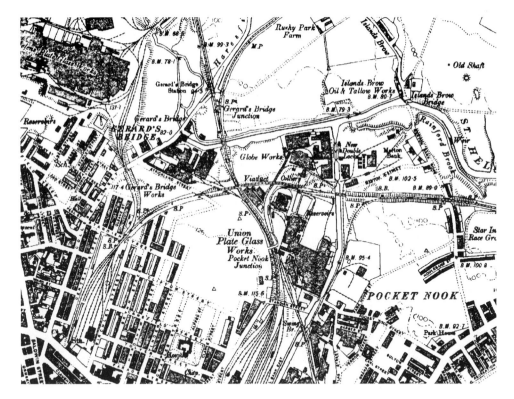

Figure 5.3   (c) 1904.

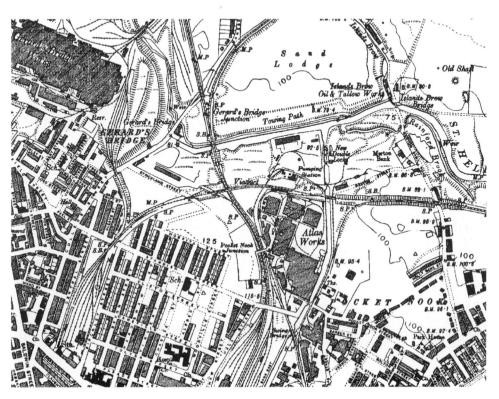

Figure 5.3   (d) 1929.

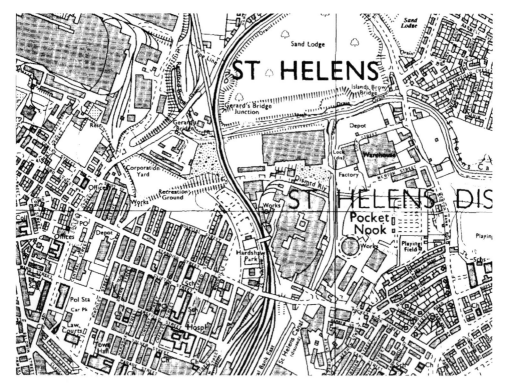

Figure 5.3 (e) 1981.

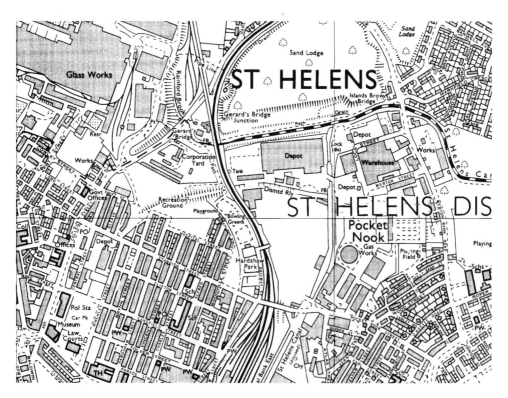

Figure 5.3 (f) 1992.

of the depot, shown to the north of the site on the 1992 map, was an alkali works. Several excavations, possibly lagoons, are shown within the site and a number of shafts are shown on the map extract. Standish Street is shown to the south of the site and old coal pits are shown to the west. The railway lines shown on the 1992 map existed in 1849 and were more extensive, including lines running into the site itself.

By 1894 (Figure 5.3(b)) a great deal more development had taken place on the site itself, which is still shown as being a plate glass works. The excavations on the 1849 map are now shown as reservoirs. The alkali works still exists and has been extended. An oil and tallow works has been developed to the north-east of the site, beyond the canal and a chemical works exists to the east of the site, on the opposite bank of the canal. A second glass works has appeared to the south-west of the site, beyond the railway and another chemical works to the north-west. In the north-west corner of the map extract is a building that was not present on the 1849 map; examination of the map beyond the boundary of the extract shows that this was also a plate glass works.

By 1904 (Figure 5.3(c)) further alterations had taken place on site, with one of the oldest buildings appearing to have been demolished. The alkali works is now called Globe Works and a colliery has appeared between it and the site. The chemical works to the east is no longer there but rail tracks are clearly visible, possibly indicating use of the site as a rail yard. Hoole Bank Street has been developed further to the east, comprising residential properties that were still present in 1992, although the name of the street had changed to Holly Bank Street by that time. Other residential development has taken place to the south-east and west of the site. The chemical works to the north-west is shown as Gerard's Bridge Works, which does not provide an indication of its use in 1904.

By the time of the 1929 map (Figure 5.3(d)) the name of the site has changed to Atlas Works and further development has taken place, with two new buildings, one of which is built over the reservoirs. Both the alkali works and the colliery are no longer shown, although several small buildings remain and a pumping station is shown. The rail tracks are no longer visible on the site of the former chemical works east of the site, although the abbreviation *Tks* is shown next to the canal — this could be either tracks or tanks. Further residential development has taken place to the west of the railway and one street is named Hospital Street, although there is not any sign of a hospital building. The chemical works north-west of the site is no longer there but there is a long building on the site, the use of which is not indicated. The plate glass works still exists in the north-west corner.

The 1981 Ordnance Survey map (Figure 5.3(e)) shows that still more development has taken place on the site; the railway to the north has been dismantled and a new building occupies the site of the former alkali works.

Reference to the 1956 and 1965 Ordnance Survey maps (not reproduced as they add little to the analysis) show that the changes took place between 1965 and 1981. The oil and tallow works is no longer shown on the map. A circular structure has appeared to the east of the canal, now disused, which is identifiable from the 1992 map as a gasholder, although the gas works is only described as Works in 1981. More residential and, apparently, industrial development has taken place to the south-east and west of the site. A park follows the curve of the railway line west of the site and the former chemical works is now a corporation yard.

5.2.2   Maps, scales and other sources of information

This case study of a small area of an industrial town gives an indication of the number of changes that can take place over a period of just less than 150 years. As well as the different uses shown on the map extracts, it is also clear that various earthworks and excavations were carried out over the period; some of these still remain while others have been removed or filled. The map scale used for the case study was 1:10000; study at a larger scale of either 1:2500 or 1:1250 might have provided even more detail. Box 5.1 contains a brief explanation of map scales used over the period studied.

Box 5.1   Map scales and projections.

The historical maps were reproduced from maps predominantly held at the scale adopted for England, Wales and Scotland in the 1840s (1:10560 or 6 in. to one mile). In 1854 the 1:2500 scale was adopted for mapping urban areas; these maps were used to update the 1:10560 maps. The published date therefore is often some years later than the surveyed date. Before 1938, all Ordnance Survey maps were based on the Cassini Projection, with independent surveys of a single county or group of counties, giving rise to significant inaccuracies in outlying areas.

In the late 1940s, a Provisional Edition was produced, which updated the 1:10560 mapping from a number of sources. The maps appear unfinished, with all military camps and other strategic sites removed. These maps were initially overprinted with the National Grid. In 1970, the first 1:10000 maps were produced using the Transverse Mercator Projection. The revision process continued until recently, with new editions appearing every ten years or so for urban areas.

(Source: Landmark Information Group, 2001)

Historical maps and street directories are not the only sources of information of use for the historical study. Geological maps not only provide information that is of use from a geotechnical standpoint when designing foundations but might also assist in the identification of potential targets for migrating contamination. Aerial photographs, often held in collections by local libraries or by commercial photography firms, may provide indications as to changes in site levels, filled watercourses and other water features that are no longer visible. The Coal Authority can provide information as to past mining activities in the area. Local authority planning and environmental health records will provide information as to previous and present site uses and details of prosecutions under environmental legislation. Environment Agency records contain information as to discharge consents, water abstraction licences, pollution incidents and river quality. Wherever possible, employees of the last occupier of the premises should be consulted and records examined to obtain details of products manufactured on the site and the storage of potentially contaminative raw materials.

Street names and the old names of public houses may provide good indications of the history of an area. For example, names such as Gas Street and the Rolling Mill public house are both very good indications of past use. Investigators should, however, be very wary of public house names that have been changed – the 'Slug and Lettuce' does not provide any indication as to past use.

5.2.3 *Reporting the historical study*

The report describing the historical study should make reference to all the information sources that have been used and the statutory bodies consulted, if only to record that nothing of an adverse nature was found. A report compiled by the Contaminated Land Advisory Group of the British Urban Regeneration Association (BURA), in conjunction with the NHBC and the RICS Foundation, contains a useful checklist for the historical or 'desk top' study (BURA, 2001, pp. 16–17).

Conducting a full historical study of this type can be very time-consuming, especially if a hand search of local authority and Environment Agency files is to be conducted, involving trips to many different places. The cost for a consultant to undertake such a study may be beyond the figure that the client is prepared to pay at this early stage where the developer may not have a binding contractual interest in the site or may be in a 'bidding' situation. An alternative is therefore to use the services of a commercial organisation, such as Landmark Information Group, to provide the historical data, see *www.landmarkinfo.co.uk*.

For the site under consideration in the case study example, the Landmark Information Group database revealed the information summarised in Box 5.2.

Box 5.2   Summary of information from a Landmark Information Group report on land at Pocket Nook, St Helens.

Within 0–50 m of the site boundary
- Shallow mining hazards and natural subsidence hazards
- 55 British Geological Society (BGS) boreholes

51–250 m from the site boundary
- One Control of Major Accident Hazards (COMAH) site
- One Notification of Installations Handling Hazardous Substances (NIHHS)
- One Planning Hazardous Substances Consent
- Six Pollution Incidents to Controlled Waters
- 15 BGS boreholes
- One Contemporary Trade Directory entry
- One post-1995 planning application for possible contaminative use

251–500 m from the site boundary
- Two discharge consents
- Nine Pollution Incidents to Controlled Waters
- One BGS Recorded Landfill site
- Two registered waste treatment or disposal sites
- 17 BGS boreholes
- 24 Contemporary Trade Directory entries
- One fuel station entry
- Three post-1995 planning applications for possible contaminative use

501–1000 m from the site boundary
- Three Air Pollution Controls
- 15 Discharge Consents
- 25 Pollution Incidents to Controlled Waters
- Eight water abstractions
- One waste transfer site
- One registered waste treatment or disposal site
- Two Control of Major Accident Hazards (COMAH) sites
- One Notification of Installations Handling Hazardous Substances (NIHHS)
- One Planning Hazardous Substances Consent
- 77 BGS boreholes
- 49 Contemporary Trade Directory entries
- two fuel station entries
- 22 post-1995 planning applications for possible contaminative use

As can be appreciated, the information available from these commercial data providers can be very comprehensive. However, for all but the simplest previously developed sites, the intending developer will need to use the services of a consultant to interpret the data.

5.3   Walk-over survey

Having completed the historical study the next stage is to carry out a walk-over survey. The purpose of this is to identify anything that might have a material effect on the redevelopment of the site. Contamination is the major issue but there may be other environmental matters of concern, such as noise and odours from adjoining properties, which should be recorded. Other than environmental matters, there may be other aspects of the site, such as remnants of industrial archaeology, that may constrain the development, or which it would be advantageous to retain. In many situations it may be appropriate for the consultant conducting the walk-over survey to be accompanied by the developer, or a member of the design team, and a representative of the last occupier.

Individual consultants will have their own methods for conducting the survey but the following is a good practical approach. Starting outside the subject property the survey should consider the security of the perimeter fences, walls and gates. If these are not secure, unoccupied properties become open invitations to fly-tipping, i.e. the illegal disposal of wastes. Even if no illegal materials have been tipped at the time the developer first visited the site, say immediately after closure of the factory, it is highly likely that by the time it comes to complete the purchase an insecure site will have been targeted by fly-tippers.

Having checked on the perimeter security the study should next focus on possible sources of contamination identified from the historical study, e.g. storage tanks, lagoons, apparent changes in level. These areas should be examined for visible signs of contamination. Such signs might include unusual colouring of the ground, an oily sheen on any water areas, discoloured and/or stunted vegetation or lack of vegetation, debris from demolition or the removal of tanks and plant.

Soil condition should be considered, together with the state of any bodies of water on the site. It may be appropriate to take samples of surface soils and of water, so the survey team should be equipped with suitable bags and jars for samples, as well as measuring equipment in order to record the locations from which samples have been removed. A comprehensive photographic record should be taken and a written description made of all features or matters of concern.

Once the locations of highest concern have been examined the survey should extend across the remaining areas of the site, photographing and recording all items of interest. Health and safety issues cannot be stressed too strongly; closed industrial sites are dangerous places. Ideally one person should not conduct walk-over surveys alone; apart from the safety issue two people are more likely to spot signs of contamination than one. If, however, someone has to conduct the survey alone they should be equipped with a mobile phone, and someone in the office should know where they are and how long the survey is likely to take. All members of the survey team should be equipped with work boots, hard hat, gloves and protective clothing.

The Department of the Environment Contaminated Land Report (CLR No. 2), *Guidance on Preliminary Site Inspection of Contaminated Land* (Applied Environmental Research Centre Ltd, 1994), goes into more detail regarding the indicators of possible contamination. Volume 1 of the report includes a useful checklist, while volume 2 describes a range of abiotic and biotic indicators that are all detectable by sight or smell.

- Abiotic indicators include: debris and structures on site; anomalies in topography and soil between the site and adjacent land or within the site; the presence of characteristic colours and odours.
- Biotic indicators are related to the biological features of the site and include: the type of animal or plant species present; symptoms of effects of contamination in any species; the condition of the soil.

(Applied Environmental Research Centre Ltd, 1994, p. 1)

5.4   Intrusive site investigation

The information obtained from the historical study and the walk-over survey can be used to design the intrusive site investigation. While the historical information may not be essential from a geotechnical perspective, it is of the utmost importance for the geo-environmental work. This is because the geotechnical investigation is primarily concerned with the proposed new buildings and structures, whereas the geo-environmental investigator is more interested in past activities. Nevertheless, the two do coincide and it is possible to design combined investigations.

Historical data may be of benefit to the designer of the foundations for the new buildings, for example in identifying water features that might have been filled and areas of contamination, both of which could possibly be avoided through a slight modification of the site layout. The information may also be required in order to prepare a health and safety plan under the Construction (Design and Management) Regulations 1994 (the CDM Regulations), see

Joyce (1995, pp. 131–133). Similarly, the geotechnical information may be of use to the environmental consultant, for example showing the presence of sand lenses in the clay underlying a contaminated site, which may constitute a possible pollutant pathway.

All too often the geotechnical investigation is designed having regard for the proposed development and then the environmental investigation is 'tacked-on', almost as an afterthought. In consequence, soil and water samples are obtained from the wrong locations, without any thought of specific areas of contamination from past uses, with inadequate logging of the investigation and insufficient sampling. The Association of Geo-technical and Geo-environmental Specialists (AGS) has produced guidance aimed at overcoming this type of problem and ensuring that both the technical and environmental criteria are satisfied. The guidance *Guidelines for Combined Geo-environmental and Geo-technical Investigation*, can be obtained direct from the AGS, *www.ags.org.uk*.

If the two investigations are to be combined, the pattern of the investigation, whether boreholes or trial excavations, or both, must be carefully designed in order to achieve the required information for both structural design and any necessary decontamination. This is briefly described in Syms (1997, pp. 79–83) and a wealth of guidance exists on the subject, including volume III 'Site investigation and assessment' of the CIRIA reports *Remedial Treatment for Contaminated Land* (CIRIA, 1995), Contaminated Land Report No. 4 *Sampling Strategies for Contaminated Land* (CRBE, 1994) and BS 10175 (BSI, 2001). Some specialist guidance is also published in respect of specific industries, such as the *Guidelines for Investigation and Remediation of Petroleum Retail Sites* (The Institute of Petroleum, 1998). The investigator should also comply with the guidance in British Standard BS 5930, *Code of Practice for Site Investigations* (BSI, 1999) and the report should confirm that the relevant guidance has been adhered to.

5.4.1   Sampling strategies

Soil samples obtained from boreholes are important to the geotechnical consultant in assessing the bearing capacity of the ground but they are only of limited use for environmental purposes, although water samples from boreholes may be essential in determining the quality of groundwater. Trial pits and trial trenches are, generally, of more use in geo-environmental investigations, as they enable the investigator to get a clearer view of the substances in the ground and their different strata, as well as providing the ability to obtain a photographic record. This is particularly beneficial where filled ground is being investigated, as the nature of the fill might change in very short distances. The nature of the investigation and its requirements might also indicate a need for changes to be made to the way in which trial pit information is logged.

The developer or landowner needs to understand how the investigation was carried out and this should be transparently stated in the report. This includes the rationale behind the sampling strategy, which is all too often missing from consultants' reports.

Figure 5.4 shows a sample log from the site in Figure 5.1, where the roughly kidney-shaped feature had been tentatively identified as an ornamental lake. The log relates to a 10 m long trial trench cutting through the north-west corner of the feature. The log clearly shows the different types of fill material encountered and the remains of organic matter at the base of the excavation, possibly decayed vegetation that had been growing in the lake before it was filled in. The bank of the lake is clearly identifiable in this and other trial trench sections.

The use of an appropriate sampling strategy is vital to ensuring that maximum information is obtained from the trial pit or trench. Sampling depths and frequency should be in line with best practice (see BSI, 1999, 2001). The strategy might, for example, include a sample from near the surface (say in the top 0.5 m of the soil), in order to ascertain the condition of the soil lying closest to possible receptors such as humans and plants, and then every metre to the base of the excavation so as to determine the extent and differing concentrations that might be present. If fill materials are encountered, the report should show that samples have been taken of each different type of material encountered, with their location and the thickness of the strata being carefully recorded. The deepest sample from a filled site should, wherever possible, be of natural ground, say 200–250 mm beneath the interface with the fill material. The site investigator may also wish to take deeper samples from the natural ground in order to assess the extent of any contaminant migration.

A trial pit record which records 'that natural ground was not encountered' is of little use in ascertaining whether or not contaminated material is migrating, whether as leachate or otherwise, into the natural ground. This has implications for the type of machinery to be used to undertake the excavations. A wheeled excavator will normally reach to a depth of 3 to 3.5 m, with a maximum of around 4 m. If the historical study and walk-over indicate that greater depths of heterogeneous fill may be present, then it would be more appropriate for the investigator to hire a tracked excavator with the ability to excavate to around 6 m. This will be more expensive than a wheeled excavator but the quality of the investigation should be improved. The report should indicate the type of equipment used and any constraints encountered, such as impenetrable obstructions, as well as any testing analysis carried out on site.

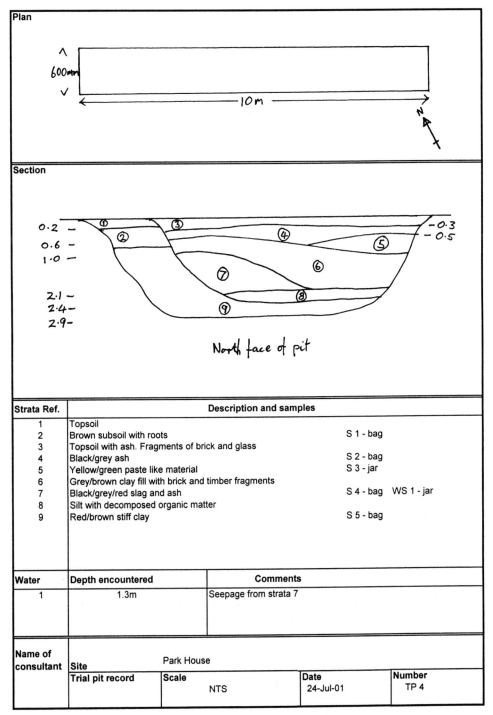

Figure 5.4   Sample log from the site in Figure 5.1.

5.4.2   *Laboratory analysis*

This part of the investigation can, very easily, be at least as expensive as the 'desk study' and on-site work combined. From the developer's perspective this is often seen as being wasted money if the project is abandoned or the site is sold to someone else. It can also be the means of saving a great deal of money and of significantly reducing the risks attaching to the development.

To give an example, the total number of samples obtained from the example trial trench in Figure 5.4 was five soil samples and one water sample. Depending upon the analytical suite used for the laboratory analysis the cost for testing each sample could range between £70 and £120, a total of up to £840 for this one sampling location. Assuming that the site had an area of 1 ha, 25 or more sampling locations could be involved, depending upon the findings of the historical study and the walk-over survey. The cost for laboratory analysis might therefore be as much as £21 000 for this 1 ha site and may be far more than the developer is prepared to pay at this relatively early point in the project, especially if the developer is in a bidding situation for the site. The alternative would be to adopt a staged approach to the laboratory work.

If, for example, the subsoil and underlying clay appear to be generally uniform across the site, then an initial phase of testing could include representative samples from say every third or fourth sampling location. The rest of the first phase testing would comprise representative samples of the bulk fill materials, such as the ash and slag, plus any anomalous materials, e.g. the 'yellow/green paste-like materials' found in strata 5 in the example. Any odorous or suspected volatile materials should also be included in the first-phase analysis.

It should be emphasised that this does not remove the need to take all the samples called for in the site investigation sampling strategy. Taking bag or jar samples, and transporting them from the site, involves negligible cost compared to the expense of the site investigation team having to return and open up the site once more to obtain additional samples. This approach is only really possible if the consultant responsible for the site investigation is on site during the intrusive work and is able to select samples for analysis on the basis of personal observations. Samples not selected for the initial analysis should be fully labelled and properly stored in a secure part of the laboratory premises.

Adopting a staged approach will, inevitably, lengthen the duration of the site investigation but the initial analysis should provide enough information for the developer to decide whether or not to proceed further with the project. Laboratories normally have a standard turn-round period of 10–12 working days. If the developer is in a competitive situation for the site it may be desirable to shorten this period so as to be able to make an early decision on the acquisition, for which the laboratory will impose a surcharge of around 25–50% for the expedited report.

The site investigation consultant should be asked to prepare an interim report once the first-phase laboratory results are available. This report should clearly state the horizons from which samples were taken in each trial pit, trench or borehole and the reasons why they were taken. It should also contain an explicit explanation as to why certain samples were selected for the initial analysis and set out recommendations for further laboratory work, based on those results.

If, on the basis of the initial results, the developer decides to proceed with the project, the remaining samples should be analysed and a full site investigation report produced. The temptation should be avoided, if no significant contamination was revealed from the initial analysis, to terminate the investigation at the part-complete stage. A full site investigation report, setting out the state of the site at the commencement of the project, is an important document and may be crucial in being able to sell the development on completion.

The analytical suite used for the analysis is extremely important and should relate to the historical usage of the site and the receptors that might be affected. All too often site investigators simply instruct the laboratory to test for the contaminants listed in Tables 3 and 4 of the ICRCL Guidance Note *Guidance on the assessment and redevelopment of contaminated land* (ICRCL 59/83, 1987) (see Chapter 6), without having regard for other contaminants that might relate specifically to past uses on the site and could form part of pollutant linkages. The site investigation report should therefore set out the reasons why the specific analytical suite was decided upon.

5.4.2   *Information on contamination*

The DoE Industry Profiles (DoE, 1996) describe the historical development and potential to contaminate, together with the types of contaminants that might be encountered, for more than 50 classes of industrial activities. The *Desk Reference Guide to Potentially Contaminative Land Uses* (Syms, 1999) also provides a quick reference to industry-specific contaminants for 39 groups of industries. Reference sources such as these should be consulted and site-specific analytical suites prepared in consultation with the testing laboratory.

The site used for the example historical study, Figures 5.3(a)–(f), provides a good illustration as to how an industrial area might evolve over time. It had a long history of use for glass manufacture and, as a result, the site may contain contaminants in the form of metals and metalloids, organic and inorganic compounds, acids, alkalis and asbestos (Syms, 1999, p. 28). It is also close to a gas works and may have become contaminated with ammoniacal liquors, coal tars, spent oxide and foul lime from that source (Syms, 1999, p. 27). In addition there were several alkali and chemical works in the vicinity of the site. The eastern boundary is a disused canal, which can act as both a pathway for contaminants and as a source of contamination, especially from silts in the bed of the canal.

5.5   The final report

It is essential that the final report draws together the various phases of the site investigation and the analytical work. The report should be clear, well-ordered and not overly technical, so as to be understood by 'non-specialist' readers, such as the developer client, financial institutions, planning officers, surveyors and lawyers. It should also include an Executive Summary as, in all likelihood, this is all that will be read by senior management.

In some cases, for example when investigation and remediation are subject to planning conditions, there may be an obligation to disclose risk-based information to demonstrate that health and environmental risks have been adequately assessed. This is not a new requirement (see for example ECOTEC and EAU, 1993, p. 2.19), but it is one of increasing importance.

The report should summarise all work carried out, the findings of the investigation and an interpretation of the results. Any variations in the programme as originally designed, and the reasons for these, should be noted. Any constraints or other difficulties encountered in the investigation itself, or in the interpretation of the findings, should be specified. Particular attention should be paid to the graphical content of the report, e.g. location plans, logs, photographs (ECOTEC and EAU, 1993, p. 3.22). The site area should also be stated in the report – something which is often overlooked by investigators – and, if plans have been reduced during the copying process, they may be misleading.

A section of the report should provide an assessment of the site investigation findings and, where appropriate, their significance in terms of any proposed development. The basis of the risk assessment, and any limitations, should be made clear. Calculations, modelling data, assumptions and safety factors should be stated in full. Any remaining uncertainties should be reported and source materials fully referenced, with the report containing an explanation as to why they have been selected.

As a minimum, the content of a final investigation and assessment report should include the items listed in Box 5.3.

Only when a fully comprehensive report has been received will the developer, in consultation with his or her development team, be able to adequately comprehend the implications of any previous uses and contamination on the proposed development. The report may outline a number of

Box 5.3 Content of a final investigation and assessment report

Introduction	Terms of reference
	Summary of previous work (including the preliminary investigation report)
	Site description and proposed end use
	Constraints on the investigation or assessment
	General field conditions at the time of the investigation
Strategy and methods	Scope of works
	Programme and any variations
	Methods used
	Health and safety provision
	Environmental protection measures
	Quality assurance plan
Field work	Description of the rationale and methods used to locate sampling positions, collect and store samples, and conduct *in-situ* testing
	Inspection and testing (e.g. boreholes, trial pits, spike tests)
	Monitoring installations
	Supplementary investigation and monitoring
Sampling and analysis	Methods and reference standards used
	Quality assurance and control
	COSHH assessment
Chain of custody	Sample receipt and storage
	Sample preparations and sub-sampling
	Sample analysis
	Sample results
	Sample disposal
Observations	General ground conditions (including field description of samples)
	Geological/hydrological regime
	Other features (e.g. flora and fauna)
Laboratory reporting	Analytical results
	Variations to analytical programme
	Accuracy, sensitivity, precision, bias
	Sample retention/disposal

Contd

Box 5.3   Continued.

Discussion of results	Results of field investigation(s) Results of laboratory analyses Limitations of the data (if any)
Assessment of findings	Detailed discussion of the rationale and procedures followed Reference data used to conduct risk assessment, risk estimation and risk evaluation
Conclusions and recommendations	Degree and extent of contamination on the site Significance of observed levels of contamination Recommendations on appropriate course of action Specification of contamination-related objectives where remedial action is recommended
Appendices	Location map and site plan Plan of sampling locations Graphic logs, boreholes, etc. (including installation details) Monitoring and analytical data Photographic records

(Based on ECOTEC and EAU, 1993, Box 3.17)

options for site remediation and it is important that the letting or selling agent, including the person responsible for sale of an investment, is involved in these deliberations, as different options may have significant implications for the end value of the development (see Chapters 6 and 7).

Above all, the report should clearly demonstrate that its predetermined objectives have been met or, if this has not been possible, it should explain why they have not been achieved. It must also record that appropriate quality control and quality assurance procedures have been followed.

5.6   Summary

Site assessment involves gaining a thorough understanding of the site conditions, including both its history and its physical state. The lack of good information regarding the history of a site may result in serious problems later in the development process, possibly turning a potentially profitable development into an outright loss. Therefore any site investigation should commence with a comprehensive review of site history. The assessment should then move on to a visual inspection of the property.

Physical investigations may be required in order to obtain information relating to both the physical (e.g. load-bearing) state of the land and its environmental condition. These investigations can be combined but, all too often, investigators focus on one aspect to the detriment of the other.

Site investigation reports should include clear descriptions as to the reasons for adopting certain methods of investigation, the distribution of investigation points and the sampling strategies for soil and water samples. The rationale behind the laboratory analytical suite should also be explained.

A great deal of guidance is available for use by site investigators and, when assessing the potential of a site for redevelopment, the developer and his advisers need to ensure that appropriate best practice has been followed. The site assessment, including geotechnical and geo-environmental information, records the state of the site at a particular moment in time. It can also comprise part of an ongoing record or logbook in the form of a Land Condition Record (LCR) (see Chapter 2).

5.7   Checklist

- Make full use of historical maps and data.
- Carry out a comprehensive site walk-over.
- Coordinate geotechnical and geo-environmental requirements.
- Report should describe sampling strategies, chain of custody for samples and laboratory testing criteria.
- Keep detailed notes.
- Final report should be comprehensive but not overtechnical.

Chapter 6
Risk Analysis

6.1 Introduction

Property development is largely about risk. Every development project involves risk to a greater or lesser extent. If the project is entirely speculative – that is, without any tenants, purchasers or investors being committed at commencement – the degree of risk will be greater than if it is partly 'pre-let' or if the investment has been 'pre-sold'. Even when a development has been entirely pre-let, the developer is still involved in risk-taking. For example, inclement weather may delay completion of the development, thus postponing commencement of the income flow and, if the tenant's agreement to lease the premises is dependent on a fixed completion date, say in order to capture a seasonal market, then the contract might be voidable. The building contractor might become bankrupt, or the prospective tenant might call in a receiver who decides to rescind the contract.

From the developer's perspective therefore, the development process involves risk right up to the point where the last unit has been completed, let and/or sold. Even then, the developer might have an ongoing liability if rental guarantees have been provided to the investor in respect of any tenants. In order to compensate for the risks involved, for the investment of finance in order to undertake the development and as a reward for the entrepreneurialism involved, the developer will require to make a profit. Even 'not-for-profit' organisations, such as housing associations, will be required to cover their costs and, in order to do so, will build in a margin to allow for unforeseen events.

Developers' profit requirements and the sensitivity analyses required to determine the impact on that profit under different 'what if' scenarios are considered in Chapter 8 on the feasibility study. The purpose of this chapter is to consider risk in relation to the land itself and particularly previously developed land.

The previous chapter described the information on contamination required to assess the suitability of the site for the proposed development. If any of that information is missing, is incomplete or has been inadequately prepared, then it is not possible to analyse with any degree of accuracy the risks attaching to the proposed development.

6.2   Greenfield development

Although the focus of this chapter is primarily on the redevelopment of pre-viously developed, or brownfield land, the question of suitability for use also applies to the development of agricultural or greenfield land. By no means all agricultural land is in what may be regarded as pristine condition. The farmer may have used the exemption provisions under the Waste Management Licensing Regulations 1994 to import fill materials in order to fill hollows in fields or to raise the levels on land liable to flooding. Whilst it is unlikely that seriously hazardous materials will have been deposited on land under the 1994 Regulations, similar activities under less regulated conditions might have resulted in the use of unsuitable materials. Even under the present regime it may be found that fill materials contain concentrations of some metals at levels significantly higher than would normally be expected as the local 'background' concentrations.

The use of fertilisers and pesticides as part of the agricultural production process may also result in higher-than-acceptable concentrations of some chemicals and poor farming practices might have resulted in spillages of gas oil from unbunded storage tanks, as well as oil and battery acid contamination from disused farm machinery. Therefore, in addition to ascertaining the phy-sical suitability of former agricultural land for the proposed development, the intending developer should also have regard for the environmental situation.

6.3   Previously developed land and the potential for pollution

As can be appreciated from the previous chapter, it is of the utmost importance, when considering a project on a previously-developed site, that the developer takes account of the possibility that contamination on the site might cause harm to the environment. This section examines ways in which harm may be caused and the following section looks at guidance documents; section 6.5 then describes the contaminated land legislation.

To take an extreme case, the development site might have been used for heavy engineering and the proposed use is for residential development with private gardens. The site has become contaminated with metals, oils and sol-vents as a direct result of the manufacturing processes, and even some pollution of controlled waters (e.g. streams and rivers adjoining the property) may be tolerated, especially if the site is in a predominantly industrial area and not in a sensitive water environment, such as over a major aquifer. All of this might change, however, in the light of the redevelopment proposal. Contaminants that were not causing harm to workers on the industrial site could be highly dangerous in a residential environment. They could be ingested or inhaled by young children and even by adults, they could be taken up in vegetables grown in gardens and they could result in stunted or weak plant growth.

In serious situations long-term health effects could ensue and the intending developer should adopt the same risk-based procedure as used under the legislation, in order to analyse the potential for harm, considering the following linkage:

Contaminant ⟶ Pathway ⟶ Receptor

For any one site there may be numerous contaminants, several viable pathways by which they might travel and, potentially, many different receptors might be harmed. As discussed in the previous chapter, the numbers and types of contaminants that might be found on a previously developed site can vary considerably according to the history of the site. There may also be more than one source of contamination within the site and different contaminants originating from each source.

The ways in which the contaminants can travel to, or otherwise come into contact with, receptors is also varied. In the water environment there may be particulate runoff or leaching of contaminants; flora, fauna and humans might also ingest waterborne contamination. Sedimentation of contaminants may occur from water into the soil and they may in turn be ingested by flora and fauna, thus entering the food chain. Humans may directly ingest contaminants from the soil – in the case of adults by inadvertent contact with the mouth when working in contaminated soil or by failing to wash hands before eating and, in the case of the pica child,[6.1] through the consumption of 'non-food' materials contained in the soil. Humans, both adults and children, can also become affected through direct dermal contact with contaminated soil. Atmospheric conditions can assist the migration of contamination, through the windborne mobilisation of dusts and their deposition elsewhere, as well as through evaporation and volatilisation.

The receptors that might be adversely affected by the contamination will differ throughout the development period and after use of the new buildings.

[6.1] A compulsive habit whereby some children eat non-food materials, such as soil (which may be contaminated as a result of past or present uses) or paint (which may contain lead).

Surface and groundwaters may become receptors at any time but are probably most at risk during construction operations. Construction workers may suffer from the ill-effects of contamination at any time during the construction process but are most at risk during the groundworks and foundations operations, as well as during the installation of services. The latter works in particular may involve workers from outside contractors who may be on the site for relatively short periods of time and, where contamination remains on site, they should be fully inducted into the health and safety requirements for the site. The Health and Safety Executive publishes guidance *Protection of Workers and the General Public During the Development of Contaminated Land* (HSE, 1991) which, although dated and in need of revision, is still largely relevant to site working operations.

Cables and services are possible receptors and damage to these from contamination may not become apparent until some time after completion of the project. Care should be taken to ensure that they are suitably protected. Attention also needs to be paid to the design of foundations if contamination is to be retained on site, (see Chapter 7), and these issues are covered by Building Regulations as well as by various Building Research Establishment (BRE) reports.

The risk of harm to vegetation can be an issue both during the development period and afterwards. For example, disturbance of the ground by engineering operations can mobilise contaminants to the extent that they could have an adverse effect on existing vegetation within the development site, e.g. retained under a planning condition or subject to a Tree Preservation Order, or on adjoining properties. Once the development has been completed, contamination in the form of phytotoxic metals, such as copper, nickel and zinc, may inhibit plant growth and, as referred to above, on residential developments other toxic metals such as arsenic, lead and mercury may be taken up through the consumption of home-grown vegetables.

Human beings living and working in the new development may become receptors if the contamination has not been adequately remediated, treated or contained and visitors may also suffer harm. Pets and other domestic animals, as well as wildlife, including invertebrates, may be potential receptors. It should, however, be recognised that, in some instances, certain species of flora and fauna may thrive quite well in environments with elevated concentrations of substances that would be harmful to other species. This situation may be disturbed and habitat destroyed as a result of remediation and development.

When dealing with a contaminated site, the risk assessment must take account of all the issues described above. The risk assessment may be qualitative, quantitative or semi-quantitative.

The term qualitative is used to refer to an assessment that identifies the presence of any contaminants in the soil or water and determines whether any receptors are currently present, or are likely to be introduced as a result of the proposed development. It then considers whether any pathways exist, or might be created during the course of the development before discussing the likelihood of the contaminants causing harm to the receptors via the identified pathways. The potential for harm may then be categorised accordingly to a scale ranging from '*very low*' to '*very high*' risk but without ascribing any numeric values to the degree of risk involved.

For many redevelopment situations a qualitative risk assessment is likely to suffice, however, in some situations a quantitative risk assessment may be called for, in which the concentrations of contaminants found on the site are compared with other reference concentrations. Quantitative risk assessments may use generic values, say from published guidance documents (see section 6.4) or set standards, although Petts *et al.* (1997, p. 206) terms these as 'qualitative'. They may also use site-specific, or use-specific, values in order to measure the degree of risk involved. This is the approach that was adopted by British Gas (now Lattice Plc) for investigating and setting remediation standards for former town gas production sites.

6.4   Guidance documents

The generic guideline values most commonly used in the UK are those found in Tables 3 and 4 of the booklet *Guidance on the Assessment and Redevelopment of Contaminated Land*, originally published by the Interdepartmental Committee on the Redevelopment of Contaminated Land (ICRCL) in 1983, of which a second edition was published in 1987 (ICRCL, 1987). This guidance relates only to a limited number of contaminants (see Box 6.1) and the

Box 6.1   Contaminants in ICRCL Guidance Note 59/83.

Table 3

Group A: Contaminants which may pose hazards to health
Arsenic, cadmium, chromium (hexavalent), chromium (total), lead, mercury, selenium

Group B: Contaminants which are phytotoxic but not normally hazardous to health
Boron (water-soluble), copper, nickel, zinc

Table 4

Tentative 'trigger concentrations' for contaminants associated with former coal carbonisation sites
Polyaromatic hydrocarbons, phenols, free cyanide, complex cyanides, thiocyanate, sulphate, sulphide, sulphur

---

Guidance Note makes it very clear that the values given in the tables should only be used in conjunction with the conditions and footnotes, yet they are often misapplied.

For each of the contaminants in Group A of the ICRCL guidance, two threshold trigger concentrations are provided: for domestic gardens and allotments; and for parks, playing fields and open space. Similarly, threshold trigger concentrations are provided for each of the contaminants in Group B, for application in any areas where plants are to be grown. The conditions for using the Guidance Note state:

> 'if all sample values are below the threshold concentrations then the site may be regarded as uncontaminated as far as the hazards from these contaminants are concerned and development may proceed. Above these concentrations, remedial action may be needed, especially if the contamination is still continuing.'

Reference is also made in the conditions to 'Action' concentrations, above which remedial action will be required, or the form of the development will need to be changed. Both threshold and action concentrations are provided for the contaminants in Table 4; these differ according to the types of uses proposed for the land.

When undertaking risk assessments on land that contains contaminants not included in the ICRCL guidance, consultants often refer to other generic guideline values, including the current and now superseded Dutch Intervention Values (Dutch Ministry of Housing, 1987) and 'Kelly' values (Kelly, 1979), also known as the GLC values as they were prepared for the former Greater London Council. Conclusions arrived at using these alternatives should be viewed with a great deal of caution as neither set of values was produced for the specific purpose of deciding on the appropriateness of land for redevelopment. The old Dutch Intervention Values were produced at a time when the remediation approach adopted in the Netherlands was one of 'multifunctionality', i.e. remediation to a common high standard regardless of the existing or proposed use, largely driven by that country's reliance on shallow groundwater for drinking water purposes. The values compiled by Kelly were produced for the former GLC explicitly for categorising the degree of hazard attaching to materials sent for disposal at landfill sites. They are still used today by some landfill operators in order to determine their charging rates. Another document that has recently been misused as 'generic guidance' for risk assessment is the *Interim Internal Guidance on the Disposal of 'Contaminated Soils'* (Environment Agency, 1997), which as its name implies is not intended for assessing risk on redevelopment sites.

Therefore, when considering qualitative risk assessments, the development team has to arrive at decisions, in the context of the site itself and the proposed development, which requires an understanding of the basis upon which the generic values have been derived and the underlying assumptions. Thus, it may be appreciated that different consultants, and indeed regulators, might arrive at diverse conclusions, albeit based on the same data.

6.4.1   *Contaminated Land Exposure Assessment (CLEA) model*

The shortcomings of existing UK guidance and the lack of set standards have been described as barriers to redevelopment but Government has adopted a more site-specific approach (see Syms, 2001). An argument often expressed against the use of uniform standards is that these have the potential to become 'norms' and may be used in all situations without having due regard to the nature of the development and its environmental setting. Nevertheless, many developers would like to see the use of mandatory standards as they would set a level playing field.

New risk-based guideline values are being developed to replace the ICRCL guidance (see Ferguson & Denner, 1993, 1994, 1995) but these have not yet been finalised (January 2002). The new values have been derived from research undertaken for the DETR and the Environment Agency (and now DEFRA), to consider what levels of contaminant intake would be unacceptable and to develop the Contaminated Land Exposure Assessment (CLEA) model, which considers human health risks via ten pathways:

(1)   Outdoor ingestion of soil
(2)   Indoor ingestion of dust
(3)   Consumption of home-grown vegetables
(4)   Ingestion of soil attached to vegetables
(5)   Skin contact with outdoor soil
(6)   Skin contact with indoor dust
(7)   Outdoor inhalation of fugitive dust
(8)   Indoor inhalation of dust
(9)   Outdoor inhalation of soil vapour
(10)   Indoor inhalation of soil vapour

Although the CLEA model guideline values have not yet been completed for use, a 'paper-based' methodology has been produced for deriving similar values for both risk assessment and risk management. The methodology is contained in a report prepared by Land Quality Management (LQM) in the School of Chemical, Environmental and Mining Engineering (SChEME) at the University of Nottingham for the Scotland and Northern Ireland Forum for Environmental Research (SNIFFER, 2000).

6.4.2   *Qualitative or quantitative – which to use?*

As mentioned above, in many cases a qualitative approach will be sufficient but, if a quantitative assessment is required, site-specific quantified risk assessments should not be regarded as necessarily superior to the use of generic qualitative methods and, in practice, it may be appropriate to use the two in conjunction with each other. According to Petts *et al*:

> 'Site-specific risk assessment applied to all sites is not a cost-effective approach to contaminated land risk management and experience is that the majority of sites can be dealt with by a qualitative [defined as using generic values] assessment (if conducted rigorously) ... a site-specific risk assessment is likely to be required where:
> - generic guidelines do not cover the contaminant(s) of concern and/or are insufficiently protective relative to the target(s) of concern in terms of their sensitivity, activity patterns, etc.;
> - generic guidelines would be overly protective as a result of conservative assumptions used in their derivation;
> - observed concentrations of contaminants exceed the generic guidelines to an extent which indicates the potential for risk to be realised;
> - local background levels are high compared to generic guidelines;
> - a site is causing considerable public concern (for example about threats to child health arising from particular contaminants) and there is a demand for fuller understanding of the risks presented by the site (a rare situation).
> (Petts *et al.*, 1997, p. 248)

Another option for assessing the degree of risk attaching to hazards contained on a site is semi-quantified risk assessment. This approach provides an indication of the risk and can be undertaken either by hazard ranking or by attaching numerical scores to all of the information relating to the site, and may be regarded as being more qualitative than quantitative. These scores relate to risk factors relevant to the contaminant–pathway–receptor scenarios of concern and, as a minimum, usually reflect the nature of the hazards, the existence of pathways and the proximity of the receptors. Cairney (1995) describes a semi-quantified approach and this method is discussed more fully in Petts *et al.* (1997, Chapter 9).

6.5   Contaminated land legislation

As part of his or her risk analysis, the intending developer will need to assess the extent, if any, to which the site may be caught up in the implications of the contaminated land legislation in Part IIA of the Environmental Protection Act 1990 and other legislation relevant to contamination, see Chapter 9. Part IIA is intended to tackle the problems of the most seriously contaminated land and the legislation applies only to land in respect of its current use including any risk to the wider environment. It may well be that, when used for the purpose that preceded the redevelopment proposals, the site did not have the potential to cause significant harm or the pollution of controlled waters but this may change as a result of the development. New pathways could be created and receptors introduced as part of the development process and the developer has to look beyond completion of the project to the end users and investors.

As referred to in Chapter 2, UK Government policy is that contamination in land should be addressed as part of the planning process. If therefore the developer, as part of the development process, intends to take action to remediate the site, for example by removing or treating the contamination, or by breaking a pathway, the regulatory authority is unlikely to take enforcement action. Should, however, the developer fail to take action within a reasonable timescale the regulator, usually the local authority, can take action to enforce remediation, including carrying out the work itself and recovering the cost from the polluter or developer as appropriate.

A three-month time period is allowed, from the date when the regulator determines that the land is contaminated, for the purpose of trying to agree voluntary action with the landowner or polluter. This applies except where urgent action is needed to prevent significant harm from being caused or where serious pollution of controlled waters is taking place. Given the reliance on the planning system to tackle the majority of contaminated sites, planning officers and planning consultants also need to consider the possible implications of the legislation. Deciding whether or not the Part IIA legislation has any implications for the proposed development must form part of the risk analysis process, although this legislation itself is not intended for contamination problems that can be dealt with under other regulatory regimes (see Chapter 9).

6.5.1   *Part IIA of the Environmental Protection Act 1990 (EPA 1990)*

Otherwise known as 'the contaminated land legislation', Part IIA of EPA 1990 was brought into being by way of section 57 of the Environment Act 1995 and became effective in England in April 2000. Similar legislation was subsequently implemented in Scotland and Wales but has not yet been introduced in Northern Ireland (January 2002). The primary legislation is underpinned by mandatory guidance and regulations (see DETR, 2000e and The Contaminated Land (England) Regulations 2000, *www.defra.gov.uk/environment/landliability/1.htm*, or for Scotland *www.scotland.gov.uk/library3/environment/contland.pdf* (the circular), and *www.scotland-legislation.hmso.gov.uk/legislation/*

scotland/ssi2000/20000178.htm (the regulations) and for Wales see *www.wales. gov.uk.*)

The legislation provides a statutory definition of 'contaminated land' as being:

'any land which appears to the local authority in whose area it is situated to be in such a condition, by reason of substances in, on or under the land, that–
(a) significant harm is being caused or there is a significant possibility of such harm being caused; or
(b) pollution of controlled waters is being, or is likely to be, caused;'

As will be noted from this definition, the degree of harm actually being caused, or likely to be caused is qualified by the word 'significant'. Although the meaning of the word 'harm' is defined in the legislation (section 78A(4), EPA 1990), the word 'significant' is not so defined. It is, however, defined in Part 3 of Chapter A of the DETR Circular 02/2000 *Statutory Guidance on the Definition of Contaminated Land* (DETR, 2000e), and deals with harm being caused to one or more of four receptor groups: human beings; ecological systems; property in the form of crops, livestock and domestic animals; and property in the form of buildings.

In order that land may be determined as being contaminated in accordance with the legislation, it is necessary for the regulator to identify at least one 'significant pollutant linkage', whereby a 'contaminant' can travel, or be transmitted via a 'pathway' to a 'receptor', or target. The extent to which 'harm' may be deemed 'significant' for possible receptors in each of the four receptor groups is given in statutory guidance contained in Annex 3 of Circular 02/2000 issued by the Department of Environment, Transport and the Regions.

So far as 'controlled waters' are concerned, it will be noted that the definition does not contain a similar significance provision and theoretically the legislation could be used for any water pollution, however minor. This is not the intention, and it is the Government's aim to review the wording and seek amendments to the primary legislation (DETR, 2000e, Annex 2, paragraph 6.2), although it should be recognised that relatively small quantities of contaminants on land may have a serious impact on the water environment.

The primary regulators under the legislation are the local authorities, and they are placed under a duty to inspect their areas for the purposes of identifying and bringing about the remediation of land that they have determined to be contaminated in accordance with this definition. Commencing in April 2000 local authorities in England were given a period of 15 months to prepare their strategies for inspecting their areas. Although by no means all local authorities had completed their strategies within the 15-month period, 91% were at formal consultation stage or had published/adopted their strategies by the end of August 2001 (Morris, 2001).

By this date, local authorities in England had determined that 23 sites were contaminated in accordance with the definition in the legislation, four Remediation Notices had been served and two Remediation Statements issued. A further eight sites had been designated as 'Special Sites' and the Environment Agency was undertaking inspections at 12 potential Special Sites (Morris, 2001).

In order that land may be determined as being contaminated in accordance with the legislation, it is necessary for the regulator to identify at least one significant pollutant linkage, whereby a *contaminant* can travel, or be transmitted via a *pathway* to a *receptor*, or target. As noted earlier, there are four receptor groups: human beings, protected ecological environments (e.g. sites of special scientific interest), domestic animals and crops, and buildings. The extent to which 'harm' may be deemed 'significant' for possible receptors in each group is given in statutory guidance contained in Annex 3 of Circular 02/2000 issued by the Department of the Environment, Transport and the Regions (DETR, 2000e). Since the reorganisation of Government departments, following the General Election in June 2001, contaminated land is now the responsibility of the Department for Environment, Food and Rural Affairs (DEFRA) see *www.defra.gov.uk/environment/landliability/index.htm* – although the responsibility for planning policy guidance lies with the Department for Transport, Local Government and the Regions (DTLR) – see *www.planning.dtlr.gov.uk/index.htm*.

6.5.2   *Appropriate persons and Remediation Notices*

Having determined that a site is contaminated in accordance with the statutory definition, the regulator then has to identify the 'appropriate person' or persons to bear all, or part, of the remediation cost. This is done using the 'polluter pays' principle but, if the polluter cannot be found, or no longer exists, the responsibility falls to the current landowner, defined as being the person entitled to receive the rack-rent. There are provisions for 'hardship', which may protect the innocent landowner from having to meet all, or even any, of the cost, in which case the regulator becomes liable for the remediation.

Regulatory authorities have the power to require 'appropriate persons' to take action to remediate land identified as being contaminated, either through voluntary action or through the use of 'Remediation Notices' (section 78E(1) of the EPA 1990). The degree of remediation required under the legislation is no more than would be necessary to render the land 'suitable for use' and to stop the land being contaminated in relation to the current use. In this context the term 'remediation' includes site characterisation relevant to remedial treatment activities. This might mean, in some cases, the alleged polluter or the landowner may have to do nothing more than undertake a site investigation and a risk assessment during the three-month period allowed for voluntary action. The investigation and risk assessment might demonstrate that, whilst contaminative substances may be present, no viable pathways exist, or no receptors are present.

It should be stressed that, as the legislation relates to the current use of the site, the degree or type of remediation required by the enforcing authority may fall short of that which is necessary to redevelop the site. A prospective developer will therefore need to consider what additional remediation may be required for future use of the land for which planning permission is being sought.

Local authorities are required under the legislation to maintain a register containing the particulars of any Remediation Notices served by the authority and details of any appeals against those notices. If the authority is satisfied that voluntary action is being taken, or will be taken, by the polluter or the land-owner to remediate the land, then the authority is required to prepare and publish a 'Remediation Statement' (section 78H(7) EPA 1990), recording the measures that are to be taken by way of remediation, who is responsible for doing them and the time-scale in which they are to be carried out.

If the authority is precluded from serving a notice because there is nothing that can reasonably be done, a 'Remediation Declaration' (section 78H(6) EPA (1990) has to be entered on the register. These declarations set out the reasons why the authority would otherwise have specified the need for remediation, and the grounds as to why it is satisfied that it is precluded from serving a notice.

Some categories of contamination may result in land being designated as a 'Special Site' (section 78C(8) EPA 1990), of which there are three broad groups: sites that involve water pollution,[6.2] certain industries[6.3] and defence sites. For such sites the Environment Agency is the appropriate regulator and if

---

[6.2] Where the pollution is such that it might affect the wholesomeness of drinking water, where it might affect surface waters to the extent that they do not meet the relevant surface water criteria, and major aquifers, as defined by reference to certain geological formations.

[6.3] Including oil refining, explosives manufacture, sites containing waste acid tar lagoons (not intended to include cases where the tars resulted from coal product manufacture, or where the tars were placed in pits or wells) and Integrated Pollution Control (IPC) sites under Part I of the EPA 1990.

a local authority identifies such sites within its area it is required to consult with the Agency prior to making a designation.

6.5.3   *Apportioning liability*

In situations where there is more than one possible 'appropriate person' the authority has to decide who should bear what proportion of the cost. The Procedure for Determining Liabilities is set out in paragraphs 9.21 to 9.49 of Annex 2 of DETR Circular 02/2000 (DETR, 2000e). The parties are categorised into two 'Liability Classes': Class A comprising the polluters and Class B the landowners. Having identified one or more liability groups, the enforcing authority should consider whether any of the members of those groups are exempted from liability under the provisions in Part IIA (DETR, 2000e, paragraph 9.33). The authority then has to decide what 'remediation actions' (RAs) may be required (e.g. preventing pollution of a watercourse) in order to remediate the land.

Each remediation action will be carried out to achieve a particular purpose with respect to one or more identified significant pollutant linkages (SPLs). Where there is only a single SPL on the contaminated land in question, all remediation actions will be referable to that linkage, and the enforcing authority will not need to consider how the different remediation actions relate to different linkages. (DETR, 2000e, paragraph 9.37). Where there are more SPLs the authority will have to decide which RAs relate to the different linkages.

In situations where there is only one polluter in the class A liability group, and that person is also the landowner, the financial responsibility for the cost of the remedial actions will normally be clear-cut but, where there are two or more persons in Class A or Class B the enforcing authority will have to determine whether any persons should be excluded from liability. To achieve this, different Exclusion Tests are applied, following a strict procedure, to the Class A and Class B persons, see Box 6.2.

Box 6.2 provides only a brief summary as to how the Exclusion Tests are intended to operate, and for the full details, the reader is referred to Chapter D of the Statutory Guidance (DETR, 2000e). Having applied the tests between the members of the liability group, and for each identified significant pollutant linkage, the regulating authority has next to decide which, if any, of the members of the liability group should be excluded, either in whole or in part. Having decided whether or not to exclude any members of the liability group the regulator then has to apportion the costs of remediation between the remaining members of the liability group. This is done by reference to the relative periods during which different persons have carried out broadly similar

Box 6.2   The six Exclusion Tests for Class A persons.

Test 1 – Excluded activities

Persons whose only involvement has been in respect of the following will, normally, be excluded from liability:

(a) providing (or withholding) financial assistance, such as a loan, grant, guarantee or indemnity;

(b) underwriting an insurance policy under which another person was insured and where that person might be held to have knowingly permitted the pollution to have occurred;

(c) carrying out any action for the purpose of assessing whether or not to provide financial assistance or to underwrite an insurance policy;

(d) consigning, as waste, to another person the substance comprising the significant pollutant, under a contract whereby that person knowingly took over responsibility for its proper disposal or other management;

(e) creating a tenancy over the land in favour of another person who has caused or knowingly permitted the contamination;

(f) as an owner creating a licence over the land, except where the person granting the licence operated the site for the disposal or storage of waste at the time the licence was granted;

(g) issuing any statutory permission, licence or consent;

(h) taking, or not taking, any statutory enforcement action in respect of the land or against some other person;

(i) providing legal, financial, engineering, scientific or technical advice in respect of the land;

(j) as a person providing services described in (i), carrying out any intrusive investigation, except where the investigation creates the significant pollutant linkage and the client is not a member of the liability group;

(k) performing any contract by providing a service or by supplying goods, where the contract is made with another person who is also a member of the liability group in question.

Test 2 – Payments made for remediation

This is intended to exclude from liability persons who have already recognised their responsibilities by making a payment to another member of the liability group for the purpose of ensuring remediation of the site. The payment, at the time it was made, must have been sufficient to pay for the remediation in question but the remediation was either not done or was not carried out effectively. If, however, the person making the payment retains any control over the condition of the land, after the date of payment, then this test does not apply.

Contd

Box 6.2   Continued.

Test 3 – Sold with information

The intention here is to exclude from liability persons, polluters, who have sold the land and, at the time of sale, have provided the buyer with information as to the presence on the land of the pollutant identified in the significant pollutant linkage. This may occur where a developer acquires land for redevelopment and accepts responsibility for remediation. In many instances the sale may involve both a reduction in price, which may have been dealt with in Test 2, and the supply of information by the vendor. For the vendor to be excluded from liability the sale has to be at arms' length and the vendor must not retain any interest in, or any right to use or occupy the land.

Test 4 – Changes to substances

The purpose here is to exclude from liability persons who deposited a substance on or in the land which, in itself, did not constitute a pollutant to the extent that it would be likely to cause significant harm or pollution of controlled waters. However, through the actions or omissions of another person, or persons, another substance has been introduced at a later date, causing the original substance to change its characteristics, by chemical reaction, biological process or some other change, to the extent that it has become a '*significant pollutant*'. For the first party to be excluded from liability it is necessary to demonstrate that the earlier substance would not have formed part of the '*significant pollutant linkage*' if the change had not taken place and that the change would not have occurred without the introduction of the second substance. It is also necessary to demonstrate that the first person could not reasonably have foreseen that the second substance would be introduced and that the change would take place.

Test 5 – Escaped substances

This test applies between those parties whose actions relate to other land and is intended to exclude from liability persons who would otherwise be liable for the remediation of contaminated land which has become contaminated as a result of the escape of substances from other land, where it can be shown that another member of the liability group was actually responsible for the escape. For this test to apply it is necessary to show that another member of the liability group caused or knowingly permitted the escape.

Contd

Box 6.2 Continued.

Test 6 – Introduction of pathways or receptors
In situations where other parties have introduced the pathway or receptor forming part of the significant pollutant linkage, the intention is to exclude from liability persons who had previously introduced the contaminant in question. The introduction of a pathway or receptor may come about through the carrying out of building, engineering or mining operations, or through a change of use in respect of the site or adjoining land. It is necessary to demonstrate that, if the later actions had not been carried out the significant pollutant linkage would not have existed. It should be noted that a local authority that gave planning or building control approval to the works, or change of use, that introduced the pathway or receptor, would not be liable because of the provisions of Test 1 relating to the granting of statutory permissions or licences.

---

operations; the relative scale of such operations (e.g. by reference to production volumes); the relative areas of land used for the operations; and a combination of these factors.

6.6 Summary

As can be seen from the discussion in this chapter, the risk analysis that intending developers need to undertake in relation to previously developed sites extends well beyond that normally associated with development projects. The greater the propensity of the former use(s) to leave a legacy of contamination (see Syms, 1999) and the more sensitive the proposed new use (housing with private gardens in which vegetables might be grown is generally seen as being the most sensitive), the more important it is for the developer to be provided with all of the information needed to arrive at the best decision.

A site may not be contaminated in the legal sense, i.e. under Part IIA of the Environmental Protection Act 1990, but the legislation is extremely important when considering the suitability of the site for alternative uses. The purpose of a risk assessment should therefore be to consider the suitability of the site for the uses proposed and whether or not, assuming those uses are implemented, there would be any implications under the legislation.

When provided with this assessment the developer, and his or her development team, will need to consider the wider implications. This will include asking such questions as 'Even if the site history and soil condition are acceptable to the regulator, will it be acceptable to end-users and investors?'

The site investigation report and risk assessment should enable the environmental consultant, possibly in conjunction with the consulting engineer, to suggest alternative means of remediation and/or treatment in order to deal with a contamination that may be present. The development team will need to analyse the suggested alternatives in respect of the proposed site uses, end-users, investors and long-term sustainability. Only then can appropriate decisions be taken in respect of remediation and treatment options.

6.7   Checklist

- Keep up to date with the environmental legislation.
- Be aware of the possibility that a developer might be classed as a 'polluter'.
- Consider possible contaminant–pathway–receptor linkages, in respect of both the existing use and the proposed development.
- Use 'guideline' or generic values with caution and ensure that they are appropriate to the situation under consideration.

Chapter 7
Remediation and Treatment Options

7.1 Introduction

When developing a site that is affected by the presence of contamination, the developer's preferred option is to excavate the contaminated soil from the site and dispose of it to landfill, often referred to as 'dig and dump'. Although many other options are now available, excavation and removal is still used in the majority of remediation projects in the UK although, as a result of the introduction of Landfill Tax (see below), possibly more selectively than had previously been the case.

From the developer's perspective this option has a number of distinct advantages:

- It can be employed for most types of contaminated sites, except those affected by radiation, anthrax and high concentrations of toxic substances considered unsuitable for landfilling.
- It provides a 'once and for all' solution, where all the contamination is removed from the site, provided the contractor does the job properly.
- It can be costed with a reasonable degree of accuracy, provided that the site investigation has been thoroughly undertaken and the quantities of material for disposal have been accurately estimated.

It also has several disadvantages:

- It is generally not considered to be environmentally acceptable, as it relocates the contamination from one place to another and defers the final treatment solution to a future generation.
- It involves a large number of heavy vehicle movements, from development site to landfill, consuming fossil fuels and with the risk of accidents occurring whilst the vehicles are on the public roads.

- It involves site operations that are noisy and which may produce harmful or unpleasant dusts and odours.

This chapter briefly describes alternative methods of preparing for development those sites that are affected by the presence of contamination and then describes case studies where sites have been prepared for development using different techniques.

7.2   Alternative treatment and remediation methods

7.2.1   *Soil treatments*

Besides removing the contaminated soil for off-site disposal or treatment, many different options exist for contamination to be treated on the development site. Treatment methods can be classified in five broad groups, as listed in Box 7.1.

Box 7.1   Classification of contaminated soil treatment technologies.

Biological treatments – degradation, transformation, sorption, accumulation or solubilisation of contaminants by living organisms existing, or introduced into the soil. May be *in situ*, e.g. bio-venting, or *ex situ*, such as landfarming, windrow turning and biopiles.

Chemical treatments – using a range of chemical reactions to destroy, transform, immobilise or mobilise contaminants. Also *in situ*, e.g. soil flushing, and *ex situ*, including physico-chemical washing and solvent extraction.

Physical treatments – separate contaminants by exploiting differences in physical, chemical and thermal properties. *In situ* soil vapour extraction and *ex situ* soil washing are the most widely used.

Solidification and stabilisation technologies – immobilise contaminants through physical and chemical processes. Mostly *ex situ*, although some work has been done on *in situ* treatments.

Thermal treatments – use elevated temperatures to achieve physical and chemical processes, e.g. volatilisation, combustion and pyrolysis, to remove or destroy substances in the soil. *Ex situ* treatments that have been widely used in Europe and the United States.

7.2.2 Full-scale treatment technologies

When it comes to treating the contamination, whether *in situ* or *ex situ*, there are many different alternatives available within the five groups listed in Box 7.1. The United States Environmental Protection Agency (USEPA) has monitored and reported upon several hundred of these through its Superfund Innovative Technology Evaluation Program (see USEPA, 1994, 1996, undated), also available on CD-ROM, see *www.epa.gov/ncepihom/*. In addition, USEPA has produced several Innovative Technology Evaluation Reports on individual processes. It would therefore appear that there is a wide range of choices for developers wishing to consider alternatives to the excavation and removal of contaminated soil. In practice, however, the choice may be more limited, as many of the processes reviewed by USEPA have only been undertaken at bench scale, or they are extremely expensive.

USEPA defines innovative treatment technologies as:

'chemical, biological, or physical processes applied to hazardous waste or contaminated materials to permanently change their condition ... Treatment technologies destroy contaminants or change them so that they are no longer hazardous or, at least, are less hazardous. They may reduce the amount of contaminated material at a site, remove the component of the waste that makes it hazardous, or immobilize the contaminant within the waste.'

(USEPA, 1996)

In the UK, Martin and Bardos (1996) have undertaken a review of full-scale treatment technologies for the Royal Commission on Environmental Pollution and Syms (1997, Chapter 6) provides an overview of the main alternatives, as well as the factors affecting the decision-making process when selecting the appropriate technologies. More recently, the Construction Industry Research and Information Association (CIRIA), supported by funding from a number of public and private sector organisations, has undertaken a review of remedial processes (Evans *et al.*, 2001).

Nine treatment technologies are covered in the CIRIA report:

(1) *Ex situ bioremediation:* an engineered soil treatment system [that] is a controlled process in which excavated soil is placed in an above-ground treatment enclosure and aerated or otherwise treated to enhance the degradation of organic contaminants only. The objective of the treatment is to degrade the contaminants to completely innocuous materials or to less toxic but stable forms. (Evans *et al.*, 2001, p. 29)

(2) *Enhanced in situ bioremediation:* the stimulation of naturally occurring

micro-organisms in order to increase *in situ* biological degradation of organic contaminants, by circulating water-based solutions through the contaminated soils. It is a technology directed at the treatment of contamination in both the unsaturated and the saturated zones. (Evans *et al.*, 2001, p. 57)

(3) *Natural attenuation:* the biodegradation, dispersion, dilution, sorption, volatilisation, and/or chemical and biochemical stabilisation of contaminants to reduce contaminant toxicity, mobility, or volume to levels that are protective of human health and the ecosystem, in the absence of intervention. (Evans *et al.*, 2001, p. 147)

(4) Soil vapour extraction: an *in situ* technique of inducing airflow through soil to enhance the volatilisation (and allow VOC removal from the unsaturated zone) and aerobic biodegradation of contaminants. SVE is also referred to as *in situ* volatilisation, soil vacuum extraction or soil venting. (Evans *et al.*, 2001, p. 73)

(5) *Air sparging:* a technique involving the injection of compressed air (and occasionally steam) beneath the water table at controlled pressures and volumes to promote site remediation. It is a hybrid technology because it induces both physical and biological remediation processes. It is commonly used to extend the application of soil vapour extraction. (Evans *et al.*, 2001, p. 115)

(6) *Bioventing:* the aeration of unsaturated soils to stimulate *in situ* biological activity and promote bioremediation through changes in contaminant mass, concentration and toxicity. The technique is widely used to treat fuel-derived hydrocarbons, though in principle it may be applied to any biodegradable contaminant. (Evans *et al.*, 2001, p. 131)

(7) *Dual-phase vapour extraction:* an *in situ* technique involving the combined extraction of vapour and liquids (groundwater and free-product contamination) from the subsurface. Vapour and liquid can be withdrawn separately, by conventional pumping with a submersible pump and a vapour extraction well, or they can be removed together under a high vacuum, by a process colloquially known as slurping. (Evans *et al.*, 2001, p. 97)

(8) *Soil washing:* an *ex situ* process that employs either mechanical separation (volume reduction) and/or aqueous leaching to remove contaminants from uncontaminated soil particles and sediments. Soil washing systems are often similar to *ex situ* chemical extraction and leaching processes. (Martin & Bardos, 1996)

(9) *Cement-based fixation:* forms of fixation whereby cement or other binders are mixed with contaminated soil in order to physically, and sometimes also chemically, reduce the mobility or availability of hazardous constituents. (Evans *et al.*, 2001, p. 175)

The CIRIA report provides guidance for good practice in the selection, design, commissioning, operation, monitoring and validation of process technologies. Each technology is described under a consistent set of headings, see Box 7.2.

Box 7.2   Soil remediation technologies in CIRIA Report C549.

Each technology is described in terms of:
- its definition
- the scientific principles underlying the process
- its applicability and selection
- plant and equipment typically required
- limitations on its use
- aspects of planning and management of the treatment including data requirements
- time-scales, health and safety, regulatory and environmental requirements, criteria for remediation
- basics of design
- guidance on specifications
- operations monitoring and evaluation
- closure and validation

7.2.3   Factors to consider

Whatever methodologies are available to remediate the land, and it will usually be more than one, the eventual selection must be made having due regard for all the relevant information and circumstances. These may be summarised as set out in Box 7.3.

Box 7.3   Factors affecting the selection of remediation or treatment methods.

Legal: international, national and local legislation, as well as any legal requirements as to remediation standards. Town planning conditions and contractual obligations, waste disposal, health and safety requirements.

Political: present and future government policies, together with public and 'corporate' perceptions. The speed of any response, as well as any possible criminal or civil liabilities. The timing of redevelopment, its end use, and its phasing relative to other activities on and around the site would be of significant importance.

Contd

Box 7.3   Continued.

Commercial: value of the land before and after treatment may have a direct influence on the selection of treatment methods, with 'high' technology being compared to 'low' technology methods, especially if any relatively untried methods are to be considered. Possible fluctuations in value would also have to be considered. The type of contract and the availability of collateral warranties, or guarantees from contractors; the time available to undertake the work and the physical space available. Cash flow requirements and the likelihood of commercial success.

Geographic: proximity of the site to domestic dwellings and other 'sensitive' structures, such as hospitals. Ease of access to the site, especially if the remediation option calls for the removal of large volumes of material. The presence of other polluted sites in the vicinity.

Environmental: proximity of the site to an aquifer or other controlled waters; these may be placed at risk during the remediation works. The hydrogeology of the site and its surroundings; any nearby water extraction points; local weather conditions.

Engineering: existing groundwater levels, whether a producing aquifer or not, and the soil type, especially its homogeneity. The volumes of materials to be treated may rule out some treatment methods as uneconomic, either because there is insufficient material to justify setting up costs, or because the volumes are too great to be handled with available plant or by currently developed processes, within the time-scale allowed. The availability of plant and equipment may also exclude some treatment methods.

Health and safety: toxicity of the contaminants and any side-effects of the proposed treatment method(s), including noise, dust, vibration and odour. The presence of any underground or overhead services; the handling requirements of the materials, including special clothing and equipment.

Managerial: availability of suitably experienced remediation companies and the ease with which the project can be managed. Quality control and assurance procedures and approvals from regulatory authorities.

Technical: limitations of treatment methods and their application; the specification of treatment criteria and analytical methods. The availability of proven methods will need to be compared with new technologies and confidence limits defined. Treatment monitoring will have to be specified, with the objective of producing an auditable report of the works undertaken.

(Based on Syms, 1997, pp. 91–92)

The selection of the appropriate soil treatment method, or methods, forms an extremely important part of the property development process. It is essential to get this right, as going back later to undertake further treatment will be very costly and may even involve demolition of, or serious disruption to, buildings on the development. When considering the selection of treatments, the development team needs to have regard for how different methods might be perceived by end-users, investors and funding institutions, as well as by the regulators. It is possible that several different treatments will be suitable for use and that different technologies may be needed to treat the various contaminants existing within a single site.

Developers would be well-advised to consult the regulatory authorities at an early stage, before final decisions are taken as to remediation methods, especially if any discharges to air or water might be involved. Many forms of treatment will require either a Waste Management Licence or a Mobile Plant Licence and these are discussed in Chapter 9.

7.3   Remediation case studies

7.3.1   *Chemical oxidisation*

In situ chemical oxidation (ISCO) is a technology designed to rapidly remediate organic contaminants in groundwater, saturated soils and, with hydraulic manipulation, the capillary fringe and unsaturated soils, through oxidation reactions induced by sequential injection of liquid chemical solutions. The nature and concentration of the chemicals vary, depending on the target contaminants and site-specific conditions. Both laboratory and pilot studies are used to determine the design quantities and concentrations of the chemicals applied. In the case study a liquid oxidant solution and catalyst were sequentially applied in order to generate hydroxyl free radical ions (OH). The hydroxyl free radical is one of the most powerful oxidising agents known and is capable of rapidly degrading hydrocarbons (particularly aromatics and shorter chain aliphatics) within groundwater and soils. Any uncatalysed oxidant decomposes to innocuous by-products, generally resulting in an increase in dissolved oxygen concentration in groundwater, which can be useful for enhancing aerobic biodegradation.

Chemical oxidation is a very powerful process causing large-scale reduction in organic contaminant loading in extremely short periods of time. It is, however, a process to be treated with respect and only operated under stringent health and safety controls. In the case study, approval was sought and received from the Environment Agency for the use of this innovative remediation technology. ISCO is currently widely used in the United States under the approval of USEPA. However, due to safety incidents resulting from the inappropriate application of ISCO, in particular the form detailed in this case study – Fenton's oxidation – several States have imposed a ban on the application of ISCO. This reiterates the importance of adequate process controls and safeguards. The case study presented is believed to be the first full-scale application of Fenton's oxidation in the UK.

Former service station site in London

In November 1999, QDS was commissioned by a major oil company to carry out the remediation of a former service station site, located in a high land value area of London. Diesel range, volatile (BTEX, i.e. benzene, toluene, ethyl benzene, xylene) and MTBE (methyl t-butyl ether) contaminants were detected within the groundwater at concentrations in excess of 70 mg/l. The client had a commitment to sell the site for redevelopment before the end of the calendar year, but faced a risk of losing the prospective purchaser unless the liabilities associated with the contaminated groundwater were significantly reduced. The task was therefore to design, install, implement and conclude a suitable remediation programme within a limited time frame. The time-scale in question was to achieve remediation of the site within a three-month period from receipt of order.

The geology beneath the site comprised River Terrace Deposits overlying alternating sand and clay beds of the Woolwich and Reading Beds. The depth to groundwater was approximately 2 m across the site.

The site itself was surrounded by other contaminated sites including a former gas works site and a former kerosene storage site. Whilst the Environment Agency ideally wanted a multilateral area remediation programme, due to the time frames involved and the unlikely event of agreeing terms with neighbouring contaminated land owners, a unilateral remediation programme was pursued. The first phase of this was to install a slurry wall around the perimeter of the site to effectively isolate the site from additional contaminant impact.

Following the successful completion of laboratory and pilot-scale feasibility trials, an intensive programme of *in situ* chemical oxidation was carried out through 32 injection wells installed across the site. The wells were installed to a depth of approximately 4.5 m with gravel packs and bentonite-cement seals to the surface. Negotiations with the purchaser's consultants and the regulators took a period of two months. This period by necessity overlapped with the system installation. Installation of the wells, site set-up and system installation and commissioning took one month. The operational injection phase lasted three days and was conducted on a continuous 24-hour basis.

The methodology involved was a batch sequencing process of chemical injection. Potable water from an adjacent source was stored in an above-ground container and dosed with an acidic ferrous solution to reach the design concentration. The acidic ferrous solution was then injected into specific wells that were subsequently dosed with 35% hydrogen peroxide. Once field-testing indicated that additional catalyst was required, the process was repeated. The ferrous salts present in the solution are designed to catalyse the conversion of hydrogen peroxide to the hydroxyl free radical, (the primary oxidising agent – it is important to note that hydrogen peroxide itself is a powerful oxidising agent). The dilute chemical solutions were injected at an average rate of 25 m^3/hr (600 m^3/day) during the injection period.

The isolation of the site, by the recent addition of a slurry wall, meant that a more intensive treatment with Fenton's oxidation could be used without risk of impacting off-site receptors. In addition this physical barrier was important in rapidly convincing the regulators that off-site migration was not an issue. In the absence of the slurry wall it is likely that the regulators would have wanted pilot test data to demonstrate that off-site migration of either oxidants, iron, sulphates or acids was not an issue. This has subsequently been demonstrated on a different site. In this context, it is important to note that the hydroxyl free radical will rapidly oxidise any oxidisable material on contact to (primarily) CO_2 and H_2O. As such, the potential for this ion to have migrated further than a couple of metres from the injection point is unlikely. Any uncatalysed hydrogen peroxide simply decomposes to oxygen and water, resulting in an increase in dissolved oxygen concentration in groundwater. Injected acids similarly are rapidly attenuated.

Pre- and post-remediation groundwater samples were collected from selected monitoring wells and submitted for laboratory analysis of diesel range organics (DRO) (C10–C40), total volatile hydrocarbons (TVH) (C4–C10), BTEX and MTBE. The results demonstrated a significant reduction in the concentrations of all contaminant compounds. The percentage reductions ranged from 89% of DRO compounds, 90% of TVH, 95% of BTEX through to almost complete removal of MTBE.

The results show a significant reduction in concentrations of all contaminant compounds in the most impacted wells and no significant change in the concentrations in monitoring well MW12. The apparent increase in concentration of DRO in MW12 lies within the acceptable range of laboratory variation for low concentrations and was not considered to represent a significant event.

Use of the powerful and innovative ISCO technology resulted in the following achievements at the site:

- Reduction in groundwater contaminant concentrations of up to 98% in less than one week.

- Remediation within a tight time-scale, which helped expedite sale of the site.
- The overall cost of the project was only 25% greater than the cost of slower physical remediation methods.
- Minimal disturbance to the site.
- No long-term operation or maintenance issues.
- No long-term impacts to the aquifer or potential receptors.

ISCO can also be applied to a wide range of other contaminants including chlorinated solvents. The application of ISCO requires extensive attention to health and safety considerations. Inappropriate application of the technology has been demonstrated to have significant detrimental impacts. Detailed below are some of the main points to note and some of the potential concerns:

- The use of ISCO to effectively treat adsorbed phase (through the process of surface catalysis) and the capillary fringe minimises the risk of rebound in comparison to more conventional technologies.
- Concerns are often expressed with regard to the long-term impact on groundwater quality from addition of ferrous sulphate (or other catalysts), acid and hydrogen peroxide. Both the type and concentration of chemicals used should be considered with both the regulatory and developer's requirements in mind.
- The presence of both sulphate and the combination of an oxygen, carbon dioxide rich acidic water can be deleterious to concrete structures. Consideration of this needs to be undertaken prior to designing both the injection system and the chemicals used.
- Bacterial denaturing can be investigated by microbiological studies during the pilot works to assess impact to the population. Site-specific details are assessed to ascertain the magnitude of the impact and mitigating measures considered.
- Off-site migration of the injected chemicals can be negated through the use of peripheral wells to be used as abstraction wells to perform two functions: hydrogeological barriers and for the provision of the carrier medium, water.
- Health and safety is a major factor when undertaking an ISCO project. As part of the design of the remediation system, engineers generally endeavour to design out as much of the risk as possible.
- Due consideration needs to be given both to the handling and injection of the hazardous chemicals involved. An inappropriate injection programme could push hazardous reactive components off site and outside of the controlled subsurface zone.
- Particular care is given to potential gas produced by the process. The combination of increased concentrations of subsurface oxygen with

volatilisation of potentially explosive petroleum hydrocarbons (in this case study) caused by the often vigorous exothermic oxidation reaction and the presence of CO_2, a by-product of the process, can present significant health and safety concerns.

7.3.2 Landfarming

Landfarming accelerates the natural microbial breakdown of coal tar. It involves the addition of water and nutrients to the coal tar, requiring no additional organic matter or special microbial formulations. The process is controlled through a cycle of tilling, covering and monitoring. It is a low-intensity, low-cost approach, although for some materials, such as the coal tar in the following case study, the time-scale for the breakdown of the contaminants may be longer than those for other bioremediation technologies.

A gas works site in Sheffield

The following case study describes work undertaken on a former town gas works site owned by Lattice Property, part of the Lattice Group, which demerged from the BG Group in October 2000. Lattice Group plc owns many former gas works sites that may have been contaminated in the past during the manufacture of town gas. To address any liabilities associated with these sites, Lattice Property undertakes an ongoing programme of site investigation and remediation. This case study was originally published as part of the DTI's BIO-WISE programme, see *www.dti.gov.uk/biowise*.

The buildings and structures at the Sheffield site were demolished in the 1960s, leaving no obvious evidence of their existence. Site maps revealed that there had been four underground coal tar tanks and their precise location was determined by geophysical mapping. Upon excavation the tanks were found to be intact and to still contain a mixture of coal tar and contaminated water.

The disposal of coal tar generally involves stabilising it with soil from the site to form a more easily handled material. This material can either be destroyed or be disposed of to designated landfill sites. Landfill disposal costs for this material are generally in the region of £40–£60 per cubic metre.

To find a cost-effective solution to landfill disposal, Lattice worked with specialist bioremediation company Advantica Technologies of Loughborough. The site owner was not under any time constraints and the consultant recommended that landfarming should be used, as it would eliminate the need to dispose of the coal tar to landfill. A risk assessment of the site was undertaken as part of the site investigation phase and the results, together with Government guidance available at the time, were used to develop the remediation process and to establish target levels. The target level decided upon for polycyclic aromatic hydrocarbons (PAH) was 1000 mg/kg.

A landfarm was prepared at the Sheffield site to isolate the contaminated material and allow the internal environmental conditions to be controlled. The landfarm was created over a concrete platform with controlled drainage.

Contaminated material from the site was screened to remove coarse bricks and concrete. This fraction was only slightly contaminated and suitable for reuse in the backfilling of excavations. The more contaminated, finer fraction was mixed with coal tar (creating some 2000 t of material) and placed in the landfarm for treatment. Samples were taken and analysed to determine the baseline level of contamination.

Every month the material was tilled, irrigated and fertilised with nutrients to promote degradation. Samples were analysed each week to monitor closely the progress being made. Field test kits for PAH, calibrated against laboratory data, provided cheap and rapid analysis. Validation was by robust laboratory methods.

After 52 weeks, the PAH concentrations in the material had decreased from 4700 mg/kg to the target level of 1000 mg/kg. Over the same period, total hydrocarbons in the contaminated material had decreased from 17 000 mg/kg to 7000 mg/kg. Although the client was pleased with the outcome of the bioremediation, the bioremediation company felt that the time-scales for treatment could be reduced. To speed up the process, a mobile landfarm was developed for use at this and other sites. This system consisted of a container with a capacity of 100 t. Using a pre-constructed container enabled on-site treatment while minimising site infrastructure requirements. The mobile landfarm was operated under guidance from the Environment Agency.

Once the container had been delivered, coal tar mixed with contaminated soil was treated for reuse on site, thus minimising the need for transportation. The container was fitted with an internal electric heater to maintain an optimum treatment temperature in cold weather.

Intensifying the process considerably reduced treatment time. This involved more frequent tilling and watering, and using the data obtained during the initial stage to adjust the pH, temperature, moisture and nutrient status of the material for optimum performance. Using the mobile landfarm, it took only 18 weeks to decrease PAH concentrations from around 3000 mg/kg to 1000 mg/kg. Assuming a more or less linear reduction under these conditions, the time taken to treat soil with a similar PAH concentration to that treated in the pens (initially 4700 mg/kg) would have been reduced from 52 to just over 33 weeks. The mobile landfarm could be used for any size of site simply by using more containers rather than building a bespoke system.

In cost terms, bioremediation using the mobile landfarm worked out at £30–£40 per cubic metre, a saving of 25–33% of the cost of disposal to landfill.

7.3.3   *Bioremediation, groundwater treatment and barrier construction*

For many sites a single treatment method may not be capable of addressing all of the problems. Therefore the development team may find it necessary to consider a suite of options, which may even include partial excavation and removal of contaminants. Identifying 'hot spots' of contamination and then either removing the material from site, or treating it either *in situ* or *ex situ* will require a very detailed site investigation and assessment. Only with the benefit of a comprehensive study will it be possible to estimate, with any degree of accuracy, the scale of the problems involved and the likely cost of the site remediation. As part of such a scheme it may be appropriate to adopt different criteria for the remediation, according to the mix of uses on the site or the exposure pathways. It is also quite likely that vertical and/or horizontal barriers will need to be installed in order to prevent any retained contamination from migrating between different parts of the site or entering from adjoining land.

The following case study is another gas works site where a combination of technologies was employed to achieve the desired remediation solution.

Former gas works, Hythe Quay, Colchester, Essex

Knight Environmental undertook the site investigation, risk assessment, regulator negotiation and subsequent remediation of the former Colchester gas works. The 2.6 ha site was operated as a gas works from 1838 to the early 1970s, when gas production ceased, the site subsequently being demolished and remaining derelict to the present day. The remediation works were required to allow for redevelopment to residential housing with gardens, three-storey flats, shops and a nursery school.

In addition to traditional coal carbonisation and associated gas purification activities, petroleum distillate (naptha) was imported to site by rail, to be reformed to produce town gas. Tar and ammonia liquors were processed and stored in underground and above-ground tanks. As a result of such historic activities, the site was highly contaminated by a variety of hydrocarbons, cyanides, sulphurous compounds, ammonium, some heavy metals and land gases. Contaminant sources were found within made ground, the upper alluvial deposits, perched groundwater and, to a lesser degree, the groundwater regime within the sand and gravel deposits. The latter stratum is classed as a minor aquifer in direct hydraulic continuity with the River Colne, located some 30 m down-gradient from the eastern boundary of the site.

The remediation scheme agreed with the Environment Agency and Colchester Borough Council Environmental Control Department was intended to reduce the risks associated with the contamination in relation to the proposed end use. The eastern part of the site was planned for redevelopment with a less sensitive end use comprising residential flats, shops and a nursery school, with the central and western part of the site scheduled for redevelopment to terraced housing with private gardens.

Principal risk drivers and objectives. In dealing with ground contamination, the remediation scheme had the following key objectives:

- Limit to acceptable levels the direct exposure of future site residents and ground workers.
- Reduce to acceptable levels the risk to controlled waters.
- Reduce to acceptable levels the risk to construction materials.
- Reduce to acceptable levels the risk to future planting in gardens and landscaped areas.
- Limit to acceptable levels the direct exposure of future residents to land-gases or vapours.

Summary of remediation scheme. It was anticipated that a high degree of site betterment and appropriate levels of risk reduction could be achieved through a remediation strategy that involved a combined approach across the site. The combined approach would provide a 'fit-for-purpose' remedial scheme and was likely to reduce the cost by targeting areas that required remediating with end use in mind.

The main elements of the remediation scheme were as follows.

(1)   *Major source removal and barrier construction*
The principal risk driver was identified as the potential uptake of hydrocarbons contained in the upper layers of the soil horizon and within perched waters. Since removal of all contaminated material on the site was not considered economically viable, the alternative solution was to:

- remove sub-surface obstructions, redundant pipework, etc. and excavate hot spots of heavy contamination in the eastern part of the site (flats, shops and school area), including underground tanks;
- excavate soil to 1 m depth over the central and western parts (housing area), remove subsurface obstructions, pipework and tanks;
- excavate hot spots of heavy contamination below 1 m depth in the central and western (housing) parts of the site;
- treat *ex situ* up to 8500 m^3 excavated hydrocarbon contaminated soils with bioremediation techniques;
- dispose to licensed landfill of 4000 m^3 contaminated, non-treatable, soils;
- remove contaminated perched water from within excavation areas, with separation of free-product hydrocarbons prior to discharge to foul sewer;

- place a vertical physical barrier (compacted clay backfill) around perimeter of excavation within housing area, to prevent further ingress of perched water into site;
- replace bioremediated soils within areas beneath proposed access roads, house footprints, or if meeting the criteria for material reuse, in the bottom layer of the clean capping layer above the capillary break; and
- place a 300 mm thick capillary break layer and geotextile layer overlaid by clean engineered backfill and topsoil up to 0.5 m above existing ground level within garden areas (forming a 1.5 m clean barrier overlying pre-existing ground).

Areas of heavy or gross contamination were those determined to contain levels of contamination in excess of the criteria agreed with the regulatory authorities.

(2)   *Monitoring of sands and gravels*

In view of the levels and distribution of contaminants encountered within the minor aquifer in the sand and gravel deposits and considering the site setting, specific remedial treatment of the groundwater was not considered likely to be of any significant environmental benefit. Some degree of local impact was apparent during the site investigation works but this was generally in the vicinity of former major subsurface structures. Samples from monitoring boreholes located on the eastern boundary (i.e. downstream direction with respect to groundwater flow) did not appear to be significantly impacted, indicating that off-site migration of contamination via this pathway to the River Colne was not likely to be significant.

In order to confirm this, both during and upon completion of remedial works, monitoring of groundwater in the sand and gravel deposits underlying the site was undertaken at six well locations for at least an 18-month period. Groundwater samples were taken for laboratory analysis prior to commence-ment of the works and at regular intervals throughout its duration, including key periods such as piling operations. If locally impacted groundwaters underlying the site showed no evident improvement during the monitoring period, further remedial action would be agreed with the regulatory authorities.

During the site remediation works, the backfill material contained within former gas holder No 1 was found to contain significant concentrations of hydrocarbons, up to 150 000 mg/kg TPH and 60 000 mg/kg total PAH. This gas holder was probably utilised at some stage for storage of tar liquors and/or petroleum distillate (naptha). Driven piles were identified within the infilled structure, which supported a large concrete slab forming extensive railway sidings. These piles were considered to present a direct migration pathway for mobile hydrocarbons, allowing vertical migration from the grossly contaminated source into the saturated sand and gravels underlying the concrete base.

This was confirmed by the significant concentrations of hydrocarbon species in a monitoring borehole located some 30 m downstream. Peak concentrations of the principal contaminants of concern were 18 000 μg/l[7.1] TPH, 18 000 μg/l napthalene and 14 500 μg/l total BTEX. Upon completing source removal, concentrations of all such compounds decreased through the process of natural attenuation. However, in order to reduce the time-scales for achieving satisfactory reduction in groundwater concentrations, an oxygen release compound (ORC) was injected into the sand and gravel horizon at 43 locations upstream and downstream from the residual source. ORC slowly releases oxygen in groundwater to increase the current rate of biodegradation. Such *in situ* treatment would have been considerably more difficult to implement retrospectively once this area of the site was redeveloped to a nursery school, housing and a car park.

ORC is proven in the USA to reduce concentrations of petroleum hydrocarbons to acceptable target concentrations in time-scales less than 150 days and the treatment included close monitoring of boreholes installed both upstream and downstream of the source area over the following months, to evaluate the effectiveness of the remedial technique.

(3)   *Foundations*

Due to the generally poorly and variably consolidated nature of the near-surface soils, traditional spread foundations were not considered feasible for the proposed development and piles were considered the only practicable foundation solution.

In order to mitigate against the potential for piles to initiate further vertical migratory pathways beneath the footprint of the proposed structures between the ground and the annulus of individual piles, an appropriate pile solution was adopted at the site. The pile design approved by the Environment Agency was the Vibro-Concrete Column method installed by Keller Ground Engineering.

(4)   *Land gas protection measures*

The site posed potential risk from soil gases including methane, carbon dioxide and volatile hydrocarbons such as benzene. Therefore the development provided for a passive gas protection system to be incorporated in each of the buildings, comprising a ventilated sub-floor void with gas/vapourproof membrane constructed into the floor in accordance with the BRE Guidance Document *Protective Measures for Housing on Gas-Contaminated Land* (Johnson, 2001).

[7.1] Micro-grams per litre, or parts per billion.

7.3.4   *Air-sparging/ozonation*

Air sparging involves the injection of compressed air, and occasionally steam, to beneath the water table. This is done at controlled pressures and volumes, so as to promote both physical and biological remediation processes. The principle behind the technology is that air will only penetrate an aquifer when the air injection pressure exceeds the sum of the water column hydrostatic pressure and the air entry pressure. When air is injected into the saturated zone below the water table, groundwater is displaced as air enters the soil voids.

Air sparging can be used for the remediation of dissolved-phase or adsorbed organic contaminants and, although it may be used in isolation, is commonly used in conjunction with other techniques, especially in extending the application of soil vapour extraction to water-saturated soils. Figure 7.1 shows a schematic layout for an air sparging system.

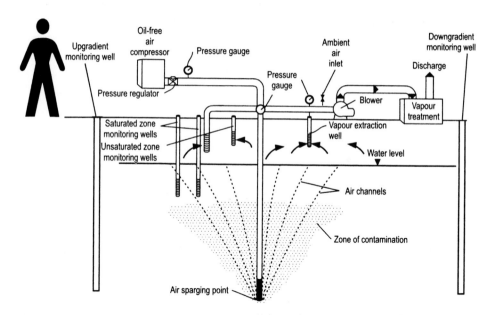

Figure 7.1   Extract from CIRIA C549 showing schematic layout of a typical air sparging system.

The underlying principles and the processes that control contaminant mass removal rates are still not well understood but the following three *in situ* processes are believed to be responsible for contaminant removal during air sparging:

(1)   Transfer of volatile contaminants from aqueous to gaseous phase by diffusion across the air–water interfacial surface area of the channels (*in situ* stripping).

(2)   Volatilisation of contaminants from the sorbed or trapped phase into air-filled channels. Direct volatilisation is the dominant process for removal of residual contamination from the saturated zone.

(3)   Aerobic biodegradation by indigenous bacteria.

(Evans *et al.*, 2001, p. 116)

The rates at which these three processes occur in the subsurface material will vary depending upon the distance from the sparge well. The following case study illustrates the use of a form of air sparging as part of a suite of remediation technologies.

Former tannery and scrapyard, Bramford Road, Ipswich

Knight Environmental provided a complete programme of technical and groundworks support including site investigation, quantitative risk assessment and remedial design for a former tannery, laundry and scrapyard proposed for residential development. The soil and groundwater within the site was contaminated with heavy metals, phenols, PCBs, methane-generating wastes, hydrocarbons (including diesel/mineral oils, PAHs) and chlorinated solvents. A cost-effective risk-based remedial strategy was implemented at the site, comprising the following corrective actions:

•   Demolition and screening of buildings, with removal of asbestos-contaminated materials.
•   Excavation and removal of contaminated 'hot spots'.
•   Horizontal barrier installation.
•   Bioremediation of 3000 t of hydrocarbon contaminated soils, by the windrow method.
•   *In situ* treatment of groundwater contaminated with chlorinated solvents (including PCE, TCE) by sparging with air and ozone.
•   Post-completion monitoring of VOC reduction in soil and groundwater.

The groundwater treatment technology adopted was a proprietary *in situ* air sparging/ozonation system imported from the USA, a technique never adopted before in the UK. Groundwater concentrations of PCE, TCE, DCE and vinyl choride (VC) have been effectively reduced from 2000–4000 μg/l to generally less than 100 μg/l for individual compounds (VC to < 1 μg/l), all of which are well below the risk-based target levels set for the source area. The works involved extensive liaison and negotiation with regulators regarding design of the remedial strategy, risk assessments, licensing the bioremediation facility and regulation of the groundwater treatment system.

7.4   Containing the contamination

Another alternative to excavation and off-site disposal is the creation of a secure containment within the development site itself. Whilst this may overcome some of the environmental disadvantages of excavation and disposal, from the developer's perspective it is somewhat less than ideal. Although there would be a saving in off-site transportation costs, on-site containment may result in sterilisation of part of the developable area of the site. Therefore, unless the containment can be constructed entirely within a landscaping area, say through the use of earth mounding, or under a vehicle parking/manoeuvring area, the value of the lost development area will have to be offset against the transport cost saving. It is also likely that the creation of a secure containment within the development site will require a Waste Management Licence under Part II of the Environmental Protection Act 1990 (see Chapter 9). Licensing require-ments will result in a need to construct the containment as an engineered landfill and lead to long-term monitoring of the contained waste, both of which may be unacceptable to the developer.

If the developer is not prepared to consider constructing an engineered landfill within the development site, he or she might wish to consider the possibility of minimising the off-site disposal of waste by sorting the con-taminated material on site and sending only the most severely contaminated soil and other wastes to landfill. The site assessment (Chapter 5) should have identified possible hot spots of contamination within the site, and these may be confirmed visually or by further chemical analysis once the remedial work is under way. It is unlikely that the volume of material eventually selected for off-site disposal can be estimated as accurately as for total disposal, as the division between material for retention on site and disposal cannot be finally decided until the site has been opened up. However, it is likely to be significantly less than for total disposal. Once the most severely contaminated spoil has been removed from site, the remaining, less contaminated material can be regraded to a reduced level for the new development, and sensitive areas, such as gardens and landscaping areas, can be provided with clean cover, e.g. clay or a geo-synthetic membrane (see Syms & Knight, 2000, Chapter 10), and finished with growing material.

Another alternative may be to simply leave the contaminated material in place, provided that it is adequately contained and not migrating, and to design the new development in such a way as to ensure the future security of the contaminated material within the site. The following case study describes a development using this approach.

7.4.1   *Development of a new warehouse in Cheshire*

This case study describes the development of a 7800 square metre warehouse on a site of 1.4 ha in a Cheshire town. The historical study revealed that land in the area had been used for industrial purposes since at least the late nineteenth century. On the 1849 map the site was shown as meadow but by 1896 a sawmill occupied part of the site. By 1929 the use had changed to leather tanning and dressing, uses that were still continuing in 1954. There was also anecdotal evidence that the site was used as a combined abattoir and tannery. In the 1980s the use changed to vehicle transport depot and warehousing, at which time most of the site was covered with reinforced concrete for parking heavy goods vehicles.

An examination of the historical maps showed that a significant part of the site had been occupied by tanning and lime pits, see Figure 7.2, over part of which a brick building had been constructed in the 1920s. At the time of the historical study this building was being used as a vehicle maintenance workshop and waste oil tanks had been placed outside. Several above-ground road fuel tanks had also been located on the site at different times, of which only one remained.

The site was located 60 m from a river, for which the water quality was classified as poor, and over a major aquifer. Several pollution incidents had occurred within 500 m of the site boundaries but none of these were attributable to the site. More than a dozen potentially contaminative industries were located within 250 m of the property, mainly connected with motor vehicle and engineering industries, and a similar number were located between 250 and 500 m from the boundaries.

An intrusive site investigation, comprising ten boreholes and 25 trial pits, was undertaken and revealed the presence of fill materials across most of the site, comprising ash brick and stone, in thickness between 1.1 and 2.3 m, overlying soft brown and black mottled silty clay. Some of the trial pits were in targeted locations identified from the historical study and other sampling locations were determined on a grid pattern. A mechanical breaker had to be used to break open the concrete for trial-pitting in most locations. In one location, close to the eastern boundary of the site, a highly offensive odour escaped from the trial pit. The material was sampled and the pit abandoned without being taken to full depth.

Laboratory analysis of samples disclosed elevated concentrations of arsenic, phenols and toluene extractable matter. Several samples were also analysed for anthrax, of which no trace was found. The samples taken from the trial pit close to the eastern boundary were found to contain fats and other animal matter, including skin, and volatiles, later identified as diesel. Further analysis of the historical maps indicated that a watercourse had existed along the eastern

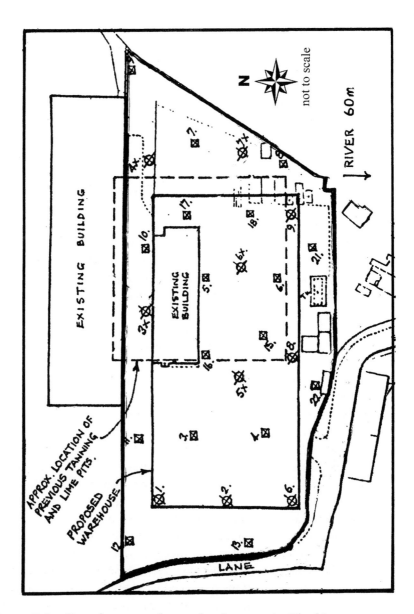

Figure 7.2   Site of new warehouse development in Cheshire.

boundary, of which no visible sign remained. It was concluded that this had been filled with animal wastes and had become further contaminated by leakage from a diesel tank on the adjoining property.

In order to determine the extent of the animal wastes and diesel contamination along the eastern boundary, and to minimise the exposure of the site investigation team, a percussive drilling rig was used to sink 16 trial holes radiating out from the original trial pit. Material from these trial holes was visually inspected and securely sampled for analysis. At the same time two deep boreholes were sunk in order to ascertain the depth of the clay cover above the sandstone aquifer, care being taken to site these boreholes in areas identified as being unaffected by contamination.

Attention then turned to the selection of an appropriate remediation and site preparation strategy. To have removed the entire contaminated fill material from the site would have involved breaking up the extensive reinforced concrete and experience from the site investigation had shown that, in places, this was up to 1 m thick. Excavation and removal would have entailed transporting an estimated 17 000 cubic metres (around 30 600 t) of material to landfill. This would have involved more than 2100 heavy vehicle movements and a cost that would have rendered the entire project unviable.

The consulting engineer suggested that, instead of removing the contamination it should be allowed to remain in place under what appeared to be an effective cover and that the new building should be constructed by 'over-slabbing' the site. The laboratory analyses had indicated that the contaminants were degrading and that there had been very little migration of contaminants into the underlying clay. As for the foundations for the new building it was proposed that a grid of driven piles be installed under the foundation pads, walls and the entire floor area of the warehouse. The precast driven piles were installed using a 5 t hydraulic top drive hammer, see Figure 7.3.

The two deep boreholes confirmed that the top of the aquifer was 20–23 m below the surface of the site, as indicated by other studies such as geological mapping, and that the initial soft silty clay gave way to firm/stiff clay at a depth of around 5 m. In discussions with the local authority environmental health department and the Environment Agency the main concern was to ensure that the piles did not create pathways from the contamination immediately below the surface down to the aquifer.

Driven piles rely on friction between the sides of the pile and the surrounding ground in order to achieve the required bearing capacity. It was agreed with the regulators that pile depths should not exceed 15 m. The piling contractor confirmed that a piling record would be taken for each pile and that, if pile set could not be achieved before 15 m depth, the pile would be downrated and an additional pile driven adjacent to the original position. The contractor also confirmed that the piles would not create contaminant pathways and that, in the unlikely event of any bulbs of contaminants being trapped on the toe of the pile these would disperse once any resistance was reached at a depth of around 7 m.

So far as the severe contamination close to the eastern boundary was concerned, agreement was reached with the regulators that the best solution for

Fig. 7.3   Precast concrete driven piling rig.

this would be for it to be excavated under tightly controlled conditions and sent to landfill. With the exception of one house, all of the properties in the area were in commercial or industrial use. Occupiers were informed of the proposed excavation works and advised to keep their windows and doors closed so far as possible. The work was also carried out when little wind was forecast. A Landfill Tax Exemption Certificate was obtained and a total of 2136 t of contaminated material was disposed of – a very small fraction of what would have been involved if a full excavate-and-remove solution had been chosen.

This approach provided a satisfactory solution for the warehouse development, utilising the extensive concrete cover that already existed. It was made possible by the fact that the site investigations had disclosed that the contamination was contained very close to the surface of the site, within the first two or three metres depth, was naturally degrading and had shown little or no propensity to migrate. The method would not have been suitable for a residential development and may not have been acceptable to an institutional investor had the site been developed other than for an owner-occupier.

7.5   Insurance

The availability of insurance in respect of site remediation works has been considered by Syms (1997, pp. 267–272). Since that time the market has grown in terms of numbers of providers of insurance cover and the extent of cover provided, as well as the number of developers and landowners seeking insurance.

So far as site remediation works are required, the developer's first interest will be in limiting the risk of cost overruns should any unexpected problems arise during the execution of the works. One way to achieve this, as discussed in Chapter 11, is to pass all of the risk onto the civil engineering contractor, or the specialist remediation contractor, responsible for undertaking the work. A prudent contractor will wish to examine all site investigation reports, and probably take independent advice from an environmental consultant, before deciding whether or not to enter into a fixed-price contract. The same contractor will probably also increase the price quoted for the work in order to allow for the increased risk and uncertainty. A less prudent contractor will not wish to examine the reports, or take independent advice, and may well not allow a sufficient margin to cover the uncertainties, with the probability that dispute or financial problems will ensue.

The alternative would be for the developer to take out insurance whereby the cost of the remediation can be 'capped' at some predetermined figure. This would operate through the developer entering into a contract under which the contractor or remediation specialist could claim for any additional costs incurred as a result of undiscovered contamination, or as a result of other specified problems. The contractor or remediation specialist would tender for the work in the normal way, having been provided with all available site investigation data. The same data would also need to be supplied to a specialist insurance underwriters, such as Certa (underwriting agents to Allianz Cornhill), *www.certa.com*, who would undertake a technical and risk assessment of the information, including the proposed remediation works. A premium would be quoted on the basis that, if the estimated cost is exceeded, the developer would bear the first part of the increase (say 5%) and the insurance company would then be responsible for any further increase.

As well as reducing the risk in respect of remediation costs, and possibly the costs themselves by not insisting on a fixed-price contract, the developer can also obtain further insurance cover, for example to extend the period of a warranty from the contractor or to protect against future regulatory action.

7.6   Summary

Among the problems identified by developers and their advisers are the lack of advice and information about alternative treatments, together with concerns about the variability of advice received from environmental consultants. Developers are also reluctant to consider treatments that require long-term monitoring, i.e. monitoring which extends beyond the development period itself (Syms, 2001). In spite of these concerns, developers do wish to be informed about the availability of alternative treatments, if only to be able to consider the options open to them.

The case studies described in this chapter illustrate only a few of the many techniques and technologies currently available to tackle soil and groundwater contamination. They also demonstrate that there are alternatives to excavation and disposal, even though some remediation strategies may include an element of off-site disposal, or treatment, as part of a suite of techniques employed. Although natural attenuation as such has not been considered, the last case study illustrates that it may not be necessary to undertake any significant removal or treatment in order to redevelop the site but there may be some implications in terms of acceptability or value.

7.7   Checklist

- Hold talks with the Environment Agency and the local authority's environmental health department in order to assess their degree of interest in the site.

- Seek to cause as few problems as possible to local residents.
- Consider any time constraints as a more environmentally acceptable remediation solution may be possible if a longer time-scale is allowed.
- Apply as early as possible for a Landfill Tax Exemption Certificate if one is needed.
- Protect the environment, try not to move contamination from one site to another without any form of treatment.

Part Three
Development

Introduction

This part considers the development processes from the feasibility study right through to the marketing of the development. This should be a very exciting stage with all the preliminary work now coming together in order to see the development 'on site'. The professional team will have been working together for some time and will now be attending progress meetings. In order to meet the deadline for handing over the building, whether it be residential, offices, industrial or commercial, the team's ability to perform will be of the utmost importance. They will all be aware of the many pitfalls – poor weather conditions, delays in the delivery of materials, etc. – that can cause delays and this is where their experience will be called on to remedy problems as quickly and efficiently as possible.

Chapter 8 deals with the feasibility study, which should consider all aspects of the project, not simply its financial viability, and will continue right through the development process. Financial appraisals are also discussed and a worked example is included.

Chapter 9 considers planning and environmental regulation and discusses the 'suitable for use' approach now being adopted in this country. This chapter also deals with planning guidance for contaminated sites and sets out the issues involved in protecting the development team on such sites.

Chapter 10 discusses the alternative means of financing a development, including debt financing, equity financing, and mezzanine financing. The chapter also deals with joint ventures, and public sector finance.

Chapter 11 sets out the work usually undertaken by the quantity surveyor, such as the tendering process. It also deals with contracts and supervision of the work. There may be more than one contract, i.e. one for site remediation and preparation and one for the construction work itself.

Chapter 12 deals with marketing, one of the most important aspects of the development process. Marketing tools such as brochures and advertisements are discussed, as well as product branding.

Chapter 8
The Feasibility Study

8.1   Introduction

Having identified a suitable site, secured options or entered into conditional contracts, progressed the development concept, design and costings to such a point that an intrusive site investigation can be designed and possible remediation options considered, the intending developer has arrived at the point where a meaningful feasibility study can be prepared. This is an ongoing process that should continue throughout the development process. Some initial aspects of feasibility should have commenced in the project inception phase, namely considering the types of rents and/or prices that might be achieved for the proposed product, together with the initial ideas on costs. However, it is only when the actual site has been secured and consideration given to the implications of historical uses for the site preparation costs, that the developer can start to 'firm up' the likely costs and income.

A feasibility study should consider all aspects of the project, not simply its financial viability. For example, the project might comprise a mix of uses, say offices, managed workspace and residential apartments, for which during the inception phase no particular location had been found. Once the location has been decided upon the developer needs to re-examine the mix of uses, so as to ensure that they are still appropriate, and consider how they relate to the surrounding community. The site may have been occupied by a major industry, which provided employment to many of the local residents, and this may have important implications for the development.

Questions need to be asked, such as: what will the development bring to the area in terms of potential employment and new housing? Are the jobs that will be created appropriate for the people who live in the area, or will a significant number of the workers be commuting into the area? If people are going to commute, what is the state of the local road network and public transport? Will there be an adverse effect on the local community, or will the new jobs provide other benefits, such as employment in support services? Is the proposed new housing appropriate to the area, or is it catering to completely new types of residents, e.g. technology workers in the new industries? If it is not in keeping with existing housing provision, how will it blend in, and what are the community implications?

These and many other questions should be addressed as part of the feasibility study in order to form conclusions about the acceptability of the development and its long-term sustainability. In many cases the local authority may give careful consideration, as part of the normal planning process, to issues such as those described above but elsewhere the planning authority may be so keen to see urban renewal taking place that these issues are not fully considered. In either event the developer should not be content to leave issues of this nature to the planning authority, as they might have significant implications for the financial well-being of the project.

Although it is not possible to fully assess the financial viability of a development project on a previously developed site, assumptions relating to possible contamination and alternative remediation options can be made following completion of the historical study and the walk-over survey (see Chapter 5). The development concept can be redefined and site-specific drawings prepared, so as to arrive at a better idea of the likely construction and sales figures. All of this can, and should, be done before the developer commissions an intrusive site investigation, as it may well be found that, on the basis of the assumptions used, the project is not financially viable regardless of the outcome of the intrusive investigation.

Assuming, however, that the financial appraisal indicates that the project is viable and this is confirmed by the intrusive site investigation, the developer should then proceed to a full feasibility study. The need to analyse the potential market for the development is dealt with in Chapter 3 as part of project inception; this should lead to fuller research and analysis of the market for the proposed development. The present chapter deals with appraising the project in financial terms.

8.2   Financial appraisals

As mentioned in the introduction to Chapter 6, property development is largely about risk and all developments involve risk to a greater or lesser extent. In order to compensate for the risks taken a developer will require to make a profit. The profit also has to reimburse the developer in respect of the capital employed on the project, although much of this may be borrowed, and for the entrepreneurialism involved in bringing the development to fruition.

The amount of profit required will depend to a large extent on the type of development involved and also on the nature of the developer undertaking the project. In the latter respect developers can be conveniently grouped into two categories – traders and investors. Trading developers are those who undertake projects with a view to selling the completed buildings to end-users or investors, with sales taking place either before the project commences on site, 'pre-sold', or upon completion of the building and letting processes. Investor developers develop primarily to hold completed projects in their own portfolios and create an investment income.

There is, however, no clear-cut line between trading and investing developers. Traders may sometimes hold completed developments, especially if they perceive a greater profit by selling at a later date (say after the first rent review), and investors may also sell investments, for example to realise capital growth and to fund new projects. In general though, there tends to be some difference in the approach to profits between the two categories of developers: the trader will want to maximise the percentage return on the development capital, whilst the investor will be more interested in the revenue return. This difference of approach has important implications for the ways in which development projects are financed, as discussed in Chapter 10.

8.2.1   Institutional leases and investment yields

For commercial developments, including industrial estates, business parks and retail stores, prospective investors and the banks providing the development finance (see Chapter 10) will want to be sure that the development is to be let on 'institutional leases'.

An institutional lease is one that will be acceptable to an investing institution, such as a pension fund, insurance company or major property company. It will usually be for a long term, say a minimum of 15 years and preferably 25 years, with provision for 'upwards only' rent reviews every five years. The basis of the rent review is usually to 'open market value', although in some instances where for example there is a lack of comparable market evidence, it may be geared to some other market or to an inflation index.

The lease will be on a 'full repairing and insuring basis' (FRI), which means that the tenant will be responsible for all repairs and decoration to the building, both internal and external, and for the cost of insurance (which may be by direct policy from an insurance company or by contribution to the landlord's master policy). The tenant will also covenant to return the premises, in good condition, to the landlord at the end of the lease, which usually means in the same condition as at commencement, fair wear and tear excepted. In other words, the landlord can expect to have a guaranteed minimum income, with all outgoings met by the tenant, with the potential for the rent to increase every five years and to receive the property back in good condition.

Provided that the tenant can be expected to remain in business for the duration of the lease, the proposed property investment can be regarded as relatively 'risk-free' by a potential landlord and by a financial institution that has been asked to provide development finance (see Chapter 10), although it may lack liquidity when compared to other forms of investment, see below.

In ensuring that the investment income is as risk-free as possible, the developer will be interested in the 'covenant strength' of the prospective tenant – that is, the ability of the tenant to pay the rent (see also Chapter 12). The ideal situation for a developer might be to accept only publicly quoted international companies with a Standard & Poor's rating of not less than AAA, but even seemingly sound companies have been known to fail. Developers, investors and bankers, whilst having regard for the credit rating of prospective tenants, will wish to make their own enquiries and satisfy themselves as to the ability of the tenant to pay the rent.

The 'quality' of the tenant(s), as assessed by a prospective investor, will influence the price that an investor is prepared to pay for the development once it has been completed and is occupied. The price itself is determined by the rate of return the investor requires from the investment. This is more commonly known in the UK as the 'yield' and in North America as the 'Capitalization' (or cap.) rate. Yield rates will fluctuate according to the state of the investment property market and its relationship to other forms of investments.

Government bonds – 'gilts' in the UK – are generally regarded as the most secure form of investment. Upon maturity the investor receives his or her money back in full (the 'nominal' value) and, until then, receives income at a given rate per cent. These bonds are also highly liquid, which means that they can be bought and sold in the market, the seller usually receiving payment the following day. The price obtainable by the vendor is likely to be at either a premium or a discount to the nominal value, according to the relationship between the interest payable on the bond and that currently obtainable in the market, e.g. on bank deposit. For example, a 7.5% bond with a maturity date of 2010 will attract a premium above its nominal value of £100 if bank interest rates are say only 6.0%; should, however, bank interest rates be above 7.5% then the bond will sell at a discount.

Exactly the same applies to property investments but these also have two important features that make them significantly different to government bonds: first, they are more illiquid and usually cannot be sold at short notice; second, their value can fluctuate, unlike the nominal value of bonds. When looking at property investments the potential investors will be looking for a combination of income and growth in the capital value, as, over the long term, property values have tended to grow at rates in excess of inflation. Therefore the higher the investor's perception of growth from a particular investment property the lower the initial investment yield he or she will be prepared to accept.

The yield rate, which an investor is prepared to accept for a particular property investment, will also depend on the fund manager's view of the market and the balance of the portfolio in relation to that market. Investment portfolios generally contain a mixture of different investments, so that some may act as a 'hedge' against adverse movements in others. Therefore, if the fund manager considers that the fund is overexposed to property, he or she will become a net seller of properties and will only buy when the yield is more attractive, i.e. higher, than for the properties being sold.

This section has provided a brief outline of some of the more important aspects of the investment property market. For a more detailed explanation and introduction to investment valuations see Baum *et al.* (1997).

8.2.2   Viability of the project

In considering the financial viability of development projects, the approach taken in this chapter is to look at financial appraisals from the perspective of the trading developer. For such a developer, profit requirements are likely to be between 15% and 25% of the project cost (land, construction, infrastructure, professional fees, finance and other costs), with 20% often being seen as the 'norm'. The lower end of the range is more likely to apply in situations where all, or a substantial part, of the development has been pre-let at an early stage in the development process, usually before the detailed design has been finalised, and the future tenant has entered into an agreement to take the lease. Such an arrangement will often enable the tenant to have some say in the final design of the finished building and to be in a strong position when negotiating rent and other lease terms.

At the other end of the profit requirement scale are developments that are entirely speculative, i.e. with no tenants identified prior to the commencement of construction, and those in designated urban regeneration areas. It should be noted, however, that where urban renewal projects have required 'gap-funding' in order to make them viable (see section 10.6 in Chapter 10), funding bodies have expected the developer to seek a lower level of profit, below 20%, on the principle that the public sector funding provides a cushion against the full exposure to risk.

8.3   An example development appraisal

In order to demonstrate the development appraisal process, a case study approach has been adopted, using a hypothetical study on the same site (of

6.312 ha) at St Helens used for the historical study in Chapter 5. Taylor Young Urban Design has prepared a masterplan for the redevelopment of the site, adhering to the principles outlined in the Urban Task Force report *Towards an Urban Renaissance* (Urban Task Force, 1999) in order to maximise the development potential of the site (see Figure 8.1).

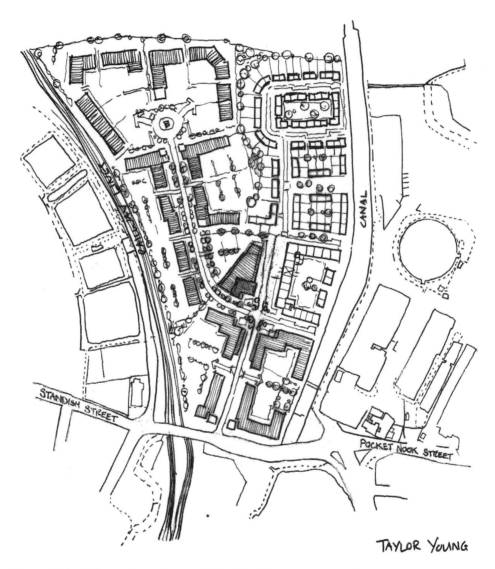

Figure 8.1   Masterplan of a canalside development, St Helens, by Taylor Young Urban Design.

The brief to the urban designers stipulated a mixed-use development with 70% of the site area (4.41 ha) being used for light industrial, office and high-technology business uses, and the remaining 30% (1.89 ha) for residential development.

The masterplan provides for 20 200 square metres (217 430 square feet) of employment space, a site coverage of 47%, with 797 car parking spaces and loading/delivery facilities appropriate to the type of use in the buildings. From an analysis of the market it was determined that the smallest unit size should be 300 square metres (3230 square feet), with 600 square metres (6460 square feet) being the 'standard' unit size that can be provided in multiples, thus ensuring maximum flexibility. The employment area is divided into three zones, with office development closest to the site entrance, leading on to mixed office and high technology units and light industry at the rear of the site.

For the residential development a mix of one- and two-bedroom apartments, as well as two- and three-bedroom houses, was decided upon. This produced a total of 136 residential units, with an average floor area of 70 square metres (753 square feet), and a total built floor area of 10 152 square metres (109 275 square feet).

8.3.1 Measurement of buildings

The normal convention for measuring buildings for the purpose of estimating construction costs is 'gross external area', that is over the external walls at all floor levels. Industrial buildings are generally let on the basis of 'gross internal area', i.e. measured inside the external walls at all floor levels but including entrance halls, staircase wells, toilets, kitchens, etc. Offices and similar buildings are usually let on the basis of 'net internal area', from which entrance halls, lobbies, lifts, plant rooms and stairwells as well as communal toilets have been deducted. In buildings let as whole floors, circulation areas, private kitchens, toilets and services exclusively used by one tenant will probably be included in the lettable area. Floor areas quoted for residential units usually exclude any circulation or communal areas and are based on the 'gross internal area' of the dwelling. The Royal Institution of Chartered Surveyors (RICS) produces a Code of Measuring Practice and further details are obtainable from *www.rics.org*.

8.3.2 The 'residual' approach

For the example development appraisal (Figures 8.3 to 8.7), the 'residual valuation' approach to development appraisal has been used. This is the traditional method for presenting development appraisals and it sets out the financial aspects of the development process in a clear and logical manner. This method has been criticised for lack of precision in calculating the financing costs applicable to the development. This is because a 'rule of thumb' method of calculating the interest is adopted which assumes that costs are incurred evenly over the (construction) contract period.

Using the normal residual approach, all costs (except promotion and letting costs) 'are divided in half and then the interest is calculated on that sum over the whole period' (Cadman & Topping, 1995, p. 91). In spite of the crudity of the approach to interest calculation, the residual valuation has its supporters as it is quick and simple to use and, provided the lack of accuracy in respect of interest charges is recognised, generally results in an overestimation of the finance costs.

For the example development appraisal, Microsoft Excel is used to overcome the inaccuracy of the 'half costs over time' calculation, by substituting a cash flow calculation (Figure 8.6) for the less accurate estimate. Each of the figures represents an individual worksheet within a single workbook and all the worksheets are linked so that changes made on one will be reflected in the others. As an alternative to using Microsoft Excel, industry standard packages, such as Visual Developer from Circle Systems, *www.circsys.com/visualdeveloper.htm*, are available. Discounted cash-flow (DCF) methods, either the Net Terminal Approach or Net Present Value, can also be used for development appraisal purposes (see Cadman & Topping, 1995; Baum *et al.*, 1997).

8.3.3   *Making assumptions*

Regardless of the method used to prepare the financial appraisal, the most important part is to clearly state all of the assumptions underlying the figures used in the appraisal. As discussed in Chapter 5, the case study site was previously used for industrial purposes and the ASSUMPTIONS MUST CLEARLY STATE THE ACTIONS TO BE TAKEN IN RESPECT OF ANY CONTAMINATION. In this case it has been assumed that a suite of remediation methods will be employed, comprising limited soil removal to landfill, some bioremediation within the residential area and containment of slightly contaminated material in the industrial and commercial areas. All buildings on the site will have to be constructed with gas protection measures in the foundations and ground floor slabs, in order to protect them from landfill gas from an adjoining site.

Figure 8.2 shows the six 'zones' of the development, divided between the commercial and residential developments. Box 8.1 shows a breakdown of the proposed development between the six development zones. At a later stage in the appraisal process, when the design has advanced beyond the masterplan stage, this information would also contain details of the site area allocated to each individual commercial building and each phase of the residential development.

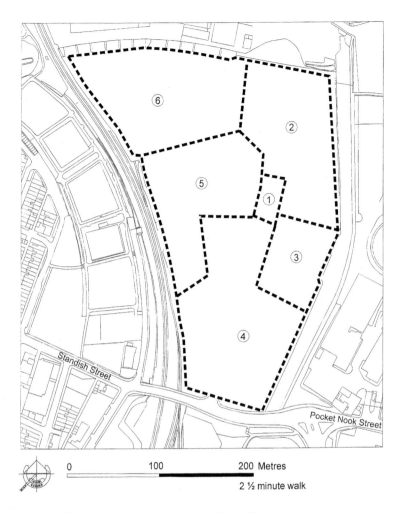

0   100   200 Metres

2 ½ minute walk

Figure 8.2   The six development zones from the masterplan.

8.3.4   *Development rents and prices*

In Figure 8.3, the commercial and industrial building areas are described according to their intended use, with the estimated rents per square metre, the expected investment yield and the gross investment value.

The residential development is shown divided between one-bedroom and two-bedroom apartments, and two- and three-bedroom houses, with the average selling price for each type and the total expected proceeds. In the feasibility study all assumptions regarding selling prices should be stated, together with information as to the comparable evidence used in forming those assumptions. In extreme cases there may be no true comparable evidence and

Box 8.1   Development schedule – case study appraisal.

Zone 1:	Use	Residential
	Massing	2 storeys
	Units	7 × 2-bedroom apartments
	Parking	1:1 in courtyard
Zone 2:	Use	Residential
	Massing	2 storeys
	Units	69 × 2- or 3-bedroom houses
	Parking	1:1 on street/in courtyard
Zone 3:	Use	Residential
	Massing	2–3 storeys
	Units	60 × 1- or 2-bedroom flats
	Parking	1:1 in courtyard
Zone 4:	Use	High-specification offices
	Massing	3 storeys
	Floor area	9500 m^2
	Parking	369 parking spaces
Zone 5:	Use	Office/employment
	Massing	2 storeys
	Floor area	6700 m^2
	Parking	208 spaces
Zone 6:	Use	Light industrial/manufacturing/employment, etc.
	Massing	1–2 storeys
	Floor area	4000 m^2 gross floor space
	Parking	160 parking spaces and loading

Total site area 6.3 ha

30% residential = 1.89 ha   70% employment = 4.41 ha
Total number of residential units   Total employment floor area
  – 136   = 20 200 m^2
At a residential density of 72 units to   Giving a total coverage of 47%
  the hectare

RESIDUAL DEVELOPMENT APPRAISAL AND CASH FLOW						
CLIENT:	**GABLE END DEVELOPMENTS**					
PROJECT:	Anystreet, Anytown					
SCHEME:	Mixed Use Development					
SHEET TITLE:	BUILDING AREAS, RENTS, YIELDS AND PRICES					

Residential Development

	Number of units	Area per unit sq.m.		Selling price per unit	Price per sq.m.	Total proceeds of sale
Zone 1						
2-bed apartments	7	67	£	75,000	£ 1,119.40	£ 525,000
Zone 2						
2-bed houses	29	72	£	79,950	£ 1,110.42	£ 2,318,550
3-bed houses	40	85	£	99,950	£ 1,175.88	£ 3,998,000
Zone 3						
1-bed apartments	20	55	£	57,500	£ 1,045.45	£ 1,150,000
2-bed apartments	40	60	£	67,500	£ 1,125.00	£ 2,700,000
TOTAL RESIDENTIAL DEVELOPMENT	136					£ 10,691,550

Commercial and industrial development

	Number of buildings	Net area sq.m.	Rent per sq.m.	Total rent per annum	Yield rate %	Total value
Zone 4						
3-storey offices	4	7600	£98.00	£744,800	7.25%	£10,273,103
Zone 5						
Offices and 'high tech'	6	5695	£ 86.00	£489,770	7.75%	£6,319,613
Zone 6						
Light industrial/business	7	4000	£ 66.00	£264,000	8.25%	£3,200,000
TOTAL COMMERCIAL AND INDUSTRIAL		17295		£1,498,570	7.57%	£ 19,792,716

DEVELOPMENT SUMMARY TOTALS

RESIDENTIAL

	number of units	average selling price	Proceeds of sale
Houses	69	£ 91,544	£6,316,550
Apartments	67	£ 65,299	£4,375,000
Commercial			
Offices	4	£ 2,568,276	£10,273,103
Offices and 'high tech'	6	£ 1,053,269	£6,319,613
Light industrial	7	£ 457,143	£3,200,000

Fig. 8.3   Breakdown of building areas, rents and prices.

the development team may have to base assumptions on information from other markets, or even experience in other towns or cities. As will be appreciated, such assumptions may have significant implications for the reliability of the appraisal.

8.3.5   *Infrastructure and construction costs*

Figure 8.4 contains the construction and infrastructure cost calculations. The basic data relating to blocks, site areas and net floor areas have been transferred from the previous worksheet. It is then necessary to adjust the net floor areas in order to arrive at the gross internal floor area (i.e. including entrance halls, lobbies, lift wells, staircases, toilets and other circulation and communal spaces) needed to calculate the construction costs for the buildings. For the purpose of the example, the net floor areas of the apartment buildings have been increased by 17.5% and the areas of the office buildings by 20% to allow for circulation and communal areas. In the case of offices and high-tech units in Zone 5, an increase of 15% has been applied to these 'hybrid' buildings.

At the earlier stages in the development process the construction costs will be based on rates per square metre, taken from price guides such as *Spon's Architects and Builders Price Book* (see Davis, Langdon & Everest, 2001) or *Laxton's Building Price Book* (see Johnson, 2001) (both published annually) or from the RICS Building Cost Information Service (BCIS), but Elemental Cost Plans, or even Bills of Quantities, with greater detail, may replace these later in the development process. Likewise the infrastructure and abnormal costs figures may be taken from price guides. In practice both these and the construction cost figures may also be based, to quite a large extent, on the recent experiences of members of the development team through their involvement with other projects.

In the example appraisal, the construction costs have been shown net of preliminaries, such as site establishment costs, and insurances. These are added at the end of the construction costs calculation at a rate of 10.5%. The civil engineering works for the infrastructure and abnormal costs have been shown inclusive of preliminaries and insurances. These figures also include any fees payable to the highways authority and statutory service providers. A contingency sum equivalent to 15% of the remediation cost has also been included.

8.3.6   *Professional fees and other costs*

Figure 8.5 contains the professional fees for the members of the project design team (see Chapter 4), as well as the fees payable in respect of planning permission and under Building Regulations (see Chapter 9). The other costs

RESIDENTIAL DEVELOPMENT APPRAISAL AND CASH FLOW							
CLIENT:	**GABLE END DEVELOPMENTS**						
PROJECT:	Anystreet, Anytown						
SCHEME:	Mixed Use Development						
SHEET TITLE:	CONSTRUCTION COSTS				Site area	6.312	hectares

Residential Development

	Number of units	Area per unit sq.m.	Net area sq.m.	Circulation area sq.m.	Gross Area sq.m.	Rate sq.m.	Total Cost
Zone 1							
2-bed apartments	7	67	469.00	82.08	551.08 £	510.00	£281,048
							£0
Zone 2							£0
2-bed houses	29	72	2088.00		2088.00 £	460.00	£960,480
3-bed houses	40	85	3400.00		3400.00 £	460.00	£1,564,000
							£0
Zone 3							£0
1-bed apartments	20	55	1100.00	192.50	1292.50 £	510.00	£659,175
2-bed apartments	40	60	2400.00	420.00	2820.00 £	510.00	£1,438,200
TOTAL RESIDENTIAL DEVELOPMENT	136	70	9457.00	694.58	10151.58		£4,902,903

Commercial and industrial development

	Number of buildings		Net area sq.m.	Circulation area sq.m.	Gross Area sq.m.	Rate sq.m.	Total Cost
Zone 4							
3-storey offices	4		7600.00	1900.00	9500.00 £	640.00	£6,080,000
Zone 5							
Offices and 'high tech'	6		5695.00	1005.00	6700.00 £	580.00	£3,886,000
Zone 6							
Light industrial/business	7		4000.00		4000.00 £	350.00	£1,400,000
TOTAL COMMERCIAL AND INDUSTRIAL	193,817		17295.00	2905.00	20200.00		£11,366,000
ESTIMATED AREAS and COST			35,740		30,352 £	536.02 £	16,268,903
Preliminaries and Insurances			10.50%			£ 56.28 £	1,708,235
TOTAL CONSTRUCTION COST						£	17,977,138

INFRASTRUCTURE COSTS		per BUILT sq.metre	per hectare OF SITE	TOTAL COST
ROADWORKS	405 linear metres	£13.34	£64,163	£405,000
MAIN DRAINAGE		£3.29	£15,843	£100,000
SERVICES		£5.11	£24,556	£155,000
LANDSCAPING		£3.23	£15,526	£98,000
FENCING TO BOUNDARY WALL		£2.47	£11,882	£75,000
SITE INVESTIGATION FEES		£1.98	£9,506	£60,000
ABNORMAL COSTS				
SITE REMEDIATION		£16.47	£79,214	£500,000
BULK EXCAVATION		£1.22	£5,862	£37,000
FOUL DRAINAGE DIVERSION		£1.38	£6,654	£42,000
OFF-SITE ROADWORKS		£2.80	£13,466	£85,000
METHANE PROTECTION TO BUILDINGS		£2.47	£11,882	£75,000
TOTAL INFRASTRUCTURE COST				£1,632,000

SUMMARY CONSTRUCTION AND INFRASTRUCTURE COSTS		
BUILDINGS		£17,977,138
INFRASTRUCTURE		£893,000
ABNORMALS AND OFF-SITE WORKS		£739,000
CONTINGENCY	15.00% of remediation works	£75,000
TOTAL COSTS		£19,684,138

Figure 8.4   Building and infrastructure cost calculations.

RESIDUAL DEVELOPMENT APPRAISAL AND CASH FLOW			
CLIENT:	GABLE END DEVELOPMENTS		
PROJECT:	Anystreet, Anytown		
SCHEME:	Mixed Use Development		
SHEET TITLE:	PROFESSIONAL FEES AND OTHER COSTS		
PROFESSIONAL FEES	RATE NUMBER		AMOUNT
Architect	4.00% of construction costs only		£719,086
Quantity Surveyor	2.00% of construction & engineering costs		£393,683
Consulting Engineer	2.25% of construction & engineering costs		£442,893
Project Manager	2.50% of construction & engineering costs		£492,103
M&E Consultant	25000		£25,000
Environmental Cons.	15000		£15,000
TOTAL PROF. FEES	10.61% of construction & engineering costs		£2,087,765
TOWN PLANNING	0.28%		£50,000
BUILDING REGS.	0.36%		£65,000
	0.64%		£115,000

	%AGE	%AGE	
OTHER COSTS	RENT	VALUE	AMOUNT
NHBC FEES		0.50%	£24,515
VOID RENT	12.50%	0.95%	£187,321
AGENTS - residential		1.75%	£187,102
AGENTS - commercial	15.00%	1.14%	£224,786
PROMOTION & P.R.		0.50%	£99,231
LEGAL FEES		0.65%	£129,104
FUNDING FEES		0.50%	£74,310
	27.50%	5.98%	£926,369

Figure 8.5   Professional fees and other costs.

described in Figure 8.5 relate mainly to marketing and disposal of the completed project and are dealt with in Chapter 12. Funding and commitment fees payable to financing institutions are also included in the other costs and this calculation has been based on 0.5% of the maximum development loan (assuming that all the development finance has been borrowed).

8.3.7   Cash flow

Figure 8.6 sets out the cash flow used to calculate the financing cost for the development. The land is acquired in the first quarter of the development and the acquisition costs are incurred in the same quarter. Work on remediation commences immediately after acquisition and so a fair proportion of this cost is also borne in the same quarter, with the work being completed in the following

RESIDUAL DEVELOPMENT APPRAISAL AND CASH FLOW

CLIENT: GABLE END DEVELOPMENTS
PROJECT: Anystreet, Anytown
SCHEME: Mixed Use Development
SHEET TITLE: CASH FLOW SUMMARY

PROJECT INCOME	%AGE	Year 1 Qtr 1	Qtr 2	Qtr 3	Qtr 4	Year 2 Qtr 1	Qtr 2	Qtr 3	Qtr 4	Year 3 Qtr 1	Qtr 2	Qtr 3	Qtr 4	Year 4 Qtr 1	Qtr 2	TOTALS
Short-term income			£3,000	£3,000	£3,000	£3,000	£3,000	£3,000	£3,000	£3,000	£3,000	£3,000				£30,000
Investment sales									£5,136,552	£5,136,552	£3,159,806	£3,159,806		£1,600,000	£1,600,000	£19,792,716
Residential sales								£525,000	£2,158,775	£2,446,275	£2,286,500	£1,250,000	£975,000	£675,000	£375,000	£10,691,550
Inflation rate %	4.75%															
DEDUCT Investors' costs									£243,986	£243,986	£150,091	£150,091		£76,000	£76,000	£940,154
NET CAPITAL RECEIPTS		£0	£3,000	£3,000	£3,000	£3,000	£3,000	£528,000	£7,054,341	£7,341,841	£5,299,216	£4,262,716	£975,000	£2,199,000	£1,899,000	£29,574,112
DEVELOPMENT COSTS																
Site Purchase		£501,838														£501,838
Acquisition costs	4.75%	£23,837														£23,837
SITE REMEDIATION		£221,700	£517,300													£739,000
Contingency provision				£75,000												£75,000
INFRASTRUCTURE			£178,600	£267,900	£267,900	£89,300	£89,300									£893,000
Construction costs - residential						£14,052	£168,381	£462,986	£946,527	£1,114,107	£1,021,937	£755,437	£314,606	£104,869		£4,902,903
Construction costs - ind./comm.				£304,000	£1,106,300	£2,406,900	£2,989,800	£2,147,800	£1,096,900	£614,300	£420,000	£210,000	£70,000			£11,366,000
Preliminaries and insurances			£142,353	£142,353	£142,353	£142,353	£142,353	£142,353	£142,353	£142,353	£142,353	£142,353	£142,353	£142,353		£1,708,235
PROF. FEES		£532,553	£417,553	£125,266	£125,266	£125,266	£125,266	£125,266	£125,266	£125,266	£125,266	£125,266	£125,266			£2,202,765
OTHER COSTS		£66,169	£66,169	£66,169	£66,169	£66,169	£66,169	£66,169	£66,169	£66,169	£66,169	£66,169	£66,169	£66,169	£66,169	£926,369
COSTS BEFORE INTEREST		£1,346,098	£1,321,975	£980,688	£1,707,988	£2,844,040	£3,581,269	£2,944,574	£2,377,215	£2,062,195	£1,775,725	£1,299,224	£718,394	£313,391	£66,169	£23,338,947
INCOME		£0	£3,000	£3,000	£3,000	£3,000	£3,000	£528,000	£7,054,341	£7,341,841	£5,299,216	£4,262,716	£975,000	£2,199,000	£1,899,000	£29,574,112
NET Quarterley INCOME/OUTFLOW		-£1,346,098	-£1,318,975	-£977,688	-£1,704,988	-£2,841,040	-£3,578,269	-£2,416,574	£4,677,125	£5,279,645	£3,523,491	£2,963,491	£256,606	£1,885,609	£1,832,831	
CUMULATIVE BALANCE		-£1,346,098	-£2,665,073	-£3,669,683	-£5,428,511	-£8,344,021	-£12,032,350	-£14,618,006	-£10,184,910	-£5,202,505	-£1,888,658	£966,590	£1,183,258	£3,068,867	£4,901,698	
INTEREST AT	7.25%		-£26,922	-£53,840	-£74,470	-£110,060	-£169,082	-£244,029	-£297,241	-£209,643	-£108,243	-£39,938				-£1,333,467
TOTAL DEVELOPMENT COST/SURPLUS		-£1,346,098	-£2,691,995	-£3,723,523	-£5,502,981	-£8,454,081	-£12,201,432	-£14,862,035	-£10,482,150	-£5,412,148	-£1,996,901	£926,652	£1,183,258	£3,068,867	£4,901,698	

DEDUCT finance cost for land £169,840
DEVELOPMENT PROFIT £4,731,858

Figure 8.6 Cash flow.

quarter. The contingency sum included against the site remediation works is assumed to have been expended in full in quarter 3. In this appraisal the commercial and residential developments have been shown separately, with construction work on the second and subsequent zones for each type of development commencing as work on the preceding zone reaches its peak. The residential development has been timed to start six months after the commercial development and the construction period for each zone is 18 months.

The construction expenditure for each zone has been calculated using an S-curve, see section 8.3.10. The site acquisition is shown in the quarter preceding commencement on site, and the first three months of the project, prior to the commencement of construction work, is taken up with site remediation. Forty per cent of the professional fees estimate and all of the planning and Building Regulation fees are shown as being paid in the first two quarters of the development; in practice it is likely that some of this expenditure will have to be met even before the site has been acquired and this is not reflected in the cash flow. The example cash flow is shown using quarterly periods, which is perfectly acceptable for the earlier studies but this might be changed to monthly periods as the development information is refined.

Short-term income from advertising hoardings and use of part of the site for car parking is included in the cash flow. Interest is shown as being calculated one quarter in arrears, and is rolled forward. In practice, interest is calculated on daily balances but this detail of calculation is not appropriate in the early stages of the development, although it is possible to simulate the 'daily balances' calculation with an appropriate formula in the spreadsheet.

The last two lines of the cash flow show the surplus adjusted to allow for the cost of financing the land acquisition, see below.

8.3.8   *Appraisal summary*

Figure 8.7 is the final development appraisal presented in the residual valuation format. This draws information from each of the other worksheets. It commences with the expected sales of the completed investment from the commercial and residential developments. The investment sales proceeds show a reduction from the gross amount in Figure 8.2, of 4.75% of the gross value, to allow for the costs incurred by the purchasing investor; these comprise stamp duty as well as surveyor's and legal fees. This deduction is required as investors, such as property companies and pensions funds, need to have regard to the total return achievable on the cost of their investments, including the land, buildings and other costs. In some situations, such as buildings let in multiple occupation in urban regeneration areas, it may also be appropriate to assume that the

RESIDUAL DEVELOPMENT APPRAISAL AND CASH FLOW						
CLIENT:	**GABLE END DEVELOPMENTS**					
PROJECT:	Anystreet, Anytown					
SCHEME:	Mixed Use Development					
SHEET TITLE:	DEVELOPMENT APPRAISAL					
INVESTMENT SALES						
	OCC. RATE	LETTABLE AREA	GROSS RENT	YIELD %AGE	YEARS PURCHASE	TOTALS
INVESTMENT UNITS	100.00%	17,295	£1,498,570	7.57%	13.21	£19,792,716
RENT per sq.metre	£86.65 AVERAGE					
ESTIMATED INVESTMENT VALUE						£19,792,716
INVESTOR'S ACQUISITION COSTS			4.75% OF EST. INV. VALUE			£940,154
NET INVESTMENT VALUE						£18,852,562
		NUMBER OF UNITS	AVERAGE PRICE			
RESIDENTIAL SALES		136	0			£10,691,550
SUNDRY INCOME	(Advertising hoardings and car parking)					£30,000
ESTIMATED TOTAL VALUE OF DEVELOPMENT						**£29,574,112**
DEVELOPMENT COSTS						
	%AGE OF TOTAL		PERIOD IN MONTHS	RATE PER CENT		TOTALS
CONSTRUCTION COSTS						£17,977,138
INFRASTRUCTURE						£893,000
ABNORMALS AND OFF-SITE WORKS						£739,000
CONTINGENCY						£75,000
PROF. FEES	10.61%					£2,087,765
STATUTORY FEES	0.64%					£115,000
ANY OTHER COSTS	4.71%					£926,369
NON-REC. VAT						
FINANCE CHARGES			42	7.25%		£1,333,467
TOTAL DEVELOPMENT COSTS						**£24,146,739**
RESIDUAL BALANCE (DEFICIT)	18.35%					£5,427,374
DEVELOPER'S PROFIT REQUIRED		16% of net value	19.60%	of development cost		**£4,731,858**
TOTAL COST PLUS PROFIT						£28,878,597
PROJECT SURPLUS/(DEFICIT) AVAILABLE FOR LAND PURCHASE						£695,516
P.V. OF £1 TO END OF DEVELOPMENT PERIOD				at 7.25%		0.7558068
Gross value of site						**£525,676**
Acquisition costs			at	4.75%		£23,837
PRICE TO PAY FOR THE SITE						£501,838
GAP FUNDING REQUIREMENT	Equates to nil		per sq.m.		nil	
PUBLIC TO PRIVATE SECTOR GEARING				1 TO		0.00
COST PER JOB/HOUSING UNIT					nil	

Figure 8.7   Development appraisal summary.

investment buildings will not be fully income producing at all times and so a 'running void' is required to allow for an element of permanent vacancy. This approach is normal in the United States and other countries where leases tend to be shorter than those generally used in the UK.

The development costs section of the residual appraisal contains the summarised information from Figures 8.3 and 8.4 and the total of this expenditure is then deducted from the net proceeds of the development in order to arrive at a balance, the residual amount from which the developer has to take a profit and pay for the site. The profit figure in the example has been calculated on the basis of 16% of the net value of the completed project, which equates to 19.6% of the development cost.

8.3.9   *Price to pay for the land*

After deducting the profit a sum of £696 516 remains for site acquisition. As shown by the cash flow, the land is paid for before the development commences; the Present Value of £1 calculation makes a provision for the payment of interest on the acquisition price up to the end of the project. In practice, earlier receipts in respect of the land element may be receivable prior to the end of the development, upon completion and sale of each building, as shown in the cash flow. This calculation may result in a slight overcalculation of interest in respect of the land. Finally, the appraisal deducts the developer's costs in acquiring the site – stamp duty, legal and surveyor's fees.

The price produced by the example appraisal may appear very low – only £79 500 per hectare (£32 300 per acre) – but it should be remembered that this is a previously developed site, with problems that would not be encountered on a greenfield site. If the 'abnormal costs' of site remediation, bulk excavation, foul drainage diversion, off-site roadworks and methane protection to buildings are added to the residual sum for the land, a total of £1 240 838 is arrived at, or £196 584 per hectare (£79 880 per acre). This may still appear to be a low figure for a development site, until the industrial nature of the surrounding area is taken into account and it is remembered that, in some locations, the result could actually have been a negative residual figure for the land purchase, needing grant aid to make the project viable.

The appraisal example described relates to a fairly simple, mixed new-build development at an early stage in the development process. The same approach can, however, be used for much more complex projects, including those involving refurbishment and conversions. Any number of worksheets can be used to set out the supporting information and the same method can be used to take account of 'gap funding' grants through the addition of a couple more rows in the cash-flow worksheet, to show the receipt of grant, and in the Residual Appraisal to summarise the impact of the grant.

8.3.10   *Estimating the expenditure and income flows*

As mentioned above, the timing of construction expenditure for each of the development zones has been plotted using an S-curve, whereby expenditure starts slowly with site set-up and preparation. It then accelerates through the main construction works of frame, walls and roof, i.e. large items of expenditure. Once these have been completed the expenditure slows down again during the finishing period, comprising decorating, ceilings, wall and floor finishes, the service installations, landscaping and other external areas. This is illustrated in Figure 8.8.

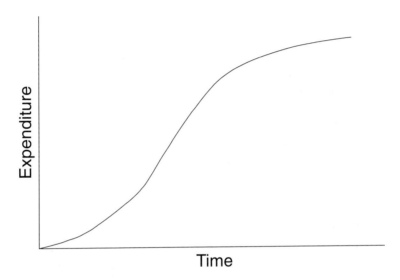

Figure 8.8   S-curve of developmental expenditure.

8.3.11   *Sensitivity analysis*

The start of construction work does not remove the need for continuing feasibility studies. Costs can change even after contracts have been signed, for example if contamination is found to be worse than expected. Possibly even more important are fluctuations in the property market, in terms of both rents and investment yields. In order to assess the likely impact of such changes on the viability of the project, the feasibility study should include a sensitivity analysis. This would examine the impact on the profitability of the development assuming different changes to the assumptions used for the appraisal. Box 8.2 shows a simplified illustration.

Box 8.2　Changes to the assumptions – impact on development profit.

Changes to assumptions	Estimated profit
Development profit as shown in the appraisal, Figure 8.7	£4 731 858
Assume investment yield for the commercial development moves out by 0.5%. Residential prices remain unchanged.	£3 563 984
Assume investment yield for the commercial development moves out by 0.5% and expected rents fall short by 5.0%. Residential prices remain unchanged.	£2 635 654
Assume investment yield for the commercial development moves out by 0.5% and expected rents fall short by 5.0%. Residential prices remain unchanged. Construction costs increase by 5.0% on both commercial and residential developments	£1 428 317

As illustrated by the example in Box 8.2, three relatively minor changes, given the duration of the project, can have the effect of significantly reducing the development profit – in this case by almost 70%. These changes could commence with a perceived downturn in the market for office and light industrial floorspace, resulting in institutional investors deciding to reduce their holdings in this type of property. This might easily produce an average 0.5% increase in the investment yields required by the institutions and a reduction in profit of almost £1.2 million.

Should this be followed by an actual reduction in demand, resulting in the developer achieving rental figures that are 5% lower than originally estimated, the profit will be further reduced by more than £900 000.

In the development appraisal used for this example an inflation neutral scenario has been assumed, i.e. any increase in construction cost and infra-structure costs is exactly matched by increases in investment values or residential selling prices. If, however, that proves not to be the case and, over the period of the development costs exceed the inflation neutral situation by as little as 1.25% per annum on average, the profit suffers a further reduction of £1.2 million.

In a strong market, the developer might have taken a moderately bullish approach to the appraisal and assumed that there would be a good investment market for office and light industrial buildings and, in consequence, project even better yield figures than those indicated by the state of the market at the time the appraisal was prepared. If actual yields had then moved out by 1% from that expectation, the profit would be further reduced, to less than £500 000 for the entire development. In other words, the commercial part of the project would have to be sold for a loss.

Assuming that the developer had actually succeeded in securing tenants for the buildings and was not left with a largely unlet development as a result of the market downturn, it may be decided not to sell the commercial development at a loss. The option then would be to retain the property until such time as yields improved, or until there was a possibility of increasing the rental income at the first rent review. This would entail the developer having to refinance the project, as the short-term development money may not be available, or appropriate in terms of interest charges, for medium- to long-term retention of the investment. It also demonstrates the argument in favour of agreeing a 'forward sale' of at least part of the commercial development, even though this might involve having to accept a reduction in price.

This example of the sensitivity of development appraisals has only used three variables; other factors, such as the development finance interest rate or the residential selling prices could also be used. Also, it has only demonstrated the potential adverse effects of changes to the variables; changes in the opposite directions would produce beneficial effects and some changes may partly counter or even cancel out other changes. Spreadsheets and commercial packages such as Visual Developer enable multidimensional changes to be shown in sensitivity matrices, and the potential impacts should be clearly understood by all members of the development team.

8.4 Other issues affecting the appraisal

8.4.1 Value Added Tax

Value Added Tax (VAT) is not normally shown on a development appraisal for a number of reasons. Essentially, if the development project is of an industrial or commercial nature (including retail and leisure use), the likelihood is that the potential tenant will be registered for VAT. Therefore, if the developer elects to charge VAT on the rent, as an output tax, he will be able to reclaim the VAT paid to the contractor and the professional team. There may be a slight impact on the cash flow, if invoices have to be settled before the VAT is recovered from Customs and Excise but, in practice, developers quite often recover the VAT before they have to settle their accounts.

Tenants who are registered for VAT (the vast majority) will be able to offset the VAT, charged by the landlord on the rent, against their trading output VAT. For the minority of tenants who are not registered for VAT or, such as charities, are exempt, the tax will have to be borne as part of their trading costs, as landlords are unlikely to absorb the VAT by way of a reduced rent.

New housing developments are exempt from VAT but tax was chargeable at the full rate of 17.5% on renovation, restoration and conversion work. Therefore, in order to be comparable with a 'new build' residential scheme, projects involving the conversion and modernisation of existing buildings need to show VAT on the expenditure as a 'non-recoverable' item, as purchasers would be most unlikely to accept a tax charge on top of the purchase price. In practice the incidence of VAT has the effect of driving down the price the developer is prepared to pay to the landowner, unless of course he is prepared to take a significantly reduced profit. In the March 2001 Budget the Chancellor of the Exchequer stated an intention to reduce the VAT on the conversion, restoration and repairs of existing residential buildings (to form new dwellings) to 5%, although conversion from non-residential use would continue to be taxed at the standard rate.

8.4.2   Landfill Tax

Landfill Tax, which came into effect in October 1996, is charged on the disposal of wastes to landfill sites controlled under the Waste Management Regulations 1994. At the present time (October 2001) it is possible for the developers to obtain a certificate exempting them from the tax in respect of soils removed from a contaminated site. It has to be demonstrated that the soil is being disposed of to landfill for the purpose of site remediation only – arisings from foundations or service trench excavations, or from reprofiling of the site are not eligible for the exemption. As with VAT, the Landfill Tax is administered by Customs and Excise and an application for exemption has to be made in advance of the disposal to landfill, normally 28 days prior to the commencement of works.

The site from which the material originates has to be specified, as too does the destination landfill, which has to be licensed to receive the type of material consigned to it. The officer dealing with the application will normally expect to see a report detailing the remediation work involved, including the expected tonnage of material to be consigned to landfill, or at least a letter from the environmental consultant confirming the figures and the reason for selection of the off-site disposal option.

The Landfill Tax was introduced to encourage recycling and to discourage the disposal of wastes to landfill when other options were available. It may therefore seem illogical to allow an exemption in respect of such a potentially large volume of waste material produced by land reclamation works. The rationale behind the exemption was to ensure that a major obstacle was not placed in the way of land reclamation as, at the time the tax was introduced, excavation and off-site disposal was by far the preferred option of the UK property development industry. Today, plenty of other options are available and, as shown in Chapter 7, are being accepted by developers. Therefore the exemption is becoming less important.

8.5   Summary

The feasibility study needs to examine all aspects of the development project, including design, market, financial and environmental issues. By the time the detailed design has been completed many months are likely to have elapsed since the project was originally conceived. Markets and public perceptions about particular types of development may have changed considerably in that time; as it may be several more months before planning permission has been obtained, they may well change again.

It needs to be recognised therefore that the feasibility study should be continually reviewed and updated. There is little point in commissioning market research at the inception stage of the project and then sticking resolutely to it for the next three to five years without taking opportunities to review the research findings. Hopefully, any reviews will confirm that the research is still valid and it may even indicate that the market has improved.

Exactly the same applies to the development appraisal component of the feasibility study. An appraisal produced on the basis of the initial sketch design may have little significance when related to the detailed design. Thus the financial appraisals should also be the subject of regular reviews.

The approach used to demonstrate development appraisals in this chapter used a spreadsheet approach, rather than one of the standard appraisal packages. This approach can be criticised for the inability to verify the data and also for the fact that alterations to the appraisal, for example by altering one formula, may have disastrous consequences if an unintended error enters the appraisal. Advocates of the spreadsheet approach like it because it provides flexibility to tailor the calculations to their requirements, which is not so readily available with the standard packages.

8.6   Checklist

- Identify the potential market.
- Identify the level of demand in order to estimate 'take-up'.

- Be aware of potential discrepancies in appraisal software.
- Use an appropriate percentage for development profit.
- Consider the need for contingency sums and, if needed, how they should be calculated.
- Clearly state all assumptions made.
- Allow for VAT and Landfill Tax if appropriate.

Chapter 9
Planning and Environmental Regulation

9.1 Introduction

The Government's policy towards tackling the UK's burden of land contamination is that the works, if any, required to be undertaken for any contaminated site should only deal with any unacceptable risks to health or the environment, taking account of its actual or intended use. This 'suitable for use' approach does not preclude an owner, occupier or developer from undertaking earlier or more thorough action if he wishes to do so. Nor does it preclude a regulatory body from requiring very thorough remedial works where the circumstances justify it (DoE, 1994, paragraph 4.2). The aims of the 'suitable for use' policy include dealing with actual or perceived threats to health, safety or the environment, returning land to beneficial use and reducing pressures on greenfield land.

One of the key factors that hinder or delay redevelopment identified in the *Releasing Brownfields* study (Syms, 2001), undertaken for the Joseph Rowntree Foundation, was a lack of 'understanding of issues by planners etc.'. This was ranked ninth out of 40 factors and 'planning constraints' was ranked 18th. The study was provided with several examples of the problems encountered by developers, such as failure on the part of the regulators to recognise the economic aspects of reusing brownfields, although a number of local authorities were also praised for their approach to urban renewal.

For their part the planning authorities often regarded the problem as being one of developers leaving it until the 'last minute' to discuss their proposals. In some cases the developers simply submitted their planning applications, with little or no prior discussion, and then expected decisions within six to eight weeks on what were quite complex land reuse proposals. To an extent, the main issue was one of 'wariness' on the part of some developers, who were reluctant to disclose too much information about their proposals until they were ready to submit a planning application, for fear that their intentions would quickly find their way into the public domain as planning officers sought the views of other departments and agencies. Such fears might take two forms: first, that premature disclosure of the developer's intentions might enable another developer to bring forward a competing scheme in a shorter time-scale; and second, that information becoming available before all the land has been secured under contract or option might have the effect of increasing owners' aspirations and drive up the price (see Chapter 4).

In spite of having concerns about the planning system, the study found there was very little support for measures such as relaxing planning controls or relaxing car parking requirements, ranked 33rd and 40th respectively. Another issue, which emerged during the course of the study, was uncertainty on the part of developers as to which regulator (local authority environmental health department or the Environment Agency) should be consulted with regard to site remediation proposals.

9.2   The interface between planning and the environment

A guide to environmental legislation is provided by the Environment Agency at *www.netregs.environment-agency.gov.uk*. Of particular concern to property developers is Part IIA of the Environmental Protection Act 1990, the 'contaminated land legislation', for under this legislation an unwary developer might become liable for remediation costs by 'knowingly permitting' a polluting activity to continue, or by causing pollution through the development works, e.g. piling or excavations creating a pathway between contaminants and receptors such as ground or surface waters.

Although of concern to developers, Part IIA of the Environmental Protection Act 1990, the 'contaminated land legislation', is not intended to be used for:

- contamination problems that can be resolved by existing powers under other regimes, for example where the contamination can be dealt with via enforcement of a condition under the Waste Management Licensing regime (Part II of the Environmental Protection Act 1990); or
- cases where the site is subject to planning and development control legislation. Here the planning authority should satisfy itself that the potential for contamination is properly assessed and the development incorporates any necessary remediation.

(Environment Agency, undated)

Nevertheless, the legislation does have important implications for developers, as part of the risk analysis process, in deciding upon the appropriate remediation and/or treatment methods to be employed in remediating any contamination present on the site, in ensuring that they do not become liable for the acts of others and in preventing their developments from being designated as 'contaminated land' at some future date (see Chapter 6).

The local authority, through its planning, environmental health and building control functions, is the primary regulator in ensuring that contamination is properly dealt with. This includes ensuring that no harm is caused to properties or persons outside the boundaries of the site. The Health and Safety Executive (HSE) will have an interest in the remediation activities, in ensuring the protection of site workers and the general public. HSE's remit would not normally be expected to extend to any off-site risks, as these would be dealt with by the environmental health department under statutory nuisance (Part III, Environmental Protection Act 1990). The Environment Agency will be interested in any works of remediation that may potentially have a deleterious effect on controlled waters – that is, ground and surface waters for which the Environment Agency has a statutory responsibility under the Water Resources Act 1991. The Agency will also need to be consulted in respect of any works affecting a landfill site licensed under Part II of the Environmental Protection Act 1990 and the Waste Management Licensing Regulations 1994.

9.3   The planning process

For town planning purposes the definition of 'development' is contained in section 55 of the Town and Country Planning Act 1990, as meaning:

> 'the carrying out of building, engineering, mining or other operations in, on, over or under land, or the making of any material change in the use of buildings or other land.'

The same section then goes on to specify operations or uses of land that shall not constitute development for the purposes of the Act, including:

- Maintenance, improvements or other alterations that affect only the interior of the building or do not materially affect the external appearance.
- Work by a local highway authority, within the boundary of a road for the maintenance or improvement of the road.
- Laying or repairing sewers, pipes cables etc. by a local authority or a statutory undertaker.
- The use of buildings or other land within the curtilage of a dwellinghouse for any purpose incidental to the enjoyment of that dwellinghouse.
- The use of land for forestry or agriculture, including buildings on the land

used in connection with those operations.

- Buildings or other land used for a purpose of any class specified in an order made by the Secretary of State.

The 1990 Act introduced a 'plan-led' approach to allocating land for development. In other words there is a presumption against development, unless land has been allocated for the use proposed in the Unitary Development Plan (UDP) in metropolitan areas, or the structure and/or local plan in non-metropolitan areas. These plans take account of the physical and economic characteristics of an area; the size, composition and distribution of its population; the communications, transport system and traffic of the area, so far as they may be expected to affect the traffic of the area, or of any neighbouring areas. They may also include other matters as may be prescribed or directed by the Secretary of State. Local authorities are required to keep the plans under review and, where matters may affect another authority, consult with that authority.

A UDP consists of two parts. Part I comprises a written statement formulating the authority's general policies in respect of the development and other use of land in its area (including measures for the improvement of the physical environment and the management of traffic). Part II of a UDP consists of:

'a)   a written statement formulating in such detail as the authority think appropriate (and so as to be readily distinguishable from the other contents of the plan) their proposals for the development and other use of land in their area or for any description of development or other use of land;

b)   a map showing those proposals on a geographical basis;

c)   a reasoned justification of the general policies in Part I of the plan and of the proposals in Part II of it; and

d)   such diagrams, illustrations or other descriptive or explanatory matter in respect of the general policies in Part I of the plan or the proposals in Part II of it as the authority think appropriate or as may be prescribed.'

(Town and Country Planning Act 1990, section 12)

Structure plans are written statements formulating the local planning authority's policy and general proposals in respect of development and other use of land in non-metropolitan areas (including measures for the improvement of the physical environment and the management of traffic). They may also contain such other matters as may be prescribed and shall be illustrated with diagrams.

Local plans consist of:

'a)   a written statement formulating in such detail as the authority think
      appropriate their proposals for the development and other use of land in
      their area, or for any description of development or other use of land,
      including such measures as the authority think fit for the improvement
      of the physical environment and the management of traffic;
 b)   a map showing the proposals; and
 c)   such diagrams, illustrations or other descriptive matter as the authority
      think appropriate to explain or illustrate the proposals in the plan, or as
      may be prescribed.'

                        (Town and Country Planning Act 1990, section 36)

UDPs, structure and local plans have to undergo a process of publicity,
consultation and, very often, a public inquiry or other hearing for the purpose of hearing objections. The Secretary of State may also call in plans.
The whole process of preparing plans, consultation and hearings, through
to final adoption may take several years. It is therefore possible that significant changes may have taken place, say in respect of employment or
demand for housing, since the plan was prepared. Such changes may
result in plans becoming out of date within a relatively short time, with
land allocations for some uses, e.g. 'employment' use, actually being far
greater than market demands would indicate. Equally, the demand for
land for other uses, such as housing, may be far greater than anticipated
when the plans were prepared. This can result in developers seeking to
change the allocated uses, which may be strenuously resisted by the local
planning authority and result in planning appeals. Given current policies
on development (see Chapter 2), developers seeking planning permission
for the development of greenfield land not already allocated for development are likely to encounter considerable resistance from planning authorities who are now obliged to ensure that brownfield land is reused.

One aspect of land availability that is very difficult to allow for during
planning preparation is the possibility of 'windfall' sites becoming available.
These are developed sites that were not available for redevelopment at the
time the plan was prepared. They might, for example, have been in use as
manufacturing plants, schools or hospitals. Whilst school authorities and
regional health authorities might be prepared to provide planning authorities
with an indication as to their future land requirements, commercial organisations are less likely to do so, especially if they are branch plants of international companies. Planning authorities are therefore left with having to
estimate the likely incidence of windfall sites based on previous experience.
This may produce a reasonably accurate estimate but there is always the possibility that the closure of a major site could result in an oversupply of development land.

9.4   Planning guidance for contaminated sites

Many windfall sites will, by their very nature, have been previously developed with buildings. Some, but by no means all, of these will be affected by contamination. The legislation dealing with land contaminated to the extent that it is causing, or likely to cause, significant harm or pollution of controlled waters is described in Chapter 5. However, these sites are only a very small proportion, the tip of the iceberg, of the total number of sites that may be affected by the presence of contaminants to some lesser degree.

It may well be that a site containing contamination is perfectly safe in its existing use. A factory may have high concentrations of contaminants in the ground, possibly arising from the on-site disposal of wastes (see Syms, 1997, pp. 152–158), but if there is no possibility of pathways being created to workers, visitors, ground or surface waters, then the site may be 'suitable for use'. A very different situation may arise if the site is to be redeveloped and, as explained in Chapter 5, the developer will have to assess whether or not the site, in its proposed new use would constitute 'contaminated land' in accordance with the legislation. Even if it does not, the developer, with advice from the development team, will have to decide upon the best course of action for any remedial work that may be required.

As referred to in previous chapters, Government policy is that land contamination should be dealt with as part of the planning process, except where there is a risk of significant harm or pollution of controlled waters. Current guidance to planning officers is contained in Planning Policy Guidance note 23, *Planning and Pollution Control* (DoE, 1994). This covers matters such as air quality and waste management, as well as contaminated land, although the guidance on planning for waste management was updated in PPG10, *Planning and Waste Management* (DETR, 1999). The DTLR also intends to issue a new guidance note dealing specifically with contaminated land.

PPG 23 states:

'very few sites are so badly contaminated that they cannot be reused at all, but the choice of new use may be restricted by contamination as well as by other planning considerations and the consequent financial implications. Each site must be considered on its merits and if necessary treated with caution.'

(DoE, 1994, paragraph 4.6)

Therefore it is important that, when determining an application for redevelopment, the local planning authority considers whether the proposal takes proper account of contamination.

The condition of the site, whether or not it is known to be contaminated, and any potential remediation are material considerations that should be taken into account by local planning authorities when determining planning applications. There may be other considerations, including:

- the possibility of land contamination arising from the proposed development, and the protection and remediation measures as appropriate;
- the impact of any discharge of effluent or leachates, which may pose a threat to current and future surface or underground water resources or to adjacent areas;
- the risk of toxic releases, whether on site or on access roads; and
- the waste generated by the development, including that arising from the preparation and construction phases, and proposed arrangements for storage, treatment and disposal.

(DoE, 1994, paragraph 3.3)

The guidance note recommends that the local planning authority consults other relevant bodies in respect of environmental issues[9.1] and states:

'in all cases, local planning authorities should make clear in their letters those issues on which they are seeking guidance. In particular, they should (i) highlight any local land uses or sensitivities which they wish the consultee to consider in deciding on their advice, and (ii) draw attention to the local topography which may affect the impact of any pollution.'

(DoE, 1994, paragraph 3.11)

Planning officers should also consult internally with their environmental health and building control colleagues in the local authority.

Annex 10 of PPG23 stresses that 'even before an application is made, informal discussions between a potential developer and the local planning authority can be very helpful'. The annex also suggests 'in districts which contain a significant number of possibly contaminated sites, the local planning authority should find it useful to include a question on contamination on their standard application form and a note to applicants on the subject'.

In situations where it is known, or strongly suspected by the local planning authority:

'that the site may be contaminated to an extent which would adversely affect the proposed development or infringe statutory requirements, an investi-

---

[9.1] The PPG recommends specifically that Her Majesty's Inspectorate of Pollution (HMIP) is consulted. The body is now part of the Environment Agency.

gation of the hazards by the developer and proposals for any necessary
remedial measures required to deal with the hazards will normally be
required before the application can be determined.'

(PPG23, Annex 10, paragraph 8; see DoE, 1994)

If, on the other hand, there is only a suspicion that the site may be contaminated, or there is evidence to suggest that any contamination may be slight:

'planning permission may be granted but conditions should be attached to
make it clear that development will not be permitted to start until a site
investigation and assessment has been carried out and that the development
itself will need to incorporate all the measures shown in the assessment to be
necessary.'

(PPG23, Annex 10, paragraph 9; see DoE, 1994)

Regardless of whether the site investigation and assessment is required before
the planning application is determined or as a condition of the planning permission, the local planning authority may also wish to consider the desirability
of including a condition that requires 'the developer to draw to the attention of
the planning authority the presence of significant unsuspected contamination
encountered during redevelopment' (PPG23, Annex 10, paragraph 11).

The study by Syms (2001, p. 10) found wide variation of experience
regarding the implementation of the recommendations in Annex 10 of PPG23
by local planning authorities – experiences ranging from 'invariably' to 'rarely'.
Not mentioned in the study report were the comments, made by a number of
developers, that this was not now an issue as they have adopted a routine of
submitting site investigation reports and, where appropriate, remediation
strategies as part of the planning application documentation, thereby pre-
empting the request for information.

Some authorities have established procedures whereby planning applications, in respect of sites where contamination may be an issue, are dealt with by
dedicated teams drawn from the planning, environmental health and building
control departments. Good practice approaches of this kind should ensure that
the issues are fully addressed, and should be encouraged. Nevertheless, it should
be emphasised that it is not the role of the planning authority to undertake
detailed risk assessments in respect of land reuse. The responsibility for
undertaking any necessary risk assessments and for providing information as to
contamination on the proposed development site is primarily that of the
developer and the development team.

9.5   Protection for workers and the public

All those involved in work on contaminated land sites (i.e. surveyors, con-tractors, transport firms, etc.) will need to make an assessment of the potential risks to health entailed in the work, and the precautions required to protect workers or the public. To enable them to do this, the client and the person in control of the site should ensure that sufficient information is provided on the nature, extent and level of contamination. The firms involved can then assess the risks to which they or their employees are likely to be exposed. Clearly the precautions to be taken by a lorry driver who remains in the cab will be dif-ferent from those to be taken by a ground worker. However, each contractor must decide what precautions are necessary and take steps to ensure those precautions are taken. Those in control of the sites should satisfy themselves that the various contractors have carried out an assessment which is sufficient and suitable and that specified control measures are provided and used. In most cases this assessment should be in writing (HSE, 1991, p. 1).

The Control of Substances Hazardous to Health Regulations 1999 (COSHH) apply to the remediation of sites affected by contamination. Where asbestos or lead are involved, the Control of Asbestos at Work Regulations or Control of Lead at Work Regulations will apply.

Achieving a good standard of hygiene is one of the most important aspects of the regime of protective measures to be undertaken (HSE, 1991, p. 7). While the level of risk will determine whether a full range of measures will be required, the development team will need to give consideration to the following issues:

- *Installation of a hygiene facility* situated at the most convenient access point to and from the dirty zone, see Figure 9.1.
- *Eating and smoking* should be accommodated by a canteen or mess room on the clean side of the site, accessed only via the hygiene facility. Regardless of the degree of contamination on the site, eating and smoking should not be permitted within the dirty area.
- *Boot wash*, situated immediately outside the entrance to the hygiene unit, with running water and either fixed or hand brushes to remove con-taminated soils. Consideration will need to be given to the disposal of waste water from this facility.
- *Cleaning of cabs* – the use of positive pressure cabs should be considered, so as to prevent the entry of contaminants, otherwise the cabs of excavators and other machines used on site should be vacuumed out so as to avoid placing the operator at risk through the build-up of contaminants.
- *Wheel-washing facilities* must be provided so as to clean the wheels and undersides of vehicles leaving the dirty area. For some sites high-pressure

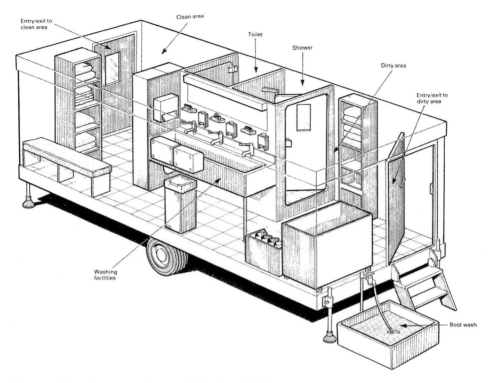

Figure 9.1 Example of a good hygiene facility.

hoses may suffice but for others, especially where vehicles will be entering the public highway, purpose-built washers with rotating brushes may be required. As with the boot wash, consideration will need to be given to the disposal of waste water. Discharge to the public sewer may not be an option (depending both on the location of the site and the nature of the contaminants) and tank storage prior to disposal at a licensed facility may be required.

- *Protective clothing* for all sites should include safety wellingtons, hard hats, hand protection and protective overalls. Disposable overalls are preferable, so as to avoid the need for laundering. PVC overalls present problems due to excessive perspiration but may be necessary in wet working conditions. They should be without pockets in order to prevent retention of contaminants. Respiratory equipment may be required for some contaminants, or where there is a risk of landfill gas being present. In addition to protective clothing for site workers, provision should also be made for regular visitors, such as surveyors and engineers, to be suitably clothed and equipped.
- *Confined space working* should, where possible, be minimised. However, if essential, then clear procedures should be developed for entry into trenches,

manholes, basements, etc. where there is a possibility of oxygen deficiency or asphyxiating or toxic gases – see *Safe Work in Confined Spaces* (HSE, 1997).

- *Control of dusts* will be particularly important on hot, dry days, when operations such as those involving excavators, etc. may produce considerable quantities of dust which can be blown off site, thus producing a possible risk to members of the public as well as site workers. Precautions, such as water sprays, may need to be introduced and, where there is a risk of asbestos dust, more stringent precautions will be needed.

- *Removal of wastes from site* will require the sheeting of open lorries or skips used for the transport of contaminated soils. There should be a clearly defined area on the dirty side of the site, close to the exit, and a gantry-type facility, such as that shown in Figure 9.2, can be used for both washing the sides of the vehicles and for sheeting purposes. Sheeting should be undertaken by site personnel and not left to the lorry driver. Detailed records must be maintained in respect of all wastes sent from the site (required under the Waste Management Licensing Regulations) and vehicle movements should be logged by site staff so as to provide an auditable trail in respect of the contaminated soil.

- *Health surveillance* of site workers may be needed in case a disease or adverse effect is related to contaminants on site and could arise in the circumstances of the individual's work. This can only be undertaken where there are valid techniques for detecting the disease or effect.

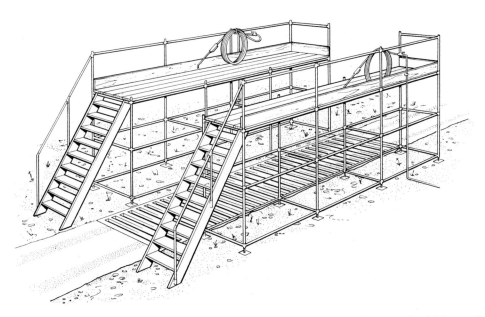

Figure 9.2 A gantry-type was facility for washing the sides and tops of vehicles and also for sheeting vehicle loads.

- *First aid* provision must be made for the protection of workers on a con-taminated land site. The type of arrangements will depend on the nature and degree of hazards at the site, the hours of work, the availability of medical services and the number of workers on site.

(Based on HSE, 1991, pp. 7–13)

Once procedures for the work have been defined, information, instruction and training programmes will need to be developed. All site workers, whether directly involved with decontamination operations or not, should receive an induction which includes information as to the history of the site, the con-taminants found and the procedures to be employed in decontamination. Health and Safety issues should form an important part of the induction pro-cess, as it is necessary to reassure personnel that they can work safely on site despite the dangers, provided proper precautions are taken. Details of all induction and training sessions should be recorded.

Site working conditions, including air monitoring and rainfall (especially important in the event of any flooding of the works) must be fully recorded. Samples of materials retained on site, say within an area considered to be only slightly contaminated, and all fill materials, such as crushed concrete, should be sent for laboratory analysis. These records will form an important part of the documentation required to demonstrate that the decontamination work has been properly undertaken.

9.6   Waste management licensing

Waste management licensing is a major bone of contention with some developers and the promoters of soil remediation technologies. But, according to the Environment Agency:

> 'it is a common misconception that remediation can only result in an environmental improvement. It has been found that some remediation activities, whilst reducing the risk of contaminants within the ground, can be the cause of pollution of the environment or harm to human health. This pollution or harm can be as a result of the mobilisation of contaminants, removal of a barrier or the introduction of a receptor.'

(Environment Agency, 2001, p. 2)

The need for the licensing of operations has been blamed for the delay to, and even abandonment of, redevelopment projects. The Environment Agency is responsible for licensing operations that involve the recovery or disposal of waste materials and this may have significant implications for the developers of previously developed sites, even those that are not highly contaminated. Whilst therefore the

Agency is not advocating that remediation activities should be prevented, it does require that the short-term risks are managed to an acceptable level.

In order to achieve this the Agency considers it essential to impose the most effective regulatory controls on operators and, in consequence, the Agency:

- fully encourages the remediation of contaminated sites and the safe regeneration of brownfield land;
- intends not to create inappropriate or disproportionate regulatory burdens or obstacles to achieve this aim; and
- is committed to encouraging the use, where appropriate, of process-based remediation technologies;
- is committed to ensuring that the use of these technologies does not create an unacceptable risk of adverse environmental impact. To achieve this [the Agency] must apply a clear, consistent and proportionate regulatory mechanism for remediation technologies.

(Environment Agency, 2001, p. 2)

For many sites this may be seen as being best managed by a waste management licence, or 'site licence'.

Operations involving the recovery or disposal of waste are subject to control under the EC Framework Directive on waste.[9.2] The waste management licensing system under Part II of the Environmental Protection Act 1990, and the Waste Management Licensing Regulations 1994, is the main means by which the Directive's requirements have been brought into operation. Under this system anyone who deposits, recovers or disposes of waste must do so in compliance with the conditions of a waste management licence, or within the terms of an exemption from licensing, and in a way which does not cause pollution of the environment or harm to human health (Environment Agency, 2001, p. 2).

The operators of waste handling facilities are required to be 'fit and proper persons' and there is a requirement for the licence to remain in force until it has been surrendered demonstrating that the land will not cause pollution. The term 'fit and proper persons' is defined in section 74 of the Environmental Protection Act 1990 and involves satisfying three tests as to:

(1) technical competence in the process or activity proposed;
(2) financial provision adequate to discharge the obligations arising from the licence; and
(3) relevant convictions in respect of offences prescribed by the Secretary of State.

[9.2] Council Directive 91/156/EEC of 18 March 1991 amending Directive 75/442/EEC on Waste.

Conditions imposed in waste management licences can involve periods of monitoring, say of landfill gases or leachates, for lengthy periods of time following completion of the remediation works. Such monitoring may be regarded as a significant encumbrance by developers who wish to sell the development once completed and fear that the value of the project will be significantly affected by the monitoring liability.

Only when the Environment Agency is satisfied that the site does not present a risk to human health or pollution of the environment can the licence be surrendered and the Agency must determine applications to surrender waste management (site) licences in accordance with section 39 of the Environmental Protection Act 1990. In determining whether pollution of the environment or harm to human health is likely or unlikely, the Agency will have regard to the use of that land and any neighbouring land as evidenced by the relevant planning authorities at the time of surrender (Environment Agency, 2001, p. 14). In such circumstances developers are more likely to opt for quick, 'once-and-for-all' solutions, such as disposal of the contaminated soils to landfill.

Such an approach may be regarded as being environmentally irresponsible, simply shifting the problem from one location to another and from one generation to the next. In practice, where landfill disposal is the selected option, it is likely to be preceded by some on-site sorting and grading of materials, with the objective of sending only the most seriously contaminated materials, or those not amenable to on-site treatments, for off-site disposal.

The sorting and grading of materials, and some on-site treatments, may require licensing by the Environment Agency. This may not necessarily mean a waste management licence, as a mobile plant licence (issued under section 35(1) of the Environmental Protection Act 1990) may be sufficient for the operations proposed. The advantage of a mobile plant licence is that it does not attach to the land, therefore once the plant has moved elsewhere the development site is no longer subject to the provisions of the waste management licensing regime – that is, unless of course there is also a waste management licence in force on the site. Figure 9.3 shows the process to be followed in deciding whether a mobile plant licence is appropriate for the operations proposed.

As mobile plant licences are not site-specific, certain provisions of the waste management licensing regime, for example the surrender test, cannot be applied but not all waste management activities can be covered by a mobile plant licence simply on the basis of the mobility of the plant (Environment Agency, 2001, p. 11). Mobile Plant is defined in the Waste Management Licensing Regulations 1994[9.3] as being:

'Plant of the following descriptions if it is designed to move or be moved by any means from place to place with a view to being used at each such place or, if not so designed, is readily capable of so moving or being so moved, but

_____

[9.3] As amended by the Waste Management Regulations 1996.

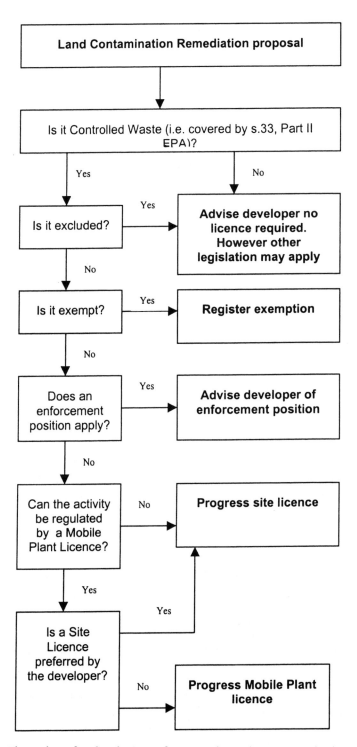

Figure 9.3   Flow chart for the decision framework used to assess whether the waste management licensing regime applies to land contamination remediation proposals.

no other plant shall be treated as being mobile plant for the purpose of Part II of the 1990 Act;[9.4]

- an incinerator which is an exempt incinerator for the purposes of Section 5.1 of Schedule 1 to the 1991 Regulations;[9.5]

plant for

- the recovery by filtration or heat treatment, of waste oil from electrical equipment; or
- the destruction by dechlorination of waste polychlorinated biphenyls or terphenyls (PCBs or PCTs);
- plant for the vitrification of waste
- plant for the treatment by microwave of clinical waste
- plant for the treatment of waste soil.'

As can be seen, this definition is fairly widely drawn in terms of mobility but, in practice, the Agency would only consider plant to be mobile if it is directly mobile (i.e. it has wheels) or it was originally conceived and designed to be moved from place to place (Environment Agency, 2001, p. 11).

Of course it is possible that the operations proposed by the developer to remediate the site require neither a site licence nor a mobile plant licence. Schedule 3 of the Waste Management Licensing Regulations 1994 contains 45 exemptions from waste management licensing, of which only six are commonly applicable to land contamination remediation activities:

(1)   Exemption 7: Spreading of waste on land for benefit to agriculture or ecological improvement.
(2)   Exemption 9: The spreading of waste on any land in connection with the reclamation and improvement of that land.
(3)   Exemption 13: The manufacture and treatment of waste soils.
(4)   Exemption 19: Use of waste for 'relevant works' ('relevant works' includes construction and maintenance of certain facilities).
(5)   Exemption 24: Brick, tile or concrete crushing.
(6)   Exemption 41: The temporary storage of waste at site of production.

Table 1 of the Environment Agency's (2001) *Guidance on the Application of Waste Management Licensing to Land Contamination Activities* sets out the criteria that are commonly applied when assessing whether a proposed activity should be considered exempt. It should be noted that the use of Exemption 19 is specifically barred for any site where 'land reclamation' in the wider context is involved. If an activity is exempt from waste management licensing, the developer must register an exemption with the Environment Agency. This excludes Exemption 24, which must be registered with the local enforcing

---

[9.4] The Environmental Protection Act 1990.
[9.5] The Environmental Protection (Prescribed Processes and Substances) Regulations 1991.

authority responsible for granting authorisation under Part I of the Environmental Protection Act 1990 for the operations involved.

9.7   Summary

This chapter has considered only some of the most important regulatory issues that may affect a development project. There are many other regulations that may need to be considered and, if in doubt, the developer or the appropriate member of the development team should establish the earliest possible contact with the relevant regulator. For the most part, early contact and a frank disclosure of the problem will bring benefits. Concealment may end in prosecution.

There are undoubted differences as to how the environmental regulations are enforced and in the relationship between town planning and the environment. Not only do these differences exist between regulatory authorities but also they even occur within the same organisation, with differing responses between areas. In the main these differences may be attributable to the problems involved in reorganising regulatory bodies at the same time as introducing new or revised legislation and guidance.

The issue of waste management licences for remediation issues is certainly a major issue for many developers and for the contractors seeking to develop or promote innovative ideas. The Environment Agency's position is that it has to comply with European law and that, so far as it is able, it tries to assist redevelopment through the use of mobile plant licences instead of imposing waste management licences. It has been suggested that some form of 'remediation licensing' should be introduced to streamline the system and provide a standardised approach to the preparation of previously developed land for new uses. This could, for example, be operated as part of the planning system in consultation with the environmental regulators. The possibility of such a system is being considered by a working party but it is likely to be some time before any changes are implemented, if at all.

9.8   Checklist

- Hold early discussions with the local authority planning department.
- Submit site investigation reports, if appropriate, with the planning application.
- Consider whether the site could be suitable for use or redevelopment in its present condition, possibly with some revision of the scheme.
- Ensure the safety of all site personnel and visitors through induction briefings and the provision of suitable safety equipment and protective clothing.
- Discuss problems with the regulators.
- Make early application for any required licences.

Note: *Development of Land Affected by Contamination Consultation Paper on draft Planning Technical Advice*

Issued in February 2002 to provide an opportunity to consult on new advice to replace the existing guidance in Planning Policy Guidance note (PPG) 23 *Planning and pollution control* (1994) and applicable only in England. Existing planning *policy* on contamination of land remains largely unchanged. The draft *advice* aims to develop existing guidance, looking at land contamination at all stages of the planning and development process.

The possibility that land may be contaminated is a material planning consideration. The draft Technical Advice Note explains the relationship of the contaminated land regime to the planning regime and, in particular, sets out the responsibilities of the parties in the development process.

The developer is responsible for:

- determining whether any proposed development will be affected by contamination and whether it will increase the potential for contamination on the site or elsewhere; and
- satisfying the local planning authority that any contamination can be successfully remediated with the minimum adverse environmental effect to ensure the safe development and secure occupancy of any site.

The local authority has the following roles:

- in most cases, the environmental health departments are the enforcing authorities for the contaminated land regime and LPAs should pay particular attention to the condition of the land where the proposed use would be vulnerable to any past contamination, this includes examination of the authority's own records to obtain information as to past usage of the land;
- responsibility for control of development, which includes (as a minimum) obtaining from the applicant a desk study to assess the possibility of contamination, the enforcement of conditions to ensure that development is appropriate in relation to all relevant circumstances and contamination, ensuring that land is remediated to an appropriate standard and maintained thereafter; and
- building control, which includes meeting the requirements to protect buildings from the effects of contamination.

The Environment Agency is a consultee on certain planning applications for development on land that may be affected by contamination, carries out technical research and publishes scientific and technical advice relevant to land contamination.

The best practice set out in the draft Technical Advice Note should ensure that, in most instances, potential contamination is identified at an early stage in the planning process, appropriate policies are developed for its use and planning applications are decided on the basis of adequate information.

Chapter 10
Development Finance and Joint Ventures

10.1 Introduction

It is probably a rare occurrence for a development company to fully fund a project from its own resources, indeed it is more likely that the developer will wish to maximise the borrowing potential of a development, so as to be able to undertake a greater number of projects at any one time. Developments can be financed in many different ways and selection of the appropriate method of finance for a project will depend on both the nature of the development and the developer's objectives.

If it is the developer's intention to sell the buildings once completed to individual occupiers, short-term development finance will be required. On the other hand, if the developer intends to let the new buildings and sell the completed investment to a pension fund, he or she may wish to identify a suitable investor at the outset, so as to combine the development finance and eventual sale as a single package. This is known as 'forward selling' the development. Alternatively, the developer may wish to hold the development in the company's own portfolio, in which case it may be appropriate to secure long-term mortgage funding.

In other words, the financing arrangement should be matched to the medium to long-term objectives of the developer and project. That is not to say that it is not possible to change the financing arrangement at a later date but some penalties may be incurred.

So far as straight development finance is concerned, this can be divided into three types: debt, equity and mezzanine. Developments can also be financed through joint ventures; these can exist between banks and developers, between two developers, land owners and developers, even public bodies and developers. In some cases joint ventures can be fairly loose arrangements, in that there is simply an agreement to cooperate in order to achieve a common objective. More commonly, however, they will take the form of a single-

185

purpose vehicle – that is, a limited liability company established solely for the purpose of carrying out the project and in which the joint venture partners hold shares.

10.2   Financing a new development

The development finance market at the beginning of the twenty-first century is somewhat different to the property boom period of the late 1980s, as there is less speculative development around. High street banks, merchant banks and building societies are all possible sources for development finance. Each finance company will have its own lending criteria and even between the same types of organisations these will differ. There is also less finance available for speculative projects, although whether it is the availability of finance that controls the volume of speculative development is difficult to answer.

Banks are less aggressive, in terms of competing to finance development, than they were before the last recession. They have a greater understanding of the risks involved, due to an improvement of the expertise within the banks. Specialist property lending teams are more prevalent and general bankers are far less likely to become involved with lending on development projects.

10.2.1   *Creditworthiness*

Before deciding whether or not to provide finance for a development project, banks will wish to review the nature of the project itself and to assess the creditworthiness of the intending developer. The project review is an essential part of understanding the degree and type of risks to which the bank might be exposed. In considering property development proposals, the bank will wish to consider the following:

- The experience of the developer in respect of the type of development proposed;
- The potential market for the proposed product;
- The robustness of the design and cost estimates provided by the development team.

The bank will also wish to consider any contingency provisions built into the development appraisal and the sensitivity analyses – the 'what if?' scenarios – should demand reduce, with the consequence that rents fall, and construction costs rise, or yield rates increase, thereby reducing the price that investors would be prepared to pay. When considering previously developed or contaminated sites, the bank will need to have regard for:

- Any impacts and costs that could arise from natural or man–made occurrences, whether direct or indirect.
- The possibility that, due to site problems, the borrower becomes unable to service its wider financial obligations, which may affect the business, its employees, suppliers, the specific project and the bank itself.
- The ownership of any security, not just property-based, offered to secure the loan, of particular importance when the site has a low base value requiring considerable expenditure on remediation
- Any potential legal liabilities, including Part IIA of the Environmental Protection Act 1990, which may affect the financial position and reputation of the borrower.
- The ability to continue or re-establish the business in the light of any unforeseen events, potentially leaving the bank having to accept responsibility for a partially remediated site.
- The possible impact on the neighbourhood, arising out of a failure of the project, which could include the effect on interrelated or interdependent lending, savings or investments.

According to Graham (2001), the developers and/or their design teams will be expected to undertake the necessary level of site investigation and to factor the technical, time and cost implications into their business plans. The banks will seek comfort with regard to the integrity of the proposals and, depending on the circumstances, may additionally require insurance, guarantees or warranties as part of the funding agreement.

10.2.2 Costs of finance

In addition to charging interest on the money loaned, usually on outstanding daily balances, the bank will wish to recover its entire incidental costs incurred in approving the loan. These will include surveyors' fees in advising on the project. For complex schemes this might include both a valuation surveyor, to advise on the value of the site in its present condition and the development once it has been completed, and a quantity surveyor to comment on the developer's cost estimates. A surveyor will also be required to prepare monthly certificates, confirming the value of the work completed on site and forming the basis for the developer to draw down the finance.

As mentioned above, an environmental consultant may be needed to advise on reports prepared for the developer or the vendor. The bank may also wish to retain its own environmental specialist to advise on certain aspects of the project as it proceeds. Legal fees and costs will be incurred in respect of the finance agreement.

All of these costs will have to be paid by the developer or, in the case of a joint venture, out of the single-purpose vehicle. In addition, the developer will be expected to pay the bank a commitment fee, around 0.5% of the total loan, in return for the bank making the money available.

10.3   Types of bank finance

This section describes the types of development finance available from banks with examples outlining the approaches adopted by two leading merchant banks – NM Rothschild & Co and Ansbacher & Co.

10.3.1   *Debt financing*

Debt financing is the conventional loan arrangement, whereby the developer borrows money from a bank, 'high street' or 'merchant', or from a building society. The bank will wish to see the developer's own feasibility study and will also employ a valuation surveyor to advise on the project. When the project is on a previously developed site the bank will almost certainly wish to see any environmental reports commissioned by the developer, or provided by the vendor of the site, and may wish to employ its own environmental consultant. Loans are limited to a percentage of the expected end-value of the project, or to a percentage of the development cost. For smaller, less experienced developers, the bank may wish to see all, or a substantial part, of the company's banking arrangements transferred to it, in order that it may keep a watch on the overall activities of the developer.

Assuming that the intending developer is an established client, with a good management team and past experience (i.e. a good track record) – in the type of development involved, Rothschild will consider providing a loan of up to 100% of the development cost. That is provided the development is pre-let on an 'institutional lease' (see Chapter 8).

Given such a situation, the bank will charge interest on the outstanding balance of the development finance at a margin of 1.5–2.5% over the London Interbank Offered Rate (LIBOR), which is the rate at which banks lend money to each other. The bank can afford to lend 100% of the development cost as the project is pre-let and it has been valued as if completed, i.e. the 'loan to value ratio' will be around 70–80%. The development finance is only paid out against surveyors' certificates that show the value of the property, as enhanced by the construction work completed to date, is less that the loan debt.

When the development project is fully pre-let a bank might normally be looking for income cover of around 12%, i.e. the guaranteed rent receivable when the building is complete as a percentage of the development cost, say with interest on the development finance at perhaps 7.5% and an expected investment yield on completion of 8%. Therefore, if the project runs into problems and completion is delayed, the bank will still receive its interest payments, although the developer's profit margin will be eroded.

A somewhat different situation exists if the property is not fully pre-let on an institutional lease to a tenant of good standing. If the development is only 50% pre-let the bank's guaranteed income cover would only be 6%, i.e. less than the interest payable on the loan. If the loan is non-recourse – that is, not secured on the general assets of the developer or with other properties offered as security – the bank would be exposed to a greater degree of risk. Nevertheless, they might still be prepared to finance the project, and even lend 100% of the development cost, without necessarily increasing the interest rate. They may, however, require a 'back end' fee on completion of the project, which will have the effect of reducing the developer's profit.

10.3.2   *Equity financing*

Equity financing involves the bank taking a stake in the project. It may acquire shares in the development company, or in a company set up for the sole purpose of undertaking the one development, known as a 'single-purpose vehicle', see section 10.4. The bank forms an integral part of the development team and, in a full equity participation project, the other members of the professional team are as responsible to the bank as to the developer. Under an equity participation arrangement the bank will take a share of the development profit in addition to interest on the development finance, although the interest may be at a slightly reduced rate.

Ansbacher and Co. tend to provide higher-than-normal loans as a ratio of end-value and then take a profit share. They will also finance entirely speculative developments, based on their judgement of the scheme and the developer's track record.

Let us assume, for example, a developer has available a sum equivalent to 15% of the development cost; Ansbacher will provide the rest and become very closely involved with the development, appointing a firm of chartered quantity surveyors and construction cost consultants to safeguard its interest. A single-purpose vehicle, outside the developer's main company, will carry out the project itself and there will be no recourse to the other assets of the developer.

The bank would charge interest on the outstanding balance of the development finance, at a rate of 2% above LIBOR, and would expect to receive a profit share of between one-third and one-half of the development profit. It will make an internal allocation between debt and mezzanine finance but this does not affect the relationship with the developer. Payments for work on site are made direct from the bank to the contractors, against quantity surveyors' certificates, so as to ensure that the funds are not diverted elsewhere.

Ansbacher will base their lending decision on a viability report on the project, taking account of the expected end-value of the project. They do not base their lending on the existing value of the land. They do not take risks on sites where planning permission has not been obtained but they may take a 'planning improvement risk' where the price to be paid for the land relates to its existing use value, i.e. the price does not include any element of 'hope value'.

In essence, the Ansbacher approach is one of 'joint venture', although the bank does not normally take a shareholding in the development vehicle.

10.3.3   *Mezzanine finance*

Mezzanine finance is important in situations where the developer is seeking to raise a higher percentage of the development finance than would normally be loaned by a bank or building society. Say, for example, that the bank was prepared to lend up to 60% of the end-value of the development but this represented only 80% of the development cost, the developer could then either provide additional collateral, in the form of other properties (even his or her own house), or seek another lender to provide the rest of the development finance. This mezzanine finance is riskier than the main funding, as it will rank second in any claims if the project fails, hence the financier will require a higher margin on the interest rate.

10.4   Joint ventures and single-purpose vehicles

As mentioned above, the simplest form is where two or more developers come together to acquire a site that is larger than either would wish to purchase on their own. This is not unusual where house-builders combine together for large developments, often producing houses that are complementary to each other in terms of styles and target markets. The agreement may cover little more than how many plots each developer is to receive, whereabouts they are to be located on the site and the proportionate cost of main roads and service infrastructure to be borne by each developer. Such agreements should also cover who is to do what in terms of matters such as obtaining planning permission and appointing civil engineering contractors. They should also contain an arbitration clause in the event that unforeseen problems are encountered and agreement cannot be reached as to how they should be resolved. An alternative to this would be for a single developer to accept responsibility for obtaining planning permission, providing the roads and infrastructure, and then selling an agreed number of plots at a predetermined price (or based on a formula) to the other developers.

Joint ventures may exist over a number of sites or development projects. For example, a manufacturer with numerous plants may be 'downsizing' or consolidating its operations in a smaller number of locations and will enter into an agreement with a developer in order to maximise the development potential out of each site. The advantage to the landowner of such an arrangement includes not having to market each site individually and negotiate terms for sales or joint venture agreements with numerous different parties. It also helps by establishing a relationship with a developer who will quickly gain an understanding of the manufacturer's operations, including the contamination or other problems that might be encountered, and the company's needs in terms of disposals and cash flow.

A typical arrangement for such a joint venture, covering one or more sites, would be to form a limited liability company, with the shares held equally between the parties. The landowner would transfer the sites into the joint venture company, as they become vacant, at open market value and the developer would inject an equivalent sum as working capital. The rest of the development finance would then be raised as debt finance, with additional sureties or guarantees (if needed) being provided by the two parent companies. With this type of model the developer partner would normally expect to receive a management fee for running the project and the development profit, or loss, would be shared equally. It is important to ensure that the company used as the development vehicle is empowered, through its Memorandum and Articles of Association, to undertake the types of projects proposed and can either retain or sell the completed buildings at the discretion of the directors. Care must also be taken to ensure that the implications regarding 'casting votes' and dispute resolution are fully understood by all concerned.

Another alternative for a joint venture between landowner and developer would be to enter into a partnership agreement, without becoming bound together in a joint venture company. Under this type of arrangement the land is either transferred to the developer at 'existing use' value, which means that the developer has the ability to use the land as security to raise bank finance, or it is retained by the landowner until the project is completed and a 'building licence' is granted to the developer. The arrangement would contain an 'uplift' provision for an additional sum to be payable to the landowner once planning permission, meeting specified criteria, has been obtained. Under this model all of the development risk is taken by the developer, the landowner may or may not receive interest on the 'land value' element and the development profit will be divided according to an agreed formula.

The division of profit may be either 'side by side', whereby the developer and land owner share all of the profit in agreed proportions, say 60/40 or 70/30 in the developer's favour, or 'horizontally sliced' whereby the developer takes, say, the first 15% of the profit, as a proportion of the development cost, the landowner takes the next 10% and anything in excess of that is shared equally. Under profit-sharing arrangements of this nature the base land value, specified in the agreement, and the development costs will be the first and second charges respectively against the development proceeds. If the development failed to make a profit then the developer would, normally, be responsible for any losses, including the repayment of bank borrowings.

10.5   Forward sales and rental guarantees

Deciding when to sell a commercial or industrial development can be very important to a developer, as it can have a significant impact on the profitability of the development. There are two main options open to the developer, but with various permutations in between. Either the developer can decide to sell the project before any work has been started on site, a 'forward sale', or wait until construction has been completed and the buildings have been fully let. On larger schemes, consisting of more than one building, the developer can also take a more flexible approach, for example forward-selling the first building but holding the second or subsequent buildings until fully let.

As with the provision of development finance, the attitude of investing institutions towards forward sale propositions will differ according to the extent to which the development is pre-let and the covenant strength of the proposed tenant or tenants. A building in a prime position, say an office block in the centre of a prosperous town or city, or a warehouse building close to an important motorway junction, let to a first-class tenant, will more readily attract an institutional investor than one in a secondary location let to a weaker tenant. If the property market is strong then there may well be considerable competition from potential investors, with the result that the yield rate achieved on the forward sale is the same, or virtually the same, as if the building was already completed and occupied. In a weaker market the developer of a well-located building, for which a first-class tenant has been secured, might have to accept a price based on a slightly higher yield, say increased by half a percentage point, but will have to weigh this against his or her judgement as to whether or not the market will weaken further before the development is completed. There may also be an added advantage in that the investing institution may be prepared to provide the development finance at a more advantageous rate than a bank or building society.

When the development is not in a prime position and is only partly pre-let it may still be possible to arrange a forward sale. However, the price achievable will show a significant discount against that which might be achieved if the building had already been completed, with the yield rate moving out by one percentage point or more. The purchasing institution will probably also require the developer to provide a rental guarantee in respect of any unlet space. Such a guarantee is likely to be time limited, say up to the first rent review period, and have a financial cap, possibly equal to the developer's profit expectation. In a worst case scenario therefore the developer's maximum loss is limited to the profit that would have been made had the development been fully let by the time construction was completed, in other words the developer could have done all the work for no reward. At first sight this may seem like a poor arrangement for the developer but it does have the advantage of minimising the downside risk, that is the degree of exposure before the developer starts to show a return, and if the development, or the market, goes badly wrong the institution will have to absorb any further losses beyond the guarantee.

10.6   Public-sector finance

In some parts of the country, and in weak market conditions, property development would have come to a complete standstill, had it not been for the availability of public-sector finance in the form of 'gap-funding'. Introduced in 1983 as the Urban Development Grant (UDG), modelled on the American Urban Development Action Grant (UDAG), gap-funding provided by the Department of the Environment (DoE) was intended to make up the difference between the cost of a development project and its investment value, or expected sales proceeds, in situations where costs exceeded value.

UDG operated in the period between 1983 and 1988, with URG (Urban Regeneration Grant) being added in the latter part of this period in order to promote area regeneration (Price Waterhouse, 1993, p. 60). In practice, very few URGs were awarded and the emphasis remained on the single building type of regeneration project, rather than wider, area-based, projects. City Grant replaced both UDG and URG in May 1988. Responsibility for the grant regime passed from the DoE to English Partnerships in April 1994, following its creation as a quasi-autonomous non-governmental organisation (Quango) sponsored by the DoE.

The aims of City Grant and its predecessors were 'to promote the economic and physical regeneration of inner urban areas by levering private sector investment into such areas'. UDG projects were also expected to 'make a demonstrable contribution to meeting the special needs of inner urban areas and creating a climate of confidence for the private sector' (Price Waterhouse, 1993, p. 5), although this was not emphasised in relation to City Grant. In terms of levering in private-sector investment, a yardstick was set – £1 of public money for every £4 of private-sector money, although this was not always achieved.

Property developers were expected to make a profit from grant-aided schemes although, as mentioned in Chapter 8, the return might have been somewhat lower than the developer would normally have expected to make in a run-down area or a poor market. Land values were often contentious issues between private-sector applicants and the grant appraisers acting for the grant-awarding body. Applicants hoped to include land in their development appraisals at a figure at least equivalent to existing use value, or even some enhanced development value, whereas the grant appraisers often took the approach that 'if the project needs grant, then the land must be valueless'. A compromise was usually reached but there were many cases where land changed hands at inflated values, without any development being carried out, in the expectation that a grant would be received, only for the purchaser to find that the appraiser would not accept, for grant purposes, the price paid for the land.

English Partnerships combined City Grant with Derelict Land Grant[10.1] to form the English Partnerships Investment Fund (EPIF) of which the Partnership Investment Programme (PIP) continued to provide 'gap-funding' for property development projects. The programme was closed in December 1999, following a ruling by the European Commission that PIP was in breach of State aid rules and therefore not compatible with the principles of the Common Market, although projects already approved continued to receive funding.

Following discussions between the Government and the European Commission, five new schemes were introduced in May 2001; these are intended to partially replace the PIP as follows:

- A direct development scheme
- Two gap-funding schemes, one for developments for a known end-user, the other for developments for disposal in the open market
- A scheme for community regeneration
- A scheme for environmental regeneration

So far as the gap-funding schemes are concerned, small and medium enterprises (SMEs) are eligible for assistance under this scheme anywhere in

---

[10.1] Previously available to provide grants of up to 100% for local authorities and 80% for the private sector of the cost of reclaiming derelict land, the grant being calculated after any increase in value was taken into account. Derelict Land Grant was available for both 'hard' and 'soft' (e.g. public open space) end-uses.

England. Where the developer is not an SME, the project must be located in an Assisted Area. If the end-user is known, is an SME, or the project is in an Assisted Area, three forms of support will be permitted: the provision of land and commercial property; business and commercial premises improvement; and physical regeneration services. Where the development is for disposal on the open market, four forms of support will be permitted: regeneration grant; joint regeneration body/private sector projects; regeneration financing aid; and regeneration services.

How the replacement schemes will be implemented in detail will be up to the individual Regional Development Agencies (RDAs) to decide; however, grants will be subject to the relevant aid intensity ceilings. One very important difference from PIP is that the new schemes do not include residential developments and it is therefore likely that new housing provision will only benefit if the housing is a minor part of a mixed-use development. The Planning and Development Faculty of the Royal Institution of Chartered Surveyors (RICS), in conjunction with the Department for Transport, Local Government and the Regions (DTLR), has produced a guidance note *Partnership Support for Land and Property Regeneration Schemes* (RICS, 2001), which is available from *www.ricsonline.org*.

Adair *et al.* (1998) considered the processes whereby private developers and investors decided whether or not to invest in urban regeneration projects. They found that funding institutions treat loan-to-value ratios for urban regeneration projects in a similar manner to other lending scenarios. They also discovered that developers perceive public-sector land assembly (see Chapter 4) to be a key risk reduction measure enabling land costs to be deferred, thereby enhancing cash flow during the initial stages of the project. The usual basis for this is that the developer constructs the new development on land acquired by the local authority, under a building agreement, with the freehold or long leasehold interest only being transferred on completion of the development, or of each building. Whilst this arrangement has a very positive advantage in reducing the developer's costs in the early stages of the development, it may create some complications in arranging bank finance, as the bank will be unable to take a charge on the land as security for the loan.

10.6.2   Public–private partnerships

These are usually seen as being a means by which the private sector meets the capital cost of public buildings or infrastructure, with the public sector then making payments in the form of rents or the costs being recouped in some other way, such as tolls for new bridges or roads. They may also be used to develop projects that contain a mix of public and private buildings, for example developing part of a college site to provide both new offices and improved teaching facilities, as in the case of the Manchester College of Arts and Technology.

Public–private partnerships can be instrumental in achieving major urban regeneration objectives, as in the case of the former coal port at Barry in South Wales, see Figure 10.1, and discussed below.

Figure 10.1   Barry, South Wales, *circa* 1950.

Case study: Barry, South Wales

Although the coal trade had ceased, prior to the mid-1980s the docks at Barry were still active, handling bananas, timber, cereals, volcanic rock and chemicals for the chemical industries in Barry. The land and rail sidings surrounding the docks continued in alternative uses, including a chemical tank farm and storage for dismantling of 600 steam locomotives. A wide range of users tenanted many of the buildings. During the property boom of the mid to late eighties, a series of redevelopment proposals emerged for part of the dockland and the Old Harbour, and were submitted to the Welsh Office as candidates for Urban Development Grant (UDG) (later changed to Urban Investment Grant (UIG) in Wales) (Griffiths, 2001, p. 2).

The proposals submitted to the Welsh Office would have required gap-funding of almost £30 million from the UDG budget and, in 1990, the Welsh Office invited the Welsh Development Agency (WDA) to consider ways in which it could assist the project. At about the same time, Dow Corning was considering the expansion of its chemical plant in Barry, at a cost in excess of £100 million, which would secure long-term chemical importing and tankage facilities. By this time also the property market had entered a downward cycle.

The WDA discussed the various proposals with dock owner Associated British Ports (ABP) (the privatised former British Transport Dock Board), and concluded that a conventional public-sector route of acquiring the land, reclaiming it and then selling on for redevelopment, was not feasible. This was due to ongoing operations in the docks, the need for maintenance and the multiplicity of tenants, as well as the complexity of rail and other service infrastructures. The development agency therefore suggested that a joint initiative approach be adopted to secure the redevelopment of an agreed area of ABP and associated lands. Each party would make agreed inputs and the returns from land disposals would be shared according to the ratio of those inputs.

The site area finally designated for the joint initiative was agreed at 79 ha (195 acres), which was to remain vested in ABP but with the WDA having a legal charge over it. The inputs by the two parties were broadly as shown in Box 10.1.

On the basis shown in Box 10.1, out of the total inputs of land, site remediation, infrastructure, landscaping, relocation and management, ABP was to contribute slightly more than 40% and the WDA just under 60%. On this basis the anticipated income from disposals would have produced £6.5 million for ABP and £9 million for the WDA. Although both parties would have been left with a loss, ABP would have resolved some potential environmental liabilities at a relatively low cost. Furthermore, ABP would derive significant benefit by securing long-term port revenue for chemical importing. The £4 million cost to the public purse would have been well below the gap-funding

Box 10.1   Inputs to the Barry Docks joint initiative.

Associated British ports	Welsh Development Agency
Land at Value	Compensation for removal of two groups
Relocation of tenants	of tanks
50% of infrastructure costs	Relocation of additional tenants
Land for new tank farm	Reclamation of land for tank farm
50% of management costs	Reclamation of route for new link road
	100% of reclamation and landscape costs
	50% of infrastructure costs
	50% of management costs
Value of inputs £9 million	Value of inputs £13 million

Source: Griffiths, 2001, p. 3)

requirement previously proposed. A substantial urban renewal project would also have been facilitated.

In order to make this joint initiative work it was essential that the initial site assessment, treatment strategy, development proposals and development appraisal were robust and conservative (Griffiths, 2001, p. 4). It was necessary to balance the WDA's broader economic regeneration aspirations for the town of Barry with the necessarily more focused commercial aspirations of ABP for its land holdings and port operations. The confidence of the local community had to be raised and support obtained for what might have been seen as yet another in a long series of doomed artist's impressions for the docks. The legal agreement had to bind and protect the interests of both parties whilst enabling decisions, spending commitments and directional changes to be made quickly and compliantly.

During the course of the project its scope was extended to include additional land and infrastructure, with the outcome that the input values for ABP and the WDA rose to £12 million and £18 million respectively. The reclamation works have removed a massive visual blight from the area and have dealt with large areas of land contaminated with asbestos, hydrocarbons and heavy metals. Rationalisation and relocation of intrusive and 'bad neighbour' uses has meant that such businesses have regrouped alongside other industries away from the town. This, together with the provision of new infrastructure, has released land for residential, retail, commercial and leisure development. In financial terms, it now appears likely that both parties may fully recoup their input investments, demonstrating the success of the joint initiative (see Figure 10.2).

Figure 10.2   Barry following removal of the redundant industries, land reclamation and provision of new infrastructure.

10.7   Summary

There are many different ways in which development projects can be financed. The extent to which banks and other financial institutions will be prepared to provide finance depends upon a number of different factors, foremost of which are the track record of the developer concerned and the institution's perception of the development project itself. Even a successful developer will have problems in arranging finance if the bank considers the project to be too risky. Pre-let or pre-sold project are easier to finance than those that are entirely speculative.

Joint ventures may provide an alternative to bank finance and they may also be entered into for many other reasons. For example, a landowner who is averse to development risk but wishes to maximise the potential of his land may enter into partnership with a developer who will exercise his skill and experience in undertaking the development project. Profits, and losses, from joint-venture projects can be shared in a variety of different ways.

Public-sector funding may play an important part in bringing the development project to fruition, especially for regeneration projects. Public–private partnerships may have the effect of reducing the cost to the public purse, whilst still enabling both parties to meet their objectives.

10.8   Checklist

- Examine the risks attaching to the selected form of finance.
- Include finance costs in the development appraisal, including any additional fees.
- If conventional funding is not available, investigate alternatives such as joint ventures.
- Gap-funding is no longer available for most residential schemes – housing would have to form a minor part of a mixed-use scheme in order to qualify.

Chapter 11

Tendering, Entering into Contracts, Monitoring and Supervising the Work

Tim Abbott

11.1 Introduction

The traditional approach to the execution of development projects was for the developer to commission an architect to prepare drawings and a specification for the proposed buildings. A quantity surveyor was also appointed to prepare voluminous bills of quantities, and a consulting engineer, either employed directly by the client, or acting as a sub-consultant to the architect, carried out the design of the remediation work. The specifications, drawings and bills of quantities would then form the basis for competitive tenders, and the remediation work was included in the building contract. This approach is still used but today there are other alternatives that the developer may wish to consider.

Franks (1990) referred to a number of key issues identified in the 1964 report by the Banwell Committee. Many of these remain important today:

- Those who spend money on construction work seldom give enough attention at the start to defining their own requirements and preparing a programme of events for meeting them.
- As the complexity of construction increases, the need to form a design team at the outset, with all those participating in the design as full members, becomes vital.
- Design and construction are no longer separate fields and there are occasions when the main contractor should join the team at an early stage.
- Some measure of selective tendering is preferable to 'open' tendering.
- The use of unorthodox methods of appointing the contractor sometimes has advantages.
- Serial tenders offer great possibilities for continuity of employment and the development of experienced production teams.
- Methods of contracting should be examined for the value of the solutions they offer to problems rather than for their orthodoxy.

(Based on Franks, 1990 pp1-2)

More recently, there have been significant developments in client–contractor relationships in the construction industry, a number of which reflect the issues raised by Banwell, almost 40 years ago. The more significant changes are considered in this chapter, along with some of the options that are open to a developer when arranging contracts for the execution of a development project.

However the process is structured, the importance of a coordinated team approach cannot be overemphasised. Poor coordination can result in an over-long development period, with a probable loss of market opportunities, and possibly a product that does not meet market requirements.

11.2   Allocation of risk

Projects involving previously developed land can involve significantly more risk than developments on a greenfield site. In particular, the site investigation may not always accurately indicate the extent of any contamination or the difficulties in carrying out the remediation works: The developer should therefore consider:

- Who is to pay the extra cost if the remediation works prove to be more expensive than was anticipated?
- Who gains the benefit, if the site proves to be less heavily contaminated, or the scope of the restoration work that is required proves to be less than was reasonably anticipated?
- How can the base line be established, in terms of what could reasonably be anticipated, in order that the extra cost or the saving can be measured?

The Institution of Civil Engineers (ICE) Conditions of Contract address the problem at clause 12. This operates on the basis that the contractor is paid for any additional costs sustained in relation to site conditions that could not reasonably have been anticipated by an experienced contractor. The concept here is that the contractor makes a reasonable assumption as to what can be expected, and includes the cost of that work in the tender price. The employer then pays the extra cost of dealing with unforeseen adverse conditions. These could, for example, include increases in the levels of contamination, or the quantities of contaminated material, or changes in the disposition of contaminated soils.

There is no parallel mechanism, however, to reduce the contract cost if conditions are better than those anticipated. The use of the ICE Conditions is therefore likely to have the effect of reducing tender values, as the contractor gains if the conditions are better than anticipated, but is protected in the event that unforeseen conditions are encountered. The difficulty with this mechanism, however, is the following uncertainties:

- on the employer's part, in relation to the final cost of the project;
- as to the period for completion, as the mechanism allows for extensions of time for any extra work involved in dealing with unforeseen conditions; and
- because the judgement as to whether the conditions encountered could reasonably have been foreseen by an experienced contractor, it is highly subjective. This issue is perhaps the most common cause of disputes in the civil engineering industry.

It may be helpful to consider the extreme positions:

(1) *Under a cost reimbursable contract, where in theory the employer bears all the risk, but gains the benefit if the conditions are better than anticipated.*

Whilst this may be considered to be an equitable way of approaching the risks, there is no incentive for the contractor to minimise costs, or to consider innovative solutions to operational problems.

(2) *At the other end of the spectrum, it is possible to draft a form of contract, or indeed to modify the standard forms, such that the total financial risk of dealing with unforeseen conditions devolves upon the contractor, who also accepts the cost of accelerating the works, to make up for the time lost in dealing with such conditions.*

Whilst a mechanism of this type theoretically provides the client with certainty as to the out-turn cost and construction period, it has two significant disadvantages.

(a) The tender price is likely to be significantly higher than would be the case if the employer accepted the risks, or if the risks were shared. The contractor is obliged to price risks which are difficult, if not impossible, to assess. He has to make an allowance for the potential cost of any additional work that may be required, and for providing extra resources to accelerate the works, to offset any delay caused by the extra work.

(b) In extreme circumstances, site remediation costs can be many times those originally estimated, and with a small or medium-sized contractor there is always the prospect of financial insolvency.

Whilst in the final analysis the developer's approach to the acceptance of risk may be driven wholly or partly by financial imperatives, which determine the contractual structure, it is nonetheless worth considering the concept of shared risk. In addition to the more obvious commercial considerations, this gives the contractor the incentive to use his knowledge and experience to minimise any additional costs that may be incurred in carrying out the works.

11.3   Selection of tenderers

Developers should consider initially whether it is intended to let the work in one or more tranches and reference is made here to section 11.5.1.

Assuming that the decision is taken to let the site remediation and infrastructure works as one contract, and the building works as another, different considerations may apply to the selection of the two lists of tenderers. The reclamation of contaminated sites normally includes bulk earth-moving work and, depending upon the remediation strategy, varying degrees of specialist engineering work. Because of the nature of the work, the engineering requirements and the regulatory issues, the earth-moving tends to be more exacting than bulk operations on other types of project. Tenderers should therefore be able to demonstrate previous experience in the successful reclamation of contaminated land.

Where the client has provided a design for the works and calls for tenders based upon that design, it is often worthwhile inviting the tenderers to offer alternatives. This is particularly relevant where a contractor has specialist knowledge of site remediation work, and is able to use his experience to propose an alternative scheme, which is either cheaper or offers better quality for a similar price.

The criteria for the selection of the building contractor may be different. It is possible, for example, that the developer has a successful ongoing relationship with a particular contractor, who has already demonstrated an ability to deliver projects on time and on budget. In these circumstances it may be considered preferable to negotiate a contract based upon prices used on previous work. The disadvantage here is the loss of the competitive element, but there are advantages in 'track record' of the contractor and the avoidance of the 'wasted' tendering costs of the unsuccessful bidders. It is arguable whether the avoidance of this unnecessary cost can be translated into savings for the developer, but it is at the very least a strong point to be used in negotiating a tender price with a preferred contractor.

In a competitive tendering situation, on either the building or the civil engineering work, it may be advantageous to restrict the tender list to three or four contractors, who have demonstrated an ability to carry out the work in question. Because of the high cost of tendering, some of the more responsible and competent contractors will not offer bids where the tender list is lengthy.

11.4   The tender documents

It is important to ensure that the tender documents clearly identify the work to be done by the contractor for the contract price. In particular, care should be taken to avoid ambiguities between the specification, drawings and bills of quantities (if any are used), as this often leads to claims for additional payment at a later date, and to the execution of unsatisfactory work. Apart from the more obvious structural, geotechnical, and design issues, the specification for remediation works should cover testing, monitoring, recording and supervision of the work.

Developers should be aware of the cost implications of the 'aggregates tax' and 'landfill tax'. As a result of this relatively recent legislation, there is con-siderable commercial advantage to be gained in treating or encapsulating contaminated materials on site, to avoid the imposition of landfill tax on off-site tipping operations. Similarly, voids created by the removal of contaminated materials may need refilling to maintain development levels. If quarried structural fill materials are used the developer will incur the costs of the aggregates tax as an integral part of the contractor's prices.

The further advantages of on-site remediation include:

- The speed of construction
- Cost
- Avoidance of disruption to local residents
- Avoidance of damage to local roads, etc.

Balanced against this are:

- The potential loss of development land, albeit (subject to the regulatory constraints) it may be possible to mitigate this problem by placing lightly contaminated materials under car parks and landscape areas.
- The risk of gas generation from certain classes of waste materials.
- The possible blight on the development, because of the presence of encapsulated contaminated material.
- The risk of environmental problems caused by the escape of leachates.

One of the recurring difficulties in site reclamation contracts is the risk that the statutory regulations governing the handling of contaminated materials, either on site or in licensed tips off site, may change during the currency of the contract. The implementation of the regulations, and indeed some require-ments, tends to vary from area to area in the UK, but the general trend is for a tightening of the regulations. This can have a significant impact on the cost of the remediation work.

If, for example, threshold levels for dealing with contaminated materials, or the contamination level at which the regulatory authorities insist that materials are placed in licensed landfills reduce, during the currency of the works, then costs can escalate very significantly. Experienced remediation contractors may be aware of this risk, and either price for it or, more likely, require some form of mechanism for recovery of any additional cost incurred.

In addition to the more general points noted in this chapter, and the particular requirements of the project, there are a number of specific issues to be addressed in the preparation of the tender documents. These include:

- Whether the rates or prices are to be fixed for the duration of the works, or alternatively, if some form of cost escalation mechanism is to be included.
- Is the contract to be let on a lump sum basis, perhaps based upon a specification and drawings, with some form of schedule of rates for the valuation of variations?
- Alternatively, is it intended that the work will be remeasured against a traditional bill of quantities, or a schedule of rates? Most of the standard forms of contract provide options to cater for the various alternatives.
- The proposed period for completion. Developers should appreciate that unreasonably short design or construction periods will impose additional risks, and possibly additional costs on the contractor, and these may well be reflected in a less competitive price for the work.
- Sectional completion dates, for defined elements of the works.
- The period allowed for the return of tenders. Again, an unrealistically short period involves the contractor in additional risk, which could be reflected in the price.
- Are there to be any liquidated and ascertained damages levied in the event of the contractor's failure to meet interim or final completion dates? If there are, then the level of damages should represent a realistic pre-estimate of the client's losses, if the contractor fails to complete. If the damages are excessive, they can be challenged in the courts. In addition, even if the damages are a genuine pre-estimate, but appear to the contractor to be excessive, he may price the risk he perceives in having to pay them as a result of delays for which he is not responsible, which may include weather, strikes, shortage of materials, etc.
- If there is a commercial advantage to the developer in securing early completion, then the offer of a bonus related to any reduction in the construction period may be advantageous. This has the added advantages of 'sweetening the pill' of the liquidated damages, and encourages the contractor to take a positive approach to the progress of the works.
- It is important to clearly specify the commencement date, as all the time-related procedures in the standard forms of contract normally rely upon this.

- Remediation work which involves bulk earth-moving is a weather-sensitive operation. Consideration should therefore be given to starting the work in the spring, or to phasing the works such that the contractor can carry out the weather-sensitive operations in the spring-to-autumn period.
- The defects correction period.
- Arrangements for the provision and release of a performance bond.
- Responsibility for insurances (employer's liability, public liability, contract works insurance and insurance for plant and equipment).
- The method of measurement, if any needs to be specified.
- The minimum amount of interim certificates.
- The bank base lending rate on contracts which provide for payment of interest on payments made late.

The tenders are an offer to enter into a legally binding contract, on the basis of the tender documents. Developers should therefore review the proposed contract at this stage, to ensure that it meets their requirements. If it does not, or the preferred bidder has qualified his tender, he should discuss and agree with the tenderer any necessary amendments, and ensure that any acceptance of the tender is made on this basis. Once a tender is accepted, an enforceable contract is made between the parties, notwithstanding any formal agreement that may subsequently be signed.

The choice of the conditions of contract is discussed in the following section.

11.5 The form of contract

11.5.1 One project, two types of work

Most redevelopment projects involving the remediation of contaminated or derelict land effectively encompass civil engineering works in the form of:

- soil remediation; or
- the disposal of contaminated materials to licensed landfills off site, and the importation of clean fill or clean cover materials; or perhaps
- the construction of on-site repository for the containment of materials with low or medium levels of contamination; together with
- the construction of the site infrastructure: roads, mains drainage, and the installation of utility services,

and building works, involving the construction of domestic, commercial or industrial units with their associated external works.

Because redevelopment projects are generally regarded as building works, many of these schemes are let using the Joint Contracts Tribunal[11.1] (JCT) forms as the basic vehicle for the contract agreement. This can create some very real difficulties, as the JCT family of contracts was designed principally to relate to building, rather than civil engineering works.

Whilst its authors contemplated the construction of pre-designed and pre-measurable foundation works, the standard building forms are, in general terms, drafted to regulate work which is constructed above ground, and which is finite and measurable. The civil engineering work on a project of this type, however, normally involves excavation, backfilling and other engineering and geo-technical work below ground level, often in materials whose levels of con-tamination, disposition, viscosity, load-bearing capabilities and other properties can only be assessed at the tender stage. These works are therefore potentially subject to significant changes in terms of scope, content and cost, and consideration should be given to the use of contract conditions which are designed to accommodate these changes.

11.5.2   *The forms of contract in common use*

The UK construction industry uses a variety of contract forms. The better known standard forms include the JCT Standard Form of Building Contract, the ICE Conditions of Contract, the ageing and now less popular General Conditions of Government Contracts for Building and Civil Engineering Works, Forms GC/Wks and CCC/Wks, the newer Engineering and Con-struction Contract (ECC) forms, which are becoming increasingly popular, and more recently a number of forms designed specifically for partnering agreements.

There are in addition numerous derivative forms, based upon the standard contracts, for example, the JCT Design and Construct Form, the ICE Minor Works Contract, the ECC Target Cost Contract. Some clients also use 'bespoke' forms written specifically for a particular project or type of work.

The JCT Conditions are probably the most commonly known and widely used in the UK construction industry, simply because of the number of pure building, as opposed to engineering, contracts which are let. The ICE Con-ditions are the most universally accepted, as they form the basis for the FIDIC contract (which is the recognised international form), the standard contracts used by many of the public utility companies in the UK, and many of the forms in current use by governments and professional organisations overseas.

[11.1] The JCT comprises a number of bodies including the Royal Institution of Chartered Sur-veyors, the Royal Institute of British Architects and the British Property Federation.

It is not possible in this short section to consider all the available contract forms and accordingly this commentary is limited to those currently in common use in the UK.

11.5.3   *The differences between the standard forms*

Possibly the most significant difference between the forms, and the point that is most relevant here, is the type of work which they were designed to cover. In general terms, the JCT contracts were designed for building works, whereas the ICE Conditions were written to cover civil engineering projects. The ECC forms and the CCC/Wks and GC/Wks contracts are promoted as covering both types of work, but tend to be used predominantly for civil, mechanical, mining and other engineering applications.

In terms of the type of work under consideration it is relevant to note that the ICE and ECC forms address the risk of unforeseen ground conditions, whereas the JCT Conditions do not. Given the problems which have been generated in the past, where both types of work have been covered by a single JCT-based contract, and the uncertainties as to the scope, content and therefore the cost of the remediation work, there is merit in letting the civil engineering work on the ICE or ECC Conditions, as these address the issues arising from the differences between the conditions which can be anticipated from the site investigation, and those actually encountered by the contractor. The construction of the buildings, once the site has been reclaimed and the infrastructure has been installed, can then be carried out under a separate JCT-based contract, which is drafted specifically for this type of work.

11.5.4   *Points to be considered in the choice of contract forms*

A helpful approach here may be to consider the objectives of the developer, as noted in the introduction to this chapter. For example:

(1)   *Is the work to be designed by independent architects and consulting engineers, or is it considered preferable to have a 'package deal', where the contractor provides design and construction?*

The more common forms now all provide alternative construct only, or design and construct options. The obvious temptation is to opt for the latter, as this offers the benefit of single-point responsibility. The disadvantage is that the contractor has considerable scope for gaining commercial advantage by savings on the quality, or possibly the scope, of the work carried out for the contract sum. This risk can however be managed or reduced by a well-considered and tightly drawn specification or 'Employer's Requirements' document, so structured that it is at the root of the contract. It is recommended that appropriate professional advice is taken as to the content of any such document, and the way in which it is incorporated into the contract.

(2)   *How critical is the completion date, and is there sufficient flexibility to award the contractor an extension of time, if he incurs problems on the reclamation operations?*

The ICE and ECC forms allow the contractor an extension of time where ground condition problems are encountered. If this benefit is withdrawn, by modifying the forms, or by using an alternative form of contract, the contractor accepts considerable extra risk and a commensurate increase in tender values can be expected.

(3)   *Who is to take the financial risks in relation to unforeseen ground conditions?*

These risks are often very significant on work of this type. It is not unknown for the final out-turn cost of remediation work on a con-taminated site to exceed the tender value by a factor of 4, sometimes due to deficiencies in the site investigation. If the contractor accepts the risk, his tender value is likely to be significantly higher, but the final out-turn cost (to the client) is more predictable.

(4)   *Is there a reason why the client wants to let all of the construction work to a single contractor?*
Alternatively, is it the intention that the site remediation work should be let to a specialist contractor as a separate preliminary works contract, and to let the building work separately? or
Is it preferable to consider a management contract, where individual specialist contractors, coordinated by a principal contractor, effectively carry out all the work?

Few contractors have in-house the capability to carry out specialist remediation work, construct the site infrastructure, and build domestic and industrial units. Under a 'traditional' contract, most contractors will sub-let specialist work, and the choice and control of the subcontractors will inevitably be motivated by commercial considerations on the part of the contractor, albeit that the position is somewhat different on a man-agement contract. Accordingly, whilst there is an attraction in single-point responsibility, in terms of managing the project as a whole, this should be balanced against the lack of control, in particular over the specialist remediation work.

Perhaps the most significant issue here is the decision as to which party accepts the financial risks inherent in carrying out the remediation work. As discussed in Chapter 5, a site investigation normally comprises a grid of boreholes and/or trial pits, orientated to include a degree of 'targeting'. This is normally done by reducing the grid interval at areas of suspected contamination, identified hot spots, or areas of particular operational difficulty. However comprehensive the site investigation may be, and no matter how thorough the historical study and the site walk-over, it only establishes the ground conditions at the position of the boreholes or trial pits, and an indication of the likely conditions below ground level. The conditions actually encountered by the contractor in reduced level or general oversite dig, or in service trench or foundation excavations, can vary widely between the points of investigation, and the scope, content and therefore the cost of the remediation work, can vary significantly from that indicated by the site investigation.

The accuracy of the investigation can sometimes be improved by reducing the grid interval, but this still may not indicate the full extent of the remediation work ultimately required, as no investigation can absolutely guarantee to find all the contamination that may be present in the site. In addition, there is the risk that the increased cost of this work may not be recovered in terms of an overall saving in the project cost, albeit that again this will depend on the apportionment of risk that the contractor and the client, respectively, accept under the terms of the contract.

11.5.5   *Partnering*

In recent years there have been a number of initiatives aimed at reducing the scope for disputes under construction contracts, and at harnessing the combined talents of the designer, supervisory consultants (architects, engineers, project managers, etc.), contractors and specialist subcontractors, in a cooperative effort to improve quality and reduce project costs and completion periods. There have been well-publicised initiatives in the UK, by Sir Michael Latham and Sir John Egan, and the process of reforming the approach to contracting has been continued by numerous public- and private-sector clients and their contractors.

Historically, many construction clients and their consultants have focused heavily upon minimising the end cost and the construction period for their projects, while contractors have been preoccupied with maximising profits and/or minimising losses. The more traditional forms of contract operate on a potentially confrontational basis, whereby the contractor can improve his profitability by identifying changes from the original concept of the project, and claiming additional payment.

Under the JCT and ICE forms, the employer's professional advisers, the architect and engineer respectively, have a quasi-judicial role in relation to such matters. The problem arises in that the architect or engineer, however professional, is the direct servant of the client, and in many cases will not always readily accept claims for additional payment, particularly if they are based on the premise that the architect's or the engineer's original design was flawed, or where they arise out of instructions that he has issued. If the contractor considers that a claim for additional payment is valid, under the terms of the contract, any reluctance or delay in accepting the merits or the quantum of the claim is a recipe for conflict.

The problem is exacerbated by the cyclical swings in workload, which have long been a feature of the UK construction industry. In periods when work is short, contractors often bid at, or below cost, and effectively gamble on making a profit from: variations to the work, additional works required as a result of poor specification, unforeseen conditions, or changes in the client's requirements. The client and his consultants often resist such claims, or at least attempt to minimise their value. This caused confrontation and has led to a lucrative and expanding workload for construction claims consultants and lawyers specialising in construction disputes.

Whilst the construction process cannot be isolated from commercial considerations, it is possible to structure the contractual arrangements in a way that encourages the parties to concentrate their efforts on the requirements of the project itself. There are various ways in which this can be achieved, but in general terms it is necessary to address the problems which previously led to conflict, in order to promote a move away from the confrontational attitudes of the past. In particular the parties should be cognisant of the following:

- Clients should assess tenders on quality, cost and the capability of the contractor to carry out the work, and not simply accept the lowest tender. The lowest tender does not always lead to the lowest out-turn cost.
- Contractual arrangements that include a sharing of risk encourage cooperation in problem-solving.
- Similarly, arrangements which include a sharing of savings encourage a positive approach, by all parties, to cost reductions
- Clear, comprehensive and unambiguous drawings, specifications and 'Employer's Requirements' documents should be provided by the client, setting out what the contractor has undertaken to do for the contract price. Poor specifications are one of the most fertile causes of claims and disputes on construction projects.
- A fair mechanism for the valuation of variations should be included in the contract. Notwithstanding the possibility of client-initiated variations, it is highly likely that on a site which has previously been developed and/or is contaminated, there will be design changes during the course of the works,

as a result of the exposure of additional areas of contamination, unforeseen site conditions, etc.

Having had regard to the foregoing issues, it is most important to ensure that the contract contains a mechanism for the speedy and inexpensive resolution of disputes.

The introduction of compulsory interim adjudication under the provisions of the Housing Grants Construction and Regeneration Act 1996, see Box 11.1, has proved very successful in persuading the parties to attempt to resolve their differences quickly and amicably.

Box 11.1   Housing Grants Construction and Regeneration Act 1996

> The Act provides that all construction contracts made in England and Wales (and there are similar provisions relating to Scottish contracts) after 1 April 1998, are to include a procedure for interim adjudication. Contracts that do not include such provisions are subject to the statutory require-ments of 'The Scheme for Construction Contracts', which provides for the resolution of disputes by adjudication within 28 days of the appointment of an adjudicator.
>
> Whilst the adjudicator's decision can be overturned or modified in a subsequent arbitration or court action, it is binding and enforceable, until such further award or decision is made. The provision therefore provides a means, for example, for a contractor or subcontractor who has been underpaid, to secure a speedy remedy. In addition, a party to a construction contract who has 'lost' in adjudication is far less likely to pursue the matters at issue in another forum, without, at the very least, attempting to settle his dispute with the other party. The courts have, to date, rigorously enforced adjudicators' decisions, even where these have been shown to be flawed, and there can be little doubt that the Act has injected realism into commercial dealings over construction contracts.

The implementation of these and similar requirements helps to achieve the underlying aim of the Latham and Egan initiatives, which was to move towards a more cooperative approach by all the parties involved in the construction process, to the ultimate benefit of the project.

Many private- and public-sector clients have acknowledged the advantages of this alternative approach, and let contracts under some form of partnering agreement. This usually involves a sharing of risk, and a sharing of any savings that accrue, if the extent of the work is overassessed in the first place, or if operational efficiencies can be developed as the work proceeds.

A common form in current use is the ECC Target Cost Contract, which works on the basis that the contractor and the client share, on a predetermined basis (for example, 50% and 50%, or 75% and 25%), any additional costs, and similarly share any savings, again on a predetermined split. There is no requirement under this form for the split on the savings to be the same as the apportionment of liability for additional cost, and there is therefore considerable flexibility in apportioning risk and reward between the parties. The form also provides other contractual mechanisms designed to encourage the parties to cooperate in value engineering, and generally in sharing ideas as to the way in which savings can be achieved and additional costs can be minimised.

There is considerable merit in operating on this basis, if the parties to the contract work in a spirit of cooperation. To a great extent, the success of the approach depends upon the development of trust between client, contractor, subcontractors and the professional team.

The Highways Agency has recently taken the initiative one step further on its most recent road maintenance contracts. Here the consulting engineer, who previously designed and supervised the work, operates in joint venture with the contractor under a 'partnering' contract with the Agency. The joint venture designs any necessary construction work, carries out all regular, cyclical and preventative maintenance work and highway inspections, supervises, and certifies the value of its own work.

In order to ensure propriety, there are various safeguards and audit procedures, but these are structured not only to protect the public purse, but to offer assistance to the joint venture in achieving the contract requirement for continuous improvement. The emphasis of the contract is on value for money and quality, and not simply on procuring the work at the least cost.

Whilst this is an imaginative extension of the current trend towards partnering agreements, it is still considered somewhat radical by many observers, and is unlikely to prove attractive to most developers, unless definite benefits can be demonstrated.

11.6   Summary

The selection of suitable contractors is essential to the success of a property development project. Experience does count when dealing with complex situations, especially where contamination or other adverse ground conditions are involved. For complex developments involving significant civil engineering works in site preparation and the provision of infrastructure, it may be appropriate to have two separate tender lists – one for the engineering works and the other for the building works.

Similarly, the developer and the professional team should consider very carefully the advisability, or otherwise, of procuring the works under a single contract. Site remediation and extensive infrastructure works are more suited to being tendered under an engineering contract, such as the ICE Conditions, with the JCT forms being used for the building elements. Regardless, however, of the form of contracts used, it is essential that the contract clearly states the nature of the work to be undertaken and is unambiguous.

Construction contracts have, by their nature, tended to be confrontational, with employers seeking to minimise the costs and contractors seeking to achieve extra profit out of the variations. The end result is, all too often, conflict that ends in court, with the main beneficiaries being the lawyers and the experts who are called to give evidence. Recent moves towards a partnering approach should help to reduce the confrontation.

11.7 Checklist

- Does the project involve contamination or extensive infrastructure works? If so, it may be appropriate to separate the civil engineering and building works.
- Consider whether the contractors on the tender list, or lists, are suitably experienced in the works involved and have the financial standing appropriate to the project.
- Does the contract documentation clearly set out what the employer requires and is it unambiguous?
- Allow sufficient time for the tenderers to give proper consideration to the project and prepare a suitable bid.
- Remember, accepting the lowest tender price may not always produce the best solution.
- Consider whether a partnering arrangement is appropriate to the project.

Chapter 12
Marketing and Sales

12.1 Introduction

The ultimate objective of property development is to find tenants or purchasers for newly constructed or converted buildings and one of the most important aspects of the process is good marketing of the product. Without adequate exposure to the market the developer cannot be assured that the best price or rent has been achieved and indeed the property may even fail to sell or let.

Newman (1997, p. 131) expresses some doubt as to whether the term 'marketing' is correctly applied when talking of property disposal. He questions whether, when instructed by a landlord to dispose of a property, the agent truly practises marketing. He does, however, recognise that in the case of a new development 'provided that the agent is brought on board at a sufficiently early stage', it is clear that a marketing role is performed.

He describes marketing as being a three-stage process of finding out what the customer will buy and at what price, reorganising internally to provide this (at a profit) and then offering the service or product. The three stages he names as Find out, Adapt and Communicate (Figure 12.1). Markets are not static; they continually evolve and change, which produces a view of marketing that is circular and continually moving forward.

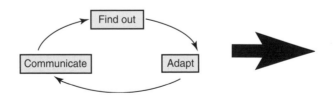

Figure 12.1 A continual process of finding out, adapting and communicating. (Source: Newman, 1997, p. 15.)

216

This circular motion continually moving forward is particularly apt when considering new developments. Marketing not only has to take account of what is available and what the market is demanding at present but also has to reflect the considerable time lag associated with property development, in order to forecast what might be available and in demand when the project is ready for occupation.

In order to succeed, the developer, and indeed the whole development team, needs to have a clear understanding of what the product comprises. Only then can decisions be taken as to how it should be marketed. This involves careful analysis of the market for the proposed buildings, considered in Chapter 3 as part of the project inception, and market research. The research should either confirm the developer's analysis of the market or enable him or her to formulate a new analysis based on the additional information. It could also result in the developer abandoning the project.

In order to have any value, property market research must be entirely objective. If it is designed to provide the answer that the developer hopes to hear, then the outcome may be disastrous for the project. Skewed results, arising for example from an unrepresentative sample, may lull the developer into a false sense of security by making the market appear to be larger than it actually is.

Developers rarely set out to market the location of their project, as opposed to the project itself, but location can form a very important part of marketing, although by no means all developments can occupy prime sites. When development projects are truly innovative, in terms of their location whether greenfield or brownfield, the developer may have to rely unusually heavily on the quality or uniqueness of the development in order to attract purchasers or tenants. It may also be more difficult for them to attract bank finance or a forward sale of the investment (see Chapter 10). Overcoming the problems surrounding developments in new or hitherto untried locations and promoting new concepts may be achieved through 'branding' of the development or the developer.

12.2   Branding

Branding is part of the broader function of marketing that consists of 'the development and maintenance of sets of product attributes and values which are coherent, appropriate, distinctive, protectable and appealing to customers' (Murphy, 1992, p. 3). He refers to the term 'marketing mix' as being used to describe the process of developing a new brand, whereby the provider of a product or service assembles a series of attributes and blends these together in a unique way.

The larger private house-builders in the UK tend to be very good at branding their corporate identities and, perhaps to a lesser extent, they also brand their developments. The television and press image of developers such as Bellway, Bryant Homes and Redrow tends to be very strong and instantly recognisable; this is carried through into the developments themselves with flags and signage. Within the constraints of planning permissions, housing developers also try to project their image through the style of their houses. Whilst the materials and some external details may change from site to site, reflecting the nature of the locality or the preferences of the planning authority, floor layouts and specifications will often make the house instantly recognisable as the product of a particular developer.

The private house-builders are very conscious of their image, which is understandable as they exist to sell houses to the house-buying public, many of whom are very discerning. Social housing developers on the other hand often give the impression of being less market conscious. Whether this is because they do not see a need to project an image, or because they have waiting lists of prospective tenants, may be debated. Many housing associations serve a local need, or specialise in providing a particular type of housing, such as sheltered accommodation for the elderly, which may not need marketing. Others serve a much wider market, both geographically and in terms of housing type, which could benefit from a degree of branding.

One such example is the Joseph Rowntree Foundation's CASPAR developments. The acronym stands for city-centre apartments for single people at affordable rents. Two of these developments have been completed to date (see Chapter 15), and the model may be replicable throughout Britain, subject to suitable sites being available.

The brand name performs a number of key roles:

- It identifies the product or service, and allows the consumer to specify, reject, or recommend brands.
- It communicates messages to the consumer. In this role the name can be either an overt or a subconscious communicator.
- It functions as a particular piece of legal property in which the manufacturer can invest and through law is protected from competitive attack or trespass. Through time and use, a name can become a valuable asset.

(Murphy, 1992 p86)

The brand name, acronym or logo can be an important marketing tool, one which can be used solely by the originator, or may be used more widely, such as through licensing or franchising, giving greater geographic coverage for the brand. It is also complex in that it may perform different functions and mean different things according to the function of the individual observer relative to the market. Furthermore, there is a risk that the branding may be imitated, with the resultant need for action to be taken against the imitator, although this is perhaps less likely in the field of property development than might be the case with consumer goods, where even the shape and colour scheme of the packaging may constitute imitation.

Unlike their residential developer counterparts, commercial and industrial developers tend not to be strong on branding as a means of projecting their corporate image. They do, however, often seek to develop strong branding for individual developments, as in the case of the BullRing case study in Chapter 15.

12.3   Marketing tools

A variety of different tools and techniques are available for the marketing of new developments. This section briefly describes some of these.

12.3.1   *Advertisements*

Developers and their marketing teams need to examine four important questions regarding advertisements:

(1)   Will the advertisement be noticed?
(2)   What is the advertisement saying?
(3)   Is the message relevant and persuasive?
(4)   Will it let or sell the development?

The worst possible scenario from the developer's perspective is for the advertisement to be noticed and to convey a strong message, which attracts prospective tenants or purchasers to visit the area, only for them to then be attracted to a competing development. This is another argument in favour of involving the marketing team at an early phase in the development process.

A great deal of property advertising gives the impression of being unfocused and, as such, may be of questionable value. The main property journals in the UK – *Estates Gazette* and *Property Week* – carry the bulk of the national property advertising. These journals are mainly, but not exclusively, targeted at property professionals. This is fine if the objective is to reach corporate property advisers or in-house real estate executives, but advertising in these journals may be less cost-effective if the target audience is end-users in a particular discipline, e.g. accountancy, law, recruitment or distribution, or if the target is a perceived sub-regional market. In order to reach this type of audience, the developer needs to consider advertising in specialist journals, newspapers and magazines, or devote a larger proportion of the advertising budget to local or regional advertising.

Even if the major part of the advertising effort is devoted to specialist or local publication, developers may still consider it appropriate to advertise in the property journals. However, this may be regarded more as prestige or corporate advertising. Advertising placed in specialist or local publications is likely to reach a relatively wide audience, although reaching a different audience to the property journals, with only a small percentage of readers actually being in the market for new premises. Given this situation, the developer may also wish to consider some of the more targeted forms of marketing discussed below.

12.3.2   Brochures

These can be anything from a double-sided A4 sheet to a multi-page sewn or stapled glossy booklet. An approach often used for large new developments, whether residential, commercial or industrial, is a pocketed folder that will last the life of the development, into which loose inserts can be placed as each phase is released onto the market. Similar loose inserts can also be used to provide information regarding specifications and more general facts about the location of the development.

The brochure should contain factual information that is relevant to the development. All too often the information they provide is of limited use as it provides only part of the story. For example, sales particulars for a new residential development might say that the tenure is leasehold but offer no further details as to the duration of the lease, the ground rent payable and whether it is subject to review. Similarly, letting particulars for a commercial property may omit to provide details of the lease term being offered or information as to the rent required. There also appears to be a growing tendency for sales literature not to provide any information as to council tax or business rates assessments, although for new developments these may not have been assessed at the time the literature was prepared.

Historically, developers and their agents in the UK have tended to provide little, if any, local demographic information in their promotion literature. To some extent this may have been attributable to a lack of ready access to such information but this has changed with the availability of online data from National Statistics, referred to in Chapter 3. It is to be hoped therefore that more use will be made of this type of information in the future.

One reason for the paucity of information contained in some sales particulars is a reluctance on the part of some agents to provide any information that may inadvertently mislead or misdescribe the property. Whilst this is obviously important, there can be a tendency to take it to extremes and even a reluctance to state fairly important facts that can easily be verified by talking to the client, the solicitor or the local authority. 'Puffing' statements, which describe properties in superlative language, such as 'outstandingly appointed' to describe a fairly standard specification house, are of little or no benefit and often irritate potential buyers who feel that their time has been wasted.

12.3.3   Direct mail

Having produced an attractive brochure that shows the development to best advantage, the next task is to get the information in front of the decision-maker. Estate agents and developers maintain lists of people and organisations known to be interested, or perhaps more accurately 'believed to be interested', in the types of properties they are marketing. These people and organisations will be the first targets for the promotional literature but then the target audience has to be widened. Mailing lists can be purchased for specific categories of organisations, such as 'financial services' or 'legal firms', and for both residential and commercial developments mailings can be organised on the basis of postcodes.

Even though direct mailing can be organised to reach fairly specific target audiences, either by activity or geography, it is still a fairly coarse method of communication. Therefore the developer has to decide whether or not to mail the full development brochure to the selected audience or whether to send a 'taster' in the form of a 'mini-brochure' or 'flyer', with a postage-paid return slip for the recipient to use in order to obtain further details. Cost has important implications here; full brochures may cost say £1–5 each, compared to less than 50 p each for a mini-brochure or even less for a flyer. Postage costs are also likely to be considerably greater for a full brochure, as if it exceeds more than three or four A4 pages it will probably cost more than the minimum postage rate to send.

Personalised mailshots, addressed to a named individual, tend to be more effective in terms of being noticed than those that are sent to 'the property director' or 'the company secretary'.

In order to attract the attention of prospective tenants or purchasers, developers have sometimes tried mailing free gifts, such as paperweights or pens. The thinking is that they will remain on the recipient's desk for a longer period than the brochure. Very often these gifts are of little actual use, are cheaply manufactured and are consigned to the waste bin immediately upon receipt. Therefore unless the gift has some specially significant relevance to the development being promoted, this form of direct mail is unlikely to be cost-effective.

12.3.4   E-marketing

Most major commercial and industrial agencies and property consultancy firms have their own websites. Many of these are extremely attractive and informative, see for example King Sturge & Co. *www.kingsturge.co.uk* and Lambert Smith Hampton *www.lsh.co.uk*. They provide means of searching their registers of available properties but, at present, the websites are probably regarded more as a corporate marketing tool than as a means of selling or letting property. Several firms, including both of those referred to here, also provide access to their research reports. Some firms, such as Insignia Richard Ellis *www.richardellis.co.uk*, provide limited online access to their research with more extensive access being available on subscription, while other firms are less open with information, preferring to use their websites simply for corporate promotion.

EGPropertyLink *www.propertylink.co.uk* is a listing service carrying property details and Estates Gazette interactive (*EGi*) *www.egi.co.uk* is a news, research and information service, containing details of property transactions, a companies database and relocation directory.

Most of the well-known residential developers, such as Bryant Homes *www.bryant.co.uk* and George Wimpey *www.wimpey.co.uk* also have websites that enable prospective purchasers to find new developments and obtain details of house types. Many firms of residential estate agents use the internet as a sales tool, either with their own websites or through marketing groups. Some of these are quite sophisticated in terms of the information provided, with full details of houses for sale, including colour photographs.

Some property investment companies, such as Bruntwood Estates in Manchester *www.bruntwood.co.uk*, include details of their property portfolios and accommodation vacancies on their websites. Birmingham Alliance, the consortium developing the new BullRing in Birmingham city centre (see Chapter 15) keeps potential tenants, and others interested in the development, informed about the development through the use of three webcams mounted on the roof of the 20-storey Rotunda, *www.thenewbullring.co.uk*. These provide regularly updated images to the website, showing work in progress on the ground. This developer has also provided an education centre as part of its site presence, catering for school visits.

12.3.5   Show suites and houses

One decision that a developer will need to take fairly early on in the development process is whether sales and/or lettings are going to be undertaken by an in-house sales team or through an estate agent. Even developers that have their own sales teams will, on occasion, use agents instead of or in conjunction with their own staff. This may come about, for example, in situations where a firm of agents has introduced a site to a developer or has been otherwise instrumental in assembling the site.

Show suites and houses can play a very important part in letting and selling offices and residential developments but a great deal depends on the staff that welcomes potential tenants and buyers to these facilities. A poor impression, created say by a lack of interest in the product, can be extremely off-putting and may result in a lost letting or sale. Unless therefore the estate agent has a well-established relationship with the developer, it may be in the best interests of the development for show facilities to be staffed by members of the developer's team, who can be fully trained in the product. Where developments are taking place on previously developed land, that training should ensure that the sales team is fully informed as to the history of the site and can respond knowledgeably with regard as to the site preparation work that has been carried out.

12.3.6   *Events and public relations*

Breaking the ground, whether it is with a silver spade or mechanical excavator, and 'topping out' ceremonies provide good opportunities to attract potential buyers or tenants to the site and to achieve publicity for the development. Press coverage through editorial columns and property pages in local newspapers and trade journals can be more effective than advertising but it needs to be properly planned and not simply regarded as an incidental spin-off.

Cocktail parties in show suites and 'agents' breakfasts' in industrial units also bring the project to the attention of people and organisations that might influence the decision-making process. The timing and duration of such events need to be carefully thought out. People are perhaps less inclined to spend what probably amounts to half a day, attending a lunch-time function than they might have done a decade or more ago. An hour at the beginning or end of the working day is probably more acceptable and more likely to attract the people who will show a serious interest in the development.

12.3.7   *Site boards and hoardings*

Perhaps the most effective and often the most overlooked means of marketing a new property development, site boards provide the best opportunity for developers to get their message across to local people and passers-by. They can include brief details of the accommodation to be provided and an artist's impression of the development. Information regarding progress of the project, such as anticipated dates for release of phases, can be shown on site boards, and bulletins regarding possible disruption, say during piling operations, can be incorporated so as to communicate with local residents.

Hoardings and site fencing are essential features of property developments, to protect both the public and the site workers, as well as to prevent theft from the site, but they need not be dull and uninteresting. With some thought, site hoardings can form an important part of the marketing package (see Figure 12.2) and developers might also wish to consider whether or not to include safe viewing areas within the site hoarding so that people can see what is happening.

Figure 12.2 Good use of hoarding around a development site.

If the new development is not situated on a main thoroughfare the developer will need to consider the possibility of finding suitable off-site advertising locations. These may include poster sites, most of which are controlled by the larger outdoor advertising contractors, where brief information about the development and directional details can be displayed. Alternatives might include finding sites at main road junctions, where information and directional boards can be displayed, although there may be difficulties in obtaining planning permission for large off-site boards. Another option, especially if suitable sites cannot be found or if there are planning permission problems, is the use of small directional arrows, containing the developer's logo and the site name, fixed to lampposts. These may be accepted by the local authority, or even insisted upon, on the principle that they indicate a clear route to the site for delivery vehicles. They also show the way for prospective purchasers or tenants, as do for residential developments the yellow AA signs with a house logo and the estate name, although they do not provide any additional information for passers-by.

Whatever is decided upon in terms of using site boards and hoardings, decisions need to be taken fairly early in the development process, certainly well before a start on site, as planning permission will almost certainly be required. Where developments receive any form of public funding, say from the European Union or a Regional Development Agency, developers should be aware that the funding body will, almost certainly, wish to see its contribution acknowledged on the site boards. It may also be necessary, or indeed desirable, to include that acknowledgement in the development advertisements, brochures and other literature.

12.3.8   *Marketing and promotion costs*

Marketing costs will vary quite substantially from one development to another, depending upon the tools employed. For strategic projects, such as the new BullRing in Birmingham, described in Chapter 15, marketing may extend over a period of several years before the development is completed and occupied. The objective of this advance marketing is to persuade tenants, especially those who will 'anchor' the development and be major contributors to its success, to sign agreements to lease at the earliest possible date. This is especially important with retail developments, as these tenants can then be used to entice other retailers – for example, Debenhams and Selfridges will have department stores in the new BullRing, with other tenants including Next, Benetton and Gap.

Although the costs vary from one development to another, for the purpose of the development appraisal a useful rule-of-thumb is to assume a figure of between half and two-thirds the commission that would be payable to the sales or letting agent (see section 4.7)

12.4   Communicating information

The marketing tools described above are largely about creating awareness and providing information. It is once the recipient has received the information that it achieves its highest importance, for it is then that the success or otherwise of the marketing will be determined.

Bevan (1991, p. 46) identified five quite distinct roles in the process of buying property:

(1)   Gatekeeper
(2)   Influencer
(3)   Decision-maker
(4)   Buyer
(5)   User

These roles may exist side by side, they may be fulfilled by individuals or groups and an individual or group may participate in all or any of the roles. He described the concept of roles in the context of buying a house but they are equally applicable to commercial or industrial property.

(1)   *Gatekeeper* – the family member who collects the details of houses from the estate agent, or the agent acting for a prospective tenant who receives details in response to a 'client's requirement' to other agents. Either may reject the development with little more than a cursory glance at the information. The reasons for rejection may be quite clear, for example the accommodation or specification does not meet requirements. However, they may be more obtuse, such as the general image conveyed by the sales particulars, the lack of information provided, or even the artist's impression of what the development will look like when completed.

(2)   *Influencer* – someone who helps to shape, or even distort, a view of the product. This could be someone already living or working on the development that complains about the failure of the developer to rectify faults in the building. It could also take the form of adverse press comment or information regarding crime statistics.

(3)   *Decision-maker* – the person who receives the information, advice and analyses of others – whether they be comments from children about moving away from their friends or representations from employees who will have to travel further in order to get to work – and then makes the decision to acquire a specific property. It has often been said that an important factor in deciding on the location of a new industrial building is travelling time from the managing director's home. Whilst this may not be entirely true, the availability of a suitable labour force is an important factor and the author is aware of one factory relocation where the final decision on a new building was decided on the view of Snowdonia that the chief executive would have from his office.

(4)   *Buyer* – the person who actually implements the deal. Bevan (1991) notes that there is often confusion between the two roles of buyer and decision-maker, although they may be the same person. It is the buyer who negotiates the price, the final specification, any extras that may be required, rent-free periods or other concessions and who instructs the lawyers in respect of the transaction.

(5)   *User* – any person or group who participates in the use of the building once it is occupied. In the case of a house this may be other family members or friends, whose opinions will influence the decision-maker.

Commercial organisations may seek to canvass the views of customers regarding any possible relocation.

One important aspect that needs to be covered is information regarding site history and remediation or site preparation. As referred to above, sales staffs need to be well-trained in order to deal with enquiries of this nature but, all too often, they do not receive any such training. Some developers are extremely open insofar as this type of information is concerned, with site managers and sales teams being able to provide technical information, even to the extent of displaying 'before' photographs in the sales office. Other developers insist that enquiries of this nature are referred to regional or head offices, or to solicitors. Regardless of how they are handled, openness must be the best policy in dealing with enquiries regarding site history and contamination, otherwise the deal will probably fail when the prospective tenant or purchaser finds out through other means. The developer may even end up in court on a charge of misrepresentation. The Scottish and Northern Ireland Forum for Environmental Research has produced a useful booklet entitled *Communicating Understanding of Contaminated Land Risks* (SNIFFER, 1999), available through the Scottish Environmental Protection Agency (SEPA).

12.5   Selling the development

One decision the developer will have to take at a fairly early point in the development process is who is going to sell the development. For many developers, such as major house-builders, the decision is usually straightforward – the company's in-house team will handle sales. Usually this means a directly employed sales force reporting to a sales manager or director, although occasionally this might mean a firm of estate agents with an exclusive marketing agreement with a developer, possibly on a local or regional basis.

For other developers without an established sales team, or who are trying to break into a new area, the preferred option may well be to appoint a local firm of estate agents or the local office of a national firm. Quite often the developer might decide to appoint the agent who introduced him or her to the site, and the agent may well expect this to happen, as site acquisition fees tend to be very small when compared to the sales or letting commissions from a large development. An important development can produce income for several years, compared to the one-off site acquisition fee, not just in terms of the commission paid by the developer but also in commissions receivable from people or firms moving onto the new development, who instruct the estate agent to dispose of their old properties.

From the developer's perspective, appointment of the introducing agent as the sales and/or letting agent needs to be considered very carefully. Unless part of a large, departmentalised firm, the introducing agent may be very good at identifying development potential and putting deals together but less good at selling the developed product. Even when this is apparent, the developer may be reluctant not to offer the sales instruction to the person who introduced the site, for fear of alienating the person or firm concerned to the extent that they will not be offered any more sites. In such a situation a frank discussion needs to be held, at which the developer can express his or her concerns and the agent can suggest ways in which the problem may be overcome.

One possibility may be to appoint two firms of agents with joint responsibility for selling or letting the development. Ideally the agents should complement each other, rather than being seen to be in competition – possibly with one agent being local to the development (quite possibly the introducing agent) with the benefit of local knowledge, whilst the other has a regional or national presence. So far as estate agents' fees are concerned, there are no fixed scales but a sole agent will be expecting around 10% of the first year's rent for an industrial or commercial letting, rising to 15% when joint agents are instructed. Fee-sharing arrangements for joint agency may vary, for example the commission may be divided equally between the agents, regardless of who does the deal, or it may be divided on the basis of 10% to the successful agent and 5% to the other firm. For residential developments the selling commission will vary according to the size of the development and the price of the house but it will probably fall in the range of 1.5–3% of the selling price; alternatively, the agreement between the developer and agent may be on the basis of a fixed sum per dwelling regardless of price.

When the developer is handling sales and/or lettings in-house, staff will have to be appointed and trained, sales offices and show units provided and furnished. The developer may have a number of regionally based key sales staff who will move from development to development, taking up their responsibilities shortly before the marketing campaign for the new development commences. Locally recruited sales people on short-term contracts may support these key staff for the duration of the development. The cost of direct selling will vary between developers but is unlikely to be any less than the cost of using agents. It may well be significantly more expensive than employing agents but the developer will have the satisfaction of knowing that the sales team is working exclusively on his or her project.

12.6   Closing the deal

The sale or letting cannot be regarded as binding until such time as the contract or agreement to lease has been exchanged; even then it should not be regarded as completed until the purchase money, or the first quarter's rent is in the bank. Deals do fail even after contracts or agreements have been signed, possibly because the requirements or financial situation of the tenant or purchaser have changed. Any deposit may be forfeit but it is unlikely to be in the best interests of the developer to sue for specific performance as the strength of the tenant's covenant may be significantly reduced (see Chapter 10), or the purchaser may not have the funds to complete the purchase.

Therefore, even after the contract or agreement to lease has been signed, developers and/or their agents need to keep a close eye on progress of the transaction through the legal process. This is especially important where an early letting or sale has been agreed and completion may be a year or more away. One situation that developers and their agents need to bear in mind, when agreeing pre-lets or forward sales, is the possibility that the market may improve before the building has been completed. There is then a temptation for the developer to renege on the deal, in the hope of obtaining a higher rent or price, with the result that the intending tenant or purchaser may decide to sue the developer for specific performance.

Procedures need to be put in place for ensuring that solicitors are properly instructed, and it has been known for them not to have been instructed because the agent thought the developer was doing it and vice versa. The solicitor needs to be made fully aware of the terms of the transaction and, most importantly, the rationale behind any special clauses or conditions to be inserted in the lease, or restrictive covenants and retained rights in the transfer. If this is not done, the intentions of the parties may not be adequately reflected in the final legal documents. It should also be clear who is to deal with enquiries before contract – solicitor, agent, developer or project manager.

The solicitor should be instructed to alert either the agent or the developer if the sale or letting appears to be running into difficulties, or if any information comes to light after contracts have been exchanged that might indicate that the transaction is in jeopardy. The agent or the developer's sales negotiator should remain in regular contact with the tenant or purchaser in order to be able to respond to any queries or problems that might arise.

12.7   Summary

Effective marketing is a fundamental part of the property development process and, like the land itself, may be regarded as an essential component, for, without successful sales or lettings, the objective of the development would not be achieved. Many different tools are available for the developer to market the project but the use of appropriate tools should be informed by good market research. It is all too easy to spend large sums of money on marketing and still fill to reach the right audience for the property.

Branding is a creative process (Murphy, 1992, p. 12). The marketing of new property developments also calls for creativity. Many of the marketing tools available today are well tried and tested but others, such as e-marketing are relatively new. The development team needs to give careful consideration to how best the target audience may be reached and this is likely to involve a combination of tools.

There are pros and cons regarding the use of estate agents as opposed to in-house sales teams. Estate agents should, theoretically at least, be able to reach a much wider audience than a developer. This includes casual enquirers passing the high street office window of the agent, a facility lacked by most developers. For the developer, the in-house team provides an exclusive service but it has to be trained and managed.

Regardless of the sales arrangements used, the developer needs to ensure that adequate procedures are in place for instructing the legal team and monitoring the transaction through to completion.

12.8 Checklist

- Prepare well-designed and informative sales details.
- Locate sales boards in highly visible places.
- Appoint a marketing team at an early stage.
- Ensure advertising is aimed at the correct audience.
- Consider how best to sell or let the development – in-house or through an agent.
- Ensure adequate procedures are in place to record details of enquirers, to instruct solicitors and monitor the transaction.

Part Four
Design

Introduction

Part Four deals with the use of land, including masterplanning. Good urban design is critical, particularly in respect of encouraging people to move back into city centres; this includes transport issues and security – both personal security and with respect to buildings. It is essential to get the mix of uses right, particularly where an inner-city site is being redeveloped. Old buildings, possibly derelict or otherwise unattractive by virtue of their use, may surround such a site and account must be taken of these issues. A number of case studies are discussed in detail.

Chapter 13 deals with land use and design and discusses the importance of good design, including density and mixing uses. It also deals with security in design and transport issues.

Chapter 14 looks at masterplanning, which provides an opportunity for land owners, developers and local authorities to work together on forward planning the evolvement of a particular area. This chapter also describes four master-plans, Sheffield city centre, Ipswich Wet Dock, Cambourne and Tower Hamlets – all very different scenarios but all working to the same aim.

Chapter 15 considers buildings and concepts, and in particular looks at three examples: a development of strategic importance in a major city centre; city-centre living; and provision of homes for key workers. The chapter also looks at how to accommodate new industrial development and briefly discusses the proposals for the new BMW Group UK head office and Rolls-Royce man-ufacturing plant.

Chapter 13

Land Use and Design

13.1 Introduction

> Good urban design is essential if we are to produce attractive, high quality, sustainable places in which people will want to live, work and relax. We do not have to put up with shoddy, unimaginative and second-rate buildings and urban areas. There is a clamour for better designed places which inspire and can be cherished, places where vibrant communities can grow and prosper.
>
> (DETR, 2000f)

These sentiments were expressed by Nick Raynsford MP, then Minister for Housing, Planning and Construction, and Stuart Lipton, Chairman of the Commission for Architecture and the Built Environment (CABE), in the Foreword to the joint DETR/CABE design guide *By Design*, which was published in May 2000. The guide seeks to provide sound, practical advice and has been drawn up around a limited number of simple but compelling principles. These include appreciating that good design is important everywhere and that the creation of successful places depends on the skills of designers, together with the vision and commitment of those who employ them. It also recognises that no two places are identical and that there is not a blueprint for good design.

Similarly, it is not the objective of this chapter to lay down design principles, or to suggest what constitutes good design. Rather, its purpose is to examine some of the main issues affecting the design of new developments. In doing so, it should be recognised that good design, whether of individual buildings or entire developments, should reflect the needs of the people who live, work or visit the newly created spaces. To quote Planning Policy Guidance Note 1 *General Policy and Principles*:

'New buildings and their curtilages have a significant effect on the character and quality of an area. They define public spaces, streets and vistas and inevitably create the context for future development. These effects will often be to the benefit of an area but they can be detrimental.... Good design should be the aim of all those involved in the development process and should be encouraged everywhere. Good design can help promote sustainable development; improve the quality of the existing environment; attract business and investment and reinforce civic pride and a sense of place. It can help to secure continued public acceptance of necessary new development.'

(DTLR, 2001a, paragraphs 13 and 15)

13.2   The importance of good urban design

Urban design is a complex phenomenon which, for all its undoubted importance, even its advocates and practitioners have difficulty grasping (RICS and DoE, 1996, p. 7). The term *urban design* is used to encompass anything from modest environmental proposals to plans for a complete new settlement. It can include the exercise of aesthetic control by the local planning authority and the physical outcome, intentional or otherwise, of the market-led development process.

The Urban Task Force placed considerable emphasis on the importance of good design in urban regeneration, with ten of the Task Force's 105 recommendations being directly related to design issues and at least a further nine having significant design implications (Urban Task Force, 1999). The Government responded to these recommendations in the Urban White Paper *Our Towns and Cities: the future* (DETR, 2000a) and has taken forward or indicated agreement with many of the recommendations.

A commitment to quality and creativity in the way in which we design buildings, public spaces and transport networks will form the basis for the sustainable city of the future (Urban Task Force, 1999, p. 39). However, in the view of Parfect and Power, 'our somewhat blinkered national pre-occupation with other issues ... does not on the whole serve to focus attention upon the need to promote enhanced urban quality within the range of our towns and cities, where most people live' (Parfect & Power, 1997, p. 19). The authors went on to express the view that the problem was not one of a lack of professional expertise in Britain but, more often, the lack of the means or perception (whether national or local), or even the political will, to harness the available expertise in an informed manner in order to deal with the problems on the ground.

According to Haughton and Hunter:

'the built environment of the city presents mixed challenges: reusing or demolishing historic buildings, which are aesthetically pleasing but seemingly functionally outdated; accommodating or removing ancient patterns of narrow streets; encouraging new architectural designs or insisting on reference to existing building styles.'

(Haughton & Hunter, 1994, p. 103)

Challenges will manifest themselves in reconciling local planning authorities' aspirations for good design and possibly the expectations of conservation groups, with the commercial viability requirements of developers whilst, at the same time, having due regard for the local context of developments. Failure to address these challenges may result in developments that fail to achieve the expected financial return, or are of mediocre design (or both) and which the local community opposes. The objectives of urban design may therefore be seen as those set out in Box 13.1.

Urban design objectives, such as those outlined in Box 13.1, achieve nothing by themselves, they can only have any impact if they are translated into fact through the development process. Urban design objectives can only be achieved through physical expression in the form of buildings, structures and spaces. Together these influence what goes on in public and private spaces; they inform and impact upon the lives of those who work, live or visit new developments. Effective design policy and design guidance is therefore likely to focus on how, in a particular context, development form can achieve the urban design objectives. Box 13.2 describes the aspects of urban form that the development team needs to consider in order to translate urban design objectives into development realities.

The DETR/CABE publication, *By Design*, contains a series of prompts that are intended to aid thinking about urban design principles. It makes the point that, in any real situation some of these prompts will conflict and some will benefit some people more than others (DETR, 2000f, p. 18). Nevertheless, they should assist the design process by ensuring that consideration is given to a wide range of concerns and assist the creative resolution of potential conflicts. All members of the development team should perhaps study them, in order that they might gain an insight into the issues involved in designing a sustainable new development. The rest of this chapter looks at some specific issues that are likely to affect the development.

13.3   Development densities

'Urban cramming' is feared by developers and occupiers alike. High-density developments bring with them connotations of streets of terraced and back-to-

Box 13.1   Objectives of urban design

Character *A place with its own identity*	To promote character in townscape and landscape by responding to and reinforcing locally distinctive patterns of development, landscape and culture.
Continuity and enclosure *A place where public and private spaces are clearly distinguished*	To promote the continuity of street frontages and the enclosure of space by development which clearly defines private and public areas.
Quality of the public realm *A place with attractive and successful outdoor areas*	To promote public spaces and routes that are attractive, safe, uncluttered and work effectively for all in society, including disabled and elderly people.
Ease of movement *A place that is easy to get to and move through*	To promote accessibility and local permeability by making places that connect with each other and are easy to move through, putting people before traffic and integrating land uses and transport.
Legibility *A place that has a clear image and is easy to understand*	To promote legibility through development that provides recognisable routes, intersections and landmarks to help people find their way around.
Adaptability *A place that can change easily*	To promote adaptability through development that can respond to changing social, technological and economic conditions.
Diversity *A place with variety and choice*	To promote diversity and choice through a mix of compatible developments and uses that work together to create viable places that respond to local needs.

Source: DETR, 2000f, p. 15.

back housing, as well as the concrete blocks and deck-access flats of the 1960s. Avoiding this image resulted, during the second half of the twentieth century, in car-dependent residential developments of 20–30 dwellings per hectare. In part this was driven by market demand, with house buyers wanting their own private space, but it was largely encouraged by the policies of local planning

Box 13.2   Aspects of urban form in new developments.

Layout: Urban structure	The layout contains the framework of routes that connect parts of the development to each other, to local areas and beyond; and spaces that separate, define and distinguish areas one from another.
Layout: Urban grain	Smaller-scale patterns of arranging street blocks, plots and buildings in a development and the way they relate to each other.
Landscape	Recognition and use of natural features and ecologies; using these as part of the new development and blending them with new landscapes.
Density and mix	The amount of development on a given piece of land and the range of uses. The vitality and viability of the development may both be determined by the density and mix. Expressed in a number of ways including plot ratio (commercial developments) or numbers of dwellings or habitable rooms for housing.
Scale: Height	The size of a building in relation to surroundings and its visual impact on views, vistas and skylines. May be expressed as number of floors or height to parapet or ridge. Can also be considered in terms of street width, e.g. for avoidance of a canyon effect.
Scale: Massing	Three-dimensional effect of the arrangement, volume and shape of a building or group of buildings, relative to other buildings and spaces.
Appearance: Details	Craftmanship, decoration, styles, lighting and building techniques combining to present the visual appearance of buildings or structures.
Appearance: Materials	The contribution made by the building or structure to the appearance and character of an area through the pattern, colour, texture and durability of the materials used.

Based on DETR, 2000f, p. 16

authorities seeking to avoid 'overdevelopment' and ensure off-street car parking for both residents and visitors.

Lewis Keeble considered the question of residential development densities and observed: 'the Englishman's preference for a semi-detached house over a terraced house if he cannot afford a detached house causes some people surprise and worry. Cost, density and appearance are all relevant to this.' He noted that a normal plot of 30 ft (9.14 m) width by 120 ft (36.55 m) produced a density of 12 houses to the acre (29.5 per hectare) but that if the plot width was reduced to 20 ft (6.09 m), the density increased to 18 houses to the acre (44.5 per hectare). Reducing the back garden depth from 60 ft (18.27 m) to 40 ft (12.18 m) further increased the density to nearly 22 houses to the acre (54 per hectare). In his view: 'many architects would regard the last named as a very satisfactory density and the first named as very unsatisfactory yet so far as architectural effect is concerned the results could be identical' (Keeble, 1969, p. 270).

The Urban Task Force looked carefully at the relationship between density and design and concluded that, the lower the density (say 20 dwellings per hectare), the larger the amount of area that is occupied by buildings, roads and open space. The result of this is to push over 60% of the houses beyond an acceptable 500 m or five-minute walking time to public transport and local facilities. This form of layout promotes excessive car use and makes it difficult to justify a bus route (Urban Task Force, 1999, p. 60).

Increasing densities to even moderate levels of say 40–60 dwellings per hectare, similar to those discussed by Keeble, rapidly reduces the land take, bringing communal facilities into closer reach and making public transport services more viable. Moreover, the critical mass of development contributes to the informal vitality of the streets and public places that attracts people to city centres and urban neighbourhoods, as well as contributing to energy efficiency (Urban Task Force, 1999, p. 60).

Development density is not only important in residential development, it can be equally important in industrial and commercial projects. In the 1970s a rule-of-thumb basis for estimating the density of an industrial development would be a coverage of 50–60% of the site area, or sometimes even slightly higher. In other words, on every hectare you could build 5000–6000 square metres of industrial floorspace, with an office content equivalent to 10% of the total, either on a single level or possibly two stories high. Service yards were often communal and parking for employees may have been fairly limited. Clear internal heights in such buildings were around 5.4 m (18 ft) to the eaves, with perhaps one or two loading doors.

With the decline of manufacturing industry and increased demand for warehousing and distribution facilities, internal heights increased to between 6 and 8 m, or even higher, office contents were either reduced to well below the

10% norm or, if the building included a sales and administration function, to more than 10%, sometimes over three floors. More loading doors were needed, for both 'drive-in' and 'tail-dock' loading, and communal yards became less acceptable.

The result of this was a reduction in development density, brought about by a need to service the newer types of buildings. Local planning authorities insisted on 30 m diameter turning circles for articulated vehicles being provided within the curtilage of each building, increased car parking provision and higher standards of landscaping. The overall effect of these changes has been to bring the development density for industrial buildings down to 35–40% of the site area.

Changes in development densities for office developments are less readily described. The attitudes of local planning authorities have differed quite significantly, often in relation to car parking provision. Some authorities, for example Manchester, have operated zero car parking requirements for city centre developments, except perhaps for a small number of spaces in the basement, but they may have insisted on large 'planning gain' contributions to parking provision on the fringe of the central area. Others may have sought contributions towards improving public transport facilities.

Business parks on city fringes are very different to central area developments. Three- or four-storey buildings, set in the midst of seas of car parking, with extensive landscaping areas, may be developed at densities of 30–35% of the total site area, or even lower for those in park-like settings. Such developments tend to be highly car-orientated, although there may be some public transport provision, with limited access to local facilities. As a result, workers wishing to eat other than at their desks or the office canteen, go shopping or undertake any type of fitness activity, have to resort to using their cars.

13.4   The public realm

Stephen Gleave (1990) defined the public realm as:

'The public face of buildings, the spaces between the frontages, streets, pathways, parks, gardens and so forth. To this can be added the activities taking place within and between these spaces and the servicing and managing of these activities. In turn, of course, all of this will be affected by the activities and uses occurring within the buildings themselves: that is the private realm.'

Gleave's definition does not necessarily indicate the ownership of 'public' spaces, as some privately owned spaces might be at least as accessible as publicly owned spaces, if not more so. The definition identifies the important components of the public realm, which the RICS sees as including:

- Roads and streets
- Squares and other formal and informal open spaces
- Trees and other landscaping
- Street furniture, signage, lighting and public art
- The public faces of buildings, their form and massing
- Various types of buildings – private, public and civic
- Circulation and parking
- Footpaths and cycleways
- Aspects of land use – for example, the mixture of land uses
- All the uses and activities which help support public life, including the management and maintenance of the public realm

(RICS, 1996, p. 7)

Property investors are the main drivers in commercial property markets in the UK. They influence not only the locations in which new developments take place but also the design specifications of those developments. So far as the public realm is concerned, if property investors plan to hold their investments for, say, six to eight years before selling them on to other investors, they might well be determined to ensure that the condition of the public realm is maintained. This might be reflected in their decision to approve higher-quality materials and more considered designs. Attention to urban design for these investors would be justified because it would maximise the profitability of the investment over the holding period (RICS, 1996, p. 25). While the investors might therefore pay close attention to detail in respect of the public realm, occupiers may be more indifferent, even to the extent that they would choose other developments if the 'quality' urban realm was accompanied by a significant uplift in rent, that is unless it was also seen to enhance the 'image' of the occupier.

A component part of the public realm is 'public art', the general perception of which is to a large extent moulded by – and also limited by – the twin traditions of statuary and commemorative architecture (Public Arts, 2001, p. 20). This perception brings with it the assumption that public art should have a monumental function and be serious in its nature, with no room for frivolity or light relief. However, this historical view of public art is changing, bringing with it a growing recognition of the opportunities that exist for artistic involvement in new development projects. Developers have been encouraged to allocate a small part of their development budget so as to introduce an element of art into their projects – the *per cent for art* – and this has often provided opportunities for new, young artists. The art component does not have to be permanent; it may, for example, exist only during the development period, and it may be subject to review or change at regular intervals.

Where the art is intended to form a permanent part of the development it is desirable to ensure that it has meaning and relevance, so that it does not appear out of place, and, most importantly, that it does not cause offence to those that will occupy or visit the development. One artist likes to consider the following for her designs for site-specific art work:

- Ideas suggested by the community.
- Designs using, or inspired by, work by the community from workshops.
- The use of natural materials which are sympathetic to the site.
- The importance of using robust materials which require low maintenance and have a long lifespan.
- The necessity to try to design-in 'vandalproofing' and with regard to safety requirements for public areas.
- An educational aspect.
- Making work that is accessible, fun and friendly.

(Harley, 2001, p. 53)

13.5   Security in design

The question of crime, against both people and property, needs to be taken into account when planning new developments. Ensuring that appropriate security features are incorporated in the design applies equally to residential and non-residential developments. A fear of crime may well be a factor in the decision-making process for the end-user – home buyer, office tenant or industrialist – when deciding whether to acquire one property in preference to another. The 'crime fear' factor may affect the decision in an unconscious manner, such as a feeling of 'lack of safeness' in a particular neighbourhood, or it may manifest itself in a more tangible manner, for example insurance premiums for cars and household contents which are based on postcodes.

The Urban Task Force (1999, pp. 126–7), 12 in referring to the Crime and Disorder Act 1998, suggested that strategies for combating crime should include:

- Policies and guidance for designing-out crime; creating lively areas with public spaces that are well-overlooked. Interconnected streets and a fine-grained mix of uses and buildings with plenty of doors that face onto streets.
- Joint action by all agencies to reduce crimes of public concern through concerted action by local authority environmental services, housing

management, schools, social services, police, probation and health services.

- Engaging residents and businesses in the fight against crime through neighbourhood watch and local partnerships on estates and in neighbourhoods, schools and public spaces.
- Practical ways for applying new statutory orders for tackling racially motivated crime, antisocial behaviour, truancy, sex offenders and child curfews.
- Bringing together the local services of the police, housing management, security, enforcement and environment management to focus on crime and vandalism hotspots.
- Improving public confidence in the police, in particular by improving the recording of racist crime and supporting its victims.

Schneider and Kitchen, in their book *Planning for Crime Prevention*, have examined the issues surrounding crime and how these are tackled by the planning process in both the UK and the United States. They observe that both countries have exhibited considerable interest in area-based initiatives to tackle crime problems, particularly in hot spots which are likely to be inner-city areas with a predominance of rented housing, concentrations of poverty, and quite probably also a concentration of people from ethnic minority communities. If these sorts of areas are typical crime hot spots, they are also areas where the experience of planners has tended to be that community-based initiatives can be particularly difficult to mount successfully (Schneider & Kitchen, 2002, p. 59 who provide several examples of initiatives of this kind).

The need to provide a secure environment may be self-evident when planning a residential development in an inner-city location but less so on a semi-rural site. Similarly, the need for security on an industrial property in a run-down city area may be more obvious than on a modern industrial estate next to a motorway junction. However, all of these developments may present their own, quite distinct, problems in terms of security, i.e. the opportunity for a rapid escape in the latter case, possibly with stolen computers or other expensive equipment, vehicles, etc.

13.5.1   *New developments can attract crime*

On one mixed-use development with which the author was involved, close to Piccadilly Station in inner-city Manchester (Syms, 1993), the objective was to encourage visitors into the area. Prior to the new development taking place the area was fairly desolate and almost devoid of activity except for a few manufacturing businesses, although it was only a few minutes walk from the city centre. The idea was to develop a mix of offices, shops, craft units and residential development – town houses and apartments. From a security perspective it was anticipated that visitors to the shops, craft units and offices would provide a form of in-built security, discouraging criminal activity. In the event, the shops and craft units failed to let, subsequently being converted to residential units, although takers were readily found for the offices and residential development.

The result was a spate of crimes, including muggings, car theft and burglaries. Ground-floor apartments were particularly vulnerable, even in daylight, but even those on upper floors were not immune. Not unreasonably, the residents started to fear for their safety and insisted that security measures were installed. This resulted in the development becoming a fully gated community, to both pedestrians and vehicles, during the hours of darkness, with access via coded keypads. During daylight limited pedestrian access was allowed, with vehicular access by keypads or intercom. Even these measures were not totally successful as car thieves attempted to remove vehicles by ramming the gates and closed-circuit television cameras had to be installed.

A few miles away in Salford a new industrial estate was developed, on a former railway goods yard, in an area surrounded by existing industries. The developer anticipated the need for security and employed a security guard outside working hours. On the night following the tenant moving into the first completed unit, the security guard was attacked, threatened and tied to his chair. The gang then made off with the newly installed computers and left the security guard with a message, saying that they would be back as and when other tenants moved in.

Both of these examples involved inner-city locations but there are plenty of examples of crimes in other areas. For example, there have been instances of car thieves, specialising in expensive vehicles, deliberately setting off the alarms of cars parked on driveways and, when the owner comes out to check on the car, stealing the keys and driving off. If the owner fails to appear they have even gone so far as to ring doorbells or knock on doors to alert the occupants to the fact that the car alarm is sounding. The author is familiar with the case of one company on a modern 'open plan' industrial estate, close to a motorway junction, which suffered from so many break-ins that the office windows are now covered with visually intrusive security bars and a 2.5 m high security fence now encloses the development. One of the problems with this development was that the landscaping – large rocks, shrubs and trees – provided many places in which the perpetrators of the crimes could hide from security personnel.

13.5.2   *Some places attract whilst others become no-go areas*

> 'Some places, whether they are certain neighbourhoods, apartment build-
> ings, corridors within buildings, parks, street corners or schools "look" or
> "feel" safer than others. Our friends tell us that they are "good" places to live
> or work or shop or travel through and the authorities report that crime there
> is rare. We shun those places that we suspect to be unsafe and tend not to
> spend our resources or time there.'
>
> (Schneider & Kitchen, 2002, p. 8)

From the developer's perspective, the look or feel of the area may be fundamental in deciding on both site acquisition and the form of the development
itself. For many developers the possibility of crime or security problems, both
during the development period and subsequently, may be sufficient to persuade
them against the project. This may reveal itself in a reluctance to become
involved with 'urban renewal' type developments.

Creating defensible space in which we feel secure is nothing new; human
beings have always defended their homes and the communities in which they
live. Today, however, the defences may appear to be less evident, or at least less
substantial, than in the days of castles and fortified manors. Cozens *et al.* (2001)
researched the views of various groups of people regarding different types of
dwellings. The groups interviewed for the research comprised planning professionals, convicted burglars, police officers and young adults. These groups
are of crucial relevance, not only for understanding crime in our cities, but also
for deriving policies which might successfully tackle this problem (Cozens *et al.*,
2001, p. 224). The study compared and interpreted data collected from the
groups, critically probing the contrasts and similarities in their perceptions, as
well as providing an overview of the aggregated data.

The members of each group were shown photographs of five different
categories of housing: high-rise flats, terraced housing, semi-detached housing,
detached housing and low-rise/walk-up flats. Two photographs were shown
for each category; where possible, these illustrated well-maintained property
and poorly maintained property. The interviews probed the concepts of ter-
ritoriality, surveillance and image. The research results illustrate the responses
from members in each of the groups. Taken overall, well-maintained semi-
detached housing was clearly perceived to be the most 'defensible' design,
followed by the two detached designs. High-rise designs were considered to be
the least defensible of all.

The authors conclude that there are obvious policy implications for planners,
property managers and housing officials to adequately and rapidly maintain the
physical fabric of residential areas, and to use caution in their allocatory
procedures, particularly with reference to high-rise and low-rise/walk-up

properties. In terms of the new-build housing projections, the requirement of high-density dwellings may well be most appropriately met by a consideration for a version of the terraced design, which was favourably considered by all the sample groups (Cozens *et al.*, 2001, pp. 244–245).

In the view of Schneider and Kitchen (2002, p. 195), it is probably correct to say that police consultation (in the UK) has by now become an established part of development control practice in many planning authorities, and that while police views on major developments do not always carry the day (because other considerations may be regarded as dominant), they are often on the table when such decisions are taken. The authors also make the point (p. 194) that planning authorities in England and Wales outnumber police forces by approximately ten to one and that the architectural liaison departments in police forces are, typically, staffed by two or three officers. They cannot hope therefore to advise on more than a small percentage of planning applications. Nevertheless, the fact that consultation takes place is very different to the situation of the late 1980s, as described in section 13.5.1, when the idea of police/planning liaison was in its infancy.

13.5.3   *Advice on design*

The DTLR guide *Better Places to Live by Design* (DTLR, 2001b) is a companion guide to PPG3, intended to assist developers in implementing the changes described in the planning guidance, see *www.planning.dtlr.gov.uk/betrplac/index.htm*. Help and advice is available for developers through the Secured by Design scheme, *www.securedbydesign.com*, which is sometimes seen as reflecting a 'fortress mentality', whereby buildings or developments are made so secure that they are totally divorced from the neighbourhood in which they are located and thus add little to the process of urban regeneration. Schneider and Kitchen (2002, pp. 195–197) recognise that there is undoubtedly some truth in this but consider it to be an oversimplification of of a complex reality. This is partly because such a perception sees Secured by Design as essentially a static concept coming from a particular and limited perspective, whereas in both theory and practice (because there are mechanisms in place for updating the available guidance) this need not be axiomatic. It also overlooks the fact that architectural liaison officers, while starting from a common base, have to deal with a wide range of situations and people.

Figures 13.1(a) and 13.1(b) illustrate different approaches on two housing developments, both of which were less than a year old when the photographs were taken. In Figure 13.1(a) the developer has relied upon high brick walls to provide a physical barrier and sense of security, whereas in Figure 13.1(b) low-growing shrubs form a deterrent. Shrubs such as low-growing varieties of

(a)

(b)

Figure 13.1 Security in the design of housing developments – contrasting approaches: (a) high brick walls are used; and (b) low-growing shrubs provide both a visual and physical deterrent.

berberis and mahonia, as well as rosa rugosa provide excellent ground cover and, with their sharp thorns, provide both visual and physical deterrent.

Both of these alternatives achieve the objective of security and both have advantages and disadvantages. The high walls in the development in Figure 13.1(a) present a very 'hard' image and, whilst this appearance may be acceptable in an urban environment, they would not be appropriate in the smaller town location shown in Figure 13.1(b). The softer landscaping of low-growing shrubs requires more maintenance than a brick wall, if only to remove litter that may be caught by the shrubs – but then brick walls can be covered in graffiti. The message is that not all security measures have to be the same, they need to be designed in a way that is appropriate to the surroundings.

13.6   Environmental performance

When planning for sustainability in a new property development, it is not just the energy consumed during the life of the building that has to be considered. Energy is involved in the extraction, manufacture and transportation of building materials and this is known as the 'embodied energy'. For the true environmental cost to be assessed, the following factors need to be considered:

- Energy used over the estimated lifetime of the building.
- Energy used in the construction process.
- The extent to which any recycled materials have been used, e.g. recovered slates, timber or crushed concrete and brick.
- The presence of pollutants, such as volatile organic compounds (VOCs) in the construction materials.
- Toxic substances used in the production process.
- Energy used in demolition and site reclamation.
- The level of recyclable material arising out of the demolition.
- The energy used in recycling materials, e.g. crushing or cleaning materials for reuse.
- Materials used in refurbishment.

(Based on Smith, 2001, p. 73)

Taking the whole cycle of construction and occupation, through to demolition and site reclamation, it is probable that most buildings consume much more energy during their lifetime than is consumed during construction and removal. Nevertheless, that does not remove the need to carefully examine the environmental costs associated with construction and in preparing land for redevelopment. For example, it would seem to be environmentally irrespon-sible to expend 100 t of fossil fuel (diesel), in excavating and removing to a licensed landfill, soil that has been contaminated by say 10 t of fuel. All other things being equal, such as other contaminants being amenable to treatment, it is probably far more appropriate in environmental terms to used an alternative method, as considered in Chapter 7.

Energy consumption during the occupied life of the building can be reduced in a number of ways, for example by:

- Careful consideration of the orientation of the building and its design, so as to maximise solar gain for heating purposes, without overheating the building and having to resort to artificial cooling.
- Recovering waste heat from living spaces and from machines such as computers, and reusing it to heat domestic water.
- Considering the installation of combined heat and power (CHP) systems.
- Improving insulation standards and designing buildings in such a way as to reduce heat loss through lack of shelter from prevailing winds in the winter.
- Providing for at least some of the energy requirements of the building to be met from renewable energy sources, such as solar, wind or water power.
- Designing buildings to incorporate natural ventilation, or even mechanically assisted ventilation, instead of using refrigerated cooling.
- Designing buildings and lighting systems to maximise daylight, with artificial lighting levels being designed to be as low as possible, while achieving the standard required, and by specifying energy-efficient lamps.
- Linking lighting controls to occupancy, with localised switching in large areas to allow lights to be dimmed or switched off in unoccupied areas.
- Providing for localised control of heating systems, with background heating in unoccupied areas, with the potential for heating levels to be quickly increased when the occupiers return.

The above list provides only a few examples of the things that a developer might consider when planning a new development. These issues are likely to become increasingly important over the next few years, with the result that firms and individuals considering the acquisition of new workplaces or homes are likely to be more searching in terms of their questions regarding the energy efficiency of new buildings.

Smith (2001) provides many more comprehensive checklists of the environmental factors that should be taken into account in designing new buildings and he emphasises the following:

- It is important that all members of the design team share a common goal and if possible have a proven track record in achieving that goal. From the earliest outline proposals through to the construction and installation, the design process should be a collaborative effort. Integrated design principles should be the rule from the first encounter with a client.

- The first aim should be to maximise passive systems to reduce the reliance on active systems which use energy.
- It is important that, at the outset, costs are calculated in a composite manner so that capital and revenue costs are considered as a single accountancy feature. This will help to convince clients that any extra capital expenditure is cost-effective, even for buildings to be let or sold on.
- Clients should be required to explain in detail the nature of office routines so that these can be properly matched to operational programmes.
- The claims made for advanced technology do not always match performance. It is important to select *appropriate* technology which achieves the best balance between energy efficiency, occupant comfort and ease of operation and maintenance. At the same time, the best compromise should be reached between optimum performance and the requirements for the majority of the year. To provide significantly greater capacity for just a few days of the year is not best practice.
- Lighting requirements should be clearly assessed to discriminate between general lighting and that required at desktop level.
- On completion, building managers should be selected for their ability to cope with the complexities of the chosen building management system.
- Appropriate monitoring is necessary to be able to assess from day to day how systems are performing. The cost of sub-meters, hours-run recorders, etc. will give valuable returns for a small cost. Energy costs should be identified with specific cost centres.

(Smith, 2001, pp. 100–101)

13.7 Mixing uses

One of the main attractions of city living is proximity to work, shops and basic social, educational and leisure uses. Whether we are talking about mixing uses in the same neighbourhood, a mix within a street or urban block, or the mixing of uses vertically within a building, good urban design should encourage more people to live near to those services which they require on a regular basis (Urban Task Force, 1999, p. 64).

The idea of mixed-use development is not new. Looking back to the industrial revolution there are countless examples of Lancashire cotton mills with nearby housing provided by the mill owners for the workers. Vertical integration of uses can be found in three-storey weavers' cottages, where the loom was placed on the top floor, above the living accommodation, so as to make the best use of natural light. Of course by no means all of these developments produced good living and working conditions. Better examples, from more enlightened employers, are to be found in the Cadbury village at Bournville in the West Midlands and Lever's Port Sunlight.

Creating a mix of uses can help to attract people to live, work and play in the same area. The mix can be at the scale of the building (one use above another), the street (one use next to another) or the neighbourhood (groups of uses next to others). Vital places often have a mix of uses which involves different people using the same parts of a building or place at different times of the day, as well as different uses happening in different parts of a building or space at the same time (DETR, 2000f, p. 32).

The DETR/CABE design guide then goes on to emphasise the importance of getting the mix right. To be successful, the uses need to be compatible and to interact with each other in a positive manner. They need to help create a balanced community, with a range of services that does not increase reliance on the car. Diversity of layout, building form and tenure of the properties created all contribute to making successful living and working environments.

Flexibility in design, with buildings of different sizes and types, allows for the possibility of changes in use over time. Well-designed social housing that is not distinguishable from private housing in mixed-tenure developments will encourage social inclusion. The subdivision of larger developments into smaller plots, each with their distinctive design and character, creates interest and diversity.

Streets and squares can have many different, often conflicting, functions which change over time. They can be places in which to dance and celebrate, but also places of horror, death or boredom (Hass-Klau et al., 1999, p. 19). In commercial areas the development of narrower, more vibrant, frontages to shops and commercial buildings will encourage small-scale activities to develop. These in turn will stimulate interest and encourage people to treat streets as part of their living spaces. This is already happening in many major cities; for example, Manchester city centre has undergone a marked change over the last decade, part driven by the trend towards city-centre living but also as a result of people staying in the city after work or coming in from the suburbs.

Hass-Klau et al. (1999) studied 20 European cities with the aim of researching the proportion of people who used the town centre for some social or recreational activity. They also enquired into the type of activity they had undertaken, its duration and location, as well as the mode of transport they used. They found that the most sociable town was Dresden, where 78% of the people surveyed had carried out at least one social activity during the day whereas, at the other end of the scale, only 31% of the people interviewed in Haywards Heath had undertaken any social activity. Haywards Heath was the smallest town surveyed but even in Reading, of similar size to second-placed Utrecht, the proportion of people engaged in social activity was only 45%, placing Reading in nineteenth place.

13.8   Cars and public transport

It is evident from the general thrust of Government policies that car use is something to be discouraged, at least so far as urban areas are concerned. Public transport is the preferred means of transport from the policy perspective but, given the extent of car usage in the UK, for it to be fully accepted a great deal has to be done in order to produce a fully integrated transport system. Unless the 'carrots' of attractive and efficient public transport becomes generally available in major towns and cities the 'sticks' of fuel taxes, central area access charges and parking levies will be less than fully effective. Motorists will complain about being penalised but will nevertheless continue to use their cars for travel to work and access to cities because they are more convenient, reliable and comfortable.

The Beeching Plan for the reorganisation of the railway system, however skilfully prepared and however valid within its own terms of reference, was in some ways useless and even harmful, because it failed to take account of the obvious fact that public transport in this country needs to be regarded as a coordinated activity rather than as the independent activities of a number of undertakings which happen to run different kinds of vehicles on different tracks (Keeble, 1969, p. 56). This comment from more than 30 years ago is probably even truer today; in spite of years of transport policies aimed at producing improvements, public transport in the UK still falls far behind that of many European countries.

Hass-Klau *et al.* (1999, p. 107) found that car use was high in the British towns and also the small German towns. When the mode of transport to the town centre by residents only (i.e. excluding out-of-town visitors) is analysed, the highest car use of all the 20 towns studied was in Horsham, at 41%, followed closely by Chichester and Winchester (each with 37%), Exeter 32% and Belfast 31%. In contrast, the lowest car use by residents to access the city centre was in Munich with only 8%, Edinburgh 10%, Dublin 11%, Utrecht 13% and Schwerin 15%. These differences are only partly explainable by the size of the town or city but, according to the researchers, the type of transport policy is more important.

In the Continental towns there did not appear to be a relationship between car use and car ownership. For example, there was similarly high use of public transport in Munich and Birmingham, at 78% and 77% respectively, yet car ownership in Munich was significantly higher than in Birmingham.[13.1] Similar comparisons could also be made in respect of other British towns and cities.

[13.1] The comparative figures were 474 and 293, although the Munich figures were more recent than those for Birmingham and the gap could have reduced by the time of the survey.

A revision to Planning Policy Guidance 13 – Transport, was published in March 2001. The main areas of guidance to local authorities are listed in Chapter 2 of this book. Some of the design implications are referred to below.

A key planning objective is to ensure that jobs, shopping, leisure facilities and services are accessible by public transport, walking and cycling. This is important for all, but especially for those who do not have regular use of a car, and to promote social inclusion. In preparing their development plans, local authorities should give particular emphasis to accessibility in identifying the preferred areas and sites where such land uses should be located, to ensure they will offer realistic, safe and easy access by a range of transport modes, and not exclusively by car. Regional Planning Guidance should set a strategic framework for this exercise through the use of public transport accessibility criteria for regionally or sub-regionally significant levels or types of development (PPG13; DETR, 2001, paragraph 19).

Local authorities should be proactive in promoting the intensive development of scarce sites around major transport interchanges and they should have a clear vision for the development of these areas, even if it means changing the allocated use of such sites. The concept of Transport Development Areas, proposed by the Royal Institution of Chartered Surveyors (RICS, 2000) is aimed at providing a mechanism to integrate development and planning to achieve higher-density development around significant transport hubs. The approach offers a number of advantages:

- The provision of funds for improving public transport facilities.
- The regeneration of many urban areas.
- Maximising the use of brownfield land and so reducing take-up of greenfield and greenbelt land.
- A more sustainable approach to land use.
- Better access to public transport by socially disadvantaged groups; reduced reliance on car use.
- A useful focus for government investment.

The Transport Development Area concept appears to have had a good reception and the need for integration of transport and land-use policies has been recognised by the Greater London Authority in the Initial Proposals for Mayor's Spatial Development Strategy for London (GLA, 2001, pp. 45–50).

Where developments are expected to have significant transport implications, Transport Assessments should be prepared and submitted alongside the relevant planning applications for development (PPG13; DETR 2001, paragraph 23). Transport Assessments replace Traffic Impact Assessments and reflect a wider approach to transport issues by including details of proposed measures to improve access by public transport, walking and cycling, so as to reduce the need for parking associated with new development proposals.

Including these assessments as part of the planning application enables local planning authorities to assess the application and provide a basis for discussion on details of the scheme, such as the level of parking, the siting of buildings and entrances. The need for further measures to improve access arrangements to the site can also be identified. The guidance states that local authorities should take account of any firm proposals to improve the access to a site (particularly where included in the local transport plan) when assessing the suitability of a site for development.

PPG13 encourages prospective developers to hold early discussions with the local authority in order to clarify whether proposals are likely to be acceptable in transport terms and to 'scope' the requirements of any Transport Assessment. Where the developer's proposals are clearly in line with planning policy (for instance where they accord with the preferred locations in the development plan and include measures to improve access by non-car modes) it should increase the likelihood of a planning permission being granted without undue delay. In such cases, the local authority may be prepared to reduce the requirements and coverage of the Transport Assessment.

For many developments a major user of space is car parking. Promoting other means of transport as part of the development scheme should have the effect of reducing the land needed for cars and facilitate a higher density of built space. Therefore instead of local authorities requiring developers to meet minimum car parking standards, the converse is likely to be true in future, with maximum levels of parking being determined for different types of development. Parking controls and charges, together with park-and-ride schemes, seek to persuade motorists not to take their cars into city and town centres but, for them to work effectively, they need to offer positive advantages.

13.9   Summary

The physical form and qualities of a place, shape – and are shaped by – the way it is used and the way people and vehicles move through it. New development should help to create places that connect with each other sustainably, providing the right conditions to encourage walking, cycling and the use of public transport. People should come before traffic. Places that work well are designed to be used safely and securely by all in the community, often for a wide range of purposes and throughout the day and evening. Local authorities, in partnership with the police, should promote designs and layouts that are safe (both in terms of road safety and personal security) and take account of crime prevention and community safety considerations. (PPG13; DETR, 2001, paragraph 28).

Given the present focus of planning policies in the UK, it would seem fairly obvious that the development proposals most likely to receive planning permission are those that seek to minimise reliance on the car and encourage the use of public transport. Proposals that include the means to improve public transport, and encourage walking or cycling in a safe environment, should find favour, possibly even to the extent of planning authorities revisiting the use allocations in local plans. Developers preparing schemes that minimise car use and maximise other forms of travel will need to be sensitive to the needs of people with disabilities; this may be through providing disabled access to public transport as part of the scheme, or through the provision of disabled parking. Good designs will also need to recognise the needs of the blind or partially sighted.

Reducing the cost of a development may result in a lowering of design quality, with the result that the building becomes less attractive in the market. It does not necessarily follow, however, that lower cost means poorer design. There are plenty of examples of high-cost buildings that fail either aesthetically or in the way they function for their occupants. Therefore it is necessary for the designers, developers and planners to consider each proposed development on an individual basis, in terms of meeting objectives, not simply repeating something that has been tried elsewhere or adhering to some mundane principles.

The choice of appropriate material is an important aspect of good design. Historical references have a part to play in this regard but they should not be allowed to influence the design to such an extent that a bad result ensures. (see Figure 13.2).

Sustainability, in terms of both the design and 'cost in use' of new buildings, is set to become increasingly important. Building occupiers and investors are likely to pay more attention to environmental issues and they, as well as planning authorities, will expect these to be reflected in new development proposals.

Figure 13.2   Stainless steel cladding may have appeared to be contextually appropriate on the former National Centre for Popular Music in Sheffield but was it the best material to use in terms of building form and location? The cladding was stained and streaked with dirt within a few months of the building being completed.

13.10   Checklist

- Try to achieve a development density appropriate to the local environs.
- Be aware of any potential for security problems.
- Take energy requirements into account, both during construction and usage, and be energy-efficient.
- Take full account of transport issues.

Chapter 14
Masterplanning

14.1 Introduction

> 'One of the great things about urban regeneration now is the knock-on
> effect that one successful development – be it architecture or urban design –
> can have on a whole city. No urban site can ever by an island "entire unto
> itself". The success of a masterplan is judged as much by its effect outside its
> time/space boundary as within its "red line". The boundaries of a masterplan
> are not clear-cut, like those for architecture.
>
> (Sir Terry Farrell, 2002, p. 9)

Masterplanning provides the opportunity for public authorities, landowners
and developers to produce a blueprint for the future evolvement of an area,
whether it is part of a town or city, or a whole new community. The masterplanning process is not just about large-scale architecture; it brings together
urban design, town planning policies and principles, transport and engineering,
economics and financial planning, real estate and markets, cultural and social
issues. It has a very definite role to play in planning the urban renewal of an area
but can be equally important in planning an urban extension. Masterplans need
to recognise, and work with, existing features and constraints within the area
that is being planned and be especially conscious about how the newly planned
area will fit within its surroundings.

Masterplans might typically cover a period of 10 to 15 years from the date of
their inception. If they are too rigid they will be incapable of being adjusted to
respond to economic, cultural or policy changes. As a result, the development
might become visually dated and labelled as being of a certain era. Therefore
masterplans need to lay down principles but also allow for flexibility in their
interpretations.

This chapter describes four quite different masterplans, all relatively new but
at different stages of their implementation. The first of these is Sheffield city

centre, where implementation of the masterplan is only just beginning, where revitalising the heart of the city is a major challenge. Second is the Wet Dock at Ipswich, lying just outside the centre of the county town of Suffolk, but almost a no-go area until the regeneration started to bring new homes, employment and leisure opportunities. The third case study is Cambourne, a new development on low-grade agricultural land to the west of Cambridge, meeting some of the demand for new homes and high-quality workspace for the expanding high-technology industries seeking to locate or expand in Cambridgeshire. Finally, to Tower Hamlets in East London, a borough of immense contrasts with the affluence of banking and finance in Canary Wharf, yet also the most deprived local authority in the UK, where a bold new masterplan sets out hopes for the future.

14.2 Revitalising the city centre – Sheffield One

'Cities evolve organically: learning, maturing, adapting. Inventive new developments alongside recycling and re-use give them a creative fusion of continuity and dynamism.'

(Rogers & Power, 2000, p. 206)

Sheffield, England's fourth largest city, has long been renowned worldwide for its steel, cutlery, engineering and toolmaking industries. Whilst these industries have declined from their peak, the city has refocused its industrial attention in more specialist areas, including special steels and precision engineering. It is the principal urban area within the south Yorkshire conurbation and Sheffield city centre is the commercial heart of the subregion. It includes a major retail centre which suffered considerably from the opening in 1990 of the Meadowhall Shopping Centre, three miles north-east of the city centre and adjacent to junction 34 of the M1 motorway.

Sheffield One, launched in February 2000, is a partnership of Sheffield City Council, Yorkshire Forward (the Regional Development Agency for Yorkshire and the Humber) and English Partnerships, and one of three pilot Urban Regeneration Companies in England, the others being in Liverpool and Manchester. It is tasked with spearheading the regeneration of Sheffield city centre in a way that will benefit the whole city and the wider subregion. The city faces an immense challenge, but also an immense opportunity to create a new future and image for itself, see *www.sheffield1.com*.

One of the first tasks of the regeneration company was to commission a baseline study of local economic conditions, which identified a number of key challenges and opportunities for the city centre, focusing on issues relating to deprivation and social exclusion, the property market, the retail, leisure and cultural aspects and the transport system. This baseline study was critical in informing the development of the Masterplan, which is to guide the regeneration of the city centre over the next 10 to 15 years. The area covered by the Masterplan is shown in Figure 14.1 but it is far more than just an artist's impression, providing as it does a comprehensive guide for change, mapping out the physical, social and cultural conditions required for sustainable investment and growth.

The masterplanning team was headed by Koetter, Kim & Associates, supported by Christopher Glaister & Company, Robert Maguire Consulting, Steer Davies Gleave, Segal Quince Wicksteed, Healey & Baker and Davies Langdon & Everest. Their vision for Sheffield is of a prosperous and commercially successful city at the heart of a city region which is reinventing itself as a new and dynamic modern economy; one that embraces both the new information and telecommunications sectors and an advanced manufacturing sector based on the area's traditional skills (Sheffield City Centre Masterplan, 2001).

The issues that have to be tackled include social exclusion, deprivation and the high levels of unemployment that exist in some parts of the city. These problems cannot be overcome in the absence of a strong and vibrant city economy. In 2000, half the city's jobs were located within the inner ring road and the Masterplan strategy aims to link to the work of other agencies, so as to ensure that the opportunities created are shared and spread into areas of need and the most vulnerable communities.

The Masterplan recognises that no single project or policy will 'turn the city around'. The vision for the future is of a cohesive central area where individual projects, programmes and strategies reinforce and support each other and the whole is greater than its individual parts. The Masterplan focuses on four strategic objectives that lie at the heart of the strategy and which are central to the transformation of the city:

(1)   **Building** a new technology-based economy in the city.
(2)   **Creating** a vibrant city as a centre for learning, culture, retail, leisure and living.
(3)   **Improving** accessibility to the city centre by all modes of transport.
(4)   **Celebrating** the public realm – bringing high-quality public spaces to all parts of the city centre and celebrating the city's green heritage.

(Sheffield City Centre Masterplan, 2001)

The economic review commissioned by Sheffield One demonstrated that the city has many of the raw ingredients necessary to encourage economic growth, and the Koetter, Kim & Associates masterplan identified the city's key strengths and the existing opportunities and clusters which should be concentrated on for maximum economic impact:

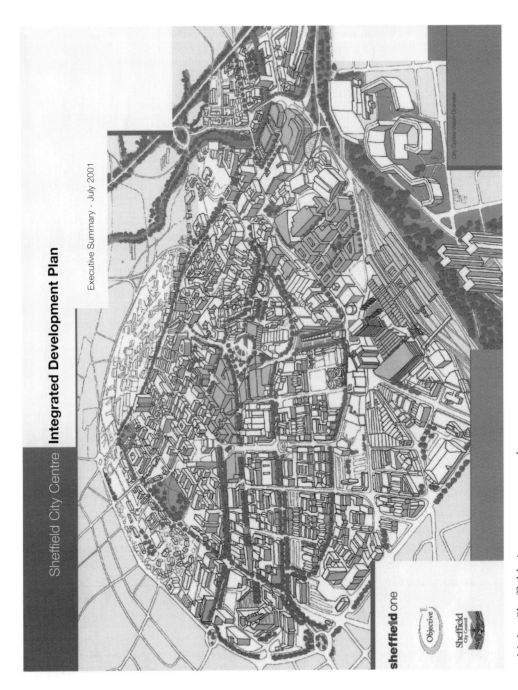

Figure 14.1 Sheffield city centre masterplan.

- Medical–related areas
- Cultural and creative industries
- Information and communication technologies (ICT)
- Biotechnology
- Sports–related activities

However, when it comes to attracting investment to develop in these key areas, Sheffield is in competition with other cities in the UK and Europe.

The South Yorkshire subregion is one of the most disadvantaged areas in the European Union and, in July 2000, was designated as an area qualifying for 'Structural Funding' under the Objective 1 European Programme. This provides a major opportunity for Sheffield city centre to achieve its vision and become a modern competitive European regional city. The purpose of Objective 1 is to stimulate significant new investment from the public and private sectors across a range of initiatives, all of which are designed to transform the economy of the subregion.

The six drivers for change, or priorities that underpin the Objective 1 programme, are:

Priority 1:   Stimulating the emergence of new growth and high-technology sectors.
Priority 2:   Modernising businesses through enhancing competitiveness and innovation.
Priority 3:   Building a world-leading learning region
Priority 4:   Developing economic opportunities in target communities
Priority 5:   Supporting business investment through strategic spatial investment.
Priority 6:   Providing the foundations for a successful programme

Following on from the City Centre Masterplan and the earlier studies, an Integrated Development Plan (IDP) was prepared to provide a comprehensive strategy and implementation plan for public- and private-sector investment in the regeneration of Sheffield city centre over a seven to ten-year period. The IDP provides the policy and management framework within which city centre projects requiring funding support through the Objective 1 European Programme can be considered, appraised and funded. The IDP identifies five strategic objectives and programmes to deliver the city centre vision:

(1)   *The economy* – to become one of Europe's high-technology centres wired into the global digital web, generating new businesses from its strong research and education institutions, acting also as a resource for the wider region.

(2)   *A vibrant mixed-use city centre* – offering something for everyone in an exciting and ever-changing environment, aiming to attract local residents and visitors from further afield. Marketing the city will be crucial.

(3)   *A connected city* – improving access and ease of movement within the city centre, including radical improvements to Sheffield station as the transport hub and gateway to south Yorkshire.

(4)   *Public places and spaces* – designing consideration for the environment and sustainability into all projects, and creating a pedestrian-dominated city core; improving public transport; managing the car; encouraging city living; reducing travel, energy consumption and air pollution.

(5)   *A compassionate city* – creating new opportunities across the socio-economic spectrum and providing bridges to well-being for vulnerable groups and the long-term unemployed, ensuring that rising prosperity in the city centre benefits those groups that traditionally have been marginalised.

The cost of achieving these objectives has been estimated to be in excess of £350 million, of which more than £57 million will come from Objective 1 funding, more than £87 million from other public funds and the balance of just over £206 million from private funds.

The regeneration of the city centre has already started – Sheffield Hallam University has spent over £70 million since 1993 on expanding and modernising its City Campus (Figure 14.2); the city council has embarked on the major 'Heart of the City' scheme and created the new Peace Gardens (Figure 14.3) and the Millennium Galleries. The 'eggbox', the 1970s extension to the Town Hall is being demolished (October 2001), to make way for a new mixed-use scheme of office, hotel, retail, leisure and residential accommodation, for which CTP/St. James was appointed as the new development partner in May 2002.

Part of the strategy set out by the Masterplan was to create a new, high-quality retail quarter around the Peace Gardens, linking into neighbouring new mixed-use areas, so as to create a 'critical mass' of high-quality urban activities within a highly compact area (Sheffield City Centre Masterplan, 2001). A survey of retailers revealed substantial unsatisfied demand for modern space in the core of the city, which some retailers such as Gap have overcome by creating their own flagship stores. In order to address the problem, Sheffield One and Sheffield City Council decided to hold a design competition in order to select a preferred development partner.

Three development teams were short-listed and, following a period of public consultation, the team led by Hammerson plc was selected. Hammerson is a major international developer and investor in retail and office property, with a high-quality portfolio valued in excess of £3 billion, comprising over

Figure 14.2 Part of the 3560 square metre (38 300 square feet) Atrium at the centre of Sheffield Hallam University's City Campus, providing direct access to five buildings with a combined floor area of 47 450 square metres (510 000 square feet) and traffic-free access by external walkways (bridge link to three further buildings containing 25 290 square metres (272 230 square feet)).

700 000 square metres of retail space and 250 000 square metres of prime offices. It is also the development manager and partner in Birmingham Alliance, which is developing Birmingham's new city centre shopping complex (see Chapter 15).

The proposed development (see Figure 14.4) will comprise a covered square – the Galleria, a curved street of shops with housing above – the Crescent, the reinstatement of an historic space at Moor Head and an improved setting for

Figure 14.3   The Peace Gardens and Town Hall, Sheffield.

the City Hall, Sheffield's concert hall. The development will be anchored by a new Cole brothers (John Lewis Partnership) store and will include a landmark building, with a new public library. Improvements will be made to existing pedestrian links and to existing buildings, with new uses being found for some of these. There will be potential for a new hotel, improved car parking and a new public transport interchange.

Other new developments will include the refurbishment and conversion of a group of listed stone-built education buildings and former offices of the city council's Education Department at Leopold Street. Here the council has appointed local developer Gleeson as its development partner.

As part of the programme to encourage the growth of technology-based businesses, the city council, in conjunction with Sheffield One, is promoting the development of an e-campus, located between Sheffield Hallam University's City Campus and Sheffield station. Subject to the outcome of a review of public transport needs in the city centre, up to 3.3 ha of land will become available for redevelopment, capable of accommodating around 60 000 square metres of floorspace, custom-made for high technology, e-commerce and knowledge economy businesses and supported by the latest ICT infrastructure.

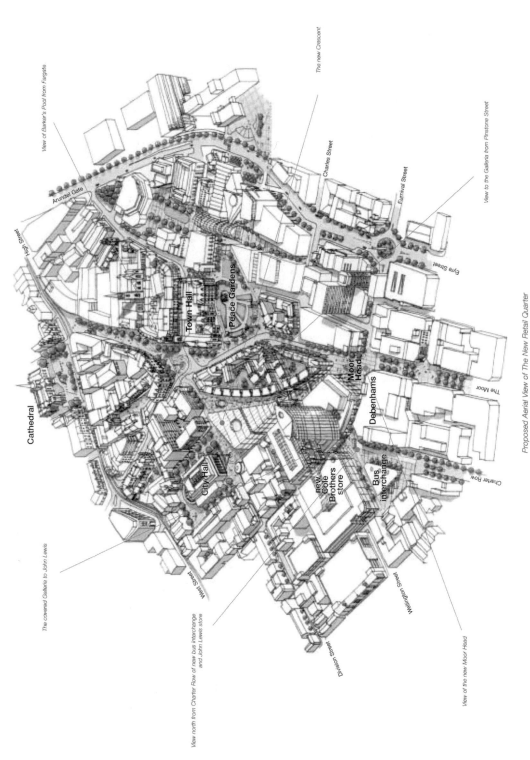

Cathedral

Arundel Gate

View of Barker's Pool from Fargate

The new Crescent

Charles Street

Furnival Street

View to the Galleria from Pinstone Street

Eyre Street

Town Hall

Peace Gardens

Moor Head

Debenhams

The Moor

City Hall

new Cole Brothers store

Bus interchange

Charter Row

High Street

West Street

The covered Galleria to John Lewis

View north from Charter Row of new bus interchange and John Lewis store

Division Street

Wellington Street

View of the new Moor Head

Proposed Aerial View of The New Retail Quarter

Figure 14.4   Artist's impression of the proposed city centre retail development.

14.3   Urban waterfront regeneration – Ipswich Wet Dock

Ipswich Wet Dock was opened in 1842 and, at that time, was the largest construction of its kind in the UK. Lying to the south of the town centre it became the focus of great commercial endeavour, bringing growth and prosperity to the town. By the late 1990s many of the quays and adjacent land and buildings were redundant and derelict. Recognising the need to rekindle the spirit of commercial and civic enterprise, the borough council produced a framework of objectives for the area, which were to:

- Provide for opportunities which will create and sustain economic regeneration.
- Provide for the integration of new and existing communities.
- Promote redevelopment which will preserve and enhance the character of the area.
- Provide for a mix of compatible uses including residential use in the Wet Dock area.
- Integrate the Wet Dock and the town centre by the development of safe and convenient pedestrian routes.
- Enhance the Transition Area between the Wet Dock and the town centre by fostering appropriate land uses including residential.

(Ipswich Borough Council, 1997)

The Wet Dock Conservation Area links, at St Peter's Street and Fore Street, with the mediaeval street pattern that joins the town centre to the Wet Dock area. This part of the town is an area in transition, in which manufacturing and warehousing activities have declined, to be replaced in part by uses such as offices, residential and recreational activities. It also contains a bus garage and several vacant and semi-derelict buildings and sites. Nevertheless, there are some attractive streets that form an important part of the character of the town.

Ipswich is still an active port, with vessels of up to 16 000 t and 8.4 m draught (5.5 m in the Wet Dock) passing up the River Orwell from the much larger port of Harwich. The port handles containers, forest products, dry and liquid bulk goods and general cargo traffic, most of which is handled in the deeper waters below the tidal lock that provides access to the Wet Dock. It also has a roll-on–roll-off (Ro–ro) facility. As part of the regeneration programme, the lock giving access to the Wet Dock has been upgraded, at a cost of £1.2 million, from one that provided limited access two hours before and one hour after high water, to one that can operate 24 hours a day.

In 1997 an Ipswich Wet Dock Steering Group was formed consisting of Allied Mills, Associated British Ports (ABP), Pauls, Bellway Homes, the East of England Development Agency (EEDA), Ipswich Borough Council, Suffolk

County Council, Suffolk College, Tolly Cobbold Brewery and the Ipswich Society. The steering group commissioned Llewelyn-Davies, in association with Campbell Reith Hill, Savills, Beckett Rankine Partnership and EC Harris, to prepare a study and propose a development framework for the Wet Dock.

It was considered essential that the study took a practical and pragmatic approach to the opportunities and difficulties presented by the Wet Dock. The study team needed to assess why previous proposals had not come to fruition and to identify three or four key areas where relatively swift progress could be made. This was important so as to give credibility and confidence to both existing and potential investors, occupiers and users, enabling them to believe that this time things were really going to happen (Ipswich Waterfront Steering Group, 1999).

In February 1998 the study team presented its final report, setting out a development framework to guide the regeneration of Ipswich Wet Dock over the next 10 to 15 years. The core study area measures 57 ha (see Figure 14.5), of which the Victorian Wet Dock occupies 10 ha. Improvement to the 13 ha Transition Area between the town centre and the waterfront was also proposed in the study. The site has a rich and colourful history, for it was here, on the northern banks of the River Orwell, that the original Anglo-Saxon town of Gipswic was founded. Much of the site is archaeologically important, particularly the north-western quayside. Most of the site is designated as a conservation area, with several listed buildings, and the Transition Area includes several scheduled ancient monuments (Llewelyn-Davies, 1998).

The study team undertook a thorough analysis of the context of the area and a study area appraisal, identifying potential markets and development constraints. Working with the steering group and others, opportunities were explored and shaped into a series of proposals, which were then evaluated and implementation mechanisms suggested. The vision was to ensure that, in a few years' time, local people, visitors and investors in housing, commercial space and leisure would come to recognise Ipswich as a great place – with the regeneration of the dockland area having played a key role in achieving this vision. The study suggested three principal aims:

(1)   To support early development on the Northern Quays
(2)   To improve pedestrian links to the town centre
(3)   To increase marine and leisure facilities in the Wet Dock

A number of engineering issues were identified in the study, which might act as constraints in achieving the stated aims; these included the following:

● Geologically, the area is a glacially eroded chalk valley, filled with sands, gravel and alluvium. The 'Island' is made ground, whilst the northern

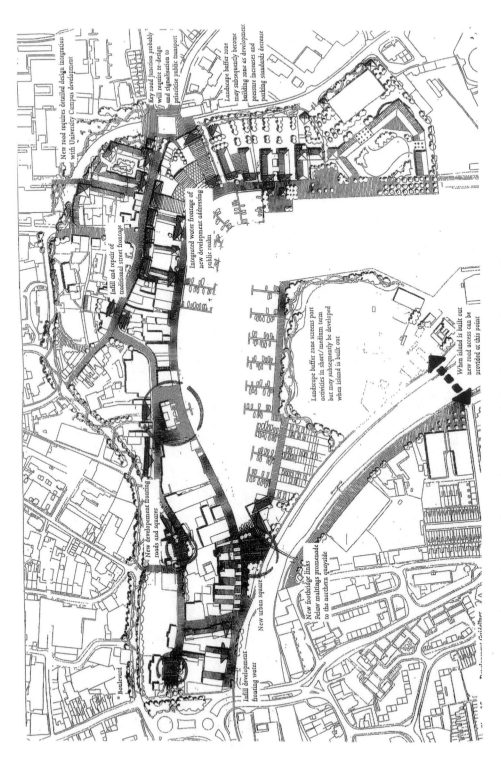

New road requires detailed design integration with University Campus development

Key road junction probably will require re-design and signalisation to prioritise public transport

Landscape buffer zone may subsequently become building zone as development pressure increases and parking standards decrease

Integrated water frontage of new development addressing public realm

Infill and repair of traditional street frontage

Landscape buffer zone screens port activities in short/medium term but may subsequently be developed when island is built out

When island is built out new road access can be provided at this point

New development fronting roads and squares

New urban square

New footbridge links Felaw maltings promenade to the northern quayside

Infill development fronting water

Boulevard

Figure 14.5 Masterplan study area of Ipswich Wet Dock development framework.

quayside constitutes successive 'town fill'. Driven piling would therefore be needed for new construction.

- Archaeology may constrain piling in some areas. Reuse of buildings and preservation *in situ* may be required, with cost implications.
- Desk studies indicated that potentially contaminated land may exist on the Island, east of the Wet Dock and off New Cut West.
- Existing flood defences, although serviceable, required upgrading to cater for a 1-in-200-year flood risk.
- Although adequate off-site services existed, an expensive drainage system would be required for development of the Island.

(Llewelyn-Davies, 1998)

From a market perspective, establishing confidence was considered to be essential but the poor environmental quality, archaeological costs, social housing requirements, piling and land remediation were considered to be stifling demand. As a result, negative land values were indicated within the Transition Area and on the Island site, producing the conclusion that gap-funding would be required in order to attract private investors. Four key markets were identified for the initial phase:

(1) *Residential* – a niche for high-quality new-build housing was perceived to exist, with a take-up rate of 50 units per annum considered achievable, and necessary to establish demand and confidence. Environmental improvements would be required.

(2) *Offices* – demand was considered to exist for quality new-build offices. A 25 000 square feet (2322 square metres) development would establish the initial critical mass.

(3) *Mixed use* – a scheme of about 25 000 square feet (2322 square metres) of restaurants, pubs and retail units, together with 20 000 square feet (1858 square metres) of studio office or workshop space was suggested.

(4) *Marina* – with the upgrading of the lock, giving 24-hour access at all states of the tide, demand existed for a second marina within the Wet Dock, supported by a yacht club.

Other possible uses were also considered for the short to medium term, including an expanded university campus and a new tourism magnet such as a Gipswic Centre.

Several strengths and opportunities were identified by the Llewelyn-Davies team, as well as a number of weaknesses and constraints. The Wet Dock was considered to present one of the best remaining inner-urban waterfront developments in the UK, with a unique sense of place, yet its potential was constrained by being severed from the town centre by the gyratory road system. The River Orwell, without which the Wet Dock would not exist, also constrained the east–west linkage, especially to the Island site which was not considered developable until market demand made it more viable.

The area presented a superb physical setting, with an attractive south-facing waterfront townscape (see Figure 14.6), with fine built heritage, comprising fine-grained mixed-use buildings, and open views of the estuary, yet it suffered from poor environmental impacts including noise, vibration, dirt, dust and air pollution. The town centre and the railway station are only 10 minutes walk away, with a new multiplex cinema to the west and University College to the east, but the immediate area suffered from an almost total lack of public transport, as well as poor pedestrian access to the waterfront.

The development framework identified four priority projects:

(1) *Public realm improvements* – improved traffic circulation, with priorities given to public transport, cyclists and pedestrians, whilst retaining access to local properties. Creation of an attractive Neptune Quayside along the waterfront and two new public squares.

Figure 14.6   Dockside walk along the restored waterfront at Ipswich Wet Dock.

(2) *Refurbishment and conversion* – restore and convert the historic buildings for a mix of uses, enabling restaurants, bars and speciality shopping to spill out into the new squares.

(3) *New build* – construct new buildings on vacant sites around the north quay, to provide a mix of residential, commercial, leisure and educational facilities.

(4) *Marina* – develop a new marina with access from the Island.

By the autumn of 2001, implementation of these recommendations was progressing well. Work on the public realm improvements had created the Neptune Quay Promenade and Bellway had completed a new housing development of 69 flats and four ground-floor retail units (Figure 14.7). Redrow Homes have acquired land next to Neptune Marina and are proposing another new residential development in partnership with the marina. Buildings have been refurbished and converted, including Felaw Maltings which has been converted into a 2797 square metre (30 000 square feet) office building. EEDA has acquired Cranfields Mill, with a floor area of 24 800 square metres

Figure 14.7   New apartments overlooking Neptune Marina at Ipswich Wet Dock.

(267 000 square feet) on a site of 0.7 ha (1.72 acres) for which a design brief was issued in September 2001 (GVA Grimley, 2001), with the intention of creating a genuine mixed-use scheme. The second marina has been developed by ABP and a floating wine bar/restaurant is moored against the quayside. The ground floor of the Old Custom House, headquarters of ABP Port of Ipswich, has been converted into a conference centre and a few doors away is Cobbolds on the Quay, a pub converted from an oast house (Ipswich Waterfront Steering Group, 2000).

Achieving the success to date has not been easy, in spite of the efforts of the steering group. According to Sue Arnold, Head of Strategic Planning and Regeneration, Ipswich Borough Council and a member of the steering group:

> 'One of the major problems with this type of project is the disparate interests of the various landowners. Virtually every section of the water frontage has different owners, all with their own agenda. It's very different to dealing with say a redundant naval dockyard or a greenfield site. Just paving the quayfront required an act of faith on the part of some owners.'

14.4   Meeting demand – masterplanning greenfield development, Cambourne

By no means all needs for development land, whether for residential, commercial, industrial or leisure uses, can be met through reusing land and buildings. Whilst there may be plenty of opportunities for reusing land and buildings in cities and towns such as Sheffield and Ipswich, elsewhere in the UK such opportunities may not exist. Cambridge is one such example, where growth in electronics- and science-based industries has created a demand that cannot be met within the existing envelope of the city.

> 'Some of the most satisfying environments in which to live are those villages and towns which have grown and matured over time and where a sense of community has evolved.'
>
> (Cambourne publicity brochure, undated)

It is the aim of the developers of Cambourne that the same sense of community will be achieved within this completely new development. Created by three of the UK's leading housing developers – Bovis Homes, Alfred McAlpine and Bryant Homes – this new community development is based on a masterplan prepared by Terry Farrell & Partners. Situated seven miles west of Cambridge, Cambourne is intended to create a new 'living environment' of homes, shops and services that will encompass the best of the past to create a more appealing community in which to live today and tomorrow.

Centred on the site of Monkfield Farm, which formerly served St Neots Abbey, Cambourne occupies a site of around 425 ha (1050 acres). The Cambridgeshire Structure Plan identified a need for new homes and employment sites. In order to meet the demand a number of options existed: expand the existing villages and market towns; increase the density of development in the centre of Cambridge; and create new settlements.

Within the area administered by South Cambridgeshire District Council, forming a 'U' to the east, south and west of the city of Cambridge, the option of expanding market towns did not exist. The alternative of creating a new settlement therefore seemed appropriate and developers put forward around ten proposals for consideration. The proposal for Cambourne came from Alfred McAlpine and Stanhope in 1994 in the form of a masterplan and development guide from Terry Farrell and Partners. The historical growth of the surrounding villages had resulted in a general spacing of around one-and-a-half miles between settlements but, at Monkfield Farm, the spacing was more like three miles to the nearest villages (Figure 14.8). This was possibly due to the nature of the previous farm in relation to the abbey, whereas village communities had grown up around other farms in the area.

The masterplan for Cambourne provided for the development of three villages and a business park, around a central high street area with shops, country pub, school, nursery and sports facilities. The three villages of Upper, Lower and Great Cambourne were each intended to have their own character and a range of architectural styles, with homes catering for individuals, growing families and the elderly alike. Small cottage-style homes will sit happily between pretty terraces and emanate outwards from the village centre into grander, detached residences in the 'unplanned' way of natural evolution (Cambourne publicity brochure, undated). A total of 3300 homes will be provided in Cambourne – 1400 in Great Cambourne, 650 in Lower Cambourne and 1250 in Upper Cambourne. Nine hundred of the housing units will be developed as affordable housing to rent or for shared ownership. A small number of self-build plots have also been provided. Different development densities will exist across the development, ranging from 30 units per hectare (12 units per acre) down to 12 units per hectare (5 units per acre), with the highest densities being around the village centres and along the roads leading from the centres. In October 2001 almost 500 houses and apartments were occupied, as were three of the buildings in the business park (see Figures 14.9, 14.10 and 14.11).

The High Street will include a market square formed by a mixture of buildings having traditional façades. For example, it is envisaged that the Exchange Building will hark back to the old East Anglian Corn Exchanges and

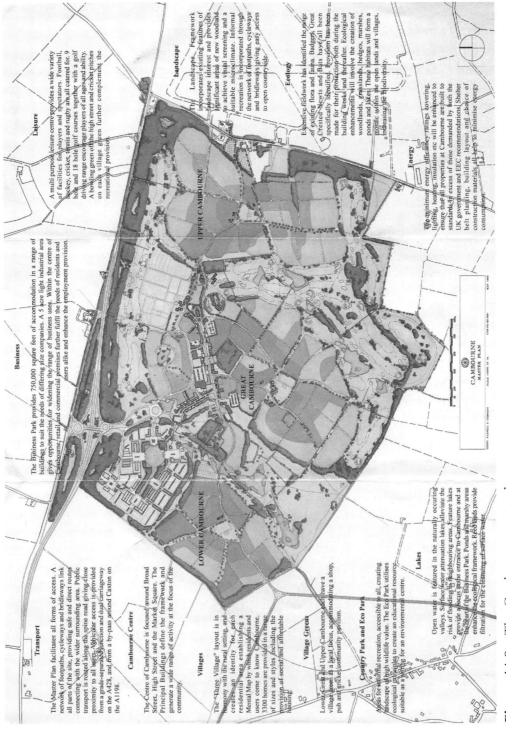

Transport

The Master Plan facilitates all forms of access. A network of footpaths, cycleways and bridleways link all parts of the site, providing safe and direct routes connecting with the wider surrounding area. Public transport is routed along the spine road giving close proximity to all users. Vehicular access is provided from a grade-separated junction and dual carriageway on the A428, and from a by-pass around Caxton on the A1198.

Cambourne Centre

The Centre of Cambourne is focused around Broad Street, High Street and the Market Square. The Principal Buildings define the framework and generate a wide range of activity at the focus of the community.

Villages

The 'Three Village' layout is in harmony with the rural setting, and creates an identity for each residential area establishing a Mental Map by which residents and users come to know Cambourne. 3300 homes are provided in a range of sizes and styles including the provision of social and affordable housing.

Village Greens

Lower Great and Upper Cambourne each have a village green as a focal point, accommodating a shop, pub and a community pavilion.

Country Park and Eco Park

Areas for informal recreation, accessible to all, creating landscape of high wildlife value. The Eco Park utilises ecological principles to create an educational resource suitable as a setting for an environmental centre.

Lakes

Open water is featured in the naturally occurring valleys. Surface water attenuation lakes alleviate the risk of flooding in neighbouring areas. Feature lakes provide a focus at the entrance to Cambourne and at the heart of the Business Park. Ponds and marshy areas enhance the ecological framework. Reed beds provide filtration for the cleansing of surface water.

Business

The Business Park provides 750,000 square feet of accommodation in a range of buildings to suit the needs of differing size companies. A 5 acre light industrial area gives opportunities for widening the range of business uses. Within the centre of Cambourne, retail and commercial premises further fulfil the needs of residents and users alike and enhance the employment provision.

Leisure

A multi purpose leisure centre provides a wide variety of facilities for players and spectators. Football, hockey, cricket, tennis and rugby are all catered for. 9 hole and 18 hole golf courses together with a golf driving range encourage players of all ages and ability. A bowling green on the high street and cricket pitches on each village green further complement the recreational provision.

Landscape

The Landscape Framework incorporates existing features of landscape interest and provides significant areas of new woodland to achieve visual screening and a suitable microclimate. Informal recreation is incorporated through the network of footpaths, cycleways and bridleways giving easy access to open countryside.

Ecology

Extensive fieldwork has identified the range of existing flora and fauna. Badgers, Great Crested Newts and Bats have all been specifically identified. Provision has been made for their protection both during the building works and thereafter. Ecological enhancements will involve the creation of woodlands, grasslands, hedges, marshes, ponds and lakes. These habitats will form a mosaic within the open lands and villages, increasing the biodiversity.

Energy

The minimum energy efficiency ratings covering lighting, heating, insulation etc will be enhanced to ensure that all properties at Cambourne are built to standards in excess of those demanded by both the UK government and EEC recommendations. Shelter belt planting, building layout and choice of construction materials all help to minimise energy consumption.

Figure 14.8 The Cambourne masterplan.

Figure 14.9   Aerial photograph of Cambourne, autumn 2001.

Figure 14.10   New houses at Cambourne.

Figure 14.11 Cambourne Business Park.

will incorporate offices and shops. Two schools were included in the master-plan and one of these, plus the nursery, has already opened. The second school is to follow later in the development. A health centre, church, library, police station and fire station are all proposed. Leisure facilities will include an 18-hole golf course, sports centre, football pitches and tennis courts. Cricket may be played on the village greens. A supermarket is to be developed by Morrisons and will be limited to the sale of food and household goods. Pharmacy and clothing sales will not be allowed in the supermarket as it is intended that these uses should be located on the High Street.

The business park will eventually occupy around 20 ha (50 acres) and provide up to 69 680 square metres (750 000 square feet) of high class office and research and development accommodation. The park is being developed by London-based Development Securities and local developer Wrenbridge Land. Three phase one buildings have been completed and are occupied by Regus Business Centres, Convergys and Citrix Systems. The first three buildings provide employment for an estimated 500 people at Cambourne (Regus providing serviced office accommodation) and, when completed, the business park is expected to employ around 5000 people.

Cambourne is situated off the A428 between Cambridge and St Neots, six miles from the M11 and 11 miles from the A1. The existing road system is inadequate to cater for the eventual size of the development, as by 2006 traffic is expected to have increased to 36 000 vehicles per day, resulting in severe congestion in some sections of the road. The Highways Agency is therefore intending to improve the existing trunk road and responses from the public indicated a high level of support, with 95.9% believing that improvement is necessary (Highways Agency, 2000). With the assistance of the local authorities and the bus companies, public transport was introduced at an early stage in the development, linking the Cambourne villages to the surrounding area and to the city of Cambridge. From Cambridge there is a fast train service, taking 50 minutes to London Kings Cross, with stopping trains taking approximately 15 minutes longer. Stansted airport is approximately 34 miles south of Cambourne, providing international air travel.

As Cambourne is developed from former farmland, the developers are seeking to work with and, where possible, retain the natural features of the land. This natural countryside will be further enhanced by environmental projects including the addition of a 32.5 ha (80 acre) country park, an eco-park, wetlands and marshes. This will include maintaining the existing water quality within the many streams and lakes. Of considerable concern was the tendency of the surrounding area to flooding, especially the village of Bourn, although Cambourne itself is not in a floodplain. Therefore an important part of the masterplan design was the introduction of a series of balancing ponds to contain stormwater. Some of these ponds remain in water at all times, and are being stocked with fish, whilst others are allowed to dry out, thus encouraging biodiversity.

14.5   Paying for regeneration – Millennium Quarter, Tower Hamlets

The London Borough of Tower Hamlets has designated an area of some 20 ha (50 acres) in the heart of the Isle of Dogs as the Millennium Quarter and, as an interim policy, has approved a masterplan. Today the Isle of Dogs is probably best known for Canary Wharf and perhaps this might give the impression that Tower Hamlets as a whole is an affluent, thriving area enjoying a 'spillover' economy from the City of London, but this would be a false impression.

Part of the east London Docklands, the Isle of Dogs and the surrounding area was once the trading hub of the British Empire but by the late 1960s it had changed from being a thriving industrial and port economy to one of the most deprived areas in Britain; overall 150 000 jobs had been lost. Now, through the joint efforts of the London Boroughs and the London Docklands Development Corporation, the Docklands has become the most attractive location for new businesses in Europe (Tower Hamlets and EDAW, 2000, p. 2). Nevertheless, serious problems still remain.

Even after all of the investment that has gone into the area, Tower Hamlets is the most deprived borough in the UK, with 15 out of 17 of its wards in the 5% most deprived. It is a destination for immigrants, refugees and asylum seekers with more than 80 different languages spoken in the borough. Nineteen per cent of the population are on Income Support, compared to 9% for the UK as a whole, and the unemployment rate is around 12%, compared to a national figure of 3.6%. Banking and finance is the largest employer in the borough, requiring high skill levels that many of the population do not possess. Sixty per cent of the housing stock in the borough is social housing, with 14 000 people on the council waiting list – about eight years' wait for a five-person home – and 45% of the population are on housing benefit, including 70% of council tenants.

This deprivation exists in one of the three leading cities in the world (the others being New York and Tokyo) and in a borough where 538 840 square metres (5.8 million square feet) of high-quality office space exists in the Canary Wharf development alone, with a further 659 600 square metres (7.1 million square feet) under construction in the same development. The proximity of Canary Wharf (see Figure 14.12) led the council to designate the Millennium Quarter development area in 1999, as the landowners and developers considered it was ripe for redevelopment.

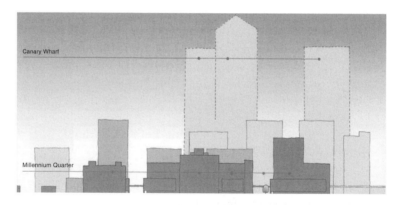

Figure 14.12   The Millennium Quarter.

Tower Hamlets Borough Council approved the consultation draft of the Isle of Dogs Planning and Regeneration Framework in March 1999 and EDAW were commissioned to prepare the masterplan in November of the same year. The Planning and Regeneration Framework established a broad strategy for the Isle of Dogs and identified a number of key focal areas for which master-plans should be prepared, of which the Millennium Quarter is the largest.

The Masterplan provides a framework to guide the future of the Quarter. It demonstrates that, together, the redevelopment of individual sites will create a sustainable urban quarter. Without such a framework, development would happen in a piecemeal way and the opportunity to realise the economic, social, environmental and urban design benefits which the Millennium Quarter could create could be lost (Tower Hamlets and EDAW, 2000, p. 2).

The majority of the existing buildings had been developed as part of the Enterprise Zone in the 1980s, providing a variety of low-density business, industrial and office accommodation. For the most part these were fairly unattractive two-storey buildings, the exception being the Glengall Bridge development, which was constructed with good materials. At the time the Masterplan was prepared, more than 30 organisations and individuals had either a freehold or leasehold interest in the land and buildings in the Millennium Quarter, excluding Glengall Bridge where there were a further 20 leasehold interests. The borough council did not own any of the potential development sites but had adopted the roads. The docks and most of the dock walls are owned and managed by British Waterways (Tower Hamlets and EDAW, 2000, p. 6).

At the end of 1999, approximately 2200 people worked for about 150 employers in the Quarter, with a diverse range of activities including business services, finance, restaurants, retail, printing and publishing. Indications were that people living on the Isle of Dogs filled no more than 15–20% of the jobs and it was considered unlikely that all of the existing firms would wish to remain as part of a long-term redevelopment of the area. However, the council considered it important to support their retention, where possible, by encouraging a mix of commercial accommodation and employment opportunities, including integrated affordable business space.

If the Millennium Quarter is to become part of the strategic centre of the London Borough of Tower Hamlets, and bring significant economic, social and environmental benefits to east London, it must meet the following challenges:

- Provide a significant increase and a diverse range of jobs which provide opportunities for the residents of Tower Hamlets and east London generally.
- Stimulate a substantial increase in office development but at a pace which reflects demand.
- Include a range of workshop and business units to maintain a diverse employment mix.
- Increase the supply of affordable housing for rent and for sale as well as respond to the demand for higher-priced housing.
- Create new visually exciting, welcoming, and socially inclusive public spaces and public realm generally.

- Secure investment to create a self-sustaining mix of uses.
- Promote travel by public transport and prevent increased car use.
- Provide more opportunities for those who live and work in the Quarter, and nearby, to use the waterfront and the water.
- Create a commercially viable, dense development without compromising the quality of the public realm and the pedestrian environment at street level.

To respond to these challenges, the Masterplan:

- Gives an understanding of the public spaces between the buildings in the Quarter.
- Shows how the streets, squares and open spaces of a neighbourhood are to be connected.
- Defines the heights, massing and bulk of the buildings and public spaces.
- Sets the relationship between buildings and public spaces.
- Determines the distribution of uses and their accessibility at ground level.
- Controls the network of movement patterns for all modes of transport and promotes sustainable transport.
- Establishes a clear planning and urban design context as a basis for assessing individual development proposals.
- Provides a mechanism for coordinating and managing the delivery of key infrastructure, public realm, community social, cultural and leisure uses.

(Tower Hamlets and EDAW, 2000, p. 7)

It is intended that the Millennium Quarter will become a vibrant and contemporary space, with the northern part, closest to the Docklands Light Railway, accommodating hundreds of companies of varying sizes. A new community will be established in the southern part of the Quarter, with buildings of a smaller scale, mostly apartments. It is intended that a distinct 'sense of place' will be created, with a high-quality public realm evident in the pedestrian network, new public gardens and plazas, and waterfront promenade (see Figure 14.13). This will not happen overnight and it is hoped that the vision for the Millennium Quarter will be realised over a 10 to 15-year period.

The Quarter already benefits from a greatly improved public transport system but, as the aim is to increase reliance on public transport, with the needs of the pedestrian and cyclist taking prominence over the motor car (Figure 14.14), the Masterplan proposes even more improvements. South Quay Station will be improved, with wider platforms and stairs, and additional bus services will be provided, linking the area with existing communities and popular destinations. A second, more direct, covered and comfortable footbridge will be provided across South Dock and the existing footbridge to

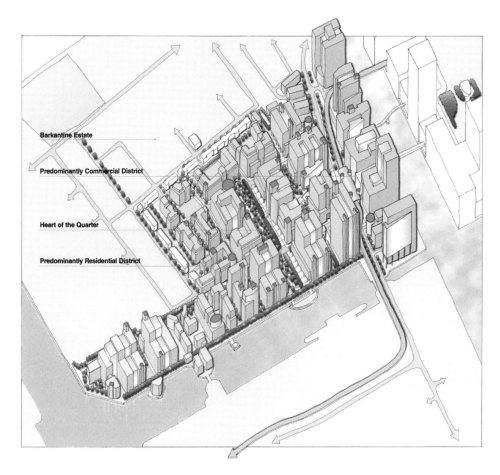

Figure 14.13   Plans for the Millennium Quarter.

Canary Wharf will be reopened once the Heron Quays development has been completed. A new, wider pedestrian crossing will be provided over Marsh Wall and the Sustrans cycle route will be completed.

All of these transport and public realm improvements have to be paid for and it is intended that they will be funded out of an estimated £23 million of 'planning gain' paid by developers under section 106 agreements. When completed, it is expected that the Millennium Quarter will provide 2000 new homes, of which 25% will be affordable housing for sale or rent, and where these are close to existing buildings, heights will be limited to three to five storeys in height. New shops, cafés, art and cultural venues will be provided in the heart of the Quarter, focused on new public spaces and Millharbour Avenue (Figure 14.15). Up to 465 000 square metres (5 million square feet) of office and commercial space, up to 25 storeys high, will be developed in the

Figure 14.14   The needs of the pedestrian and cyclist will take precedence over the motor car in the improved Millennium Quarter.

north of the Quarter. It is estimated that 20 000 new jobs will be located in the area (Tower Hamlets and EDAW, 2000, p. 14), compared to the 2200 that existed when the Masterplan was prepared.

14.6   Summary

This chapter has looked at four very different reasons for masterplanning new developments. In Sheffield the driver was to create a plan that would not only produce economic and physical regeneration in the city centre but to spread the benefits further afield to tackle social and cultural problems in disadvantaged areas of the city. For Ipswich the objective was to bring life back into the old docks, preserve the historic old buildings and find new uses for them and to link the waterfront to the town centre. At Cambourne the new development on a greenfield site provided an opportunity to create a new

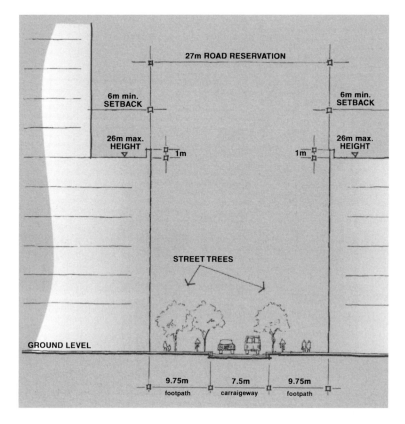

Figure 14.15   The social development of the heart of the Millennium Quarter.

community, and for the Millennium Quarter in Tower Hamlets, the expectation is one of significant urban renewal and enhanced quality of life for the residents of the area.

The challenge for cities like Sheffield is not merely to aspire to catch up, but to anticipate the next business trends and requirements and try to be ahead of the game (Sheffield City Centre Masterplan, 2001). The city has the potential to transform itself and to seize new opportunities. Investment and redevelopment are taking place but there is still a long way to go. In Ipswich, residential, business and leisure activity have brought new life to the Wet Dock. The public realm is being improved and more development is about to happen, but for the Area of Transition between the Wet Dock and the town centre not much has happened. The redevelopment of this area will be an important step in linking the town centre and the dock.

At Cambourne, the developers have adhered fairly well to the Masterplan in terms of the general layout but less well in terms of the design guide. Although some new housing designs have been introduced, there does seem to be some loss of opportunity to introduce innovative designs and layouts. The present lack of any shops or a public house does mean that the development gives the impression of being two housing estates, separated by green fields, a school and a play school. Employees on the business park also complain about the lack of facilities and have to drive to one of the surrounding villages in order to eat at lunch-time. Cambourne was designed at a time when there was less pressure to increase development densities and, so far as Great and Lower Cambourne are concerned, there may be little opportunity to make any significant changes. Perhaps Upper Cambourne, where development has not yet started, may provide an opportunity to be more innovative in terms of designs and densities.

Millennium Quarter is very different to the other three studies although, like the Ipswich Wet Dock, it could be termed an urban waterside development and, like Sheffield, it is an urban area. However, it is also very unlike both of these in terms of the great disparity between the 'haves' and the 'have nots'. Implementation of the masterplan will take a long time to produce any long-term tangible benefits for the local community but it deserves the opportunity to succeed.

Public consultation is an important aspect of the masterplanning process. In the case of the Millennium Quarter, EDAW consulted a wide range of interests and held meetings with resident groups, borough council elected councillors, landowners and developers. The Government Office for London and the London Planning Advisory Committee both supported the process. The Masterplan was also the subject of a public exhibition and a public seminar. Similar processes were also undertaken for each of the other case study Masterplans.

14.7   Checklist

- Masterplans need to be innovative and look to the future
- Due to the complexities involved in planning large mixed-use schemes, masterplans may take many years before they are completed.
- Local employment requirements need to be taken into account.
- A masterplan can bring together many landowners, who might be unable to develop their sites in isolation.

Chapter 15
Buildings and Concepts

15.1   Introduction

Many examples of good design could be included in this chapter, for example it could list the winners of the latest Civic Trust awards, *www.civictrust.org.uk/awards/2001*, or of the Royal Institute of British Architects (RIBA) awards *www.riba.org.uk*. Instead, the approach has been to describe a few buildings falling into different categories or scale of development. The first example is of a development of strategic importance in a city-centre location. Second, a look is taken at city-centre living and the problem of providing homes for key workers. Third comes the question of reusing buildings and fourth locating modern industry in suitable surroundings.

15.2   Strategic redevelopment – the new BullRing, Birmingham

The regeneration of Birmingham city centre is of strategic importance for the city, comprising a phased redevelopment of around 16.2 ha (40 acres). Creating 8000 jobs, the regeneration scheme of which the new BullRing forms a major part, will inject over £800 million into the local economy. The Birmingham Alliance, a partnership between Hammerson plc, Henderson Global Investors Ltd and Land Securities, is working with the city council to ensure a phased and structured approach to Europe's largest city-centre retail regeneration project.

Over 7.2 million people live within an hour's drive of Birmingham city centre, with the largest professional/financial sector outside London, but it lacks the retail capacity to service this catchment. Birmingham is the UK's leading conference city, home to the International Convention Centre and the National Exhibition Centre, employing 320 000 people in the service and leisure sector – 71% of total employment in the city. There are three universities in the city, with a student population approaching 50 000, and it is a major centre for telecommunications, information technology and the development of knowledge-based industries.

The new BullRing will provide 110 000 square metres (1.18 million square feet) of prime retail space on 10.2 ha (25 acres), parking for 3200 cars, plus a 4500 square metre state-of-the-art indoor market which opened in September 2000 (see Figure 15.1). Work on the new BullRing started in June 2000 and the development is due to open in Autumn 2003. It replaces the 1960s Bull Ring shopping centre, which contained 32 500 square metres (350 000 square feet) of supermarkets, retail stores and retail markets, plus the landmark Rotunda, a circular office building. However, the commercial history of the site is much older than the 1960s development.

In 1166 Birmingham was given the right to have a market, beneath the spire of St Martin's church in the Bull Ring and, over the next 800 years the village was transformed into a world-class industrial city, gaining titles such as 'the toyshop of Europe' and 'the city of 1000 trades'. Archaeologists working on the final dig at the new BullRing have found strong evidence of a wealthy and prosperous lifestyle in the city, dating from mediaeval times and continuing throughout the sixteenth and seventeenth centuries. Four excavations on the site have uncovered evidence of thirteenth and fourteenth century town planning; mediaeval bull horns and a fish-shaped lead weight; the boundary of the Lord of Birmingham's twelfth century deer park; a mediaeval communal well; and a superbly preserved chair, believed to date from the mid-seventeenth century. Evidence was found to indicate that Birmingham was a thriving industrial centre, with a central tanning industry, in the thirteenth and fourteenth centuries – long before the Industrial Revolution.

The new BullRing development builds on the historic street patterns of the city and will, once again, link New Street and High Street to St Martin's Church, the markets and Digbeth beyond. A new pedestrian walkway next to St Martin's Queensway will be called Swan Passage after a nearby ancient route called Swan Alley, which appears on the 1731 plan of the city. Other old names to reappear will be Jamaica Row and Spiceal Street, which first appeared on plans from 1795. Jamaica Row is believed to have derived from a pub called the Black Boy after King Charles II, who was dark-skinned. Spiceal Street was a later variant of Mercer St, the street of the city's cloth merchants. Both will form new pedestrian routes.

The development is immediately adjacent to New Street Station, Birmingham's principal rail station and a bus interchange. The nearby Moor Street Station is to be refurbished as part of the project. The city's inner ring road, or 'concrete collar', which has acted as a constraint against expansion of the city centre, has been broken, providing a link to the east side of the city.

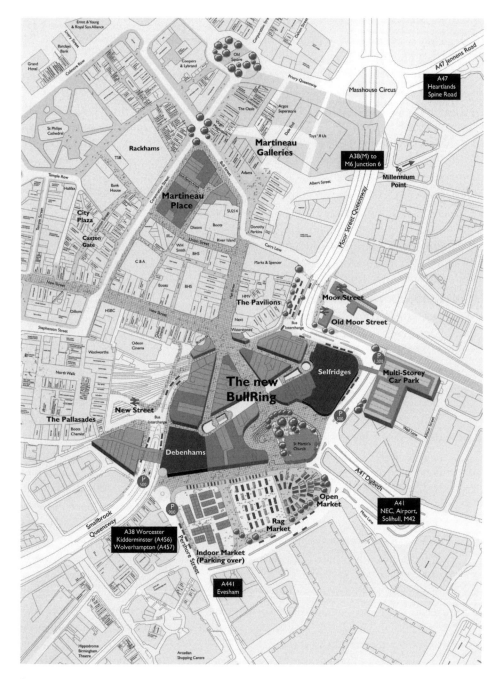

Figure 15.1   The new BullRing development plan.

Figure 15.2   A forest of tower cranes at the new BullRing.

By mid–June 2001 there were around 400 people working on the site and 10 tower cranes (see Figure 15.2). Excavation for foundations has involved the removal of around 180 000 cubic metres of soil and rock, peaking at 400 vehicle movements per day. Approximately 65 000 t of concrete from the old Bull Ring has been crushed and recycled as structural fill material for off-site use, with small quantities being used on the site for haul roads and ramps. Around 12 000 t of steel has been removed for recycling. Four hundred piles, up to 19 m long, have been installed using continuous piling techniques. Some of these piles are only 1.5 m (5 ft) from the sides of the railway tunnels serving New Street Station.

The large, strategic nature of this development is such that it can only be undertaken by a developer of considerable substance or, most probably, as in this case a consortium of developers and investors. Involvement of the city council is also an essential component of such a development, both in terms of planning and execution. The sheer scale of the demolition and excavation works requires a great deal of thought, especially when they are in such close proximity to major infrastructures and public areas.

15.3   Affordable city-centre living

In spite of an upsurge in residential development in city centres such as Leeds, London, Manchester and Nottingham, there is considerable concern that this provision of new housing is not meeting the needs of the people who need to live in these central areas. 'Yuppie' loft apartments tend to be priced beyond the means of key workers in hospitals, the police and fire services. The result is that these people, who often work unsocial hours, are being forced to live considerable distances from their places of work. In London in particular, high house prices and a declining quality of life are forcing or encouraging thousands of Londoners out of the capital and into the provinces, Johnston (2001), with figures from the Office for National Statistics showing that in 12 months 230 000 people left the capital and 163 000 arrived from within the UK.

One approach to resolving the problem of providing homes in city centres is that adopted by the Joseph Rowntree Foundation with its CASPAR developments (City-centre Apartments for Single People at Affordable Rents) two of which have been completed in Birmingham and Leeds. The philosophy behind CASPAR comes from the Government's housing projections that some 80% of all new households formed in the period up to 2021 could be accommodating single people, whilst most new housing for sale is designed for families. For those moving around for job reasons and not yet ready to put down roots, it is easier to move in and out of renting without the responsibilities of maintenance, gardening and DIY (Joseph Rowntree Foundation, 2000, p. 4).

Other considerations may also apply; for example, those not in a fixed relationship will not wish to take out a mortgage in two names but conventional two-bedroom apartments or houses may not be affordable by a single wage-earner. Divorcees may be encumbered with financial commitments that make it impossible to consider purchasing a home, whilst recent graduates with loans to repay may not be ready to take on mortgage debts. For all of these and other single people working in city centres but not in highly paid jobs, renting may be the answer. However, they may not qualify for subsidised social housing, and monthly rents in private-sector housing may actually be significantly higher than mortgage repayments. Thus they are in a trap.

Research commissioned by the Joseph Rowntree Foundation, undertaken by Caroline Oakes and Eleanor McKee, studied consumer views of market renting in Leeds. Extended group discussions with middle-income working single men and women, and young childless couples, discovered:

- Attitudes to renting were changing: whilst purchase was still seen as the ultimate goal by most, renting was found to be growing in popularity, not least because it offers greater flexibility/freedom and allows spending on other priorities.

- The highest priority for renters was location: whilst people might be prepared to overlook certain aspects of the dwelling itself, they would not be prepared to move into an area that lacks appeal for them.
- There was a clear division between the 'urbanised' who appreciated the 'buzz' and social anonymity of city life and the 'country life'/'suburbanised' who wanted a quieter pace, more outdoor pursuits and often had family ties outside the city centre.
- The car remained important (even though mileage would be much reduced for those who would cease to commute). Secure parking was regarded as essential.
- The interior was regarded as more important than the external appearance, but there was a clear preference for renovated/old buildings.
- Preference was for part-furnished accommodation, providing only curtains, carpets, fitted kitchens and wardrobes.
- No one wanted a designated communal area which was there solely to encourage neighbourly contact.
- Participants expected to pay rents from £80 to £110 per week for one/two bedrooms.

(Findings from Oakes and McKee, 1997)

The research indicated a demand for rented housing in city centres and the Foundation decided to put the research to the test. Although the participants in the focus group discussions indicated a preference for renovated older buildings, e.g. a former warehouse overlooking a canal, the Foundation decided to opt for new buildings on the basis that the costs should be more predictable.

The research confirmed that a central location was very important and that the apartments should be light and bright, with sufficient space for two people and/or occasional visitors, including children. Personal security was perceived to be more important by women than by men, but secure car parking was a high priority for men. A discount for those not wanting a parking space was a popular concept. The specification should include main appliances, as well as carpets and curtains.

The locations chosen for the first two CASPAR projects, Birmingham (CASPAR I) and Leeds (CASPAR II), were both within walking distance of the main commercial, cultural and leisure areas, and main-line railway stations, with all central amenities easily accessible by cycle routes. Top architects were chosen to provide award-winning contemporary designs and each scheme has larger-than-usual one-bedroom apartments (around 50 square metres), with one secure parking space provided for each apartment. Tenants who do not have a car have their rent reduced by around £45 to £50 per month. The apartments meet the 'Secure by Design' criteria and are served by lifts. Space standards achieve the Lifetime Homes criteria for accessibility and adaptability, making the apartments suitable for a large proportion of disabled people.

CASPAR I (Figure 15.3) occupies a site of 0.2 ha (0.49 acres), producing a development density of 225 residential units per hectare, CASPAR II (Figure 15.4) on a slightly larger site of 0.345 ha (0.85 acres) – due to the configuration of the roads and green space around the perimeter – achieves a density of 130 units per hectare. Therefore these developments both achieved an even higher density than the suggestions advanced in the Urban Task Force report but it must be recognised that these developments are addressing a particular market and are on very small sites. Therefore they are not representative of housing needs as a whole. Nevertheless, given the projected nature of new household requirements, they do indicate that very much higher densities can be achieved.

Figure 15.3   A view of the CASPAR I apartment block, Birmingham.

Sites for the first two projects were selected in consultation with the local authorities and, whilst negotiations for purchase were under way, a design-and-build competition was held for teams of contractors, architects and quantity surveyors. Trustees from the Joseph Rowntree Foundation and independent specialists undertook judging of the competition entries. Five teams were short-listed and each was awarded the sum of £5000 to work up a detailed

Figure 15.4   The CASPAR II apartment block, Leeds.

proposition against a brief that included meeting Lifetime Homes accessibility/ space standards and a total design-and-build cost of around £50 000 for each apartment (Joseph Rowntree Foundation, 2000, p. 8).

The final outcome was that the cost budgets were exceeded, resulting in an average cost per apartment of £51 900 for the Birmingham scheme and £52 300 in Leeds, both excluding land. Site contamination on both sites was found to be worse than originally anticipated. The innovative construction techniques used at Leeds reduced the build time when compared to Birmingham but the Leeds site, being larger, was also more expensive per unit. Thus the final costs including fees and land came out at £65 200 per apartment for Birmingham and £69 900 for Leeds. These figures need to be compared to the Total Cost Indicators, fixed by the Housing Corporation, of £60 600 for Birmingham and £57 300 for Leeds.

No grants or subsidies were received in respect of either of the CASPAR projects. After deduction of all costs involved, the two schemes are producing a return on capital employed of 6.4% in Birmingham and 6.1% in Leeds.

The CASPAR projects provide affordable homes in city centres for those people who wish to rent their home but what about others who wish to buy? A study by the National Housing Federation[15.1] found that, in over half of all English counties outside of London, an income of over £30 000 a year is needed to buy an average-price home. In 18 English counties and all but four London Boroughs, to buy a home with a 95% mortgage (borrowing three times annual income), a household needs to earn over £40 000. In only one London Borough – Barking and Dagenham – is an income of less than £30 000 needed to buy an average-price home (National Housing Federation, 2001), *www.housing.org.uk*.

These facts make stark reading when compared with Government figures showing that over 70% of households earn below the £30 000 mark (Office for National Statistics, 2000), *www.statistics.gov.uk/statbase*. The National Housing Federation argues that the Government's £250 million Starter Home Initiative, that will help 10 000 workers over three years with the cost of their home, is likely to far outstrip supply.

One possible solution to the problem of providing affordable housing for purchase in city centres has been suggested by architects Piercy Conner. Their aim is to produce miniature flats, based on the compact designs of catamarans and caravans, aiming at a selling price of £70 000 in central London to allow low earners to get on the capital's property ladder (Baker, 2001). The micro-flats will measure about 23 square metres (250 square feet) and have a double bedroom, living room, shower room and kitchen. Buyers will have the option to add a balcony or dining room.

15.4   Reusing buildings

Although the principal focus of this book is on new-build development, albeit mostly on previously developed land, the potential to reuse buildings must not be ignored. The following case study illustrates this potential.

15.4.1   *The Match Works, Speke, Merseyside*

The Match Works is the conversion of the former Bryant and May factory by developers Urban Splash. The landmark Grade II listed building is one mile from Liverpool John Lennon Airport and 10 minutes from Liverpool city

---

[15.1] The National Housing Federation is the representative body of around 1400 'not for profit' independent social landlords – commonly known as housing associations – providing over 1.4 million homes.

centre. The architects, Shed KM, have contrasted the details of the existing building with clean modern lines for its new use as quality offices. Set in an expansive landscaped area, the building has views across the River Mersey.

Following closure of the factory in the early 1990s the factory complex was acquired by the Speke-Garston Development Company. The Speke-Garston Development Company was established in 1996 and is a joint venture between the Northwest Development Agency and Liverpool City Council, backed by £18 million of European Objective 1 funding. It is spearheading a £50 million drive to breathe new life into the industrial heartland of south Liverpool. It provides a one-stop-shop for new investors, offering comprehensive advice and information on property, technical and environmental issues.

The Match Works building is part of a larger development of the 6.4 ha (15.75 acre) former match factory. Having acquired the whole site, the Speke-Garston Development Company set about finding a development partner with the vision to take forward the redevelopment project. Urban Splash was selected as the preferred developer from a final short-list of three developers.

So as to facilitate conversion to offices of the listed building at the front of the match factory site, and to provide car parking, two bays of industrial buildings at the rear were demolished. The converted building now provides 8004 square metres (86 154 square feet) of office accommodation over three levels (Figure 15.5). Six pavilion units of different sizes, with ground and mezzanine floors, each have their own separate entrances and a curved service pod at the rear (Figure 15.6) containing designer kitchen and toilet facilities.

At first-floor level the accommodation is open plan, providing 2684 square metres (28 890 square feet) of offices, as one or two suites. The first floor is accessed through the central entrance area, under the Water Tower, by lift and staircase. Good natural light comes through large feature windows and there is a floor-to-ceiling height of 4 m. The West Wing provides two further suites, at ground and first-floor levels, of 232 square metres (2497 square feet) each, finished to the same specification as the main building.

A short distance from the Match Works is the former terminal building of Liverpool Airport, now renamed the Liverpool John Lennon Airport. The old art deco terminal building has been replaced by a modern terminal but has found a new lease of life through conversion to a Marriott Hotel (Figure 15.7).

Based in Manchester and Liverpool, Urban Splash was founded in 1993 by Tom Bloxham and Jonathan Falkingham who identified a market for well-designed mixed-use developments. They were convinced that many redundant or underused historic buildings in the central areas of the two cities had a real future and could be adapted for exciting new uses. Since it was founded, the company has refurbished many well-known buildings by utilising con-

Figure 15.5 The Match Works, Speke, Liverpool – front view.

Figure 15.6 The Match Works, Speke, Liverpool – rear view.

Figure 15.7   The Marriott Hotel, Speke.

Figure 15.8   An external view of Smithfield Buildings, Manchester.

temporary architectural solutions to complement the quality of the original architecture. The company is perhaps best known for its conversions to provide loft-style apartments and has won many awards for its developments, of which Smithfield Buildings in Manchester (Figures 15.8 and 15.9) is probably best known, having been featured in many television programmes.

Figure 15.9   A view of the interior of Smithfield Buildings, Manchester.

15.5   Providing for modern industries

As discussed in Chapter 2, Government planning policies place a great deal of emphasis on the reuse of previously developed land for residential purposes and, as seen from the masterplanning case studies in Chapter 14, mixed-use projects are often seen as the best way forward for major urban regeneration schemes. It could, however, be argued that instead of developing former industrial sites for housing and commercial uses, they should be used to accommodate new industrial developments.

Several counterarguments may be advanced against the reuse of former industrial sites for new industries. These include:

- Inadequate highway infrastructures in inner-city areas for modern heavy-goods vehicles (HGVs).
- Lack of a suitably trained workforce.
- Inappropriate image of the area for new industry.

The following case study describes a new industrial development in a greenfield-type location that, nevertheless, makes good use of the previous activities on the land.

15.5.1   *Rolls-Royce Manufacturing Plant and UK head office for BMW Group*

When BMW acquired Rolls-Royce from the Volkswagen-Audi Group, following the sale of Rolls-Royce and Bentley by Vickers plc, they acquired only the name – no factory premises, tools, dies or workforce. It was therefore necessary to find a site on which to build a new factory.

The selected site, near Chichester in West Sussex, was chosen on the basis of its transport links to airports and seaports and the specialist skills of the local work-force. The site is adjacent to the Goodwood Estate and vehicle testing will be carried out on the nearby Goodwood Motor Circuit. Detailed planning and environmental studies were undertaken before the site was finally selected. As the site already had planning permission for gravel extraction it was possible to take account of the planned excavation, partially sinking the buildings into the ground.

Nicholas Grimshaw and Partners, architects of the Eden Project in Cornwall, won an international competition to design the £60 million manufacturing and office complex, with a floor area of about 46 500 square metres (500 000 square feet). The development will accommodate approximately 350 people in development, design, production, marketing and sales, as well as commercial and office operations. The manufacturing facilities will produce an entirely new Rolls-Royce saloon to be launched by the BMW Group in 2003.

The scheme places considerable emphasis on sensitive landscaping and the use of environmentally friendly production techniques. A living green roof further reduces the impact on the local topography so, from a distance, the buildings will blend into the landscape. The approach down a sweeping driveway will reveal glimpses of natural stone walls and, at the heart of the development, a courtyard will allow views of every part of the manufacturing process (Figure 15.10). The finely detailed façades will reveal the quality of the restrained architecture.

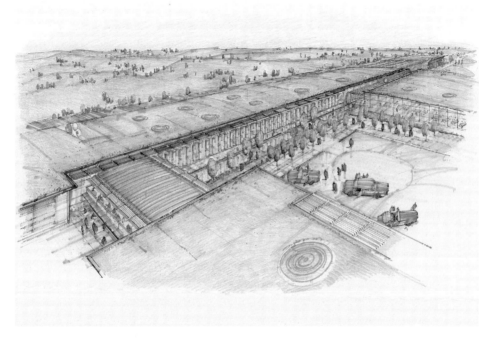

Figure 15.10   Proposed new Rolls-Royce factory at Goodwood.

The development comprises three main elements: a Pavilion, assembly building and paintshop, together with associated services and storage buildings. The Pavilion houses the design studio together with administration and customer relations functions. The assembly building's form and location are designed to optimise the production line.

A large proportion of the development will be naturally ventilated and the design maximises daylighting through careful orientation of the buildings. The landscaping scheme is conceived to create a positive impact on the surroundings through the use of planting, natural materials and screen banks.

The intention of the architects and their client is to create a finely crafted, contemporary building that works in harmony with its natural setting. In this way the new manufacturing plant and head office will reflect the ethos behind the Rolls-Royce name, where technology and tradition are brought together with exceptional results (Nicholas Grimshaw and Partners, 2001) *www.ngrimshaw.co.uk.*

15.6   Summary

This chapter has considered a small selection of different developments and concepts. It is not intended to cover a broad spectrum of development forms, instead the purpose has been to look at how designers and developers have tackled a variety of different problems.

The new BullRing in Birmingham is a major strategic development in the centre of the city, replacing an old centre with a poor reputation that was scorned by the people of the West Midlands. It is a massive commitment in terms of investment and duration of the project. A fundamental issue was that of replacing the market, which had been located in this part of Birmingham for hundreds of years, a problem that was solved by giving priority to its relocation in the early stages of the development.

Housing for key markets is a serious problem in London and the South-East, where nurses, police and fire service personnel, teachers and other essential workers cannot afford to purchase even the lowest-priced properties, let alone buy a family house. In consequence, they are being forced to live many miles from their places of employment and possibly live in employer-provided accommodation between shifts. The Government's proposals to provide financial support will only assist a small number of these key workers and, whilst initiatives such as the provision of homes over (or adjacent to) non-residential uses will also assist, this issue is likely to remain a problem for the foreseeable future. It should also be recognised that similar problems exist in other major cities, where workers are forced to live some distance from their place of employment. Problems such as these do not help to make progress towards sustainable development. CASPAR and similar schemes help to redress the balance but even these may be priced out of the market.

Reusing buildings can make an important contribution, not only in preserving heritage but also in terms of renewing the vitality of an area. The Match Works and the Marriott Hotel are important components in the regeneration of the Speke–Garston area of Liverpool. Smithfield Buildings and the numerous other residential and mixed-use schemes in Manchester city centre have transformed the city over the last decade.

We should not forget, with the present focus on reusing land for residential and mixed-use developments, that land is also required for uses that cannot be incorporated into mixed-use schemes and for which much previously developed land may be unsuitable. Finding solutions such as that proposed for the new Rolls-Royce factory may not always be possible, but the potential should be explored.

15.7   Checklist

- New buildings should fit into their surroundings.
- Developers and designers should take account of any historical aspects when proposing new buildings.
- Security needs to be taken into account in the early design stages.
- Do not overlook the possibility of reusing old buildings.

Chapter 16
Planning for the Future

16.1   Introduction

Parts 2 to 4 have considered three essential components of the development process:

(1)   *Land* – the essential raw material of any development project.
(2)   *Development* – the activity of providing new buildings and infrastructure, of using or reusing land and buildings.
(3)   *Design* – the essential drawing together of all the elements in such a way as to produce a product that is sustainable, attractive, good to live, work or spend leisure time in, and that is economically viable.

It has not been possible to cover the above three components in the fullest detail; indeed, this was not the intention of the book. There are plenty of good texts or other sources of reference dealing with specific issues in more detail and many of these have been cited in the text. Rather, the purpose was to consider the components of the development process from the perspective of the planner, surveyor, architect or developer confronted with the challenge of creating a good and profitable development.

It was appreciated at the outset that this book was being written at a time when many important events were occurring in terms of planning and development policies, urban regeneration and land use in Britain. However, the extent of change was perhaps not fully appreciated, although it rapidly became apparent as the writing progressed. It could be argued that perhaps a book of this type is a little premature and that time should be allowed for policies to be fully formulated and implemented. Such an argument could, however, result in the book never being written for, in the field of urban development, change is always happening.

In particular, it was known that a consultation draft of new planning guidance for the redevelopment of contaminated land was likely to be issued in November 2001 and the Green Paper on the reform of the planning process in December. The work has therefore sought to describe the situation, as it existed in November 2001, when the manuscript was delivered to the publisher. It was nevertheless appreciated that further changes may occur, or policy changes may be announced before the publication date. Therefore, in order to ensure that the book is as up to date as possible, provision was made for this chapter to be completed at the latest possible moment before the book went to press.

16.2   The problems with planning

The town planning system as it currently exists in England and Wales is now over 50 years old, having its origins in the 1947 Town and Country Planning Act. Whilst, in some respects, it functions in an adequate manner in allocating land for specific uses and in providing a regulatory regime, it is also heavily criticised. Some of the shortcomings of the present system were highlighted in the study of stakeholders in *Releasing Brownfields* (Syms, 2001), and the Planning Green Paper *Planning: Delivering a Fundamental Change* (DTLR, 2001c) describes the problems in some detail and these are briefly described below.

16.2.1   Complexity

The problems of complexity can be defined as the system being remote, hard to understand, and difficult to access.

- A multi-layered structure, with up to four tiers in some areas, means that plans are often out of date, inconsistent with one another and with national guidance.
- National planning guidance is long, often unfocused, and mixes policy (which must be followed) with practice advice.
- The rules applying to different types of development are often unclear.
- The planning appeal procedures can seem obscure and it is sometimes hard to understand the basis for decisions.

16.2.2   Speed and predictability

The problems surrounding lack of speed and predictability are perceived as: preventing instead of ensuring good development, lack of community involvement, and the inevitable frustration for business.

- The speed of decision-making is both slow and variable between authorities.
- There is a lack of predictability, with the outcome of applications frequently being uncertain because of insufficient clarity about the criteria used to judge the application.
- The process of updating plans is expensive and takes several years, and may be seen as unaffordable by some authorities.
- The lack of speed in dealing with appeals and call-ins; the failure to meet deadlines.

16.2.3 Community engagement

The present system often fails to engage communities.

- The processes leading to the adoption of a plan are so protracted that few community groups, or businesses, can afford to sustain their involvement – perceived as favouring those with the deepest pockets and greatest stamina.
- Planning committees can make decisions without applicants or objectors being able to present their case.
- Some planning procedures are legalistic and, in consequence, effective participation may require specialist knowledge or access to professional advice.

16.2.4 Customer focus and standards of service

The present system lacks customer focus and planning departments are over-stretched.

- The inability to obtain straightforward advice about how to submit a planning application and, once it has been submitted, to access information about progress; 'e-business' is poorly developed.
- User-friendly information is not always available and, because they are so burdened with householder applications, local planning authorities are often unable to give sufficient attention to complex industrial and commercial applications.
- There are serious skill and resource shortages in most planning departments and elected councillors serving on planning committees are often insufficiently well trained.

16.2.5　Enforcement

There is a need for effective action.

- There is a perception – often accurate – that planning regulations are not being sufficiently enforced, resulting in a lack of confidence in the system.

16.3　Proposals for change

The problems outlined in the previous section are very real. They deprive us of the system we need to plan for a sustainable future. They make the planning system the subject of constant attack and its decisions suspect. This in turn has seriously demoralised the planning profession and damaged its ability to recruit new blood. Until there is a clear sense that the system has overcome these problemss, it will not attract the degree of public confidence that a good planning system deserves (DTLR, 2001c, paragraph 2.8).

16.3.1　Addressing the concerns of business

A major focus of the Green Paper is the Government's intention that there will be a fundamental change in planning so that it works much better for business. It intends that businesses will be able to submit applications against a background of understanding the basis on which the applications will be considered and in the knowledge that they will get a fast decision. In some areas new 'Business Planning Zones' will allow planning controls to be lifted where they are not necessary and new handling targets will distinguish business from householder applications. For the largest planning applications, delivery contracts will be drawn up between local planning authorities and applicants, setting timetables for reaching decisions and providing for penalties if they are not met.

16.3.2　Changes to the 'plan-led' system – the Local Development Framework

Whilst the Green Paper restates a commitment to a 'plan-led' system of development control, it acknowledges a need for fundamental reforming. This includes simplifying the plan hierarchy, reducing the number of tiers and clarifying the relationship between them. It recognises the need for shorter, better focused, plans at the local level, that can be adopted and revised more quickly. The need for greater community involvement in the process of plan preparation and improved integration with other local strategies and plans is also recognised.

The Green Paper therefore proposes the abolition of structure plans, local plans and unitary development plans. These would be replaced with a new single-level plan – the Local Development Framework – consisting of:

- A statement of core policies setting out the local authority's vision and strategy to be applied in promoting and controlling development throughout its area.
- More detailed action plans for smaller local areas of change, such as urban extensions, town centres and neighbourhoods undergoing renewal.
- A map showing the areas of change for which action plans are to be prepared and existing designations, such as conservation areas.

(DTLR, 2001c, paragraph 4.8)

It is envisaged that plans produced on this basis would take less time to prepare, amend and keep up to date. Plan preparation normally would be undertaken by the relevant district, unitary and National Park authorities (DTLR, 2001c, paragraph 4.17), but authorities may wish to work together in order to produce joint frameworks. This may be seen as being particularly advantageous for smaller authorities. The Green Paper sets out an expectation that Local Development Frameworks should be prepared in months rather than years.

The Green Paper proposes that the Local Development Framework should contain a Statement of Community Involvement, setting out how the community should be involved in both the continuing review of the Framework and in commenting on significant planning applications (DTLR, 2001c, paragraph 4.22). This statement will set the standard for good practice and will provide a simple and clear guideline that will enable the community to know with confidence when and how it can expect to be consulted. It will also provide a benchmark, enabling applicants to understand what is expected from them in terms of community consultation. For large developments, it is proposed that compliance with the terms of the Statement and its requirements for engaging the community, should be a material consideration supporting a planning application.

16.3.3 Action plans

Action plans should form a new focus for community involvement in developments affecting neighbourhoods or other local areas (DTLR, 2001c paragraph 4.24). As part of the process, local authorities will have the opportunity to seek direct participation from local people in shaping the future of their communities. This will include obtaining the views of local people on the type of development they would like to see and how it is to be laid out, the intention being one of taking planning closer to the people it most directly affects.

16.3.4   *Speeding up the process*

The Green Paper seeks views as to how the time taken for adoption procedures may be reduced, making it less time-consuming and adversarial. Options might include: wide public participation followed by adoption by the council; an examination before an independent chair to test the adequacy of the plan and its preparation process; or a public informal hearing of representations before an inspector (DTLR, 2001c, paragraph 4.26). It is envisaged that, under either of the two latter options, the report of the chair or the inspector would be binding on the local authority. The Green Paper also envisages that the Secretary of State would retain a reserve power of direction to amend Local Development Frameworks. This would only be used in exceptional circumstances, such as where national or regional policy has been incorrectly applied, or where the Statement of Community Involvement was inadequate (DTLR, 2001c, paragraph 4.28).

One of the main complaints levelled at the existing system by property developers is that, due to the time taken to prepare and adopt plans, they are frequently out of date even before they come into effect, yet alone after two or three years of operation. The Government considers it essential to its new approach that Local Development Frameworks are kept up to date. It is in the authority's own interests and those of the business and the wider community to ensure that the Framework takes full account of any changes to planning policies at national and regional levels (DTLR, 2001c, paragraph 4.30). It is considered unlikely that core policies will be subject to frequent change; nevertheless, local authorities will be required to keep them under continuous review. Local authorities will be required to publish the statement of core policies each year and to keep a continuously updated version of the Framework on their website.

16.3.5   *Role of the counties*

In 'non-unitary' areas, the present arrangement is that county structure plans address strategic issues, including house building, the broad location of new employment sites, improvements to the transport infrastructure, and policies on the development of built-up areas or the conservation of the countryside. In areas administered by unitary authorities, part 1 of the unitary development plans deals with similar issues. In the Government's view the county is no longer the most appropriate level at which to decide many of the key strategic planning issues and, as many of these cut across county boundaries, they should be dealt with at regional or subregional levels. The Green Paper seeks views as to whether the counties should have a role in assisting the regional, district and unitary authorities in preparing their plans (DTLR, 2001c, paragraph 4.37). It does not, however, propose changing the role of the counties in respect of the preparation of Minerals and Waste plans, or in deciding applications on these land uses (DTLR, 2001c, paragraph 4.38).

16.3.5   Regional policies

The Green Paper states that regionally based policies are needed for issues such as planning the scale and distribution of provision for new housing, including setting a brownfield target and the growth of major urban areas (DTLR, 2001c, paragraph 4.39). Regional involvement is also needed for coastal planning, regional transport, waste facilities and for major inward investment, as well as other aspects of the Regional Development Agencies' (RDAs') economic strategies. The revised guidance on the preparation of Regional Planning Guidance (PPG11 'Regional Planning'), published in 2000, emphasised the need for guidance to be more concise, avoid unnecessary repetition of national policy, address specific regional or subregional planning issues, be outcome-centred, focused on delivery mechanisms and be subject to annual performance monitoring.

In the view of the Government many of these objectives have yet to be achieved (DTLR, 2001c, paragraph 4.41):

- RPGs are still long and insufficiently strategic – they continue to restate national policy or defend local interests.
- RPGs are insufficiently integrated or coordinated with other regional strategies.
- There is overlap and duplication between regional and county plans.
- The process of preparation can lead to RPGs avoiding difficult decisions.

The Green Paper therefore proposes that:

- Regional Planning Guidance will be replaced with new Regional Spatial Strategies (RSSs);
- the RSS will be given statutory status – the Local Development Frame-

works and local transport plans should be consistent with it unless there is more recent national policy;

- the content of the RSS is to be more focused – outlining specific regional or subregional policies, setting targets and indicators, cross-referring to but not repeating national policy;
- each RSS shall reflect regional diversity and specific regional needs within the national planning framework;
- the RSS shall be more fully integrated with other regional strategies and provide the longer-term planning framework for the Regional Development Agencies' strategies and those of other stakeholders, and assist in their implementation; and
- the preparation of sub-regional strategies should be promoted, where necessary, through the RSS process.

The Green Paper does not specify precisely which bodies will be responsible for preparing Regional Spatial Strategies and recognises that these might vary from area to area. They should, however, satisfy four main criteria (DTLR, 2001c, paragraph 4.46):

(1) They should demonstrate that they are representative of key regional interests – groups comprised solely of local authorities will not be acceptable.
(2) The planning bodies should consult a broad range of regional stakeholders through focus groups or planning forums (as advised in PPG11).
(3) They should work closely with all groups to ensure delivery of the strategy.
(4) They must be capable of taking a strategic regional view addressing, where necessary, difficult regional choices.

It is intended that the regional Government Offices will be closely involved in the preparation of Regional Spatial Strategies. After public examination, the Secretary of State will seek to implement the recommendations arising, except if they are inconsistent with national policy or if they adversely affect another region (DTLR, 2001c, paragraph 4.48). No changes are proposed in respect of the Mayor's role in the arrangements for planning in London.

16.3.6   *Planning Policy Guidance*

At present, national planning policies are principally set out in 25 Planning Policy Guidance notes (PPGs) (see Chapter 2), and 15 Mineral Policy Guidance notes (MPGs). In addition to these there are numerous circulars, policy statements and good practice guidance, many of which have been referred to in earlier chapters, as well as advice on procedures and other material. Planning policies and other guidance have an important role in enabling the Government to achieve its objectives for housing, transport, urban regeneration and a range of other policies. National policies must be taken into account by planning authorities when they are preparing local plans or regional planning policy.

Whilst therefore the importance of planning policies is recognised by the Green Paper, and are generally considered to be a success, the volume of national planning policy is considered to be too onerous. For example, the PPGs alone run to a total of 852 pages (DTLR, 2001c, paragraph 4.57) and the amount of guidance imposes a considerable burden on the planning system. Much of the guidance is insufficiently focused, with little differentiation between policy and advice, whilst in other respects it is too prescriptive. It is also of uncertain status – in some instances being a 'material consideration' when a planning application is assessed but in other respects not adequately reflected in plans and decisions. The Green Paper also states that there has been a failure historically to provide sufficient guidance on the Government's policies for delivering the country's major infrastructure needs (DTLR, 2001c, paragraph 4.58).

For the future the Government intends that national planning policy should concentrate on the important policy issues that need to be resolved at national level, leaving regional or local issues to be resolved at those levels. The intention is to set out national policies in a clear manner and not to cloud them with ancillary material and detailed instructions. It proposes to:

- review all PPGs and MPGs, asking whether they are all needed and seeking much greater clarity of expression – describing them in terms of objectives and outcomes to be achieved;
- separate policy guidance from practical implementation – making a clear distinction between national *policy* which should be followed and *advice* which can be interpreted more flexibly;
- issue national statements about major infrastructure needs – setting a clear policy framework for investment decisions that have national significance.

It is proposed that the review of planning policy guidance will initially focus on PPG1 (General Policy and Principles), PPG4 (Industrial and Commercial Development), PPG6 (Town Centres and Retail Development), PPG7 (The Countryside), PPG15 (Historic Environment) and PPG16 (Archaeology). It is expected that PPG5 (Simplified Planning Zones) will be withdrawn and that new guidance will be issued in respect of the proposed new Business Zones. The review is expected to be timetabled over a two-year period, so that core policies will be ready when the new Local Development Frameworks are introduced following legislation. In the meantime, local planning authorities are expected to continue to implement fully the provisions of existing PPGs (DTLR, 2001c, paragraph 4.63).

16.4   Development control

As well as proposing changes to the policy aspects of planning, so as to speed up the system and make it more understandable, the Green Paper proposes some fundamental changes in relation to development control. This is the process by which decisions are made on applications to develop land or buildings or to change their use. It is at this point that people are most likely to encounter the planning system (DTLR, 2001c, paragraph 5.1). Although a system for regulating development is needed to protect the public interest, the present system is not well understood and is not customer-friendly. Businesses in particular complain about slowness and the lack of certainty in the existing system, both of which have important implications when it comes to making investment decisions.

> 'Most people only have limited experience of the planning system. They may encounter it because they wish to start up or expand a business, extend their house or because they are consulted on a planning application submitted by someone else which may affect their property. Whichever is the case, for many people and small businesses, the development control process is unfamiliar. We have got to make it much more understandable, more service-orientated and responsive to customers.'
>
> (DTLR, 2001c, paragraph 5.6)

16.4.1   Changing the system

The Green Paper therefore proposes that a fresh look be taken at the system of development control, so as to produce a system that:

- is responsive to the needs of all its customers and offers a new culture of customer service;
- delivers decisions quickly in a predictable and transparent way;
- produces quality development; and
- genuinely involves the community.

It proposes to:

- introduce a planning checklist so that people know how to submit a good-quality planning application;
- tighten targets for determining planning applications and deal with the delays caused by statutory consultees;
- encourage masterplanning to improve the quality of development;
- promote better community involvement by offering community groups advice on planning;
- introduce delivery contracts for planning for major developments;
- introduce new 'Business Zones' where no planning permission is required for certain forms of development; and
- seek better and tougher enforcement against those who evade planning requirements.

(DTLR, 2001c, paragraph 5.5)

Pre-application discussions between applicants and local planning authorities will be encouraged, with local planning authorities being able to charge fees for such discussions so that they do not constitute a drain on resources. Such fees will, however, have to be set at such a level as to ensure that they do not discourage applicants from seeking early discussions.

16.4.2 A 'one-stop shop'

Where possible, it is proposed that a 'one-stop shop' consent regime might be introduced to deal with situations where more than one approval might be required for a single development. Specific references are made in the Green Paper to alterations affecting listed buildings and to parallel consents with pollution control authorisations. A major bone of contention with property developers, revealed during the *Releasing Brownfields* study (Syms, 2001), was the need to obtain Waste Management Licences for many remediation methods applicable to the preparation of contaminated or 'previously developed' land (see Chapters 7 and 9). The delays associated with obtaining these licences and, to a lesser extent, Mobile Plant Licences, are seen as a major hindrance to urban renewal and can have a significant impact on the cash flow of a development. One reform that could be introduced to reduce this problem would be a uniform Remediation Licence, dealt with as part of the planning system in consultation with other regulators, for all land that is to be redeveloped.

16.4.3 Appeals against non-determination

At present, if planning applications are not determined within eight weeks of being submitted, and if the applicant has not agreed to an extension of time, the applicant is at liberty to lodge an appeal for non–determination. This often means that property developers will lodge two identical applications, in the anticipation that they may well need to appeal on one, whilst continuing with negotiations in respect of the other application. This is wasteful of resources for both the developer and the planning authority.

Advice received from business organisations suggests that businesses would be prepared to waive the right to appeal against non–determination if, in exchange, they had greater predictability about when a decision will be made and were kept informed about the progress of the application. The Green Paper therefore proposes that, for bigger applications, local authorities and developers should at the outset agree a timetable for delivering a decision (DTLR, 2001c, paragraph 5.26) and that this should be set out in a contract. Such an arrangement should have the effect of removing the need for twin-tracking planning applications.

16.5   Compulsory purchase and compensation

The Planning Green Paper sets out proposals for fundamental changes to the way in which the planning system operates; several daughter papers address specific issues in more detail. One of these deals with compulsory purchase and compensation. These were identified in the *Releasing Brownfields* study (Syms, 2001) and in other studies, such as Yates (2001), as being important issues that prevented, or at least delayed, urban renewal projects.

Most development takes place as a result of proposals brought forward by private sector developers. However, sometimes it is necessary for local authorities and other bodies such as transport undertakers and utility providers to take a proactive lead in assembling land for development (DTLR, 2001d, paragraph 1.1). Studies in this area have found that, in many instances, local authorities have been reluctant to use their compulsory powers to facilitate development, for reasons such as the lack of financial or human resources. Developers, for their part, have been unwilling to underwrite the process due to a lack of certainty in respect of both time and cost.

The Government is committed to making the system of compulsory purchase a more efficient and effective means of achieving land assembly by making the procedures and compensation arrangements: *simpler*, *fairer*, and *quicker*. The daughter paper sets out the Government's proposals for changes to the laws and procedures relating to compulsory purchase, compensation and the disposal of compulsorily purchased land. It covers acquisitions under all enabling powers, including those exercised by Government ministers, agencies (including Regional Development Agencies (RDAs)), local authorities and privatised bodies. It relates to England and Wales, and the National Assembly for Wales was consulted during its preparation.

The main problems were perceived to be as follows.

- The piecemeal way in which the current system has evolved. The existing legislation is complex and difficult to understand; much of law rests on past decisions by the Courts. There is therefore a need to consolidate, codify and simplify the law.
- There is uncertainty as to whether the powers available to local authorities, in particular, are adequate for the functions they are now expected to perform.
- Consequently, local authorities are discouraged from making use of their powers, with the result that, when it becomes inescapable, they have little expertise and often create further delays through error and inexperience.
- The concerns of those whose land is to be taken escalate to outright opposition because they are worried about the inordinate length of time which the compulsory purchase process can take from inception to relocation and whether they will be compensated adequately for the sacrifice which they are being required to make.
- Those wishing to invest in the development of the land to be acquired are also deterred by the length of time which the process can take, and so are reluctant to make the sort of commitment which acquiring authorities feel they need in order to be able to justify using their compulsory purchase powers.

(DTLR, 2001d, paragraph 1.7)

The Government considers it of vital importance that bodies charged with delivering development proposals in the public interest should have available an affective and efficient tool which enables them, where necessary, to compulsorily acquire land. This requirement exists whether the object is the regeneration of inner-city areas, the effective reuse of brownfield sites or the construction of new infrastructure projects. However, any compulsory purchase system has to strike a fair balance between the needs of acquiring authorities and the interests of those whose property is being expropriated. It is essential for the latter to be properly protected, but that should not mean that the acquisition of private property, with appropriate compensation, can never be justified (DTLR, 2001d, paragraphs 1.8 and 1.9).

The consultation paper therefore proposes that unnecessary complexity be reduced by investigating the scope for amending/repealing section 17 of the Acquisition of Land Act 1981 and, if practicable, providing a single, consistent and up-to-date definition of 'statutory undertaker' in relation to the compulsory acquisition of land.

Advice will be provided to local authorities on matters such as appointing a named case manager where appropriate and on steps which they might usefully take during the period leading up to the making of a compulsory purchase order. In particular, this might minimise the time required to secure confirmation of the order. These steps could include:

- Entering into informal agreements with those from whom land is required, setting out terms for its sale by agreement when required – including a contractual agreement that the amount of compensation payable can be referred to the Lands Tribunal for determination, if necessary.
- Making effective use of mediation and other alternative dispute resolution (ADR) techniques to reduce the level of objection based on fear and ignorance or concerns about the compensation payable.
- Ensuring that all potentially relevant statutory bodies are kept fully informed of the authority's intentions in sufficient time to be able to undertake any parallel procedures which may be required to facilitate the release of the land required.

(DTLR, 2001d, paragraph 3.4)

In addition, the consultation paper proposes the following:

- That acquiring authorities be granted powers enabling them to confirm their own orders where no statutory objections are sustained. This will need to be subject to a notification procedure to protect the interests of potential objectors.
- To remove some of the inflexibility in the current arrangements. For example, there may be scope for widening the procedure for amending orders to include cases where the purpose of the compulsory purchase order has been clear from the outset but the wrong statutory provision has been quoted, and by providing a general power to facilitate the partial confirmation of orders.
- To take steps to help people check the position as it affects their properties, by providing a formal notification procedure where an order is withdrawn and introducing requirements to register the status of all orders (from the time at which they are made, onwards) as local land charges.
- To significantly improve the time taken by the Secretary of State DTLR in deciding whether to confirm orders once the Inspector has reported.

(DTLR, 2001d, paragraph 3.9)

An important issue, in the eyes of developers, has been the limitation of compensation payable on compulsory acquisition to 'open market value' with no additional payment to reflect any enhanced value that might be attributable to the proposed scheme itself (see Chapter 4). In other words, there is no incentive for the landowner to arrive at an agreed settlement with the acquiring authority without taking the compulsory purchase process to its ultimate conclusion.

The consultation paper notes that the Government has concluded that retaining the concept of *open market value* provides the fairest basis for assessing the compensation payable for land taken. It does, however, recognise a need to encourage acquiring authorities to adopt a generally more flexible approach than hitherto in negotiating the open market value of any particular site in order to reach agreement more quickly.

While it rejects the concept of a premium payable on top of open market value *as an element in the valuation of the land* being acquired, it is considered right that those who have had their property compulsorily taken from them should receive an additional '*loss payment*' in recognition of the physical and psychological upheaval which that causes. It is therefore proposed to extend the principle currently enshrined in the concept of 'home-loss' payments to cover economic activities (including farms). In order to retain flexibility, it is proposed that the actual amounts payable will be defined in secondary legislation.

16.6   Planning obligations

Also known as section 106 agreements (Town and Country Planning Act 1990), planning obligations are typically made between local planning authorities and developers, negotiated as part of the process of granting planning permission. Their purpose is to ensure that developers contribute towards the infrastructure and services considered necessary to support their developments. The contributions may be in kind or take the form of financial contributions. Planning obligations are also used to ensure the provision of affordable housing, either on the developer's site or elsewhere.

Ideally, planning obligations should enhance the quality of the development and the wider environment, as well as making a contribution towards sustainability. The system should also be transparent to everyone involved in the planning process, including the community. In another consultation paper, *Planning Obligations: Delivering a Fundamental Change* (DTLR, 2001e), the Government states that the present system falls short of its objectives.

Although there are some examples of innovation and good practice, there are concerns that the system can operate in ways that are unfair, inconsistent or lacking in transparency. The agreements also may take an unacceptably long time to negotiate and involve high legal costs, the result sometimes being unacceptable delay leading to abandonment of the development project. There is widespread consensus that the system and the way it operates needs to be changed (DTLR, 2001e, paragraph 1.8).

16.6.1   *Proposals for reform*

The consultation paper puts forward proposals for reform and improvement of the system, including a proposal that local authorities should set standardised tariffs for different types of development through the plan–making process. The Government intends to use planning obligations as a positive planning tool that complements its proposals to reform the planning system and, to this end, they should be refocused to deliver sustainable development. This means that they should be used as a mechanism to ensure that development provides social, economic and environmental benefits to the community as a whole (DTLR, 2001e, paragraph 2.2).

As discussed above, the planning Green Paper proposes that new Local Development Frameworks should replace the present system of local plans. These frameworks will embrace core policies including, amongst others, the use of planning obligations. One set of policies would set out the arrangements for determining the schedule of tariffs and how they would apply, the criteria for negotiation or exemptions and the approach to monitoring and accounting. A parallel set of policies would cover the purposes to which the receipts from the tariff would be put. This would reflect the priorities for spending within the local area, set in the context of the authority's strategies for housing, transport, regeneration, education, health, 'liveability' and public open space, recreation and other community benefits (DTLR, 2001e, paragraph 4.5).

It is proposed that local authorities should have discretion to determine the types, sizes and location of development on which the tariff would be charged and that there should be local discretion about how the receipts are spent. However, the application of the tariff and the ways in which it is spent would be subject to national policies and guidance. It is also envisaged that a wider range of developments would be subject to the tariff than is currently the case with planning obligations. The Government expects that smaller developments would not be liable to pay the tariffs and is seeking views on a threshold; one option would be to exempt developments below 200 square metres gross commercial floorspace or 150 square metres of residential floorspace (DTLR, 2001e, paragraph 4.13).

16.6.2   *Affordable housing*

Under the tariff-based approach, a much wider range of types and sizes of development would contribute to affordable housing, including commercial development. The Government recognises that on-site provision may not always be appropriate in, for example, some commercial developments or where residential developments are very small in scale. There would therefore be a need to ensure that sufficient sites are available on which to build affordable housing (DTLR, 2001e, paragraph 4.23).

Current planning policies referred to in Chapter 2 place considerable emphasis on the reuse of land, converting existing buildings for housing use and on bringing empty homes back into use. As part of the drive towards sustainability in development, the consultation paper proposes that the tariffs should be used not only to develop new property but to convert existing buildings and to bring empty property back into affordable residential use (DTLR, 2001e, paragraph 4.25). The overall intention of all these proposals is not only to increase the supply of affordable housing but to ensure that both commercial and residential developers support its provision within a simplified, predictable and transparent framework (DTLR, 2001e, paragraph 4.29).

16.7   Planning fees

Another of the daughter papers relates to *Planning Fees* (DTLR, 2001f). The Government's policy over a number of years has been to raise planning fees to a level where they should cover 100% of the estimated relevant local authority costs in providing the service and then to maintain them at that level. Local authorities in England complete a quarterly statistical return showing the amount of fee income, which they have received. Fees have not, however, been increased since 1997.

In 1999, DTLR asked the Planning Officers Society to look at current fee-related costs as part of a wider pilot exercise that they were undertaking. That involved around 25 authorities measuring their core planning costs between July and December 1999 using a new definition produced as part of the Government's Best Value initiative. Those authorities were also asked to measure their fee-related costs over the same period. Although some useful work was produced, several of the original sample dropped out during the exercise, leaving an insufficiently large number on which to base a revised fee calculation.

Research has also been undertaken for the Scottish Office (now the Scottish Executive) by Paula Gilder Consulting. In summary, the seven objectives of that research are to:

- examine the direct and indirect costs of the various aspects of the planning service;
- suggest a common framework for cost accounting;
- examine, in relation to development control, the breakdown of costs relating to determining applications and those related to other aspects;

- indicate the broad scale of costs of monitoring and enforcement of minerals permissions;
- consider the reasonableness of the fees;
- devise an ongoing information system for monitoring costs of determining applications;
- advise on any other cost information that should be regularly reported.

The overall findings, based on detailed studies of eight local authorities, were that costs varied between authorities and that this was exaggerated if clearly defined headings were not used.

On development control, the key findings were as follows:

- Costs from other departments add about a third to budgeted costs.
- Approximately 50–70% of total development control costs relate to fee-earning activities.
- Around 50–70% of total costs are recovered from fees, but because of the wide variations this does not imply full cost recovery.
- Little information is kept on costs incurred on different types of application (relativities).
- The general consensus among officers is that the fee scale should be stretched – i.e. lower bottom and higher top.

The conclusion reached from these researches was that some revision is needed in respect of planning fees, although not involving a comprehensive increase in fees, and suggestions are advanced in the consultation paper, see *www.planning.dtlr.gov.uk/consult/greepap/planfees/index.htm.*

16.8   Regulatory impact appraisal

Development in England is defined in section 55 of the Town and Country Planning Act 1990 (as amended) and, unless specifically excluded, all development requires planning permission from the local planning authority. Even though a large proportion of development by householders and statutory undertakers does not need a planning application, there were about 550 000 planning applications in 2000 and the number of applications has been rising each year. About half of all planning applications are for minor household developments and a quarter are for minor business or commercial developments. The rest include a small number of applications for major commercial/industrial applications, plus change of building use, listed building consents and advertisements.

The main thrust of the Planning Green Paper is intended to reduce the degree of regulation that currently encumbers the planning system. In summary, the Green Paper proposals have the following aims:

- Nationally, it is proposed that 852 pages of national planning policy guidance be reviewed to seek much greater clarity in its expression and describe them much more in terms of aims and objectives.
- It is proposed that the hierarchy of plans should be simplified, with local plans, unitary development plans and county structure plans replaced with new Local Development Frameworks. The new system will reduce uncertainty caused by out-of-date plans.
- There will be new targets for faster planning decisions by local and central government.
- There will be a number of other proposed changes to the development control system, making it faster and more user-friendly.

(DTLR, 2001g)

The complete set of proposals and their likely regulatory impact is set out in Table 16.1

Table 16.1   Planning Green Paper – regulatory impact.

Proposal/chapter reference	Regulatory impact
Chapter 4: A fundamental change for plans **Local planning** We will abolish structure plans, local plans and unitary development plans and replace them with a new Local Development Framework (LDF)	Simpler system will lessen regulatory burden on users
LDF to consist of statement of core policies, detailed action plans and map, setting out area-based designations	Simpler system will lessen regulatory burden on users
Decisions on planning permission to be made in accordance with statement of core policies and action plans where in place	In line with current system
LDF to be continuously updated to ensure consistency with national and regional policy, with statement of core policies published each year and comprehensive review every three years (or in line with revision of Community Strategies)	Simpler system will lessen regulatory burden on users
LDF to include a Statement of Community Involvement, setting out how community is to be involved in review of LDF and decisions on planning applications	No regulatory impact (NRI)
Local authorities to be encouraged to work with Local Strategic Partnerships (LSPs) to establish effective mechanisms for community involvement	NRI
Local communities to shape vision, objectives and strategy in LDF and be particularly involved in preparation of action plans	NRI

Contd

Table 16.1　Continued.

Proposal/chapter reference	Regulatory impact
Regional and subregional planning	
Statutory Regional Spatial Strategies (RSS) to replace Regional Planning Guidance	Simpler system will lessen regulatory burden on users
RSS to be better integrated with other regional strategies	Simpler system will lessen regulatory burden on users
Subregional strategies to be prepared, where necessary	NRI
New arrangements for preparing RSS, involving RDAs and representatives of public, business and voluntary sectors	NRI
National planning	
Government to review all PPGs and MPGs, considering in each case whether it is needed, and separating national policy and advice	Simpler system will lessen regulatory burden on users
Chapter 5: A fundamental change in development control	
Improving customer service	
Government to work with Local Government Association to develop user-friendly checklist for planning applicants	Clear requirements will reduce costs and delays for applicants and local planning authorities (LPAs)
To encourage pre-application discussions between applicants and local authorities	New expectation of local authorities, but improved quality of application should reduce costs and delays for applicants and LPAs
New expectation that applications to be dealt with by a nominated officer	More effective service for users of planning system
E-planning and Planning Portal	Easier access to planning system for users
Government to move quickly to standardise application and administration procedures under different consent regimes	Reduction in burden arising from multiple and different regulatory regimes
Faster delivery	
New performance targets for local authority handling of planning applications	Reduced delays
Delivery contracts for large applications which cannot be dealt with within normal time-scales	Greater certainty for applicants and LPAs
Consultation paper to be published proposing changes to the basis of planning obligations	See RIA on Planning Obligations Paper
Reduction in the number of statutory consultees for planning applications	Reduced delays
A new duty on statutory consultees to respond within a statutory time-scale	Reduced delays

Contd

Table 16.1   Continued.

Proposal/chapter reference	Regulatory impact
Statutory consultees to be able to charge a fee for providing a substantive response, provided it is given within 21 days	Provides incentive for better service. Increased costs from fees should be offset by savings from better service
Increased use of standing advice by statutory consultees	Reduce delays
To introduce new mechanisms for monitoring performance of consultees, and, where they are dependent on Government funding, to link future funding to satisfactory performance	Increased speed of response
Regional Development Agencies to be able to make representations on major investment proposals likely to h ave an economic significance that extends to the region or subregion	NRI
Introduction of new Business Planning Zones (BPZs), where no planning consent necessary if development in accordance with tightly defined parameters	Significant reduction in regulatory burden on developers within BPZs
Masterplanning of major developments, in place of outline consents	More certainty for applicants
Repeated applications not to be accepted unless a material change in circumstances	Reduce unnecessary costs on LPAs and third parties but restriction on ability of developer to pursue repeated applications
Local authorities to be able to refuse to accept 'twin-tracked' applications	Reduce unnecessary costs on LPAs and third parties but restriction on ability of developer to pursue twin-track approach
Permissions and consents to be time-limited to three years	May have impact on value of land towards end of period of permission, if not developed
On appeal for non-determination, planning inspector to pick up local authority's case file and take over jurisdiction	Reduced delays for applicants
Deadline for launching appeals to be reduced from six months to three months	Will constrain applicants' ability to appeal by reducing the time window in which they can decide

Source: DTLR, 2001g

The economic benefits of these proposals are difficult to quantify, as it will depend on detailed implementation. A full Regulatory Impact Appraisal will accompany the final proposals that follow the consultation on the Green Paper.

16.9   Summary

In the period leading up to publication, the Green Paper on planning reform was sometimes described, by Civil Servants and consultees, as having 'white edges' or 'white stripes', implying that it was something more than just a consultation document. This does indeed appear to be the case as it seeks to consult on some issues, such as the future role of counties in the plan preparation process, whilst laying down firm policy in other areas, for example the abolition of structure, local and unitary development plans and their replacement by Local Development Frameworks.

Clear separation between matters of policy, which must be taken into account by planning authorities, and advice or guidance that can be applied more flexibly, will be an undoubted improvement. Leaving regional and local issues to be resolved at those levels should also be a significant improvement, provided that national policies are not made so onerous as to unreasonably impinge at the regional and local levels.

If they are fully implemented, the proposed changes to the planning system should have the effect of speeding up the process and making it more open and transparent. Even the suggestion that fees should be charged for pre-application discussion will probably be acceptable to property developers, provided they can see that they are receiving value for their money.

The proposed changes to the system of planning obligations should have the effect of creating a fairer and more open system, and one that is more readily understandable by applicants. If, as indicated, the tariff system is applied more widely than the present system, it should have the effect of transferring some element of development value to the wider public benefit. As developers are unlikely to reduce their profit requirements, the cost will have to be borne out of the land value, or met out of higher property prices, provided of course that the market accepts these.

However, by no means everyone is in favour of the proposals to streamline the town planning process. Concerns have been expressed that involving parliament in the decision-making process for projects of 'national' interest is seen as reducing public participation through the transfer of power to politicians. Public inquiries will not be allowed to challenge the 'principle, need or location' of such plans and, in the view of Coward (2001), this is a return to Victorian ways, in which control is to be wrested away from those affected.

As there will be no automatic right to object, the fate of an area could be decided in an afternoon's parliamentary discussion.

'Soon people will be up in arms about the outrageous implications of having no say at all about the building of chemical plants, radioactive waste disposals and open cast mining in their community. Whether they will also grasp the similar attack on environmental protection and democracy in plans to reform local planning is harder to say.'

(Coward, 2001)

Note: *Land, Development and Design* has been written at the end of an important period for urban regeneration in England and at the beginning of what promises to be a very interesting period as the new policies and guidance come into effect.

The Royal Institution of Chartered Surveyors, in its response to the Planning Green Paper, acknowledged that the review process and future planning policy would benefit greatly from a clear statement of government policy on the purpose of the planning system. It notes that there is a need to change the culture, endemic in the planning system, of over-prescription and obstruction, whilst agreeing that the system must promote and ensure sustainable development.

However, the RICS feels that the Green Paper and associated government announcements may have the unwanted effect of increasing public expectations to unrealistic levels, which would have the effect of increasing, not decreasing, the adversarial nature of planning. Complexity must be reduced further but the government's proposals will result in a complex system of local action plans under the local development framework (*www.rics.org*). This will increase the burden on local planning authorities and, thus, the tighter timescales for reviewing plans are unlikely to be attained. In order to meet expectations resources must be increased for LPAs.

The Yorkshire branch of the Royal Town Planning Institute, in conjunction with Leeds Metropolitan University and Sheffield Hallam University, has published the proceedings of a conference on the Green Paper[16.1]. Perhaps the greatest concern expressed in the papers and discussions, was about moving from where planning is now to where it should be in the future under the development plans framework. There was some doubt as to whether the new framework would genuinely simplify the process and about whether it will actually be easier for customers of the planning service to comprehend. Related to this was concern about how all of this will mesh with all the other types of plans and strategies that exist at all spatial scales. 'Joined-up thinking' has to be applied not just across activities at all levels in this hierarchy but also between levels.

There was a worry that the Green Paper appears to have taken a very optimistic view both of the time that proper public consultation takes and of the extent to which it can be presumed to lead to consensus in the contemporary world and in the world of tomorrow. Once again there was concern about resources, stemming from a recognition that, in essence, the community will get what it is prepared to pay for.

[16.1] 'Certainty, Quality Consistence and the Planning Green Paper: can planning deliver the goods?', report of the proceedings of a conference held at Leeds Civic Hall, 13 February 2002.

Appendix 1
Sample Option Agreement

THIS AGREEMENT dated

is made **BETWEEN:-**

(1)
    ("the Owner")
and
(2)
    ("the Developer")

IT IS AGREED

1. DEFINITIONS AND INTERPRETATION

1.1   "Associate" means a company which is a member of the same group as the Developer within the meaning of Section 42 of the Landlord and Tenant Act 1954

In this example case, the developer operated its 'landbank' through a separate company from its development operations. This is not unusual, the function of the 'landbank' company being to resolve any planning problems before the land is transferred to the development associate.

1.2   "Local Plan" means the local plan within the meaning of Section 36 or the unitary development plan within the meaning of section 10 of the Town and Country Planning Act 1990 for the area in which the Option Site is situated

1.3   "Notice of Exercise" means a written notice in the form set out in the Schedule 1 exercising the Option

The 'trigger notice' whereby the option is taken up by the developer. The original draft gave the developer the opportunity to take the land in several small tranches. This was felt to be inappropriate.

1.4   "Open Market Value" means the value of the Option Site assessed as between a willing buyer and a willing seller on the open market with the benefit of Qualifying Planning Approval in accordance with Practice Statement PS 4.2.1. of the RICS Appraisal and Valuation Manual

A clear definition by which the valuers, or the expert, can arrive at the price to be paid.

1.5 "Option" means the option granted by clauses 3.1–3.6

1.6 "Option Fee" means the sum of twenty-five thousand pounds (£25,000)

1.7 "Option Period" means a period of eight years beginning on the date hereof but subject to extension in accordance with the provisions of clauses 3.2 and 3.4

In the original agreement this could be extended almost ad infinitum through manipulation of the planning process.

1.8 "Option Site" means the land situated at .... and shown edged red on the Plan and comprising .... or thereabouts

1.9 "Plan" means the plan annexed

1.10 "Planning Agreement" means an agreement required by a Local Authority under Section 106 of the Town and Country Planning Act 1990 or Section 33 of the Local Government (Miscellaneous Provisions) Act 1982 or Section 278 of the Highways Act 1980 or under any similar legislation in connection with the grant of the Qualifying Planning Approval

Could include items such as the provision of access to adjoining land, social housing provision, play areas, etc.

1.11 "Planning Appeal" means all or any of the following as the case may be:-

1.11.1 An appeal under Section 78(1) of the Town and Country Planning Act 1990 against a refusal of a Planning Application or the grant of a planning permission pursuant to a Planning Application which is subject to conditions which the Developer in its absolute discretion deems unacceptable or

1.11.2 An appeal under Section 78(2) of the Town and Country Planning Act 1990 against the non-determination of a Planning Application or

1.11.3 The reference of a Planning Application to the Secretary of State for the Environment under Section 77 of the Town and Country Planning Act 1990

1.11.4 An application under Section 73 of the Town and Country Planning Act 1990 for the discharge or variation of any condition attached to any planning permission issued pursuant to a Planning Application and which is not a Qualifying Planning Approval

1.12 "Planning Application" means an application made by or on behalf of the Developer for a Qualifying Planning Approval and the Developer will submit a Planning Application within 3 months of the allocation of the Option Site within the Local Plan for residential use and PROVIDED THAT if the Option Site has not been so allocated within 5 years of the date hereof then the Developer will obtain an opinion from leading planning counsel as to whether a Planning Application should be submitted in any event and will take such action as is advised by such opinion and the Developer will provide a copy of such Planning Application to the Owner's agents for approval before its submission (such approval not to ve unreasonably withheld or delayed) and in the event of the Owner's agents not making any comment within 30 working days of the provision of a copy then such approval shall be deemed to have been given

The land in question was not zoned for development and, under the original draft agreement, the developer could have held the land secure under the option until the end of the eighth year without any obligation to test whether or not planning permission might be obtainable and then, right at the end of the agreement, lodge a planning application, thus effectively extending the term of the agreement.

Under the original draft agreement there was no provision for the owner or his agent to be able to comment on any planning application.

1.13 "Planning Challenge" means an application to the Court (including an application for leave to apply for a judicial review) which may result in any planning permission granted pursuant to a Planning Application or a Planning Appeal being modified or found never to have been valid and in this connection a Planning Challenge will be regarded as finally determined when judgment has been given on the application and any further proceedings arising out of the application and all appeal procedures have been exhausted or when the period for any appeal has expired without any such appeal having been made

1.14 "Price" means such sum as shall be calculated in accordance with the provisions of clause 5 hereof

1.15 "Price Notice" means a written notice given by the Developer to the Owner in accordance with the provisions of clause 4

1.16 "Qualifying Planning Approval" means a planning permission issued pursuant to a Planning Application permitting the development of the Option Site for residential and ancillary purposes or for such other purposes as are consistent with any allocation of the Option Site in the Local Plan

1.17 The masculine includes the feminine and the singular includes the plural and vice versa

1.18 References herein to numbered clauses or schedules are unless otherwise stated references to the clause or schedule of this agreement bearing that number

1.19 The clause headings used herein are for ease of reference only and shall not affect the interpretation of this agreement

2. PLANNING APPLICATIONS

2.1 The Developer will seek at its own expense (but subject to the provisions of clause 2.3) and use all reasonable endeavours to obtain Qualifying Planning Approval including making any Planning Appeals and/or any representations in the course of the preparation or amendment of the Local Plan which the Developer in its absolute discretion considers advisable and will use all reasonable endeavours to maximise the Open Market Value of the Option Site

Under the original draft agreement the developer could have applied for permission to build a minimal number of houses on the site and there was no obligation to maximise its value.

2.2 The Developer will keep the Owner fully informed of all material progress of its negotiations with the Local Planning Authority and will supply copies of all relevant notices correspondence decisions and appeals and will on written request provide the Owners with copies of all relevant documents

The original draft did not include any requirement to keep the owner informed as to progress.

2.3   The reasonable costs and expenses incurred by the Developer in seeking a Qualifying Planning Approval may be deducted from the Price if the Options are exercised up to a maximum sum of £50,000 but for the avoidance of doubt shall be borne by the Developer if the Option is not exercised

From the landowner's perspective it is essential to cap the figure for planning permission costs that may be deducted from the purchase price, as some planning appeals can result in costs running well into six figures.

3. GRANT OF OPTION

3.1   In consideration of the Developer paying to the Owner the Option Fee the Owner grants to the Developer an option during the Option Period to purchase the freehold estate in the Option Site in its entirety on the terms of this Agreement and subject as mentioned in clause 6 but otherwise free from incumbrances

3.2   If at the expiration of the Option Period the Developer has not received a Qualifying Planning Approval but is awaiting:

3.2.1 the result of any Planning Application
3.2.2 the result of any Planning Appeal
3.2.3 the result of any Planning Challenge

THEN the Option Period shall be extended to a date 10 working days after the expiry of the period of 3 months after the Developer receives the result of such outstanding Planning Application or Planning Appeal (by which for the avoidance of doubt shall be meant receipt by the Developer of written notification of the issue of a planning permission or the decision of the Secretary of State for the Environment's decision as the case may be) or a date 10 working days after the Planning Challenge has been finally determined (as appropriate) PROVIDED THAT any Planning Application has been made at least 6 months prior to the expiry of the Option Period

3.3 The Owner agrees not to dispose of any legal or equitable interest in any part of the Option Site to any person other than the Developer unless at the time of such disposal the purchaser or transferee executes and delivers to the Developer a Deed of Covenant in the form set out in Schedule 2

3.4 The Owner agrees to accept until the expiry of the Option Period a restriction on the Owners' title that no dealings may be registered without the consent of the Developer and the Developer agrees to provide such consent promptly on receiving the appropriate Deed of Covenant pursuant to clause 3.3 PROVIDED THAT the Owner shall be entitled to grant a grazing licence in relation to the Option Site or part thereof but so that no security of tenure shall be established over any part of the Option Site

3.5 The Owner agrees to countersign any Notice of Exercise given by the Developer which complies in all respects with the provisions of this Agreement

3.6 If the Option is exercised the Option Fee shall form part of the Price but if the Option is not exercised the Option Fee shall be retained by the Owner

4. PRICE NOTICE

4.1 A Price Notice may be given by the Developer at any time before the expiration of the Option Period.

4.2 When a Price Notice is given the Price shall be determined in accordance with clauses 5 and (if applicable) 7. Within twenty working days after such determination the Developer may exercise the Option by giving Notice of Exercise to purchase the Option Site at the Price so determined

4.3   In the event of a Price Notice having been
      served in accordance with clause 4.1 hereof
      the Option Period (whether or not extended
      in accordance with clause 3.2) shall (if the
      Option Period would otherwise have expired)
      be extended (or further extended) to the date
      which shall expire twenty working days from
      the date on which the Price is agreed or
      determined in accordance with clause 5 or 7

5. PRICE

5.1   The Price shall be 87.5% of the Open Market
      Value at the date of the giving of the Price
      Notice if the Price Notice is served within five
      years of the date hereof and 90% of the Open
      Market Value at the date of the giving of the
      Price Notice if the Price Notice is served after
      the expiry of five years from the date hereof
      less the sum of twenty five thousand pounds
      (£25,000) already paid to the Owner

This discount against full value gives the developer the incentive to maximise the development potential of the site, is a return for the efforts involved and represents the margin for the 'landbank' company. The differential provides an incentive for the developer to seek planning permission at the earliest date possible.

5.2   The Owner and the Developer shall upon
      service of a Price Notice endeavour to agree
      the Price but if within 20 working days after
      the date of any Price Notice the parties have
      not agreed the Price then either party may
      refer the matter to an Expert appointed under
      clause 7

A reference to an expert is probably more appropriate than an arbitration reference in this type of situation as the developer may have more market data than the landowner, thus potentially disadvantaging the latter.

6. EXERCISE OF OPTION AND GENERAL CONDITIONS

6.1   Notice of Exercise will be valid if received by
      the Owner during the Option Period

6.2   Receipt by the Owner of the Notice of
      Exercise signed by the Developer (and also if
      the law so requires countersigned by the
      Owner) shall constitute a binding contract for
      the sale and purchase of the freehold estate in
      the Option Site at the Price free from
      incumbrances except as mentioned in this
      clause 6 and including the following terms:-

6.2.1 Title to the Option Site shall commence with a conveyance on sale dated [...........] and made between [....] registered at HM Land Registry under Title Number [....] and will be deduced in accordance with Section 110 of the Land Registration Act 1925

6.2.2 An abstract or office copy entries of the Registers and filed plan as the case may be of the title to the Option Site having been produced to the Developer or its Solicitors prior to the signing hereof of the Developer will purchase with full knowledge of all matters therein contained and shall make no objection nor raise any requisition in respect of such title save as regards matters arising after the date hereof

6.2.3 The Owner shall convey or transfer the Option Site with full title guarantee

6.2.4 The Standard Conditions of Sale (Third Edition) shall apply so far as consistent with the express terms of this Agreement

6.2.5 The contract rate referred to in Standard Condition 1 shall be 4% per year above the base rate from time to time of Royal Bank of Scotland PLC

6.2.6 Completion shall take place twenty working days after the coming into effect of a binding contract in accordance with the provisions of this clause

6.2.7 Vacant possession of the Option Site will be given on completion

6.2.8 The Option Site is sold subject to the rights and other matters contained or referred to in a Conveyance dated the .... and made between .... and ....

7. APPOINTMENT OF EXPERT

Any dispute regarding the provisions of this agreement shall be referred to a person having appropriate professional qualifications and experience in such matters ("the Expert") appointed jointly by the parties or in default by the President for the time being of the Royal Institution of Chartered Surveyors (or on his behalf) on the application of any party. The decision of the Expert shall be final and binding upon the parties and the following provisions shall apply to the Expert:

An expert can take evidence from the parties but, at the end of the day, has to make a decision based on his/her opinion and knowledge of the market, whereas an arbitrator will decide the case based on the weight of evidence presented by the parties.

7.1   The charges and expenses of the Expert shall be borne equally between the parties or in such other proportions as the Expert may direct

7.2   The Expert shall give the parties an opportunity to make representations to him before making his decision

7.3   The Expert shall be entitled to obtain opinions from others if he so wishes

7.4   The Expert shall make his decisions having regard to such representations made by the parties as he thinks fit but shall give reason for his decision

7.5   The Expert shall comply with any time limits or other directions agreed by the parties on or before his appointment

8. OWNER'S OBLIGATIONS

8.1   The Owner will offer all reasonable support to any Planning Application and if the Developer so requests will enter into any Planning Agreement and/or agreement required by any service undertaker in respect of the drainage or provision of any access or service for the Option Site subject to the Developer indemnifying the Owner against all costs charges claims expenses and liabilities thereunder and in particular the Developer will make all appropriate representations in respect of any review of the Local Plan and the Owner will support al such representations

The developer will normally expect the landowner to support any action taken in seeking planning permission.

8.2 During the currency of this Agreement the Owner shall not use the Option Site except for its existing use as at the date hereof or any other operations which would not materially increase the expense of any subsequent development

An important aspect of this would be to prevent any activity, such as temporary storage of waste materials, that might lead to contamination of the site.

8.3 The Owner shall not during the currency of this Agreement grant or create any easements rights privileges or tenancies affecting the Option Site except with the prior written consent of the Developer

Not unreasonably, the owner agrees not to do anything that might prevent development of the site once planning permission has been obtained.

8.4 The Owner shall (at the request and cost of the Developer and conditional upon the Developer purchasing the Option Site) enter into any deeds of easement by which third parties grant easements for the benefit of the Option Site the Developer paying any consideration and indemnifying the Owner against all claims costs charges expenses and liabilities thereunder

In some situations it may be advantageous, to both developer and landowner, if some infrastructure provision is made before planning permission has been obtained.

8.5 The Owner shall permit the Developer to enter the Option Site at reasonable times and upon reasonable prior notice for the purpose of carrying out any soil or other investigations or survey the Developer doing as little damage as reasonably possible and making good promptly any damage which is done and paying compensation for any damage that cannot be made good

9. DEVELOPER'S COVENANT

The Developer will within six calendar months after completion of the purchase erect a proper and suitable stock proof hedge or fence along the boundary of the Option Site and the land retained by the Owners shown coloured green on the Plan

The site in the example was grazing land and the owner also owned two adjacent properties. In this case there was no need for other covenants but in other situations there may be a need to require the developer to provide road access and service connections to retained (and future developable) land.

10. NOTICES AND EXPIRY DATES

Any notice notification or payment under this
Agreement may be given or made by or to the party
concerned or the Solicitors for that party. Where an
expiry date is not a Working Day then the period
concerned shall expire on the next Working Day.
Any notice or payment shall be effective only if
given or made by 2.30 p.m. on the day in question

11. MERGER

Any obligation or liability hereunder which still
remains to be observed performed or honoured shall
survive completion of any conveyance or transfer to
the Developer

*This enables the 'landbank'
company to transfer the site to the
development company but not to
generally offer it for sale in the
market.*

12. ASSIGNMENT

The Developer shall be entitled to assign this
Agreement to an Associate PROVIDED THAT the
performance of the obligations hereunder is
guaranteed by the Associate's Parent Company

SCHEDULE 1

By this Notice [the Developer] gives notice to [the
Owner] of exercise of the Option granted under the
terms of an agreement dated [. . . . .] made
between the Owner of the one part and the Developer
of the other part in relation to the land therein defined
as the Option Site. The Owner shall sell and the
Developer shall purchase the said land for the sum of
[. . . . . .] and otherwise upon the terms and conditions
set out in the said agreement as though the same were
set out in full in this Notice
Dated . . . .
Signed on behalf of the Deveoper
Signed by the Owner

. . . .

SCHEDULE 2

COVENANT BY PURCHASER OR
TRANSFEREE
DEED OF COVENANT
Date . . . .

1. PARTIES
    1.1   . . . . ["the Developer"]
    and
    1.2   [Name] of [address] ["the Purchaser"]

2. BACKGROUND
    2.1   This Deed relates to an Option Agreement
          ("the Agreement") made on [date]
          between [owners' names] and the Developer
          in repect of land at [place – the plan attached
          to the Agreement ("the Option Site"]
    2.2   The Purchaser intends to acquire the
          freehold estate [in the part of] the Option
          Site [shown edged blue on the attached plan
          ("the Property")]

3. COVENANT
    The Purchaser covanants with the Developer that
    on completion of the acquisition of [the Option
    Site] [the Property] by the Purchaser:
    3.1   The Purchaser will notify the Developer that
          completion has taken place and
    3.2   The Purchaser will perform the obligations
          of [name of Owner] under the Agreement in
          so far as they relate to [the Property] [the
          Option Site] as if the same had been set out
          herein in full
    Executed and delivered as a deed by [Purchaser] in the
    presence of: . . . .

    SIGNED by a duly authorised person for [the
    Developer]

References

Adair, A., Berry, J., Deddis, W., McGreal, S. & Hirst, S. (1998) *Accessing private finance: the availability and effectiveness of private finance in urban regeneration*. Research report for the Joseph Rowntree Foundation and RICS, RICS Research, London.

Adams, D. (1994) *Urban Planning and the Development Process*. UCL Press, London.

Adams, D., Disberry, A., Hutchison, N. & Munjoma, T. (1999) *Do landowners constrain urban redevelopment?* Research report for the Economic and Social Research Council, University of Aberdeen.

Anon (2001) Can't live with it, can't live without it – Britain's dinosaur housing market. City Comment, *Daily Telegraph*, 31 August.

Applied Environmental Research Centre Ltd (1994) *Guidance on preliminary site inspection of contaminated land*. Contaminated Land Report No. 2 (CLR2), two volumes. Department of the Environment (now Department for the Environment, Food and Rural Affairs), London.

Baker, E. (2001) Mini flats will ease London homes crisis. *Daily Telegraph*, 28 August.

Barrett, S., Stewart, M. & Underwood, J. (1978) *The land market and the development process. Occasional Paper 2*, School for Advanced Urban Studies, Bristol.

Baum, A., Mackmin, D. & Nunnington, N. (1997) *The Income Approach to Valuation*, 4th edn. Thomson Learning, London.

BCIS (Building Cost Information Service Ltd) (2001) *Review of consultants' fees on construction projects*. RICS, London.

Bevan, O.A. (1991) *Marketing and Property People*. Macmillan, Basingstoke.

British Urban Regeneration Association (BURA) (2001) *Breaking Old Ground*, the BURA Guide to Contaminated Land Assessment and Development. BURA, London.

BSI (British Standards Institution) (1999) *Code of Practice for Site investigations*, BS 5930. BSI, London.

BSI (British Standards Institution) (2001) *Investigation of Contaminated Sites Code of Practice*, BS 10175. BSI, London.

Byers, S. (2001) A speech to the Institute for Public Policy Research, introducing a debate into the future of the planning system, leading to a proposed Green Paper, 26 July, 2001.

Cadman, D. & Topping, R. (1995) *Property Development*, 4th edn. E & FN Spon, London.

Cairney, T. (1995) *The Re-use of Contaminated Land: a Handbook of Risk Assessment*. Wiley, Chichester.

Cambourne (undated). A publicity brochure describing the development of three new 'villages' and a business park. Cambourne Concept Centre.

CB Hillier Parker (2000) *The sequential approach to retail development*. Research report for the National Retail Planning Forum, British Council of Shopping Centres and DETR, CB Hillier Parker, London.

CBI (2001) *Planning for productivity: a ten-point action plan*. Planning brief issued by the CBI, London.

CIRIA (1995) *Remedial Treatment for Contaminated Land, Volume III: Site Investigation and Assessment*, Special Publication 103. CIRIA, London.

Collins, N. (2002) Homing in on monstrous regiment that does its bit to limit building. City Comment, *Daily Telegraph*, 8 January, p. 38.

Connellan, O. (2001) Land pooling. Paper presented to the RICS Cutting Edge Conference, Oxford, September.

Contaminated Land (England) Regulations 2000. Statutory Instrument 2000/227. The Stationery Office, London.

Coward, R. (2001) A green light to the developers. *The Guardian*, 18 December.

Cozens, P., Hillier, D. & Prescott, G. (2001) Crime and the design of residential property – exploring the perceptions of planning professionals, burglars and other users. *Property Management*, **19** (No 4), 222–48.

CPRE (Council for the Protection of Rural England) (2001) *Sprawl patrol – first year report*. CPRE, London.

CRBE (Centre for Research into the Built Environment) (Nottingham Trent University) (1994) *Sampling Strategies for Contaminated Land*. Contaminated Land Report No 4 (CLR4). Department of the Environment (now Department for the Environment, Food and Rural Affairs), London.

Davis, Langdon & Everest (2001) *Spon's Architects and Builders Price Book*. Spon Press, London.

DETR (Department of the Environment, Transport and the Regions) (1996a) *Household Growth: Where Shall we Live?* Green Paper, The Stationery Office, London.

DETR (Department of the Environment, Transport and the Regions) (1996b) *Planning Policy Guidance Note 6:Town Centres and Retail Developments*. The Stationery Office, London.

DETR (Department of the Environment, Transport and the Regions) (1999) *Planning Policy Guidance Note 10: Planning and Waste Management*. The Stationery Office, London.

DETR (Department of the Environment, Transport and the Regions) (2000a) *Our Towns and Cities: the future*, the Urban White Paper. The Stationery Office, London.

DETR (Department of the Environment, Transport and the Regions) (2000b) *Planning Policy Guidance Note 3: Housing*. The Stationery Office, London.

DETR (Department of the Environment, Transport and the Regions) (2000c) *The*

Town and Country Planning (Residential Development on Greenfield Land) (England) Direction 2000. DETR, London, www.planning.dtlr.gov.uk/circulars/0800/index.htm.

DETR (Department of the Environment, Transport and the Regions) (2000d) *Tapping the Potential – Assessing Urban Housing Capacity: Towards Better Practice.* DETR, London. www.planning.dtlr.gov.uk/tpauhcbp/index.htm.

DETR (Department of the Environment, Transport and the Regions) (2000e) *Environmental Protection Act 1990: Part IIA Contaminated Land*, Circular 02/2000. DETR, London.

DETR (Department of the Environment, Transport and the Regions) (2000f) *By Design – urban design in the planning system: Towards better practice.* Design guide produced in conjunction with Commission for Architecture and the Built Environment (CABE). Thomas Telford Publishing, London, or www.planning.gov.uk/bydesign/index.htm.

DETR (Department of the Environment, Transport and the Regions) (2001) *Planning Policy Guidance Note 13: Transport.* The Stationery Office, London.

DoE (Department of the Environment) (1994) *Planning Policy Guidance Note 23 – Planning and Pollution Control.* HMSO, London.

DoE (Department of the Environment) (1995) *The Use of Conditions in Planning Permissions*, Circular 11/95. The Stationery Office, London.

DoE (Department of the Environment) (1996) *Industry Profiles*, 47 volumes. DoE, London.

DTLR (Department for Transport, Local Government and the Regions) (2001a) *Planning Policy Guidance Note 1: General Policy and Principles.* DTLR, London or www.planning.dtlr.gov.uk/ppg/ppg1/index.htm.

DTLR (Department for Transport, Local Government and the Regions) (2001b) *Better Places to Live by Design: a companion guide to PPG3.* DTLR, London or www.planning.dtlr.gov.uk/betrplac/index.htm.

DTLR (Department for Transport, Local Government and the Regions) (2001c) *Planning: Delivering a Fundamental Change.* Green Paper, DTLR, London or www.planning.dtlr.gov.uk/consult/greenpap.

DTLR (Department for Transport, Local Government and the Regions) (2001d) *Compulsory Purchase and Compensation – the Government's Proposals for Change.* DTLR, London or www.planning.dtlr.gov.uk/consult/greenpap/compurch/index.htm.

DTLR (Department for Transport, Local Government and the Regions) (2001e) *Planning Obligations: Delivering a Fundamental Change.* DTLR, London or www.planning.dtlr.gov.uk/consult/planoblg/index.htm.

DTLR (Department for Transport, Local Government and the Regions) (2001f) *Planning Fees.* DTLR, London or www.planning.dtlr.gov.uk/consult/greenpap/planfees/index.htm.

DTLR (Department for Transport, Local Government and the Regions) (2001g) *Planning: Delivering a Fundamental Change, Regulatory Impact Appraisal.* DTLR, London or www.planning.dtlr.gov.uk/consult/greenpap/pdfcria/index.htm.

Dutch Ministry of Housing (1987) *Soil Clean-up Guidelines (Leidraad bodemsanering).* Dutch Ministry of Housing, Physical Planning and the Environment, The Hague.

ECOTEC and EAU (Environmental Advisory Unit) (1993) *The WDA Manual on the Remediation of Contaminated Land*. Welsh Development Agency, Cardiff.

Environment Agency (undated) *Contaminated Land, Part IIA of the Environmental Protection Act 1990*. Information leaflet, Environment Agency, Bristol.

Environment Agency (1997) *Interim Guidance on the Disposal of 'Contaminated Soils'*, 2nd edition, Environment Agency, Bristol.

Environment Agency (2001) *Guidance on the Application of Waste Management Licensing to Land Contamination Remediation Activities* (version 2.0). Environment Agency, Bristol.

Evans, D., Jefferis, S.A., Thomas, A.O. & Cui, S. (2001) *Remedial processes for contaminated land: principles and practice*. CIRIA (Construction Industry Research and Information Association) report No. C549, CIRIA, London.

Farrell, Sir T. (2002) *Ten Years: Ten Cities. the work of Terry Farrell & Partners 1991–2001*. Laurence King Publishing, London.

Ferguson, C.C. & Denner, J.M. (1993) Soil remediation guidelines in the UK – a new risk based approach. Proceedings of *Developing Clean-up Standards for Contaminated Soil, Sediment and Groundwater*, Washington DC, 10–13 January, 205–211.

Ferguson, C.C. & Denner, J.M. (1994) Developing guideline (trigger) values for contaminants in soil: underlying risk analysis and management concepts. *Land Contamination and Reclamation*, **2** (No 3), 117–23.

Ferguson, C.C. & Denner, J.M. (1995) UK action (or intervention) values for contaminants in soil for protection of human health. In: *Contaminated Soil '95*, (eds W.J. van den Brink, R. Bosman & F. Arendt, pp. 1199–200, Klewer Academic Publishers, Dordrecht.

Franks, J. (1990) *Building Procurement Systems: A Guide to Building Project Management*. Chartered Institute of Building, London.

GLA (Greater London Authority) (2001) *Towards the London Plan: Initial Proposals for the Mayor's Spatial Development Strategy*. GLA, London.

Gleave, S. (1990) Urban Design 1: Introduction. *Architects Journal*, **24**, October.

Gore, A. & Nicholson, D. (1985) The analysis of public sector land ownership and development. In *Land Policy: Problems and Alternatives* (eds S. Barrett & P. Healey), pp. 179–202. Gower, Aldershot.

Graham, D. (2001) Contaminated land: a funder's view. Paper presented at *CIRIA Conference on Land Contamination: How to Turn Risks into Opportunities*, 25 September, London.

Griffiths, G. (2001) 'Large scale urban regeneration projects – Barry waterfront case study. Paper presented at *CIRIA Conference on Land Contamination: How to Turn Risks into Opportunities*, 25 September, London.

GVA Grimley (2001) *Cranfields Mill, Ipswich: development brief*, September.

Harley, J.B. (1975) *Ordnance Survey Maps: A Descriptive Manual*. Ordnance Survey, Southampton.

Harley, J. (2001) Working in communities. In: *Making Places: Working with Art in the Public Realm*. Public Arts, Wakefield.

Hass-Klau, C., Crampton, G., Dowland, C. & Nold, I. (1999) *Streets as Living Space*. Landor Publishing, London.

Haughton, G. & Hunter, C. (1994) *Sustainable Cities.* Jessica Kingsley Publishers and the Regional Studies Association, London.

Health and Safety Executive (1991) *Protection of Workers and the General Public During the Development of Contaminated Land.* HMSO, London.

Health and Safety Executive (1997) *Safe Work in Confined Spaces*, Legal Series 101. HSE Books, Sudbury.

Highways Agency (2000) *Trunk Road Improvement: Caxton Common to Hardwick*, announcement of preferred route. Highways Agency, London.

HM Treasury (2001) *Finance Bill 2001*, clause 70 and schedules 22 and 23, tax relief for remediating contaminated land or summary at www.hm-treasury.gov.uk/news-room and www.hm-speeches/press/2001/press_38_01.cfm.

ICRCL (Inter-departmental Committee on the Redevelopment of Contaminated Land) (1987) *Guidance on the Assessment and Redevelopment of Contaminated Land*, ICRCL 59/83 (2nd edn). ICRL, London.

Ipswich Borough Council (1997) The Wet Dock area. In: *Ipswich Local Plan*. Ch. 5, Ipswich Borough Council.

Ipswich Waterfront Steering Group (1999) *Ipswich Waterfront*, issue 1, summer.

Ipswich Waterfront Steering Group (2000) *Ipswich Waterfront*, issue 2, summer.

Johnson, R. (2001) *Protective measures for housing on gas-contaminated land.* BRE report 414, Building Research Establishment, Garston.

Johnson, V.B. (2001) *Laxton's Building Price Book.* Butterworth-Heinemann, Oxford.

Johnston, P. (2001) House prices cause migration from London to the provinces. *Daily Telegraph*, 31 August.

Joseph Rowntree Foundation (2000) *The Secrets of CASPAR.* JRF, York.

Joyce, R. (1995) *The Construction (Design and Management) Regulations 1994 Explained.* Thomas Telford, London.

Keeble, L. (1969) *Principles and Practice of Town and Country Planning*, 4th edn. Estates Gazette, London.

Keeping, M. (2001) The negligent conveyancing of polluted and contaminated land. *Property Management*, **19** (No 4), 249–64.

Kelly, R.T. (1979) Site investigations and material problems. Paper presented at 'RECLAN' Conference. Published in *Reclamation of Contaminated Land*, Society of Chemical Industry, London.

Landis, J. (1998) An overview of GIS technology in real estate. In: *GIS in Real Estate: Integrating, Analyzing and Presenting Locational Information.* Appraisal Institute, Illinois.

Landmark Information Group (2001) Note concerning map scales on Envirocheck report maps.

Law Commission (2001) *Compulsory purchase and compensation: a scoping paper.* Law Commission, London.

Llewelyn-Davies (1998) *Ipswich Wet Dock Development Framework.* Final report (unpublished).

Martin, I. & Bardos, P. (1996) *A review of full scale treatment technologies for the remediation of contaminated soil.* Report for The Royal Commission on Environmental Pollution, EPP Publications, Richmond.

Morris, J. (2001) An anniversary of Part IIA – the Environment Agency's viewpoint. Paper presented at *CIRIA Conference on Land Contamination: How to Turn Risks into Opportunities*, 25 September, London.

Murphy, J.M. (1992) *Branding: A Key Marketing Tool*. Macmillan, Basingstoke.

National Housing Federation (2001) *Homes for the rich alone*. Report on an analysis of house price figures, 14 August.

Newman, N. (1997) Marketing in commercial property. *Estates Gazette*, London.

Nicholas, Grimshaw and Partners (2001) 'Rolls-Royce manufacturing plant and head office for BMW Group', press release.

Oakes, C. & McKee, E. (1997) *City-centre Apartments for Single People at Affordable Rents: the requirements and preferences of potential occupiers*. York Publishing Services, York.

Office for National Statistics (2000) *Family Spending: a report on the 1999–2000 Family Expenditure Survey*. The Stationery Office, London.

Office for National Statistics (2001) *Land Use Change in England*. The Stationery Office, London.

Oliver, R. (1993) *Ordnance Survey Maps: a concise guide for historians*. The Charles Close Society for the Study of Ordnance Survey Maps, London.

Parfect, M. & Power, G. (1997) *Planning for Urban Quality: urban design in towns and cities*. Routledge, London.

Petts, J., Cairney, T. & Smith, M. (1997) *Risk-Based Contaminated Land Investigation and Assessment*. Wiley, Chichester.

Price Waterhouse (1993) *Evaluation of Urban Development Grant, Urban Regeneration Grant and City Grant*. Part of the Inner City Research Programme for the Department of the Environment, HMSO, London.

Public Arts (2001) *Making Places: working with art in the public realm*. Public Arts, Wakefield.

Raggett, B. (1999) Revitalisation through redevelopment: using positive planning to break down barriers to regeneration. Proceedings of the *National Symposium Compulsory Purchase: An Appropriate Power for the 21st Century*.

RICS (Royal Institution of Chartered Surveyors) and Department of the Environment (1996) *Quality of Urban Design*. A study of the involvement of private property decision-makers in urban design, Department of Land Management and Development, University of Reading, and DEGW. RICS, London.

RICS (Royal Institution of Chartered Surveyors) (2000) *Transport Development Areas*. Report based on research by the Symonds Group, RICS, London.

RICS (Royal Institution of Chartered Surveyors) (2001) *Partnership Support for Land and Property Regeneration Schemes*. RICS, London.

Rogers, R. & Power, A. (2000) *Cities for a Small Country*. Faber and Faber, London.

Rose, D. (2001) Comment on the CBI 'Planning for Productivity' paper. *Planning*, 27 July.

Roulac, S.E. (1998) Introduction to *GIS in Real Estate: Integrating, Analyzing and Presenting Locational Information*. Appraisal Institute, Illinois.

RPS Consultants Ltd (1994) *Documentary Research on Industrial Sites*. Contaminated Land Report No. 3 (CLR3). Department of the Environment (now Department for the Environment, Food and Rural Affairs), London.

Schneider, R.H. & Kitchen, T. (2002) *Planning for Crime Prevention: a Transatlantic Perspective*. Routledge, London.

Sheffield City Centre Masterplan (2001) Prepared by a team led by Koetter, Kim & Associates, Sheffield One.

Smith, P. (2001) *Architecture in a Climate of Change: a guide to sustainable design*. Architectural Press, Oxford.

SNIFFER (Scottish and Northern Ireland Forum for Environmental Research) (1999) *Communicating Understanding of Contaminated Land Risks*, SNIFFER Project No. SR97(11)F. Scottish Environmental Protection Agency, Stirling.

SNIFFER (Scottish and Northern Ireland Forum For Environmental Research) (2000) *Framework for deriving numeric targets to minimise the adverse human health effects of long-term exposure to contaminants in soil*. Report by Land Quality Management, SChEME, The University of Nottingham.

Straw, M. (1999) Town centres of contention. *Estates Gazette*, 4 September, 129–31.

Syms, P.M. (1993) Piccadilly Village, Manchester: a case study in waterside urban renewal. In: *Urban Regeneration: property investment and development* (eds J. Berry, S. McGreatl & B. Deddis) pp. 307–21. E & FN Spon, London.

Syms, P.M. (1997) *Contaminated Land: the practice and economics of redevelopment*. Blackwell Science, Oxford.

Syms, P.M. (1999) *Desk Reference Guide to Potentially Contaminative Land Uses*. ISVA (now RICS), London.

Syms, P.M. (2001) *Releasing Brownfields*. Research report prepared for the Joseph Rowntree Foundation, RICS Foundation, London.

Syms, P.M. & Knight, P.E. (2000) *Building Homes on Used Land*. RICS Books, London.

The Institute of Petroleum (1998) *Guidelines for Investigation and Remediation of Petroleum Retail Sites*. The Institute of Petroleum, London.

Tower Hamlets and EDAW (2000) *Millennium Quarter Master Plan Isle of Dogs*. London Borough of Tower Hamlets, September.

Urban Task Force (1999) *Towards an Urban Renaissance*. Final report of the Urban Task Force, E & FN Spon, London.

USEPA (United States Environmental Protection Agency) (undated), 'Information Sources for Innovative Remediation and Site Characterization Technologies'. CD-Rom, USEPA National Centre for Environmental Publications and Information (NCEPI), Cincinnati, Ohio.

USEPA (United States Environmental Protection Agency) (1994) *Superfund Innovative Technology Evaluation Program: technology profiles* (7th edn). Office of Research and Development, Washington DC.

USEPA (United States Environmental Protection Agency) (1996) *A Citizen's Guide to Innovative Treatment Technologies for Contaminated Soils, Sludges, Sediments and Debris*. Technology Fact Sheet, USEPA National Centre for Environmental Publications and Information (NCEPI), Cincinnati, Ohio.

World Commission on Environment and Development (WCED) (1987) *Our Common Future*. Oxford University Press, Oxford.

Yates, L.A. (2001) *To what extent do recent recommendations made for the revision of compulsory purchase powers overcome the problem of bringing forward regeneration in towns and cities?* Unpublished MSc dissertation, Sheffield Hallam University.

Copyright Acknowledgements

Index